The
Marketing Research
Process

Third Edition

The
Marketing Research
Process

Third Edition

MARGARET CRIMP

![Prentice Hall logo] **Prentice Hall**
New York • London • Toronto • Sydney • Tokyo • Singapore

First published 1990 by
Prentice Hall International (UK) Ltd
66 Wood Lane End, Hemel Hempstead
Hertfordshire HP2 4RG
A division of
Simon & Schuster International Group

Typeset in Garamond 10/12 pt
by MHL Typesetting Ltd, Coventry

Printed and bound in the United States of America

British Library Cataloguing in Publication Data

Crimp, Margaret
    Marketing research process.
    1. Marketing. Research
    I. Title
    658.8'3

    ISBN 0-13-556515-4

3 4 5   94 93 92 91

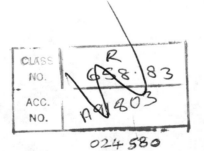

Contents

Preface to the Third Edition

The impact of new technology on the marketing research process was anticipated in the second edition of this book. During the past four years, techniques that were once innovative have become common practice. Changes in the techniques used to gather data, and in the ways in which data are used to generate marketing information, have necessitated considerable rewriting.

This third edition of *The Marketing Research Process* continues to take the route followed in the first two, tracing the development of a product or service from the strategic choice of a likely market, via the development of a brand, through to monitoring and the evaluation of performance with a view to planning ahead. As before, the marketing questions are asked first and the marketing research methodology designed to reduce uncertainty, if not to supply firm answers, follows.

Technological development has prompted research suppliers to expand existing shared-cost services and to launch new ones; subscribers to their services are being encouraged to access the databanks direct. Access is facilitated by computer bureaux 'hosting' syndicated data from diverse sources. The habit of accessing direct using desktop micros spreads as computer-educated managers become responsible for the planning of marketing strategies.

It is possible to explore inviting 'what if?' avenues with little understanding of how the data were collected, with no feel for the kind of analysis the recorded figures will stand, to pursue dead ends and to miss real opportunities.

This edition of *The Marketing Research Process* accordingly includes an appendix on 'The principles of analysis' by John Bound, formerly lecturer in marketing research at the University of Strathclyde and currently a visiting research associate at the London Business School, working with Professor Andrew Ehrenberg. John Bound takes account of the computer packages available to analysts and concludes: 'The way data become information needs understanding if the marketer is to appreciate the potential and the limitations of the research.' The third edition benefits from his having taken on this assignment.

Acknowledgements

John Davis's appendix on statistical tests continues to ensure real understanding of what these tests amount to, important when computer programs for carrying them out are so readily available. The development of DIY, 'suck it and see' investigation (see Preface) makes John Bound's 'The principles of analysis' particularly relevant.

These two appendices add weight to *The Marketing Research Process* and I am grateful to their authors. I would also like to express a special thanks to Phyllis Vangelder, who edits The Market Research Society's publications. I want to thank her for her patience in answering questions (no one is better informed about the MR industry); and for the MRS abstracts, which any researcher in the social and marketing fields should consult.

In preparing this third edition I have been at pains to establish the effects of new information technology on common practices in marketing and in MR. I also knew that my knowledge of qualitative methods needed updating. I want to thank the following, who have helped me to pursue one or both of these ends, but first make it clear that any signs of omission, commission or interpretation are mine: Ruth Badger, Nielsen Marketing Research; Tim Bowles, MRB Group; Jenny Davis, British Market Research Bureau; Karen Day, BBC Broadcasting Research Department; Tony Fawley, TABS; Alan Frost, Frost International; Wendy Gordon, The Research Business; Phil Gullen, J. Walter Thompson Company; Bridget Hall, Donovan Data Systems; Judie Lannon, J. Walter Thompson Company; Janet Mayhew, Joint Industry Committee for National Readership Surveys; Peter Menneer, BBC Broadcasting Research Department; Rory Morgan, Research International; Keith Morris, Independent Data Analysis (IDA); Kathy Rees, Frost International; Jack Sutcliffe, Unilever Marketing Division; David Taylor, Outdoor Advertising Association; Tony Twyman, Media Consultant; Juliet Young, Applied NPD.

Margaret Crimp
January 1989

An introduction to the marketing research process

The first part of this introduction is an overview of the marketing research process. It aims to show why and where research data and information are important to the strategic design, execution and evaluation of marketing plans.

The second part describes the structure of the market research industry and considers the impact of technological development on the industry and on the way in which it operates.

1.1 Focus on the market

It is now generally agreed that the health of a company largely depends on its capacity to interpret the behaviour, attitudes and needs of the individual consumers or industrial users who make up its market. We cannot say that good health entirely depends on effective focus on the market. A company's plans and performance are affected by forces over which it has little or no control, forces such as the following:

- The economic climate.
- Government action.
- Changes in the law.
- Technological developments which may make what it has to offer old-fashioned.
- The activities of competitors, who may be quicker to exploit the technological developments.

In a mixed economy, a company's ability to carry out its plans also depends on whether institutions and individuals are able and willing to invest in its shares. Whether investors are able is largely outside the company's control. Willingness to invest will be influenced by the company's market performance, for a decision to invest is often taken on the advice of analysts who study market form.

1.2 Consumer and industrial markets

The company's sales will largely depend on the buying behaviour of consumers or industrial users, or of organizations such as local authorities.

It may be marketing goods or (and this is a growth area) providing services such as the hire of office machinery, computer facilities or transport.

Consumer goods may belong to the category of those which are used up quickly, or fairly quickly (ice-cream, detergents, toothpaste), in which case they are fast-moving consumer goods: or they may be more durable and infrequently bought (motor cars, washing machines, power tools for DIY), and be classified as consumer durables.

We shall be interested in the frequency with which products are bought when we come to design market experiments and to build market models. For fast-moving consumer goods repeat purchase is an important criterion, as well as getting the product tried (penetration). For most durable goods, penetration is the criterion.

Industrial goods fall into three categories:

1. Materials (e.g. timber) and parts (e.g. timing devices).
2. Capital items (e.g. generators).
3. Supplies (e.g. lubricants) and services (e.g. advertising).[1]

We are also interested in the frequency with which goods are bought when planning research in industrial markets. Success in marketing goods in categories (1) and (3) depends on repeat purchase as well as penetration, while items in category (2) are infrequently bought by any one customer.

Derived demand: in an industrial market the ultimate consumer may be some stages away; but there are industrial markets in which the ultimate consumer is close at hand, so that it pays the company to study the behaviour of consumers as well as that of its industrial customers.

> The behaviour of consumers buying motor cars, cooking stoves or washing machines soon affects the sale of timing devices to the car industry or to the manufacturers of domestic durables.

1.3   Feedback and market intelligence

If our company is marketing an infrequently purchased industrial good (say machinery used in the manufacture of shoes) to a limited number of customers (shoe manufacture is concentrated in a few hands) with little competition to meet, then we can rely on sales and technical representatives to give early warning of events which might affect our sales forecasts. Most companies trade under rather different conditions. Let us consider the obstacles to communication with its market faced by a company marketing consumer goods, knowing that suppliers of industrial goods often face similar problems.

1.3.1 Obstacles to communication

Most companies marketing consumer goods depend on buying-decisions made by a large number of individuals spread over a wide area, increasingly in more than one country. The company will only be in direct contact with these individuals if it sells by mail order, or if (like Avon Cosmetics) it operates door-to-door selling. Otherwise, intermediaries stand between the company and those who finally consume its products.

The company may be selling direct to the retail organizations controlling the outlets where its product is bought, or to wholesalers (possibly to a voluntary group of wholesalers such as Mace) who break bulk and pass goods on to retail outlets. The company may sell direct to large retailers, such as Tesco and Curry, and wholesale to those with less clout. Finally, in its dealings with intermediaries, and at the point of sale to consumers, the company's product meets competition.

1.3.2 Where feedback falls short

Feedback from sales representatives is a useful source of marketing intelligence, especially in industrial markets, but information derived from its own sales records and its own representatives' reports will not enable a company to focus effectively on the following:

- The behaviour, attitudes and needs of the consumers in its market.
- The behaviour, attitudes and needs of the intermediaries on whom it relies to make its goods available to consumers.
- The activities of competitors and the response of consumers and intermediaries to these activities.

'Market research is the means used by those who provide goods and services to keep themselves in touch with the needs and wants of those who buy and use those goods and services.'[2]

1.4 Stages in the marketing research process

Marketing research has two basic purposes:

1. To reduce uncertainty when plans are being made, whether these relate to the marketing operation as a whole or to individual components, such as advertising.
2. To monitor performance after the plans have been put into operation.

The monitoring programme has two functions: it helps to control execution of the marketing company's operational plan and it makes a substantial contribution to longer-term strategic planning. The research data collected in order to monitor performance provide important inputs when markets are modelled.

If 'research' and 'marketing' are fully integrated, as in the process outlined below, radical and unexpected changes of plan can be avoided: unless, of course, one of the uncontrollable forces mentioned in section 1.1 comes into play without warning.

> We refer from now on to 'product', avoiding the expression 'product or service'. Apart from being clumsy, the 'or service' is superfluous. The service offered to consumers by banks, tour operators, local authorities and research agencies (to give some examples) are the products of these bodies and they are susceptible to substantially the same marketing research treatment as the goods we call 'products'.

The choice of a product field for investigation will depend on the company's financial, technical and productive resources, on its corporate aspirations and management style, and on its marketing experience. A particular product field may look promising because the company is operating in a related field, because it knows the distributive channels serving it, because the brands in the field are susceptible to technological change or because a company has been acquired, to cite some obvious reasons.

The first research objective is to establish whether there is an opportunity for a new brand in this product field.

> A 'brand' is a product or service which has been given an identity; it has a 'brand name' and the added value of a 'brand image'. The image is developed in advertisements and in all the other communications associated with the product, including its packaging.

(The following overview of the stages in the marketing research process will be helpful to some as a map of the route to be followed in this book; but an overview is necessarily condensed and others may prefer to proceed to Chapter 2, via section 1.5 on the market research industry.)

The market is explored (Chapter 2)

All available sources of facts and ideas are consulted with a view to defining the characteristics of buyers and users in the market; the channels through which products reach them; how the products and brands available to them are perceived; ways in which they are used; where they fall short. Some of these data will be in the form of available statistics, others in the form of ideas and these ideas may suggest unsatisfied, or only partly satisfied, wants.

> Unless a marketing company is operating in a familiar field, exploratory research is a necessary preliminary to the formulation of research objectives and to the design of more conclusive research.

The market is described (Chapters 3–5)

In order to design a descriptive survey of the market we need to know the parameters of the survey population, whether this be a population of households, individuals, firms or retailers. We also need to know how the survey population stratifies and whether some strata (groups) are more meaningful to our purpose than others. If a minority group looks like being significant, the sample must include a sufficient number of its members to justify singling the group out for separate consideration. For an industrial, trade or other 'non-domestic' population stratification is based on the relative business importance of groups: on volume of production or turnover, rather than on the number of industrial establishments or shops to be found in different groups.

Exploratory research will have suggested what topics should be covered when data are collected and in what detail the topics need to be treated. The method adopted to collect the data will largely depend on the nature of the data required and the characteristics of the survey population. The budget and the time available also influence research design.

The market is segmented (Chapter 6)

The object of the marketing process, taken in its entirety, is to locate a target group of consumers or users who have an unsatisfied need which could be met by a branded product. The descriptive survey will probably be so designed that it provides the data for a segmentation study.

There are two basic approaches. Consumers or users can be sorted into groups with 'like' buying requirements according to demographic characteristics, buying behaviour in the product field or beliefs and attitudes held in common (consumer typology). Alternatively, the types of product or brands in the field may be grouped according to the benefits or shortcomings they are seen to share by those who buy or use them (product/ brand differentiation). Either way, a descriptive survey of this kind must be carried out on a sufficiently large scale to allow for the sample to be broken down for detailed analysis of the data.

Markets may also be segmented using one of the geodemographic systems based on the electronic analysis of census and other government data. These analyses tell us where product users are likely to be found, but not what brands they use and why.

A fruitful segmentation analysis defines a target group in the market and specifies the characteristics of a product to suit this group. This serves to focus product development and the research associated with product development.

The brand is developed (Chapter 7)

Ideas, or concepts, for products to meet the need that has been located are tried out on the target group using qualitative methods. Ways of advertising the brand are likely to be tried out at the same time.

This is a weeding-out process. We hope to be left with the profiles of one or two possible branded products, but our data, though rich in ideas, lack statistical support. We proceed to set up experiments.

The product as perceived by buyers and users is an amalgam of formulation plus packaging plus price plus communication: i.e. it is a brand. In the experimental programme these components may be tested individually (atomistic approach) or in combination (holistic approach). Both methods are considered.

We are not yet out in the market, these screening 'go/no-go' experiments being of a 'lab.' type. Communications research (a large subject) is reserved for Chapters 8 and 9.

The 'message' is tested (Chapter 8)

In consumer markets advertising is the most important means of communicating the characteristics of the new brand to prospective buyers and users. Other means of communication are public relations, promotions and, particularly significant in industrial markets, the sales force.

We concentrate on advertising research because here the need to reduce uncertainty is greatest. While advertising can add considerable value to a brand, this added value is achieved at some cost.

We are 'pre-testing' at this stage, i.e. conducting experiments in controlled but unnatural contexts. Post-testing is covered when the 'mix' goes into the field (Chapter 10).

Market-simulation models are increasingly being used to eliminate non-starters and fine-tune the mix before the brand is tested in the market.

The media are selected (Chapter 9)

The advertising industry (advertisers, advertising agencies and media owners) provides a wealth of shared-cost data relating to main media categories (television, newspapers, magazines). The 'support media' (radio, outdoor and cinema) are also researched.

Viewers and readers are classified in some detail and it is possible to 'marry' the target group to the audience using the standard regional, sex, social-grade, age-group, etc. demographic classifications. We may, in addition, decide to buy shared-cost or syndicated research which collects product-use and media-'consumption' data from one and the same individual.

The effectiveness of the media plan cannot be measured until the advertising campaign has been launched, and we will then be faced with the problem of disentangling the effect of the media selection from the effect of the creative work and of the other elements in the mix.

The 'mix' is tested in the field (Chapter 10)

There are certain important components of the mix which cannot be tested until plans for the brand are sufficiently advanced to allow for a test launch. Distributive, selling and merchandising decisions do not lend themselves to 'lab.'-type experimentation.

Syndicated retail-audit data will guide channel decisions with trend data showing the relative importance of different types of retail outlet and how these are being used by competitors.

Penetration and repeat-purchase data derived from consumer panels enable brand-share predictions to be made. The data also show what kind of consumers are buying, and in what quantity and how often they buy.

The ultimate criterion is contribution to profit, but the immediate measure of performance is an estimate of retail sales or consumer purchases and the share of all sales or purchases in the product field these represent.

Sales reflect the impact of the marketing mix as a whole. It is difficult to isolate the effect on sales of individual items in the mix, but repeated and carefully timed surveys enable us to record how consumers are responding to the brand and the image the advertising associates with it.

Tests in the market often require a large financial commitment. This is especially so when a brand is being introduced. In addition, the marketing company's reputation with the retail trade is at stake and competitors are alerted. Micro-market testing (mini-test market) may be used either to shorten the duration of a full market test or to sidestep it and go straight to launch. Here again market-simulation models, based on data accumulated during development of the brand, are now being used to assess performance.

Performance is monitored and the future forecast (Chapter 11)

After the product or service has been launched, trend data are collected relating to the major components in the 'mix', so that 'own' marketing performance may be compared with that of competitors on a continuous basis.

The immediate task of the monitoring programme is to control the operational plan:

- To keep track of the passage of the brand along the distribution channel to the ultimate buyer or user.
- To keep a running record of its market share.
- To assess the effect of the communications programme and, more particularly, the effect of the advertising campaign.
- To ensure that the sales force is being deployed as effectively as possible.
- Depending on the nature of the product, to record how the brand is being used.

The research procedures used will be those which are also employed to measure the effect of experiments in the field — retail audits, consumer panels, usage and attitude surveys. The data derived from the monitoring programme are used when the future of the brand is being forecast.

The 'marketing research system' is one of four components of the 'marketing information system',[1] the others being the 'internal accounting system', the 'marketing intelligence system' and the 'marketing management-science system' (see Figure 11.1).

The marketing research system makes the major monitoring contribution in consumer markets, but the internal accounting system is critical when marketing costs are related to sales revenue. The marketing intelligence system makes a significant contribution to the monitoring programme of a 'non-domestic' company, while the marketing management-science system covers the use of modelling procedures to describe, diagnose and predict.

Sales achievement is, of course, dependent on the marketing support allocated to the brand in terms of sales-force time, advertising expenditure and promotional offers: i.e. sales achievement is dependent on marketing costs. The monitoring programme needs to provide data relating to competitors', as well as 'own', marketing costs in order that sales may be forecast and contributions to profit estimated.

> The trend data stored in data banks are used by marketing companies not only to monitor performance but also to construct market models. These are commonly used to predict the effect on sales of changes in the marketing mix, variables such as 'adspend' or retail selling price.

Econometric models are widely used. These are based on aggregated data and availability of back-data is important. In order to construct an econometric model, each input variable must be supported by a sufficient number of readings.

Micro-behavioural models are disaggregated or individual data to simulate the responses to market stimuli of individuals, the respondents acting as 'electronic consumers'.

1.5 The marketing research industry

'Hi-tech' developments present the MR industry with opportunities but, as in all industrial revolutions, these opportunities constitute challenges. Equipment and working practices become outmoded, new skills are required and roles within the industry change. Marketing is a comparatively innovative field and the rate of change is accelerating. There is a risk inherent in this information explosion:

> Data are available now as by-products of many different systems. Generally, however, they are by-products and they are data. Their representativeness and accuracy are often unknown or incalculable. Market researchers are not concerned with simply data, they are concerned with information. Information has relevance, validity, and application for its users — data do not.[3]

1.5.1 The marketing research industry now

Marketing companies buy research from different types of research supplier and commission research work in a variety of ways. Syndicated continuous panel services and other large-scale shared-cost surveys will typically be bought from one of the thirty-two companies (1987) belonging to the Association of Market Survey Organisations (AMSO). Companies have been amalgamating in the research field, as elsewhere in industry, and the MR industry includes some very substantial operators offering a wide range of research services. To qualify for membership of AMSO a supplier of research must have achieved a specified turnover and be equipped to undertake full-scale national surveys. The AMSO companies have a total turnover of £177 million (1987).[4]

Among the largest operators, all with turnovers exceeding £2 million and listed here in alphabetical order, are the following:

- AGB Research, BMRB, Burke Marketing Research.
- MBL Group, MIL Research, Millward Brown Market Research.
- MORI, Nielsen Marketing Research, NOP Market Research.
- Research International, Taylor Nelson Research.

All are AMSO members. The thirty-two AMSO companies handle 75 per cent of consumer research. Some AMSO companies, for example AGB, MBL Group and Nielsen, have turnovers well in excess of £2 million.

Apart from the general service agencies, there are research suppliers specializing in particular marketing applications, for example in product, packaging, pricing or communications research, and the marketing company may have occasion to commission one of these specialist suppliers. The marketing company may choose to plan its own research programme and then buy fieldwork from a fieldwork supplier. The data may then come back to the marketing company as computer print-outs from an agency specializing in electronic data processing. Translating the data into a report and recommendations is then the sole responsibility of the marketing company.

For exploratory and diagnostic work the marketing company may employ a consultant. Typically, the consultant may be a psychologist qualified to hold 'depth' interviews and group discussions and to interpret the results; or a mathematician with statistical expertise equipped to apply multi-variate techniques to the wealth of data a large marketing company has on file.

The services offered by research agencies are set out in the *MRS Yearbook*, a wide-ranging and essential source of information about the MR industry.[5] It will be seen that all the large companies include syndicated services in their product line. These make a major contribution to turnover and account for the outstanding performance of companies such as AGB and Nielsen, the latter a subsidiary of Dunn and Bradstreet.

Data collected during the course of retail audits, consumer panels, tracking studies and omnibus surveys (all of which feature in this book) constitute rich databases. In-house computer terminals, linked to a host bureau's mainframe computer, make it possible for a company to access a number of databases through one supplier (always provided the company subscribes to the services filed in the host's databank). Donovan Data Systems' service to the advertising industry is a case in point.

In 1986 the Technical and Development Committee of the MRS carried out a Research Suppliers Survey.[6] The survey covered companies on the MRS register of organizations providing market research services. These companies are, in effect, the MR industry and they contributed more than £8 million to the UK trade balance in 1986. The survey, the first of a planned series, shows the following:

- The MR industry is worth £222 million.
- 76 per cent of this total relates to research in consumer markets with 9 per cent on 'retail/wholesale', 9 per cent on 'business/industrial', 4 per cent on 'medical' and 1 per cent on 'agricultural' markets.
- But fast-moving consumer goods (accounting for 38 per cent of the £222 million) no longer dominate research spending.

'Studies involving group discussions or depth interviews, with findings based on content rather than numeric analysis, account for £32 million turnover.'[6] Qualitative work of this kind is widely used when markets are being explored, products and services developed and unexpected findings from quantitative surveys probed. Such work seeks to uncover the motivations lying behind consumer behaviour and to measure the numerical importance of the behaviours observed. Research in the United States relies more exclusively on the 'justification by numbers' supplied by quantitative work. The Research Suppliers Survey shows that 'the activities of the whole industry are predominantly concerned with improving clients' understanding of customer needs, motivations and opinions rather than measuring existing behaviour.'[6] The two data-collection methods most commonly used in qualitative research, depth interviews and group discussions, are also used in industrial and other 'non-domestic' enquiries where the interviewer is often seeking information from an expert.

1.5.2 Impact of the new information technology

Computerization has speeded up enormously the gathering, storage and retrieval of research findings and it has encouraged the examination of multi-variate relationships between data from different sources.

Major innovations will be met as this book follows the marketing research process, but here are some influential examples:

- Now that 82 per cent of adults are available on the telephone, computer-assisted telephone interviewing (CATI) is widely used. Instead of ringing code numbers on a questionnaire, the interviewer punches keys and the respondent's answers are fed straight into the computer (see section 3.5.2).
- Article numbering has made possible the electronic recording of the passage of goods along the distributive channel. Manual auditing of stock into and out of retail outlets continues but, in addition to their traditional auditing service, Nielsen now offer Scantrack, based on electronic point of sale (EPOS) capture, while AGB are considering the application of electronic data capture to their consumer purchasing panels. It is possible to give panel members the means to scan the codes on their purchases as they unpack them.
- The introduction of push-button handsets (peoplemeters), to capture the television-viewing habits of the individuals in a household, saves the individual viewer on a panel from the need to keep a diary, thus reducing error and accelerating data capture.

Turning to the computer's multi-variate facility, we see the following:

- The computer makes it possible to 'marry' data from diverse sources: for example, the postcode groups households. There are on average seventeen households to a group. Applicants' postcodes are recorded on government forms such as the vehicle licence form. Respondents' postcodes are recorded by government surveys, such as the General Household Survey, and when commercial surveys are carried out. Using the postcodes recorded on computer files, it is possible to 'flesh out' and locate consumer targets in a market (see section 4.2.3).
- CACI's ACORN (a classification of residential neighbourhoods) is used to the same end. Electronic data processing has made possible the rapid

scrutiny of relationships between the many population variables published in the census, and to cluster these in a meaningful way. ACORN was the first geodemographic analysis; but it now has competitors (Pinpoint, Mosaic, SuperProfiles).

1.5.3   The Market Research Society

Most of those who work in MR are members of The Market Research Society. The society is a professional body based on individual membership; it is not a trade association. The membership, which currently (1988) approaches 6,000, was last surveyed in 1985.[7]

Members employed by:	%
Research supplier (including consultancy 6% and self-employed in market research 8%)	46
Advertising agency	9
Client (private sector)	33
Client (public sector)	3
Other (including academic institution 4%)	8

Base   2,665

Members enter the profession with a variety of academic qualifications; in addition, 12 per cent of the total membership hold the Diploma of The Market Research Society (1988), a professional qualification. The percentage in the youngest age group (16−24) is markedly larger: 25 per cent. Professional status has recently been strengthened by the appointment of the first professor of marketing research (at the City University).[8]

Members of the society subscribe to a code of conduct[5] which puts a premium on confidentiality, and the anonymity of the respondent is carefully protected. This is critical because market research depends on the collection and storage of data provided by individuals. In addition, the Data Protection Act of 1984 relates to 'any file of personal data capable of being processed automatically'[9] — 'personal' means any information relating to a living individual which allows you to identify that individual. Further, a ' "data user" is anyone who controls the contents and use of personal data'. It is as well for the MR industry that the habit of protecting the individual's privacy is well ingrained. In fact the Act is more beneficial to the industry than harmful, for its makes it more difficult for bogus organizations to sell under the guise of conducting research ('sugging').

In addition to enforcing the code of conduct, the society operates the interviewer quality control scheme. The fifty-five companies which have been audited by the IQCS inspectors are listed in the *MRS Yearbook* (1988).

The guide to the Data Protection Act quoted above is issued jointly by the MRS and AMSO. The society liaises with a number of associations representing special research interests. Members of the associations listed below are usually members of the MRS as well (for further particulars see the 'Useful addresses' section of the *MRS Yearbook*). The Market and Social Research Liaison Group consists of the following:

- Association of British Market Research Companies (ABMRC).
- Association of Market Survey Organisations (AMSO).
- Accounts Planning Group (APG).
- Association of Qualitative Research Practitioners (AQRP).
- Association of Users of Research Agencies (AURA).
- Industrial Market Research Association (IMRA).
- Social Research Association (SRA).
- The Market Research Society (MRS).

Finally, for anyone entering or in market research, the publications of the Society are essential for their academic rigour and practical use and they are set out at the end of this introductory chapter.

Sources and further reading

1. P. Kotler, *Marketing Management, Analysis, Planning and Control*, 4th edn (Englewood Cliffs, NJ: Prentice Hall, 1980).
2. The Market Research Society, *Guide to the Practice of Market and Survey Research* (London, 1980).
3. Blyth, Chairman's introduction, *MRS Yearbook* (1988).
4. *MRS Newsletter*, no. 266 (May 1988).
5. *MRS Yearbook* (1988).
6. The Technical and Development Committee's Research Suppliers Survey, *MRS Newsletter*, no. 249 (Dec. 1987).
7. *Journal of The Market Research Society*, vol. 28, no. 1 (Jan. 1986).
8. *MRS Newsletter*, no. 262 (Jan. 1988).
9. MRS and AMSO, 'Registering under the Data Protection Act for the purpose of carrying out survey research' (Dec. 1985).

See also

Garrett, A., 'How to home in on the target market', *Marketing Week* (29 May 1987) (Geodemographic systems).
Piercy, N. (ed.) *The Management Implications of New Information Technology* (London: Croom Helm, 1984).

Market Research Society publications

Serials

MRS Newsletter (monthly)
The *Newsletter* carries news of society activities and acts as an instrument of communication amongst its membership. From time to time supplements on specialized topics are published: these have included *Data Processing* (September 1974); *Fieldwork* (March 1975); *International Marketing Research* (March 1976); *Qualitative Research* (March 1977); *UK Marketing Research Industry* (September 1978); *New Product Development* (March 1980) and *Fieldwork and Data Processing* (December 1980).

Journal of The Market Research Society (quarterly)
JMRS, a refereed academic journal, is firmly established as the professional journal of marketing research in this country. It provides a medium for the publication of original contributions to the theory and practice of marketing research as well as more informal notes on cases and research in progress.

Market Research Abstracts (bi-annually)
Market Research Abstracts is the only series of abstracts published anywhere in the world which covers all fields of marketing and advertising research, as well as relevant papers in statistics, psychology and sociology. Over 400 papers and articles are abstracted each year from some forty different English-language journals. The *Abstracts* includes the following as regular section headings: survey techniques; statistics, models and forecasting; attitude and behaviour research; personality and social psychology; communications; advertising and media research; specific applications of research; industrial market research; market research and general applications; new products development.

Survey (quarterly)
A new journal, *Survey*, was launched in June 1983. *Survey* goes out to all 5,500 members of The Market Research Society and 10,000 selected non-members who are senior executives in manufacturing companies, national and local government, advertising agencies, and also to Members of Parliament. From January 1985 it became a regular quarterly publication. The aim of the editorial content is to interest and attract opinion-formers and decision-makers. This is achieved by demonstrating the scope of market research when professionally completed to solve management or marketing problems.

Interviewer Newssheet (quarterly)
The society endeavours to publish articles and information of particular interest to interviewers. The publication also acts as a forum for interviewers to voice their ideas and concerns.

Annuals

Market Research Society Yearbook

International Research Directory 1989
This is jointly sponsored by The Market Research Society and the British Overseas Trade Board, and is now in its seventh edition. It lists details of some 1,300 market research organizations in over sixty countries, plus the names and addresses of all major national market research associations. It is more comprehensive than any other similar directory and is regarded as a basic document.

Conference Papers
Collected papers of the MRS annual conferences.

Other publications

Country notes
These provide information on research procedures, e.g. social classifications, sampling methods and sources of information, as well as a useful list of hints on special local aspects to be taken into account. The series now covers no less than thirty-six countries all over the world, including Australia, Austria, Belgium, Brazil, Canada, Colombia, Denmark, Finland, France, Greece, Hong Kong, India, Indonesia, Ireland, Italy, Japan, Kenya, Malaysia, the Netherlands, New Zealand, Nigeria, Philippines, Singapore, Spain, South Africa, Sweden, Taiwan, Thailand, Trinidad, Turkey, the United Kingdom, West Germany and Zimbabwe.

Regional volumes
These bring together in convenient form the relevant country notes (as described above) for two major trading areas: the European Community, and South East Asia and Australasia.

MRS/AMA conference proceedings
The proceedings of this joint venture held in 1974 were published under the title Changing Values and Social Trends: How do Organisers React? The problems of defining and measuring the rapid changes in the social climate were discussed by senior researchers from both sides of the Atlantic.

An Evaluation of Social Grade Validity
The conclusions of a Joint Industry Working Party based on extensive re-analysis of published and unpublished data, part of which was undertaken by the Cranfield School of Business Management, are presented in this report.

Guide to the Practice of Market and Survey Research
The Market Research Society has published this guide in order to explain to those outside the survey research industry what market researchers do and what market and survey research in general is about.

Standardised Questions
This publication was originally published in July 1972; a new edition was published in October 1984. It examines the most commonly used method or methods of asking certain types of questions and of recording the answers.

2 Exploring the market

A marketing company is considering entry into a product field. It has been suggested that a survey of the buying habits, attitudes and perceptions of consumers in this market be commissioned to establish whether there is an opportunity for a new brand. But *ad hoc* surveys are expensive and there is available today a volume of information about many product markets. In any case, exploratory research is a necessary preliminary to survey design unless the market is already familiar.

Whether the exploratory procedures discussed here are adopted in whole or in part will depend on the company's prior knowledge of the market. Clearly, the company would not be pondering the possibility of entering the market without some prior knowledge, while, when/if it reaches the stage of commissioning a survey, the research agency may be able to make a contribution based on its experience.

2.1 Why the exploratory stage is important

In the first place the exploratory stage is important because it is necessary to establish what is already on record about the market of interest and the kind of product or service envisaged. As we shall see, most markets are well documented: there is a wealth of information, both statistical and literary, stored in databanks, while on-line information systems make it possible to access these data without long and laborious searches through journals, published reports and newspapers. However, the available data may not focus closely enough on the product market in question and the decision may be taken to commission an *ad hoc* survey. Now, in order to design a cost-effective survey, it is necessary to have available data relating to the following:

- The parameters of the survey population.
- The ideas held by this population about the product field.
- Ideas about the brands available in the product field.

To put this another way, it is necessary to be informed about the population and topics of interest, given the field to be surveyed.

Statistical data are required about the population in order to design the sample. In order to describe the varying habits and attitudes of different groups in the population, for example different age groups, it will be necessary to break the sample down. A minority group may look like being of particular interest. The sample design must provide for the collection of data from a sufficient number of consumers in this group.

Similarly with the topics of interest: in order to design the questionnaire, or any other data-collection instrument, it is necessary to have explored consumer behaviour and attitudes with regard to the type of products and brands available and the context in which these are used: motoring, clothes washing, do-it-yourself, etc. The designer of the survey risks two 'sins': the *sin of omission* — not treating a topic in sufficient detail, or failing to provide sufficient respondents in a group which has marketing significance; and the *sin of commission* — collecting data which proves to be immaterial or unactionable, or breaking the sample down to a wasteful extent. It would, for example, be wasteful to provide for a breakdown of the sample into four social classes where two would be sufficient, as in many 'fast-moving' product fields.

In an early edition of his *Marketing Management*,[1] Kotler gave a definition of marketing research which takes account of the importance of informed conjecture in research design:

- Marketing research is systematic problem analysis, model-building and fact-finding for the purpose of improved decision-making and control in the marketing of goods and services.
- The key expression is 'model-building'.[2]
- A model is a set of assumptions about the factors which are relevant to a given situation and the relationships which exist between them.

The research planner undertakes exploratory research in order to arrive at 'a set of assumptions' on which to base the research design. Obviously, the more thorough the exploration, the firmer the assumptions.

2.2 The exploratory process

In our well-documented society it is difficult to conceive of a market about which there is no information available, over and above the company's own records. Available information is called secondary data, while that derived from a new research study is primary data. Since search of secondary data takes place before the collection of primary data, use of the terms 'secondary' and 'primary' can be confusing, and often leads to an elementary mistake in examinations!

Exploratory research includes all or some of the following activities:

- Secondary data search $\left\{\begin{array}{l}\text{Internal sources} \\ \text{External sources, including} \\ \text{government statistics and} \\ \text{syndicated sources}\end{array}\right.$

- Consulting experts

- Observational studies

- Consulting people in the market $\left\{\begin{array}{l}\text{Group discussions} \\ \text{'Depth' interviews}\end{array}\right.$

- Buying into an omnibus survey

Let us take each of these exploratory activities in turn.

2.3 Secondary data search: internal sources

Internal sources can be divided into two categories: the company's operating records (what Kotler calls 'the internal accounting system'[3]) and reports on file, including research previously carried out by the company.

The operating records

These will cover subjects ranging from the cost of raw materials (if this is a manufacturing company) to sales of the company's output. Transport costs, sales costs, advertising and other promotional expenditures are marketing costs, to be set against sales revenue. Packaging and warehousing costs may also be regarded as marketing costs.

Whether or not the operating records are kept in such a way that they can be used to allocate marketing costs to specific branded products, and to help monitor marketing performance, indicates whether the company is truly focused on the market. Records of this kind were originally designed to enable accountants to account for costs incurred and the sales manager (or sales director) to control the sales force. The kind of detail and analysis needed for these purposes is not the same as the kind of detail and analysis needed by a marketing director, or brand manager, striving to predict the contribution to profit likely to be made by a particular branded product or service.

Acquisition of a mainframe computer plus article numbering and the availability of software systems developed by companies specializing in this field (such as Donovan Data Systems and SPSS) can considerably improve the planning utility of a company's internal records.

Analysis by region

In consumer markets it is helpful if sales records can be related to IBA*
television areas, even if the company is not a television advertiser. Large
companies tend to be television advertisers and the data generated by
syndicated services (retail audits and consumer panels) are generally
presented in this way. So are the statistics relating to readership of
newspapers and magazines.

In the case of industrial markets, sales are best recorded by Standard
Region for comparison with the wealth of information published by the
Government Statistical Service.

Analysis by industrial application

Focus on an industrial market is sharper if sales and costs are recorded
by the use to which the industrial customer is putting the product. If this
happens to equate with a Standard Industrial Classification, the figures
derived from internal records can be related to a wide (and international)
range of statistical data.

Analysis by size? Or by numbers?

For industrial and trade customers, how they group by output, sales or
turnover is more significant when designing research than how they group
by the number of industrial establishments, or the number of shops, in
a category. On the other hand, for consumers it is the number of
individuals in a particular group that we are interested in.

Where internal records fall short

The company's own sales figures do not tell us about the following:

- How big a customer is.
- How much business the competitors are doing with our customer.
- What our potential sales are.

Reports from sales representatives and from staff belonging to technical
and professional bodies convey intelligence about competitive activity,
but we now need to extend the search to include data deriving from
sources outside the company.

*See pp. 203—4 re anticipated take-over by the Independent Television Commission
(ITC).

2.4 Secondary data search: external sources

We will consider this large subject under three headings: government statistics; other published sources; and syndicated sources. Appendix 1 (at the end of this book) lists the more commonly used sources, and includes an introduction to 'electronic desk research'.[4]

Companies operating in industrial markets will rely on the first two when making research plans. Consumer companies are likely to make use of syndicated sources if they operate on a large enough scale to warrant the cost.

2.4.1 External sources: government statistics

The most prolific source of secondary data is the Government Statistical Service.[5]

> The Government Statistical Service (GSS) comprises the statistics divisions of all major departments plus the two big collecting agencies — Business Statistics Office (BSO) and Office of Population Censuses and Surveys (OPCS) — and the Central Statistical Office, which co-ordinates the system.

The reference to 'all major departments' reminds us that government statistics are collected for the purpose of government: they do not always fit a particular marketing purpose, but every effort is made to meet business requirements and data additional to those published are often made available on request.

A list of GSS publications is available from the address given in Appendix 1. The *MRS Yearbook* includes a useful review of GSS output by department. Two offices are of particular interest to market researchers: the Business Statistics Office of the Department of Trade and Industry and the Office of Population, Censuses and Surveys.

The Business Statistics Office processes returns made by samples of industrial establishments, retailers and suppliers of services and these are published in a series of regularly updated business monitors. There is a production series, a service and distributive series and a miscellaneous series. The last covers a range of subjects such as motor-vehicle registrations, cinemas, finance and overseas travel. The monitors are published monthly and quarterly.

The validity of these published statistics depends on the care with which businesses make their returns. The anonymity of businesses supplying data is carefully safeguarded, and the Business Statistics Office does not tell companies who their competitors are.

The work of the Office of Population, Censuses and Surveys is particularly relevant to the planning of surveys because it is concerned with the size and distribution of the UK population by age and social grade, with the way in which the population is housed and the amenities it has, or does not have, including telephones and a range of durable goods. The last census was taken in 1981 and the next one is due in 1991. Census data, together with other 'lifestyle' statistics collected by the OPCS, constitutes the computer input of geodemographic systems such as ACORN. The OPCS carries out two continuous surveys which illuminate social trends: the Family Expenditure Survey and the General Household Survey.

The CSO databank holds the macro-economic statistical data listed in Appendix 1. This is more immediately relevant to researchers concerned with industrial products and services than to those in fast-moving consumer markets.

Exploratory research for a marketing project. The following approach to 'government statistics' may help the business studies student engaged on exploratory research for a marketing project:

- Write for *Government Statistics: A Brief Guide to Sources*, free from the CSO (see Appendix 1 for address).
- Consult the *Guide to Official Statistics*, published annually by the CSO.
- Consult the cumulative and recent lists of government publications.
- Familiarize yourself with the *Monthly Digest of Statistics, Economic Trends* and *Population Trends* (quarterly).
- Take note of the classifications used for population, production and distribution.
- If there is a Government Bookshop near you, visit it.
- If you are in London, make use of the Statistics and Market Intelligence Library (see Appendix 1 for the addresses of the Government Bookshops and the Market Intelligence Library).

2.4.2 External sources: other published sources

Marketing information is also published by banks, stockbrokers, trade and professional associations, media owners, local authorities and government-sponsored organizations such as the National Economic Development Office. Appendix 1 lists commonly used sources, including sources of information about overseas markets.

It would be tedious to discuss these sources individually: it might, however be helpful to mention *Retail Business* (Economist Publications) and *Mintel*, both published monthly. These journals summarize data from government and trade sources relating to a wide range of markets. One or both can be found in most libraries with a marketing section. But it is possible to avoid library searches by subscribing to an on-line system such as TEXTLINE, MAGIC, MAID or HARVEST (see Appendix 1).

Ours is indeed a well-documented society, but published data do not always fit requirements and they are often out of date. It is essential to find out how the original data were collected.

2.4.3   External sources: syndicated sources

A consumer marketing company of any size is more likely to consult the trend data supplied by the research agencies who operate retail audits and consumer panels. This syndicated research enables comparisons to be made between estimates of own sales and those of competitors, evaluation of performance usually being based on 'brand share'. ('Estimates' because the data derive from *samples* of retail outlets or consumers. A panel is a sample maintained over a specified time so that trends may be observed.)

The traditional retail audit records sales to consumers through a panel of retail outlets. Auditing is a method of data collection based on observation (see Table 3.1). The estimate of consumer sales is arrived at as follows:

| Opening stock for period (checked at last audit) | + | Net deliveries since last audit | − | Stock held at present audit | = | Sales to consumers during period |

The interval between manual audits is often, but not invariably, two months. As well as estimating consumer sales, the retail audit monitors the distributive, selling and merchandising programmes associated with brands in the product field. The number of brands recorded in the reports bought by subscribers depends on their individual requirements and on the amounts subscribed above a minimum: i.e. the size of the 'all others' category varies. The Nielsen Company, Retail Audits and Stats MR are substantial operators in the retail field.[6] It is to be expected that EPOS will obviate the need for most manual point-of-sale auditing, and that automatic services such as Nielsen's Scantrack will take over. Scantrack reduces the reporting interval from bi-monthly to monthly.

The consumer panel records estimates of consumer purchases, and gives useful information about the characteristics of those who buy and about their buying habits. The data yielded by retail audits and consumer panels are compared in Table 10.1. For a survey designed to describe consumers in a product field, consumer-panel data make a big contribution to informed assumptions. Most panels relate to products purchased frequently but panel data relating to a wide range of durables are available (e.g. the AGB Home Audit). Durables are audited once a quarter. The fast-moving purchases are either recorded by means of an audit carried out by an interviewer once a week, or the data are recorded by the purchaser in a diary designed for easy marking up and rapid data processing. The reporting interval is four weeks. We need to distinguish between three types of panel:

1. Household panel: a record of housewife purchases, the most widely used being the Television Consumer Audit (TCA) and the Attwood Consumer Panel, both owned by Audits of Great Britain (AGB).
2. Individual panel: a record of purchases made by individuals for their own use; e.g. the AGB Personal Purchases Index.
3. Special-interest panel: a panel such as the Motorists' Diary Panel operated by Forecast (Market Research), a Unilever subsidiary. This panel is devoted to the recording of petrol and engine oil purchases, plus information on accessories, servicing and car insurance.

The range of the data available from consumer panels relating to repeat-purchase products is summarized as follows:

- Trends in the total volume and value of consumer purchases in the product field.
- The demographic characteristics of those buying in the product field, such as age, social class, size of family.
- Buying behaviour in the product field: average amount bought, frequency of buying, and, since these data record individual purchasing of individual brands (i.e. the data are 'disaggregated'), repeat-purchase and loyalty patterns can be established.
- All this information is recorded within IBA television areas and by the type of retail outlet at which purchases were made.
- Seasonal patterns can be seen.

But data derived from consumer purchasing panels do not answer either of the following:

- How products and brands are used.
- How buyers perceive brands in a product field.

Any attempt to collect use and attitude data from the members of a purchasing panel would contaminate the purchasing data. Data derived from new panel members are ignored until they have been given time to settle back into their habitual purchasing patterns.

For both retail audits and consumer panels 'back data' may be available if the company is not already subscribing. The range of these data will relate to the requirements of subscribers, but important product fields and major brands in those fields will have been covered.

The first purpose of audits and panels is to monitor the effect of marketing programmes (see section 10.4.1); while the accumulated trend data constitute important inputs to diagnostic predictive models (see sections 10.4.3 and 10.5.2).

BMRB's Target Group Index (TGI) serves a strategic planning purpose. The TGI annual reports, based on a sample of 25,000 adults, relate individual product field and brand purchases to media 'consumption'. The 86-page questionnaire (placed by interviewers for self-completion) covers 4,500 brands in 500 product and service fields, as well as the respondent's media habits and attitudes. Questions are also asked about attitudes towards, for example, drink, diet and health, home and DIY; and a lifestyle system called Outlook, useful for segmenting markets, is based on the answers (see Chapter 6).

Postcodes are recorded and so it is possible to relate the product–media data to specific locations (see section 4.2.3). It is also possible to relate TGI data to the ACORN classification of neighbourhoods based on the Census of Population and on lifestyle indicators (such as 'without a bath', or 'two-car family') included in the census data (see section 4.2.4). AGB's consumer panels and BMRB's Target Group Index (TGI) generate very substantial databases. These may be accessed either direct by subscribers or via a 'host' data service. It is still not common practice for end users to be 'on-line'.

Given an adequate research budget, it is possible to explore most consumer markets in considerable detail.

2.5 Consulting experts

If a company is considering entry into a new product field, the research planner may feel the need to seek expert advice. Much depends on how thoroughly he/she has been briefed.

The expert may be on the staff, say a research chemist in the research and development (R & D) department or a home economist in the test kitchen; or it may be necessary to go outside to consult a heating and ventilating engineer or a paediatrician, to quote two possible outside experts.

In a consumer market there is a clear distinction between seeking the advice of experts and seeking to clothe the secondary data statistics by encouraging individuals in the market to talk, either alone in 'depth' interviews or in groups (see section 2.7).

In industrial markets the distinction between 'experts' and 'buyers' is muddied by the industrial buying process. The industrial buyer is often buying at the behest of company experts. Indeed, as we shall see, determining just who makes the buying decision presents a problem when designing industrial marketing research surveys (who should be asked the questions?).

2.6 Observational studies

Strictly speaking, audits and diaries represent data collection by means of observation (see section 3.4). Here we consider observation as an exploratory aid for the research planner.

If the product field is unfamiliar it may be advisable to go out and observe, for example, the following:

- How motorists behave on the forecourt of a filling station.
- How housewives buy bread.
- How retailers shop in a cash and carry wholesaler's.
- How customers behave in a DIY centre.

It all depends, of course, on the nature of the product and the planner's experience as a consumer.

At this exploratory stage we are not collecting statistical data. Our purpose is to get better acquainted with what goes on in the market as part of the business of arriving at our 'set of assumptions' (see section 2.1).

2.7 Consulting people in the market

If the market is reasonably well documented, the search so far will have told us what demographic variables are likely to affect the behaviour of consumers with regard to the product field.

We will have a good idea whether age is a critical variable, or whether social class, having or not having children, living in the north compared with living in the south, going out to work or being a housewife full-time, and so on, are important criteria.

Who buys and who uses

We also hope to know whether we have to take account of a distinction between 'who buys' and 'who uses' in this market, when deciding what sort of consumers to consult. Electric razors and male toiletries are often bought by women for men. Who determines the kind of holiday the family takes? The model of family car? The kind of bicycle the child shall have?

We need to know as much as possible about consumers, and users, in the market because we are going to encourage a limited number of consumers to talk freely and at length about their behaviour in the product field, their attitudes towards what is available in the way of products (or services), their wants and their preoccupations.

We shall either contact them as individuals or bring them together in groups of about eight — a number small enough to encourage general discussion and large enough to make it likely that the group will hold a variety of ideas. This kind of research, which seeks to illuminate the motivation behind consumer behaviour, is described as 'qualitative'; as compared with the 'quantitative' type of research study, designed to produce statistics.

Qualitative research

Individual, intensive or 'depth' interviews and group discussions are the two most commonly used qualitative research methods. It would be possible to conduct a sufficient number of lengthy, unstructured interviews to draw statistical conclusions, and indeed this is sometimes done. The more cost-effective approach is to do enough *qualitative* work to reveal most, if not all, of the ways in which consumers behave in the market and of the attitudes they hold; then to use this rich data to design a *quantitative* study of a sample sufficiently large to allow conclusions to be drawn as to *how many*, and *what sort of*, consumers behave and think in the ways shown by the qualitative study.

In industrial and other 'non-domestic' markets, where information is often being sought from experts and a formal questionnaire out of place, individual, intensive or 'depth' interviews are frequently used, as are group discussions.

The 'depth' interview and group discussion are both clinical methods. 'Depth' is in inverted commas because depth interviews in market research are shallow compared with the interviewing techniques used in psychotherapy. 'Extended' or 'intensive' are better descriptions but 'depth' is still in common use. Individual, depth or intensive interviews are used when the subject might prove embarrassing or if it is necessary to avoid interaction between group members. The interview may be 'non-directive' or 'semi-structured'. In the first case the interviewer, having established a relaxed atmosphere, leaves the respondent free to come up with an experience, attitude, need or idea that bears on the subject which, at the exploratory stage, is likely to be broadly defined as, for example, 'feeding the family'. For a semi-structured interview, the interviewer is equipped with an agenda or check-list designed to ensure that specific aspects of interest are covered.

Group discussions have cost and time advantages. A group of consumers with an interest in common, such as motoring, child-rearing, taking holidays or DIY, can develop a dynamic so that more ideas are discussed over a shorter time than would emerge from the same number of depth interviews, however skilful the interviewer at establishing rapport. The type of group most commonly used is described here. Groups based on synectical and brainstorming techniques (see Sampson[7]) are more appropriate to new-product development (Chapter 7).

Designing the groups

The number and make-up of the groups depend on the variability in the consumer market shown by the secondary data search. If the market is not sufficiently well documented a limited number of questions in an omnibus survey (see section 2.8) will establish the main variables.

Any variable which is known to be significant is allowed for in the design of the groups, not forgetting regional differences. The groups can either be of like (homogeneous) or of unlike (heterogeneous) types. A mixture of types in each group could reveal a greater variety of experience and ideas: or it could have the opposite effect. In many product and service markets, social grade is no longer a discriminator where buying behaviour is concerned, but in the United Kingdom it is still usual to distinguish between middle class (ABC_1) and working class (C_2DE) when designing groups.

Discussions are tape-recorded and they are often filmed so that body language may be observed. (Should participants not be told about this recording beforehand, their permission to use tape and film must be sought after the session; this is in the MRS code of conduct.)

Risk of bias

Group discussions are recorded on tape and later transcribed. Statements expressing habits, attitudes and wants are listed verbatim. The lists are cut up into individual statements and the statements are sorted into piles. Then the discussion is summarized, using the respondents' own words as far as possible.

In qualitative work of this kind there is clearly a risk that the results may be biased:

- Group members may not be representative of the market.
- The interviewer may influence the course of the discussion.
- The content analysis may not truly represent the experience and attitudes of the group.
- The report writer may impose a doctrinaire psychological interpretation on the content.

Value of qualitative work at later stages

Qualitative methods are used extensively in the search for product and advertising ideas and in the development of concepts arrived at during the exploratory stage. The qualitative techniques employed during product and advertising development are discussed in Chapters 7 and 8.

In essence, whether used to explore or to develop, the validity of qualitative work depends on the recruitment of suitable market members for discussion and the choice of suitable stimuli to enable these to formulate and express their own thoughts and motivations.

2.8   Buying into an omnibus survey

The Market Research Society's monthly newsletter carries a regular feature in which research suppliers advertise their omnibus surveys.

- The research *supplier* draws the sample, administers the questionnaire, processes the data, reports results.
- The research *buyer* takes space in the questionnaire, pays according to the number of questions asked and the statistical breakdowns required.

Establishing market characteristics

The number of questions you will include in an omnibus questionnaire is limited, but sufficient to establish basic market characteristics; and your market may be the subject of a specialist omnibus. There are, for example, motoring omnibuses and baby market omnibuses as well as the more general omnibus surveys based on a sample of all the adults in Great Britain, or on a sample of all the households.

There are omnibus surveys relating to the EC, 'all-Ireland', Scotland, Hong Kong, the Middle East, Malaysia to pick an arbitrary selection from one issue of the MRS newsletter.

The samples are specified and carefully drawn. The omnibus survey is an important item in the research supplier's range of products. The surveys are conducted at regular intervals and are relied on for a regular contribution to revenue.

An omnibus survey would, for example, be a good way of establishing what sort of people are in the DIY market, their DIY equipment and their most recent DIY job done.

Effect of the shared questionnaire

This is an efficient and inexpensive way of establishing the nuts and bolts of a market: but the questionnaire is likely to range over a number of subjects so that it is difficult to engage the respondent's attention in more than a superficial way. This does not apply quite so much to the specialist omnibus, but the questionnaire still represents the interests of a number of sponsors.

The development of computer-assisted telephone interviewing (CATI) makes it possible to capture and process omnibus data very quickly, e.g. 'Questions by Friday noon, results by Monday noon.'

2.9   Importance of informed assumptions

It is unlikely that all these exploratory avenues will be followed in any one piece of exploratory research. The objective can be reached by a variety of routes and the objective is sufficient certainty about the following in order to design a cost-effective research study.

- The structure of the population to be sampled, whether this be one of individuals, households, firms or retail outlets.
- The topics that are relevant to the marketing problem.

Variation in the population

We need to be sufficiently well informed about the population to be able to design a sample which takes account of those variables likely to lead to marketing action, for example:

> If AB class behaves in a markedly different way from C_1 in this market, then we are going to have to ensure that our sample includes enough ABs for us to have confidence in the representativeness of the AB results. If AB and C_1 behave in much the same way, then making separate provision for AB would be wasteful. But we must avoid the risk of getting results in and finding we want to make recommendations about AB as a separate group, but cannot (or ought not!).

Topics of interest and level of generality

Here again, we have to avoid sins of both omission and commission. Let us take an example:

> Qualitative work has given us a list of statements expressing motorists' attitudes towards driving a car. We want to quantify these attitudes by putting them to a sample of motorists. Do we need to distinguish between how he/she feels about driving the car when going to work, ferrying children to school, taking grandparents for a run; or is it sufficient for our purpose to establish how the motorist feels about driving in general?

The answer will affect the design of the questionnaire, the time taken to answer it (or fill it in), the complexity of data processing and the cost of the survey.

2.10 Conclusion

This chapter assumes company interest in a particular market and considers how this market may be explored. The time spent on the preliminary investigations reviewed here will depend on the company's familiarity with the market.

We have seen that there is a wealth of published and syndicated data available. These data, together with some qualitative work, may fit our particular interest so well that there is no need for further data collection. We are, however, more likely to find that the data, while illuminating about the general characteristics of the market and of the distributive channels serving it, are not focused closely enough on the habits, attitudes and requirements of the consumers we are interested in to meet our purpose. Exploratory research has put us in a better position to define research objectives and to design primary research, tailored to our objectives.

Sources and further reading

1. P. Kotler, *Marketing Management, Analysis, Planning and Control*, 1st edn (Englewood Cliffs, NJ: Prentice Hall, 1966), Chap. 10.
2. J. Rothman, 'Experimental designs and models', in R.M. Worcester and J. Downham (eds), *Consumer Market Research Handbook* (2nd edn, Wokingham: Van Nostrand Reinhold, 1978; 3rd edn, Amsterdam: North-Holland, 1986), Chap. 3.
3. P. Kotler, *Marketing Management, Analysis, Planning and Control*, 4th edn (Englewood Cliffs, NJ: Prentice Hall, 1980), p. 603.
4. P.N. Hague, *The Industrial Market Research Handbook*, 2nd edn (London: Kogan Page, 1987).
5. *Government Statistics: A Brief Guide to Sources* (London: Central Statistical Office).
6. *Organisations Providing Market Research Services in Great Britain* (London: The Market Research Society), updated yearly.
7. P. Sampson, 'Qualitative research and motivation research', Chap. 2 in R.M. Worcester and J. Downham (eds), *Consumer Market Research Handbook*, 3rd edn (Amsterdam: North-Holland, 1986).

See also

*   Appendix 1 of this book.
*   J. Morton-Williams, 'Unstructured design work', Chap. 2 in G.W. Hoinville,

R. Jowell and Associates (eds) *Survey Research Practice* (London: Heinemann Educational, 1978).
- *MRS Newsletter*, monthly feature 'Omnibus surveys'.
- N. Newson-Smith, 'Desk research', Chap. 1 in R.M. Worcester and J. Downham (eds), *Consumer Market Research Handbook* (2nd edn, Wokingham: Van Nostrand Reinhold, 1978; 3rd edn, Amsterdam: North-Holland, 1986).

Problems

You are employed in the research department of a chain of food stores with national (but rather uneven) distribution.

1. You have been asked to report on developments in the market for wine consumed in the home. How would you tackle this problem?
2. Write a report drawing on the sources you have consulted (the consumer market for wine is well documented).
3. How would you proceed if you were asked to report to management on the distribution of wine to the retail trade in Great Britain?

3 Describing markets: design choices

Exploratory research may yield results that are sufficiently conclusive to obviate the need for a descriptive survey of the market population. In this chapter, however, we assume that:

- exploratory research has put us in a position to formulate hypotheses about the characteristics of the population we are interested in;
- the extent to which these characteristics of habit and attitude are held is open to question.

This chapter is designed to give a general view of the decisions which have to be made, and the choices of research procedure available, when markets are described. Sample design and data-collection methods are considered in more detail in Chapters 4 and 5.

3.1 Stages in the survey procedure

The order of events from review of marketing objectives to provision for monitoring performance is illustrated in Figure 3.1 which shows a good relationship between the marketing and marketing research functions in a company. Marketing objectives are fully discussed with those responsible for designing research and the discussion includes consideration of possible courses of action *before* the research plan is made. In Figure 3.1 the supplier may be a research agency offering a range of services or an organization specializing in one research function, e.g. data collection or data processing (see section 3.2).

In addition, Figure 3.1 illustrates a procedure which provides for second thoughts about the nature of the marketing problem after exploratory research has been carried out. Had research been ordered without due discussion of marketing objectives and possible courses of marketing action, the research department would not be in a position to judge whether the research problem could be better defined. Taking the stages in Figure 3.1 in turn:

- Exploratory research and the formulation of hypotheses were considered in Chapter 2.

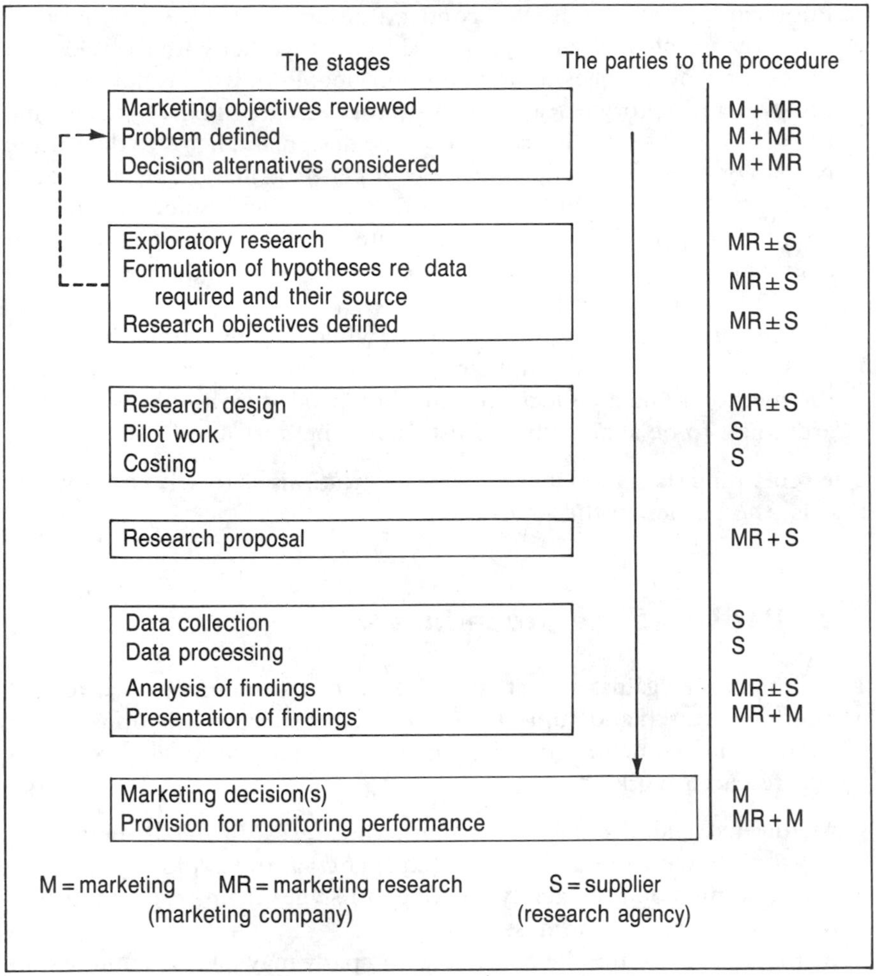

The stages	The parties to the procedure
Marketing objectives reviewed	M + MR
Problem defined	M + MR
Decision alternatives considered	M + MR
Exploratory research	MR ± S
Formulation of hypotheses re data required and their source	MR ± S
Research objectives defined	MR ± S
Research design	MR ± S
Pilot work	S
Costing	S
Research proposal	MR + S
Data collection	S
Data processing	S
Analysis of findings	MR ± S
Presentation of findings	MR + M
Marketing decision(s)	M
Provision for monitoring performance	MR + M

M = marketing   MR = marketing research   S = supplier
    (marketing company)   (research agency)

**Figure 3.1
Stages in the
development of
a market
survey**

- Research objectives are not a repetition of marketing objectives. The marketing objective might be to enter the market for accelerated freeze-dried convenience foods and the marketing problem the definition of the launch range. The research objectives might then be to establish the demographic characteristics of those using the main categories of convenience food, to define their attitudes towards products they had tried, how they had prepared them, when they had used them, and where what was available fell short of requirements.
- The research design is based on choice of data-collection method and of sampling procedure. The possible choices are reviewed later in this chapter. Cost is, of course, an important constraint.

- Pilot work is trying out the proposed design — the questionnaire or other recording device it is proposed to use together with the selection of respondents for questioning, or observing. Pilot work is not the same thing as exploratory research. Exploratory research helps to determine the research design. Pilot work tests the design and helps to determine costs. For example, in the early days of pet-food marketing, a research agency underestimated the cost of fieldwork. Pet owners like to talk about their pets and, in the event, interviews took longer than had been anticipated. If sufficient pilot calls had been made, this problem would have been averted.
- The research proposal specifies when, where and by whom the survey is being carried out. It summarizes the research objectives, specifies the method of data collection, sampling procedure and how the data are going to be analysed, and estimates the cost involved.

The remaining stages in Figure 3.1 raise questions as to who does what: that is, the parties to the procedure.

3.2 Parties to the procedure

The initials set against the stages in Figure 3.1 stand for marketing, marketing research and supplier. In consumer surveys it is unusual for the sponsoring company to carry out its own fieldwork. The extent to which research work is 'put out' varies:

- At one extreme the sponsor's marketing research department may collaborate with an outside research agency at the exploratory stage, then commission the agency to cover all stages from research design to presentation of findings.
- At the other extreme, the marketing company may merely commission fieldwork and electronic data processing — handing over the questionnaire, specifying the sample and receiving back computer printouts of the analysis.

If the working relationship between marketing and marketing research is a good one, interpretation of the findings will be a joint operation so that the significance of the findings is fully (marketing) and properly (marketing research) exploited.

Development of the new information technology is beginning to divide 'data users' from 'data gatherers' and, where large sophisticated users are concerned, to exclude the gatherers from diagnosis of the data (see section 1.5). This divorce is, however, more likely to develop where large-scale, routinely captured trend data are concerned. There are many research contexts where co-operation between user and gatherer remains important, for example when beliefs and attitudes are being explored, and when the components of a new branded product or service are being developed.

3.3 Design choices

The research design will be the product of the choices set out in Table 3.1. Selection of data-collection and sampling procedures will, of course, depend on the research objectives and the funds available for research.

In this chapter we are focusing on the use of surveys to describe markets but we might have decided to take a qualitative rather than a quantitative approach. Qualitative work is invaluable, indeed essential, at the exploratory stage. But when market description is going to affect marketing decisions involving substantial expenditures, findings based on statistically significant numbers of cases carry more conviction than those based on small numbers of cases, even though the data yielded by the few are likely to be richer in ideas and detail than those collected in a large-scale survey.

It is possible to have the best of both approaches: to collect the ideas at the exploratory stage and then to design a survey which quantifies the significant ones.

We are now going to review the design choices set out in Table 3.1 before focusing more closely on sampling techniques and on questionnaire design. But we must not under-rate the importance of qualitative work, for the qualitative approach is widely used in the search for new product ideas and the formulation of brand propositions (Chapter 7), and in the creation and development of advertising campaigns (Chapter 8).

Table 3.1
Design choices

Data collection	
Questioning	Observing
personal	personal
telephone	diary
postal	instrumental
computer	electronic
Sampling	
Probability	Purposive
simple random	quota
systematic random	judgement
multi-stage drawn with pps*	
Random Location	

*drawn with probability proportionate to size of population (see section 4.2)

3.4 Questioning or observing?

In essence, there are two ways of collecting survey data: by asking questions or by observing behaviour. In practice, the distinction between the two is by no means cut and dried.

As an example of observing, from time to time motorists are held up while traffic is funnelled past an observation post. The post is manned by observers with recording instruments and clipboards. The passage of all vehicles is recorded but every nth vehicle is stopped. The driver of the nth vehicle is asked where he/she has come from, is going to, the purpose of the journey and, perhaps, some questions designed to show if this is a one-off journey or a routine one.

This example illustrates the strength and limitation of observing as a method of data collection. The strength is its objectivity. Given that the recording instrument is in order and that traffic is sufficiently slowed down for the necessary observations to be made (e.g. commercial vehicles, passenger cars, etc.), risk of bias is reduced to a minimum. The data are not influenced by how questions are asked nor by the respondent's capacity to answer. But the weakness of the data is that they will tell us nothing about the purpose or frequency of journeys unless a sample of commercial vehicles and cars is stopped and questions are asked.

It is sometimes claimed that data derived from observation are more objective than those derived from questioning. This holds good if the data are automatically recorded by instruments, provided the sample being observed is representative of the population concerned.

In the television-audience research carried out by AGB for the Broadcasters Audience Research Board (BARB), meters attached to panelists' sets automatically record whether the set is switched on and, when on, what station is being received. But in order to know the size of the television audience it is necessary for individual viewers to record their presence in front of the set. Peoplemeters (press-button handsets or key pads) have taken the place of diaries for this purpose. It is, of course, less onerous for the viewer to press a button at the start and at the finish of a viewing session: the risk of human error is reduced (but not eliminated) and passage of the data from viewer to databank is accelerated.

Diaries are used for a wide variety of marketing purposes. They have long been the means by which consumer purchases are recorded. Most are so designed that the respondent is only required to mark coded positions and the data are electronically 'mark-sensed' when the diary is returned to the research company (see Table 11.2). But as the choices being offered to consumers proliferate — manufacturers' brands, retailers' 'own labels', generic products, varieties within brands, special offers — it is easy for the wrong position in the diary to be marked or for a purchase to be overlooked.

Observation and recording of the passage of goods along the distributive channel now generally rests on the electronic scanning of bar codes. Nielsen's syndicated Scantrack service is based on a panel of retail outlets with checkouts equipped to read bar codes so that data may be recorded electronically instead of by manual audit.

But in the United Kingdom observation of consumer purchasing behaviour is still dependent on diary records. There has, however, been considerable development in the use of electronic methods outside this country and major research suppliers, such as AGB and Nielsen, operate internationally. Application of AGB's experience in electronic methods of data capture to the consumer purchasing panels which the company operates is a matter of time.

There are two approaches to be considered: in the first case, an interviewer keys in the panelist's answers to a structured questionnaire; in the second, the panelist is equipped by the research company with a modem, together with an electronic device to read the bar codes as the shopping is being unpacked. The modem connects the domestic telephone to the company's mainframe computer and the data are transmitted as the bar codes are read. The second approach appears to be the more efficient. It is, for example, being used by McNair Anderson's Brandscan service in Australia.[1]

Distribution checks are also used to observe retail selling prices. The observations may be made by the marketing company or by a research agency offering trade research services. The distribution checks may be made regularly to yield trend data or on an *ad hoc* ('one-off') basis. This use of observation is cheaper than the continuous audit based on a panel and it gives a marketing company the chance to conceal its interest from the retail trade: but the data yield is limited to what can be seen at the point of sale.

Human observation is also used in comparison shopping. Retailers are as interested in comparing consumer prices as are the consumers themselves. The John Lewis Partnership's claim to be never knowingly undersold is supported by observation research of this kind.

When observations are being made by people, reliability of the record will be affected by whether the observer has anything else to do at the time. When self-service was first introduced to the petrol station forecourt the behaviour of motorists was observed to see if they had difficulty in following the instructions on the pump. The behaviour of those being observed may be affected by the fact that they are being watched, however discreetly. When the observer is disguised, say as a forecourt attendant, he is liable to be distracted from the business of recording observations. Hidden cameras get round this difficulty, but the rules of The Market Research Society require that the subject be informed before use is made of data collected in this way.[2]

The use of observation as a method of data collection has been stimulated by developments in the electronics field. 'Mechanical' methods are used in the development of pack designs (see section 7.4.1), the pre-testing of advertisements (section 8.4.3) and in the measurement of television viewing (section 9.3.2). The use of 'impersonal' methods is discussed in these contexts, and in the context of retail auditing (section 10.5.1).

3.5   Conveying questions to respondents

We can ask questions in a personal interview, by telephone, through the post or by computer. The choice depends on the following:

- The subject of the survey.
- The nature of the survey population.
- The research budget.

Surveys vary in the ease with which the required type of respondent may be contacted and in the length and complexity of the questionnaire. In deciding between personal, telephone and postal interview the criterion is the cost of each *satisfactorily* completed questionnaire. This must, of course, be estimated in advance, the estimate being based on the prior experience of the research agency or of the marketing company and on the results of pilot work (see section 3.1).

3.5.1   In a personal interview

Face-to-face interviewing is still the commonly used method of collecting survey data in this country; whereas in the United States telephone interviewing has largely taken over. In 1986, 85 per cent of the 17.5 million interviews undertaken by research suppliers in Great Britain were personal interviews.[3] But personal interviewing is labour-intensive and costly. During the 1980s economic pressure and intensification of competition have stimulated marketing companies to demand faster and cheaper data. The development of computer-assisted telephone interviewing has helped research suppliers to meet this demand.

For a questionnaire of any length or complexity, satisfactory completion is most likely to be achieved in a personal interview. Given proper training, an interviewer has the opportunity to establish rapport with a respondent and to achieve this without biasing answers to questions. In addition, the face-to-face interview offers the opportunity to show supporting material, such as cards listing all possible answers to multi-choice questions or scales to help respondents rate how strongly they feel about a subject. And it is possible to include open-ended questions which demand verbatim written answers. Computer-assisted telephone interviewing does not lend itself to open-ended questions. Finally, as we shall see, interviewers play a critical part in the selection of respondents for the quota sampling widely used in survey research.

We discuss the design of questionnaires, including the risk of interviewer bias and The Market Research Society's interviewer quality control scheme in Chapter 5.

3.5.2 By telephone

Before the development of computer-assisted telephone interviewing conducted from a central location, the telephone offered little, if any, advantage in cost and time over face-to-face interviewing. The developing popularity of telephone interviewing is due to the following:

- The demand for information *now*. CATI makes it possible to collect, analyse and despatch research findings in as little as twenty-four hours.[4]
- The spread of telephone ownership. Eighty-two per cent of adults are available on the telephone.[5]
- Increases in fieldwork costs and the reluctance of interviewers to work in certain areas and in the evening.
- The improved and more cost-effective control of fieldwork when telephone interviewing is centrally located.
- The opportunity to record and process results as questions are answered.
- The ability to avoid clustering in nationwide surveys (see section 4.2.1).
- Where fast-moving packaged goods are concerned, buying habits are much the same for those without as for those with telephones.[6]

CATI is now widely used to update trend data and in omnibus surveys. On the other hand, CATI is not cost-effective for small samples, demands structured questionnaires with pre-coded answers, does not lend itself to long questionnaires ('Ideally a telephone interview should not last longer than fifteen minutes'[4]) nor to subjects which cannot be quickly introduced to respondents. The Market Research Society's Development Fund (MRDF) has published on the use of telephone interviewing.[5] 'Telephone availability' analyses answers to the question 'Have you your own telephone?' put to adults aged fifteen and over in the National Readership Survey (a meticulously designed probability sample representative of the adult population of Great Britain). The analysis shows the following:

- The telephone is readily available to A, B and C_1 social grades, but a sample drawn from telephone directories would not give due weight to D and E grades:

Social Grade	A	B	C$_1$	C$_2$	D	E	Total
Adults %	98	96	94	85	74	55	82

- Telephone penetration varies by region:

ITV regions (adults %)
Highest   London 88   Southern 87   Anglia 86
Lowest   Lancs., Yorks., Tyne Tees: all 78   Border 74
(There are twelve ITV regions.)

'Comparing telephone and face-to-face interviews', a methodological research survey financed by the MRDF and based on carefully matched samples, both defines population differences and investigates respondent reactions to telephone and face-to-face modes.[5] We consider differences in reaction to, for example, open-ended questions, rating scales and type of subject being asked about in Chapter 5.

In the meantime, the following MRDF findings have important research design implications:

- The refusal rate was found to be nearly three times as great for the telephone as for the face-to-face approach:

	Face-to-face	Telephone
Available for interview	89%	67%
Full productive interviews	63%	45%

- There was 'a very strong indication that most respondents prefer the face-to-face personal contact with an interviewer and find it a more rewarding experience.'[5]

It is clear that to represent the general population by a sample available and willing to respond on the telephone involves *weighting* not only by region, sex and age (common practice whether the sample be a probability or a purposive one — see Chapter 4), but also by social grade, to ensure due representation of DE habits and attitudes in the total.

The telephone is a useful means of reaching business respondents. Here the problem is one of deciding who should be asked the questions. Who makes the decisions? The professional buyer? The managing director? The chief chemist? A committee? The telephone has a useful screening function and it is also used to put straightforward questions; but in more searching business enquiries the telephone call will precede an interview.

The renting out of lists of decision-makers derived from databases has created the risk of an 'irritant factor',[7] key decision-makers being contacted at a considerable frequency.

The convenient storage and rapid retrieval of data now possible encourages marketing companies to make marketing use of the telephone, for example to locate targets for goods and services. There is a danger of overkill, particularly when the target is a non-domestic one. Sugging (in which the voice on the telephone pretends at first to be conducting a research enquiry) is a dubious form of telemarketing frowned on by telemarketers as well as market researchers.

3.5.3 By post

The response rate achieved by a postal survey is likely to be low (30—40 per cent), unless the survey population consists of members of a special interest group: e.g. new car buyers, fellows of the Royal Horticultural Society, members of the Wire-haired Dachshund Owners' Association. Here we can expect a better than average response to a postal questionnaire, provided the questionnaire is about new cars, gardening or wire-haired dachshunds.

For a subject of more general interest, mailing questionnaires may prove more expensive than anticipated. It is necessary to take into account the following considerations when comparing costs with personal interviewing:

- The number of completed questionnaires returned.
- The cost of follow-up letters and other inducements to stimulate response, e.g. a ball-point pen to fill in the questionnaire.
- The cost of reply-paid envelopes.
- Possibly the need for some personal interviews, for the responses may add up to what appears to be a biased sample.

A postal questionnaire may be read from beginning to end before questions are answered, so that the particular interest of the company sponsoring the research is revealed from the outset, instead of gradually. In addition, we cannot be quite sure that the answers recorded represent the respondent's own habits and attitudes with regard to the subject of the enquiry.

There are, of course, occasions when a family or household response is required and the postal questionnaire gives all members a chance to join in. It may be necessary for documents to be consulted in order to answer the questions: for example, to consult the log book in an enquiry about motor cars.

There may be a case for combining data collection methods. If the questionnaire is long, or if the respondent is being asked to keep a diary record, questionnaire or diary may be placed during a personal interview. The introductory interview will add to the research costs but it is likely to secure a higher response rate so that cost per satisfactorily completed interview may be improved. Today mailed questionnaires have to compete with an ever-increasing volume of direct mail.

3.5.4 By means of a computer

There has been considerable development in computer-aided interviewing since the early experiment described in the second edition of this book: O'Brien and Dugdale's experiment, in which administration of questions via a VDU and keyboard is compared with oral administration.[8] Since then, Frost International have built up a substantial business based on data captured in computer-driven self-completion interviews.[9]

Here, our concern is with the different ways in which questions may be administered, and the Sandpiper procedure is a good example of computer-aided interviewing.

> The questionnaire relates to a particular market, say the market for private cars, and to the attributes consumers associate with them. (The attributes are generated by exploratory research as described in Chapter 2.)
>
> The respondent sits facing a microcomputer screen either at home or in a hall.
>
> Cars and the attributes on which the respondent is going to rate them are displayed as shown in Figure 3.2.
>
> The respondent rates each car in turn on, in this case, 'large/roomy' by moving a pointer along the 0–10 scale. Figure 3.2 shows the comparative strengths and weaknesses of these six competitors where this particular attribute is concerned.
>
> A longer list of cars and some forty discriminating attributes will be covered during the session which will last between forty and ninety minutes.

**Figure 3.2
Interacting with
a computer**

Source: Frost International's Sandpiper shared-cost service

It is to be expected that this method of administering a long list of scale items is less susceptible to the fatigue/boredom effects considered in Chapter 5 than the self-completion of a printed questionnaire.

Logistical and cost factors are likely largely to confine computer-assisted interviewing to shared-cost operations for some time to come. It is, of course, in the syndicated area that the big research money is made. As another example, in the Netherlands Gallup operate a consumer panel in which the respondent is provided with a home computer with a disk drive, a modem and a diskette with an interview and communication programme.[10]

The original Frost system, Scribe, was designed to meet the strategic needs of international marketing companies who bought exclusive access to a tailor-made database of consumer attitudes, needs, beliefs and intentions held in a mainframe computer.

Emergence of the micro-computer made possible the development of Sandpiper, a shared-cost system which brought the Scribe market-simulation model within the means of a wider range of marketing companies. We consider a number of market models later in this book.

3.6   Probability or purposive sample?

A glossary of sampling terms is given in Figure 3.3. Whatever the type of design, the object is to draw (or select) individuals from the population in such a way that the sample represents the population being surveyed, whether this be one of consumers, retail outlets, industries or organizations.

> We want to ensure that the sample is large enough to pick up variations in behaviour and attitude which are relevant to our marketing plans, and to be reassured that these variations appear in much the same proportions in the sample as in the survey population. (The expression 'in much the same proportions' is used because the statistics derived from samples are estimates. One can be pretty sure that a properly designed and managed survey will yield sample estimates which reflect population values but one cannot be 100 per cent sure.)

3.6.1   Probability (or random) sampling

It is possible to calculate how close to population values the sample estimates are likely to be, and the statistical procedure is described in Chapter 4. But, strictly speaking, this procedure should only be used if

- every individual or item in the population has a known chance of being included in the sample;

Probability sample. Each member of the population has a known (and non-zero) chance of being selected into the sample.

Purposive sample. Selection of sample members is dependent on human judgement.

Stratification. The population is divided into homogeneous groups (strata) whose relative size is known. Strata must be mutually exclusive. A random sample is taken in each stratum.

Proportionate sample. A uniform sampling fraction is applied to all the strata, i.e. the proportion of *n* (the number in the sample) to *N* (the number in the population) is the same for all strata.

Disproportionate sample. Where there is a marked variation in the sizes of the strata in a population, it is more efficient to use a variable sampling fraction. To calculate the sample estimates for the population as a whole, estimates derived from individual strata are weighted according to their relative size. A disproportionate sample is also used when the characteristic to be studied is markedly variable across the population, e.g. unemployment.

Quota sample. A method of stratified sampling in which selection of sample members within strata is non-random.

Simple random sample. All the population members are listed and numbered and the sample is drawn in one stage.

Sampling frame. A specification of the population which allows for the identification of individual items. The frame should be complete, up-to-date and without duplication of items.

Systematic sample. The sampling interval is calculated (let $N/n = k$). The first member of the sample is drawn at random from a numbered list; k is added to the number of the randomly selected member. This identifies the second member and the procedure is repeated.

Multi-stage sample. The sample is drawn in more than one stage, usually after stratification by region and type of district. Three-stage drawing is quite common: first, constituencies; second, ward or polling districts; third, electors using the register of electors as a sampling frame.

PPS. With probability proportionate to size of population/electorate: used in multi-stage drawing and associated with the use of a systematic interval. A range of numbers, equivalent to its population, is attached to each item on the list (e.g. each constituency, each polling district) before the draw is made. A number between one and the total population, divided by the number of sampling points, is drawn at random (or generated by computer). This indicates the starting point; the list of items is then systematically sampled, the probability of selection being proportionate to the size of each item.

**Figure 3.3
Glossary of
sampling terms**

• the draw for the sample is made using a random procedure so that human judgement does not enter into the selection or rejection of individuals or items.

To meet these requirements it is necessary to be able to locate every individual in the survey population on a list. For some populations this is an easy matter. For the student body of a university, polytechnic or other academic institution, for the membership of a professional body such as The Market Research Society or for the account or budget customers of a retail store, suitable sampling frames are readily available.

Each individual on the list is identified by means of a number and numbers are drawn at random until the sample has been filled. This is a simple random sample.

If the survey population is of any size, we may decide to adopt a systematic procedure.

Let us assume we need to draw 500 individuals from a survey population of 5,000: the sample members will amount to 1/10 of the survey population. We draw the first numbered individual at random, say this is the individual numbered 5. We then program a computer to generate the names of the individuals numbered 15, 25, 35 and so on until the sample is filled; i.e. to add 10 four hundred and ninety-nine times.

This is a systematic sample and this drawing technique is generally used in probability sampling. We have to be sure that the names are recorded on the sampling frame in a sufficiently random order, and that there is no periodicity in the listing. Application of the fixed interval to a list recorded in a hierarchical way, say the army list, could produce a biased sample.

For a national survey the register of electors is likely to be used as a sampling frame. (There is, in fact, a separate register for each polling district.) The Post Office's postcode file may also be used. This is a frame of addresses. (When the postcode file is being used in probability sampling, it is necessary to list individuals living at the randomly drawn addresses, to number them and then make the final draw, see section 4.2.3.)

When the survey population is large and widely dispersed a probability sample will commonly be drawn in more than one stage — this is multi-stage sampling.

It would be possible to draw a sample of, say, 2,000 adults from the adult population of 44.8 million in Great Britain in one stage but:

- The sample members might well be found to live at addresses scattered throughout Great Britain without regard to region or population density.
- Dispersal of calls would make it difficult to organize fieldwork and to supervise investigators.
- Scattered calls would add to the time taken to complete fieldwork and so to the cost of the survey.

A more cost-effective procedure is to divide the population into geographic groupings (geographic stratification) which take account of region and population density and to draw the sample in more than one stage. We might for example, draw a sample of constituencies within regions at the first stage, of polling districts within this random sample of constituencies at the second stage, and of electors from the registers for the selected polling districts at the third stage. A procedure for selecting non-electors at random is described in Chapter 4 where multi-stage drawing with PPS is considered in more detail.

A sample is drawn in more than one stage in order to cluster calls. This improves administrative efficiency and reduces fieldwork costs, but if calls are unduly clustered we may end up with a sample which does not represent the variety in the population as a whole.

The decision as to how many constituencies to draw and then how many polling districts, is based on informed judgement. If we were using the postcode file as a sampling frame we would have to decide how many postcode areas, and sectors within areas, to draw.

The national census tells us a good deal about variation in the geodemographic distribution of the population, how locations vary by level of unemployment, types of house tenure, enjoyment of basic housing amenities such as baths and toilets, size of immigrant population. Census data are used to classify residential neighbourhoods. ACORN has been developed as a market-analysis system by CACI using work carried out by Richard Webber.[11]

> ACORN applies published census statistics and classifies areas of about 150 households (census enumeration districts) into 38 different neighbourhood types. The ACORN classification takes into account 40 different variables encompassing demographic, housing and employment characteristics. The 38 neighbourhood types aggregate up to 11 neighbourhood groups.[12]

ACORN now has competitors: Pinpoint, Mosaic (set up by Richard Webber) and SuperProfiles.[13] All use census data; how they differ is discussed in Chapter 6. In the meantime, use of ACORN analysis in sample design is developed in Chapter 4 and illustrated in Table 4.2.

The census is taken every ten years and the next one is due in 1991. The market research industry is anxious that enumeration districts should be re-coded to accord with postcode boundaries. This would greatly increase the research value of the census because postcodes are now routinely collected in large-scale research operations and the postcode provides a link between different sources of data. Each postcode defines a group of about seventeen households (large users of the post have individual codes) and the Post Office address file and central postcode directory are available on optical discs. Adoption of the postcode as 'the main unit of spatial location'[14] is being pursued by The Market Research Society.

It is common practice for research agencies to use a master sample of first-stage units for all their survey work. The field force will be recruited and supervised in randomly drawn constituencies, administrative districts or postcode areas representative of the distribution and environmental circumstances of the population as a whole. Fieldwork might, for example, be concentrated in 200 out of 635 constituencies. Samples will be drawn in these constituencies as required.

A random procedure may be used up to and including the selection of respondents, or up to and including the selection of sampling points, as in random-location sampling.

In random-location sampling final selection of respondents is based on quotas. Quota samples are widely used in marketing research: cost–benefit analysis favours their use. In probability sampling, the randomly drawn individual must be interviewed. A one-hundred-per-cent response is difficult, if not impossible, to achieve, but at least three calls must be made at the address, and sometimes interviewers are instructed to make more than three. The cost of call-backs is added to the cost of drawing respondents from a sampling frame. The fieldwork for a national survey is likely to cost twice as much when probability methods are used throughout the drawing of the sample.

A probability sample design has two particular advantages:

1. Random drawing of the sample from the population makes it possible to establish a statistical relationship between the sample estimates and population values.
2. If names and addresses are drawn by a random process there is less danger of the composition of the sample being affected by the interviewer's likes and dislikes.

The reports published by the Office of Population Censuses and Surveys are based on probability samples. Government departments have to be prepared to answer politically loaded questions about sample estimates. It helps to be able to establish the statistical significance of the findings and to know that human judgement has not entered into the selection of respondents.

Psychologists and sociologists tend to use probability methods. They work in areas where motivations are often obscure and this makes it difficult to control the purposive selection of respondents.

Probability methods are also used to set up and maintain panels of consumers for the collection of trend data relating to buying behaviour or media habits. This is done on a shared-cost basis and the use of a probability method to draw a pool of panel members encourages confidence in the findings. The panel is stratified to mirror the major demographic characteristics of the population as shown in official statistics, and members are selected from the randomly drawn pool as required.

3.6.2 Purposive sampling

In marketing research it is common practice to use quota samples. In developed countries a good deal is known about the structure of populations whether these be consumer, trade, industrial or organizational populations, and the records are regularly updated. Governments collect and publish statistics, as do professional, industrial and trade associations (see Appendix 1, 'Access to secondary sources'). A quota sample takes account of this wealth of statistical data.

Let us assume that we are going to select a quota sample from the adult population of Great Britain.

We stratify the population by region. We may use the government's ten Economic Planning Regions, or the Independent Broadcasting Authority's thirteen television areas. These are often used in marketing surveys because of the importance of television as an advertising medium.

We stratify the population by social class group and by age group. These demographic characteristics are frequently used in the design and control of quota samples.

Social-class classification

A   Higher managerial, administrative or professional
B   Intermediate managerial, administrative or professional
C_1 Supervisory, clerical, junior administrative or professional
C_2 Skilled manual workers
D   Semi-skilled and unskilled manual workers
E   State pensioners, widows, casual and lowest-grade earners

This has always been one of the most dubious areas of market research investigation, but is also one of the most widely used classification systems. Along with age, it is generally used as a control in selection for quota sampling and therefore has to be assessed before the interview begins. A great deal of unsuccessful effort has been put into developing a classification system that is easy and simple for the interviewer to apply in the field with a reasonable degree of reliability and validity. The current convention is to use a socio-economic grouping, based exclusively on 'occupation of head of household'.[15] This is described in great detail in a document published by the National Readership Survey. (For JICNARS see also section 9.4.) In 1987 a sub-committee of The Market Research Society's Technical and Development Committee found that the NRS classification method was still in general use. Their report on socio-economic grouping is available from the MRS.[16]

The adult population of Great Britain breaks down as shown in Table 3.2.

An interviewer's daily assignment may be anything from ten to twenty calls, depending on the nature of the survey. (Length of questionnaire is critical.) For the sake of simplicity let us assume that a quota has been set based on 100 calls for five days' work. The interviewer is instructed to contact eighteen ABs, twenty-three C_1s, twenty-eight C_2s and thirty-two DEs. Among these 100 interviews, twenty are to be with age group 15–24, eighteen with age group 25–34 and so on. The social class and age controls are independent of each other. The interviewer might end

By social class (%)				Rounded total
AB	**C₁**	**C₂**	**DE**	
18	23	28	32	100

By age (%)						Total
15—24	**25—34**	**35—44**	**45—54**	**55—64**	**65 +**	
20	18	17	13	13	19	100

Table 3.2 Adult population of Great Britain by social class (%) and age (%)

Source: JICNARS National Readership Survey (Jan.—Dec. 1987)

up with a group of calls showing a distorted relationship between age and social class, so it is better practice to set the quota with interrelated controls, but this adds to the cost of fieldwork.

It may be possible to combine groups so that the interviewer's task is simplified, saving time and cost. It may not, for example, be necessary to distinguish AB class (upper middle) from C₁ class (lower middle) or the 25—34 age group from the 35—44 group. These decisions depend on the nature of the product field or service being surveyed and the extent to which exploratory research indicates that behaviour and attitudes vary by social class and age. For most fast-moving packaged goods, class is a weak discriminator and a breakdown of the sample by three social-class groups — middle class, skilled worker and unskilled group — would be relevant for planning and control. In Table 3.3 it is assumed that four age groups and three social-class groups will adequately reflect the variability in the population.

Quota samples are often controlled by social class and by age because other relevant data are classified in this way, an important example being the continuous surveys on which media planning is based (see Chapter 9). But other controls may be relevant, such as size of family and whether a housewife works outside the home. In a survey relating to convenience foods or to durables the interviewer is likely to be required to collect data from a laid-down proportion of 'gainfully occupied' housewives (22 per cent of housewives work full-time, and 21 per cent work part-time).

In other words, *the selection of respondents is purposive*. They are chosen to fit a quota designed to mirror relevant characteristics in the

Social class	Age				Total
	15—24	**25—44**	**45—64**	**65 +**	
ABC₁	7	13	11	7	38
C₂	6	10	9	6	31
DE	6	10	9	6	31
Total	19	33	29	19	100

Table 3.3 Sample quota of four age groups and three social-class groups

Note: Based on JICNARS Readership Survey (July '82—June '83)

population. They are not drawn from the population by a random procedure. This is the essential difference between purposive and probability sampling.

A quota sample is as reliable as a probability sample in practice, though not in theory, when the following requirements are met:

- Up-to-date statistics relating to the structure of the population are available.
- The quota is set in such a way that important population characteristics are interrelated, such as age and social class, age and size of family or age and working outside the home.
- Classification questions are carefully designed so that, for example, the occupation of the head of the household is established with some certainty.
- The interviewer's choice of location is restricted. This is not always possible but where the decision as to which door to knock at is taken out of the interviewer's hands, the main criticism of quota sampling is removed.
- The selection of respondents features in the interviewer's training programme.

It is difficult to control selection of individuals for interviewing if contact is made away from the home, in the street or at work. In the case of people at work, an important control is the nature of the work. The numbers of men and women employed in the main categories of job are readily available and the published statistics can be used to design a suitable quota.

> If selection of respondents is not controlled in this way the sample is likely to contain too many readily accessible workers, such as men working on building sites and in public transport, at the expense of those working on assembly lines or in offices.

3.7 Proportionate or disproportionate sample?

This is an important decision when making design choices. It is likely to affect both the cost of a survey and the validity of the sample estimates derived from it. In asking the question 'Proportionate or disproportionate sample?', we are implying that the population can be divided into groups (or strata) whose relative weight is known. We considered three commonly used stratification factors when describing the selection of a quota sample of adults from the British population: region, social class and age.

In a proportionate sample each stratum has its population weight:

$$\frac{n \text{ (number in the sample)}}{N \text{ (number in the population)}} \text{ is } \textit{uniform} \text{ for all strata}$$

In a disproportionate sample we oversample small-sized strata at the expense of large-sized strata, but restore their due weights in the population when we come to consider total results or proportions of the total results:

$$\frac{n \text{ (number in the sample)}}{N \text{ (number in the population)}} \textit{varies} \text{ from one stratum to another}$$

For the proportionate sample we used a uniform sampling fraction and for the disproportionate sample a variable sampling fraction. Exploratory research will have cleared our minds as to which strata in the population should be considered as separate and individual groups.

> Let us assume we are going to survey the habits and attitudes of adult males with regard to shaving. We are interested in all males of shaving age but have a particular interest in the 15−19 age group because males in this group are developing their shaving habits and attitudes. But the group represents a small percentage of the male shaving population. If we use a uniform sampling fraction we either end up with too few interviews in this group and about the right number in other, larger groups; or we provide for a sufficient number in the 15−19 age group and conduct many more interviews than we need in the larger groups. Obviously, we would deploy the research budget to better effect if we used a variable sampling fraction, 'oversampled' the small group and restored their weight to the larger groups when the data relating to all men were processed by the computer.

Disproportionate samples are often the most cost-effective. (Questions of sample size and of confidence in sample estimates are dealt with in Chapter 4.)

In a stratified sample, whether a uniform or a variable sampling fraction is used, the risk of sampling error is reduced. If we drew the sample of adult males at random, without stratification, we might find ourselves with a 15−19 age group whose size did not equate with official statistics. By ensuring that each group is given its due population weight we remove a possible source of error.

There are more opportunities to use stratification in the design of purposive samples than in the design of probability samples. Any reliable statistical data about the structure of the population, relevant to the marketing objectives, can be used to stratify a purposive sample. For a probability sample it is necessary to be able to identify individuals within the strata in order to be able to make a random draw.

If we are going to use the register of electors as a sampling frame we can stratify geographically before making the draw because the registers tell us where people live: but social class and age of the respondent (to quote two commonly used ways of classifying respondents) are not known until *after* the interview. We can stratify after the interview and reweight in accordance with official statistics.

3.8　The judgement sample

Table 3.1 on 'design choices' shows two types of purposive sample: quota and judgement. We have seen that judgement enters into multi-stage probability sampling as well as into purposive designs. But the description 'judgement' is particularly applicable to industrial and trade-research sampling.

In industrial and trade research we are concerned to sample output or sales turnover. Our base for sample design is output or turnover and not the number of establishments or shops in a particular industry or trade. The multiples are only 8.5 per cent of grocery outlets (Nielsen) but in 1983 they accounted for 73 per cent of grocery sales while Sainsbury and Tesco between them handled 30 per cent (AGB/TCA).

When we consult secondary data sources at the design stage (see Appendix 1) we soon realize that in many fields there are a few concerns so large that, if they were excluded from a sample in a probability draw, sample estimates would be unlikely to represent values in the real industrial or trade world. Any survey of the manufacturers of paints should include ICI Paints and any survey of the grocery trade should include Tesco. In this circumstance our sample design is:

Census of dominating firms + Sample of the rest

If no one concern is so dominant that it must be included in the sample, we are likely to find that a comparatively small proportion of the industrial or trade population we are surveying (say 20 per cent) does a substantial proportion of the business (say 80 per cent); the '80:20' rule.

Stratification by volume/value is accordingly an important factor in the design of industrial or trade surveys. Table 3.4 shows how the Government Statistical Office stratifies establishments in the 'food, drink and tobacco' category.

This type of official information makes it possible to set quotas, provided our market fits the official classifications. Informed judgement is needed in the design of a sample to represent the market for, say, a timing device used in a variety of industries, or one to represent the distribution of soft drinks sold through a variety of outlets.

Given that the market has been stratified by volume/value there follows the problem of identifying the enterprises in each stratum. The official

Employees N	Establishments		Gross Output		
	N	%	£000	%	
1– 10	1,862				
11– 24	1,498				
25– 99	1,172				
	4,532	79.2	1,382.0	13.3	
100– 199	425	7.4	842.5	8.1	
200– 499	459	8.0	1,820.6	17.7	
500– 999	181	3.1	1,451.8	14.0	
1,000–1,499	50	0.9	643.0	6.2	
1,500& +	84	1.4	4,205.5	40.7	
	5,731	100.0	10,345.4	100.0	

Table 3.4 Stratification by value of output

In this case 4,532 establishments, each with less than 100 employees, account for 13.3 per cent of gross output, while 84 establishments with 1,500 or more employees account for 40.7 per cent.

Source: Census of Production

statistics provide information about the structure of industries and trades, but firms return this information on the understanding that names are not published. Fitting names to strata requires skilful judgement in the use of secondary sources.

Where it is possible to establish a complete list of firms within strata a probability design is theoretically possible (an example is given in section 4.3), but purposive selection of firms within strata is the more general practice.

Survey design calls for the exercise of judgement, and research suppliers operating in this area are exceptionally well informed. They have on file detailed information about individual markets and every opportunity is taken to update this information.

3.9 Conclusion

In survey research cost-effective allocation of often scarce resources depends on the following:

- Close collaboration between those who are commissioning the research and those responsible for its design and execution, both while the research proposal is being developed (Figure 3.1) and when the findings are interpreted.
- Estimating what proportion of questionnaires (or other means of collecting data such as diaries) are likely to be satisfactorily completed

before deciding whether to contact respondents in a personal interview, over the telephone or through the post (section 3.5).

- Using a disproportionate design when groups of interest in the population show marked variations in size (section 3.7).
- Using quota samples when the parameters of the survey population are well documented, provided sampling points are specified and the selection of respondents is controlled (section 3.6), and there is proper provision for the training and supervision of the field force.

To use a probability sample where a quota sample would be suitable is to incur opportunity costs: the opportunity within the research budget to enlarge the sample or carry out further research.

Sources and further reading

1. J. Jephcott, 'A breakthrough in household panels', *ADMAP* (Sept. 1986), pp. 52–4.
2. Code of conduct of The Market Research Society and the Industrial Marketing Research Association, effective from 1 January 1988. *MRS Yearbook* (1988), pp. 58–76.
3. *MRS Newsletter*, no. 249 (Dec. 1987), p. 10.
4. J. Weitz, 'Why the telephone', *MRS Survey* (Summer 1986), pp. 15–17.
5. MRDF research projects: 'Telephone availability' (1987); 'Comparing telephone and face-to-face interviews' (1986); 'Telephone interviewing facilities' (1987).
6. G.P. Hyett and G.M. Allan, 'Collection of data by telephone: its validity in consumer research', paper given at the MRS conference, 1976.
7. G. Hurley, 'Telemarketing and telephone market research: an unholy alliance?', *MRS Newsletter*, no. 256 (July 1987).
8. T. O'Brien and V. Dugdale, 'Questionnaire administration by computer', *Journal of The Market Research Society* (Oct. 1978), p. 228.
9. K. Gofton, 'Using a model approach', *Marketing* (6 Feb. 1986).
10. W. Saris and W. Marius De Pijper, 'Computer-assisted interviewing using home computers', *European Research*, vol. 14, no. 3 (1986), pp. 144–50.
11. R.J. Webber, 'The national classification of residential neighbourhoods: an introduction to the classification of wards and parishes', *PRAG Technical Papers* (Nov. 1977).
12. *Users Guide, CACI Market Analysis*.
13. A. Garrett, 'How to home in on the target market', *Marketing Week* (29 May 1987), pp. 57–60.
14. P. Mouncey, 'Making sense of the census', *MRS Newsletter*, no. 261 (Dec. 1987) pp. 16–18.
15. A.R. Wolfe (ed.) *Standardised Questions: A Review for Market Research Executives*, (2nd edn, London: The Market Research Society, 1984).
16. J. Bound, 'The use of socio-economic grading', *MRS Newsletter* (Dec. 1987), p. 12 (introduction to a report on the subject available from the MRS).

See also

- M. Collins, 'Telephone interviewing in consumer surveys', *MRS Newsletter*, no. 211 (Oct. 1983).
- L. England and P. Arnold, 'Telephone, mail and other techniques', in R.M. Worcester and J. Downham (eds), *Consumer Market Research Handbook*, 3rd edn (Amsterdam: North-Holland, 1986).
- C. Greenhalgh, 'How should we initiate effective research?', *MRS Conference Papers* (1983). Includes a definition of the research brief.
- C. Husbands, 'The telephone study of voting intentions in the June 1987 General Election', *Journal of the Market Research Society*, vol. 29, no. 4 (Oct. 1987).
- W. Sykes and G. Hoinville, 'Methodological research on telephone interviewing', *MRS Conference Papers* (1984).

Problems

1. 'The design of a survey, besides requiring a certain amount of technical knowledge, is a prolonged and arduous intellectual exercise' (Oppenheim). Discuss.
2. Faced with the following assignments, what method of data collection would you propose in each case? List main topics of interest and explain your choice of method.

    (a) A survey of voting intentions at a general election.
    (b) A survey to establish where and in what way gardening tools are selected by the population of an expanding town in the south-east, a town served by a variety of traditional and modern retail outlets.
    (c) A survey to establish car accessories in use on the vehicles of private motorists, together with those not on the vehicle but desired.
    (d) A survey designed to show regional differences in the use of equipment by commercial laundries.

    (There is a question about sample design, given these assignments, at the end of Chapter 4.)

4 Describing markets: focus on sampling

We have seen that there are two particular advantages to be gained from using a probability sample:

1. Human judgement does not enter into the selection or rejection of respondents.
2. It is possible to measure the extent to which values in the population may vary from the estimates yielded by the sample.

In this chapter we focus on the second advantage and consider the application of probability theory to sampling in consumer and in non-domestic markets.

4.1 Basic statistics

4.1.1 Sample estimates and population values

In size most samples are small fractions of the population. It is not necessary to draw a large proportion of the population into the sample to achieve valid results. Samples of 2,000 or less are commonly used to represent the 44.8 million adults in Great Britain. Validity of the sample estimates depends on the following:

- The size of the sample in relation to the variability in the population where the subject of the survey is concerned (if habits and attitudes were uniform throughout the population, the responses of one individual would suffice).
- The care with which the sample has been drawn.
- There being an adequate number of respondents in any one group which is to be considered in isolation.
- Avoidance of 'non-sampling errors' when the data are being collected and analysed, errors such as 'interviewer bias' and use of ambiguous questions (Chapter 5).

There are, of course, very many possible samples of 2,000 in a population of 44.8 million. Can we be confident that the sample we happen to have drawn is a representative one? We cannot. But we can take individual sample estimates and establish what the relationship between sample estimate and population value is likely to be. Figure 4.1 summarizes notation in common use and gives the formulae referred to in this section. Let us consider a population value, say, the foot size of adult women. Distribution of female foot sizes is, of course, of moment

	Notation	
	Population (values)	Sample (estimates)
Number of items	N	n
Mean	μ or $\overline{X}$	$\overline{x}$
Standard deviation	σ or S	s
Standard error of the mean	—	$s_{\overline{x}}$ or s.e. $(\overline{x})$
Proportion	π or P	p
Standard error of the proportion	—	s_p or s.e. (p)

Sampling formulae

Standard deviation $\sqrt{\dfrac{1}{n}\Sigma(x-\overline{x})^2}$

See section

Standard error of the mean $\dfrac{s}{\sqrt{n}}$ Applies variables   4.1.2

Standard error of the proportion   Applies attributes   4.1.3

$\sqrt{\dfrac{p(1-p)}{n}}$ or $\sqrt{\dfrac{p(100-p)}{n}}\%$ or $\sqrt{\dfrac{pq}{n}}$ q is the proportion without the attribute

To estimate sample size: 4.1.4

Let Z stand for the number of standard errors required by the confidence level (in market research it is usual to work at the 95 per cent confidence level, i.e. to set limits of ± 1.96 (or 2) standard errors around the sample estimate); Let E represent the range of error around the sample estimate acceptable to the decision maker; then the formula for estimating sample size is —   4.1.1   4.1.1   4.1.4

    for variables using the standard error of the mean

$$n = \frac{s^2 \times Z^2}{E^2}$$

    for attributes using the standard error of the proportion

$$n = \frac{pq \times Z^2}{E^2}$$

Figure 4.1 Survey research, sampling: basic statistics

Source: C.A. Moser and G.K. Kalton, *Survey Methods in Social Investigation*, 2nd edn (London: Heinemann Educational Books, 1971)

to shoe manufacturers. If we were to plot foot sizes, one by one, on a piece of squared paper we would see a pattern emerge. In due course the plottings would be seen to be symmetrically distributed around their mean. If we outlined the shape of the distribution, as shown in Figure 4.2, we would see that the foot sizes filled the area beneath a normal curve.

Distance from the mean is measured by the standard deviation, which takes account of the variability in a population. A normal distribution would show the following characteristics:

- 68 per cent of the area occupied by our plottings of shoe sizes would lie within -1 and $+1$ standard deviations from the mean.
- 95 per cent would lie within -2 and $+2$ standard deviations (or, to be exact, ± 1.96).
- 99 per cent would lie within -3 and $+3$ standard deviations (or ± 3.09).

Provided we are considering a sample of at least thirty people and the sample has been drawn using a probability procedure, we can use knowledge of the normal distribution to relate our sample estimates to values in the population as a whole.

It is possible to prove mathematically that the means of all the possible samples in a population equal the population mean.

- Draw the ten possible samples of 2 from the five women with foot sizes ranging 3, 4, 5, 6 and 7.
- Average the foot size of each sample of 2.
- Take the mean of the ten averages.

The answer is 5, which is the mean of 3 + 4 + 5 + 6 + 7.

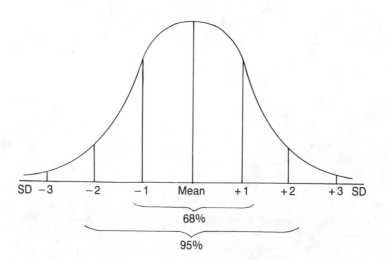

**Figure 4.2
A normal
distribution**

If we were able to draw all the possible samples of women from a population and to plot the average shoe size of each sample, we would find that the distribution of our plottings of means took the same symmetrical shape around the mean of all the average sizes as that shown in Figure 4.2.

Mini-exercises apart, we are not going to be able to draw all possible samples from the survey population, so how do we use this finding to calculate how much confidence we can have in an estimate given by our one sample?

4.1.2 The standard error of the mean

We do not expect our sample estimate to be exactly the same as the population value. We are going to make an allowance for possible error and the size of the allowance will depend on:

- Variability in the population — if all women had the same foot size there would be no risk of error.
- The size of the sample.
- The confidence level we choose to work at.

Variability in the population is measured by the standard deviation. Without a census, we do not know how foot sizes vary in the population as a whole, but we can consider the distribution of foot sizes shown by our sample and calculate the standard deviation of these. We know the size of our sample, and we choose at what level of confidence we want to work.

Research data relate to amounts spent by samples of the population on a variety of items: items such as rent, rates, holidays, car insurance, petrol and, perhaps most frequently, food and other fast-moving necessities.

Let us assume that the average daily amount spent on food and necessities by a sample of 400 households is £6 and that the standard deviation from the mean shown by the 400 budget totals is £1.60 or 160p. Then the standard error of the mean is given by:

$$s_{\bar{x}} = \frac{s}{\sqrt{n}} = \frac{160p}{\sqrt{400}} = \frac{160p}{20} = 8p$$

If we choose to work at the 68 per cent level of confidence we allow for a possible sample error of ± 8p and conclude that the sample estimate of £6 represents a population value lying between £5.92 and £6.08.

But in choosing the 68 per cent level of confidence we run a one-in-three risk of our sample mean being outside the range of all possible means covered by ± one standard deviation. If we allow for ± two standard errors of the mean, this risk is reduced to one in twenty.

> At the 95 per cent level of confidence our sample estimate of £6 represents a population value lying between £5.84 and £6.16.

We have increased confidence at the cost of precision. To achieve a more precise estimate at the 95 per cent level it would be necessary to increase the sample size. However, to halve the allowance for error it would be necessary to multiply the sample size by four. The 95 per cent level is common practice in marketing research. The cost of working at a higher level of confidence is out of proportion to the benefit received. In any survey of human behaviour and attitudes there are possible sources of error other than those which can be statistically measured.

4.1.3 The standard error of a proportion

In marketing research we are often considering attributes rather than variables. Attributes, such as being able to drive a motor car, are either present or not present whereas variables, such as the amounts spent on petrol, have a range of values. Variables are reduced to means/averages; attributes to proportions/percentages.

The distribution of a population according to whether or not its members have a particular attribute is called 'binomial distribution' from bi-nomen meaning two names:[1] for example, adults in Great Britain can be called 'drivers' or 'non-drivers' according to whether or not they hold a driving licence.

Let us assign the letter P to the drivers (using a capital letter because P relates to drivers in the population and not to drivers in a sample of the population). Then let us assign the letter Q to the non-drivers; $P + Q = N$ (the population). If we are working in proportions, N is 1, or 100 if we are working in percentages: so Q is either 1 minus P or 100 minus P.

If we were to draw all possible samples from the population, the proportions shown to be drivers would vary, but distribution of the sample ps in relation to the population P is known and so, as with the standard error of the mean, it is possible to make allowance for sampling error. The standard error of a proportion takes account of n, the number in the sample, and p, the proportion with the attribute.

> If p is the percentage or proportion with the attribute and q the percentage or proportion without, the standard error is calculated as follows:
>
> $$s_p = \sqrt{\frac{pq}{n}} \text{ often written as } \sqrt{\frac{p(1-p)}{n}} \text{ or } \frac{p(100-p)}{n} \%$$

Most market research data are presented in the form of percentages rather than proportions so we use percentages in the following example:

A survey shows that 40 per cent of the women in a town drive cars. The estimate is based on a sample of 600. How precisely can this estimate be interpreted at the 95 per cent level of confidence?

$$s_p = \sqrt{\frac{40 \times 60}{600}} = \sqrt{4} = \pm 2\%$$

At the 95 per cent level of confidence, a likely range of error is ± twice 2 per cent. The sample estimate of 40 per cent indicates that the true proportion probably lies between 36 and 44 per cent.

4.1.4 Estimating sample size

The formulae given in Figure 4.1 suggest that in order to estimate sample size we need to put figures to the following:

- The standard deviation anticipated for individual variables (s).
- The proportion/percentage likely to hold each attribute (p).
- The number of standard errors required by the confidence level (Z).
- Action standards set by the marketing department, the acceptable error (E).

The data needed to estimate s and p are an important product of exploratory research. If secondary sources do not give the necessary clues, an omnibus survey may be used (see section 2.8).

When exploratory research has suggested that p is 40 per cent, the range of acceptable error (E) is ± 2 per cent and the confidence level requires allowance for $2s_p$, then:

$$n = \frac{pq \times Z^2}{E^2} = \frac{40 \times 60 \times 4}{4} = 2,400$$

Were we prepared to tolerate an error of ± 4 per cent the required sample size would be 600:

$$n = \frac{40 \times 60 \times 4}{16}$$

Doubling the allowance for error makes it possible to quarter the sample size. (Conversely, in order to halve the standard error, it is necessary to quadruple the sample size.)

Since surveys cover a variety of characteristics, and we are likely to want to consider these for a number of sub-groups within the total sample, the full statistical procedure is unduly laborious.

It is, however, essential to have decided in advance how the results of a survey are going to be analysed and what measurements will be the most important. It is unfortunate if a particular estimate arouses marketing interest, and this estimate is found to be based on the habits or attitudes of so few individuals in the sample that a conclusion cannot be drawn. In determining sample size it is common practice to ensure that there are at least fifty, and preferably 100, individuals in the smallest sub-group likely to be considered in isolation.

Sample size is, of course, often constrained by cost. We start with a budgetary allowance sufficient to buy a certain number of interviews. In the following example we can afford a total of 1,500 and we compare the efficiency of a design using proportionate stratification with one using disproportionate stratification (see section 3.7).

A population of 50,000 persons is distributed over three areas: 10 per cent live in area A, 40 per cent in B and 50 per cent in C. Exploratory research has stimulated marketing interest in an age group which accounts for 20 per cent of the population in each area. We want to be able to consider the habits and attitudes of this age group in relation to the population as a whole. Given that we can afford 1,500 interviews, and that we are required to use a probability design, how should we proceed?

Design using a proportionate sample

Area	Population N	$N\%$	Sampling fraction N/n	Sample n	Special-interest group of 20% (n)
A	5,000	10	33.3	150	30
B	20,000	40	33.3	600	120
C	25,000	50	33.3	750	150
Total	50,000	100	33.3	1,500	300

With a proportionate design we have an unduly small number of the age group in region A and a generous allocation to B and C.

Design using a disproportionate sample

Area	Population N	$N\%$	Sampling fraction N/n	Sample n	Special-interest group of 20% (n)
A	5,000	10	10	500	100
B	20,000	40	40	500	100
C	25,000	50	50	500	100
Total	50,000	100	33.3	1,500	300

We make a judgement decision to allocate the 1,500 interviews we can afford, giving 500 to each region, so using a variable instead of a uniform sampling faction. This gives us a satisfactory number of interviews in each of the three regions with the age group we are particularly interested in.

We shall, of course, have to restore their due weight to the three regional populations when calculating total results for the three regions as a whole. Had we not been committed to a probability design, we could have sampled disproportionately by age as well as by area, setting quotas to achieve the following allocation of calls:

Area	Population N	Sample n	Special-interest group of 20% (n)	Remaining 80%
A	5,000	500	250	250
B	20,000	500	250	250
C	25,000	500	250	250

The computer would be programmed to restore due weight to totals by area and by age, and a more cost-effective design would be achieved.

4.1.5 Effect of design on sampling error

The basic formulae given in Figure 4.1 relate to simple random samples. In a simple random sample all the individuals in the population go into the draw and the sample is drawn in one stage.

- If we stratify the population and draw a simple random sample from each stratum, we reduce the sampling error. If we sampled a population of polytechnic students without prior stratification we might, by chance, draw too many engineers and too few business studies students, or too many full-time students and too few part-time ones. In a survey relating to courses we might need to be sure that engineering and business studies were duly represented, while for a survey about amenities we might want to ensure that the attitudes and behaviour of part-time students carried due weight. There is here a clear case for stratification, whether we are considering courses or amenities, and we can use a probability design because the student records enable us to assign students to strata.

- If we draw in more than one stage, with probability proportionate to size of population, we increase the sampling error. The multi-stage procedure has the effect of clustering the members of the population included in the sample. The effect of this has been investigated using estimates derived from simple random sampling as the criterion. The standard errors arrived at using the formulae given in Figure 4.1 are corrected for design effect by multiplying them by a design factor of between 1.0 and 2.5. Even the National Readership Survey (section 9.4.4) 'recognised as having a particularly good sample design'[2] has been estimated to have a design factor of 1.4. The size of the design factor depends on the closeness with which calls are clustered when the sample is drawn. Clustering has a stronger effect on sampling error than stratifying.

- If the sample embraces 10 per cent or more of the population (as might occur in a survey among students), we apply a correction factor, known as the finite multiplier, $\sqrt{(N - n/N - 1)}$. This has the effect of reducing the standard error: but surveys are usually based on smaller sampling fractions.

4.1.6 Weighting samples

We have seen that in both probability and purposive sample designs, data derived from reliable sources, such as the Government Statistical Service, are used to stratify the population *before* individuals are drawn/selected for interviewing. But some of those drawn/selected may be unavailable for interview, or they may refuse to be interviewed. In telephone interviewing a substantial proportion of those approached may refuse (section 3.5.2). The sample we achieve may be unbalanced when compared with the population as known. 'Weighting' aims to rectify this. The procedure is described by Ehrenberg:

> If an unstratified sample of 10 has given 6 boys and 4 girls and we *know* that boys and girls are 50 : 50 in the population, the results in each stratum can be 'weighted' to bring the sample into line with the population proportion (e.g. by multiplying all the girls' readings by 1.5). This kind of 'posterior' stratification is usually less effective than prior stratification. The weighted portion of the sample has an undue effect on sampling errors (e.g. an untypical girl would count for 50% more than an untypical boy).[3]

Weighting by region, sex and age is standard procedure in a sample drawn from the general public. In the case of telephone surveys 'telephone-accessible weighting' is used. DEs are up-weighted (together with the oldest and youngest age groups). Ehrenberg's caveat is relevant here. The MRDF's methodological survey ('Comparing telephone and face-to-face interviews') found that DEs with a telephone may behave differently from those without.

Specification of 'any weighting methods used' is among the 'relevant details' which members of The Market Research Society are required by the code of conduct to provide to clients. Computerization makes possible the programmed application of weights. This may reduce vigilance as to 'an undue effect on sampling errors'.

4.2 Drawing procedures

4.2.1 Drawing with probability proportionate to size (PPS)

The PPS procedure is associated with multi-stage sampling. Let us assume that the first-stage sampling unit is the constituency. The 633 parliamentary constituencies in Great Britain are first stratified by region using either the government's ten Economic Planning Regions or the Independent Broadcasting Authority's twelve. The order in which the constituencies are listed within regions is important because we are going to draw the first constituency at random and then take a systematic interval (see section 3.6.1).

Every individual in the population must have had a chance of being included in the sample when we get to the end of the drawing process: but first of all we want to ensure that the regional distribution of constituencies, together with their varying population densities, are duly represented in the sample.

Having stratified by region, we may take account of population density by sorting each region's constituencies into four groups: 'conurbation' (those lying entirely within a conurbation — an aggregation of urban districts, e.g. Greater London), 'other 100 per cent urban', 'mixed urban and rural' (constituencies in which 50 per cent or more of the population live in urban administrative districts), and 'rural' (less than 50 per cent live in urban administrative districts).

Thus far the ordering of the list of 633 constituencies is as follows:

Region 1
Conurbation constituencies.
Other 100 per cent urban constituencies.
Mixed urban and rural constituencies.
Rural constituencies.

Region 2
Conurbation constituencies.
Other 100 per cent urban constituencies.
Mixed urban and rural constituencies.
Rural constituencies.

And so on until all the regions have been covered.

We have four strata relating to population density within each of ten regions (assuming we are using the standard regions). Within each of these strata (or cells) it is quite usual to list the constituencies in descending order according to the ratio of Conservative to Labour (or Labour to Conservative) votes cast at the most recent general election. This is done because voting tends to correlate with social economic class. The final list is therefore stratified by an approximation to social economic class as well as by population density and regional distribution. This is implicit stratification, i.e. stratification is 'implied' in the way in which the first-stage sampling units (in this case constituencies) are listed.

In order to draw with PPS, it is necessary to accumulate the electoral populations of the constituencies, so that each constituency is represented by a range of numbers equal to the size of its electorate (Table 4.1). Let us assume that we have decided to draw a master sample of 200

Constituency*	Electorate	Electorates accumulated	
Hall Green	67,683	67,683	
Selly Oak	64,631	132,314	
Yardley	57,574	189,888	. . . 175,000 drawn at random
Northfield	78,873	268,761	
Perry Barr	51,794	320,555	Add *N/n*
Erdington	64,341	384,896	228,725
Stechford	61,115	446,011	. . . 403,725
Edgbaston	68,645	514,656	
Handsworth	45,018	559,674	Add *N/n*
Sparkbrook	45,910	605,584	228,725
Ladywood	33,989	639,573	. . . 632,450
Small Heath	46,602	686,175	
N	686,175		
N/n	228,725		

Note: The three constituencies selected with probability proportionate to their electoral populations are Yardley, Stechford and Ladywood.

* Ordered according to the ratio of Conservative to Labour votes cast at the 1979 general election

constituencies and that the total number of electors on the registers is 40,000,000.

> *N/n* = 40 million over 200 = 200,000.
> Draw a number at random between 1 and 200,000, say 85,000.
> The constituency with this number in its range is the first drawn.
> Add the sampling interval of 200,000 to 85,000 = 285,000.
> The constituency with this number in its range is the second drawn, and so on.
> The sampling interval of 200,000 is added on 199 times.

The procedure used to draw first-stage sampling units with PPS is illustrated in Table 4.1. The twelve Birmingham constituencies are listed according to the ratio of Conservative to Labour votes cast at the 1979 election in each constituency: then electorates are recorded and accumulated. If we were drawing from the complete list of 633 constituencies in Great Britain (the UK total is 650; there are 17 constituencies in N. Ireland), Birmingham's twelve would be well down the list in region 7, and a substantial number of electors would have accumulated before Hall Green was recorded. However, for the purpose of this example we start with Hall Green, and this constituency is represented by the range 1–67,683.

The decision as to how many constituencies to carry out fieldwork in is based on informed judgement. There are available statistical data to show how the population varies. Geodemographic systems such as ACORN are based on these data. Savings in cost and improved supervision have to be weighed against undue clustering of sampling locations. There is less risk of undue clustering if respondents are selected at the second stage, i.e. after the constituencies have been drawn, but this would still produce rather a widely dispersed sample.

At the second stage wards or polling districts may be listed, their electorates accumulated and a second draw made using PPS.

> Let us assume that we are drawing a sample of 3,000 people using a master sample of 200 constituencies. The varying sizes of the constituencies have been allowed for in the PPS procedure so we have to make fifteen calls in each constituency. The extent to which we cluster the calls will depend on the subject of the survey and the extent to which habits and attitudes vary where this subject is concerned. We could, for example, draw five names from each of three polling registers or three names from each of five registers to get our fifteen per constituency; for here again variation in the size of polling districts will have been taken into account in the PPS drawing procedure.

4.2.2 Drawing from the register of electors

The names and addresses of all British subjects aged eighteen and over who are entitled to vote and have registered are listed in the register of electors. The returns are made in October and the register is published in February of the following year. From the marketing point of view the main weakness of the register as a sampling frame is the fact that it excludes young adults and immigrants. There are procedures for including 'non-electors' in the sample but let us first draw the electors.

> Let us assume that we are making five calls in each of three polling districts drawn with PPS. In one of these three polling districts there are 845 electors listed on the register and numbered 1 to 845 (N/n = 845/5 = 169). We draw a number at random between 1 and 169. Let us say this is 109. By adding the sampling interval onto the random start we draw the following respondents:

> 109 Marks, Ann M., 10 Bran End Road.
> 278 Low, James W., Brambles, The Spinney.
> 447 Fellows, Jean B., 40 Garden Fields.
> 616 Crisp, Elizabeth M., Mill Cottage, Rosemary Lane.
> 785 Humphreys, Christopher A., 12 High Street.

We stop at this point if the intention is to interview electors, but our interest is more likely to be in all adults, 'non-electors' as well as 'electors'. The following procedure makes it possible to extend the draw to non-electors while giving every adult a known (and non-zero) chance of being included in the sample:

- A name and address are drawn from the register using the method described above.
- The interviewer works to a sample issue sheet: all the electors at the same address as the selected elector are listed in the order of the register on the sample issue sheet.
- The selected elector is starred.
- The total number of electors at the address is the sampling interval.
- Suppose there are e electors at the address of the starred elector, then starting with the starred elector every eth name following is starred. The added starred names (if any) will all be non-electors and they constitute the non-elector sample.

This procedure cannot determine the number of non-electors in the sample in advance, but the probability of selecting a given non-elector is the same as the chance of selecting any given elector, provided he/she lives in a household where there is an elector!

4.2.3 The postcode address file as a frame

The procedure of drawing a sample in more than one stage with PPS is being applied to the postcode units in the same way as to parliamentary or local government units, as compared with constituencies or administrative districts, wards and polling districts.

These different units are best explained by taking a typical postcode, RM3 6HS:

RM	This is the postcode area denoted by the letters at the beginning of the postcode. There are 120 areas in the United Kingdom.
RM3	The postcode district denoted by the first half of the postcode. There are nearly 2,690 districts in the United Kingdom.
RM3 6	The postcode sector of which there are 8,880 in the United Kingdom.

RM3 6HS   The complete postcode. The 21.75 million addresses in the
United Kingdom are covered by 1.5 million postcodes.

Each postcode defines a group of, on average, seventeen houses. However,
'large users' of the post, that is any address receiving over twenty pieces
of mail a day, have their own unique postcode.
  Every address in the United Kingdom, except those in the Isle of Man
and the Channel Islands, is postcoded.[4]

There are 180,000 'large users'[5] each with its own postcode and this computer file constitutes a useful sampling frame for use in 'non-domestic' markets (see section 4.3).

It will be readily appreciated that, with the postcode file as a sampling frame, it is possible to draw a national sample in more than one stage, stratifying by postcode area, treating districts and sectors as first- and second-stage units, and arriving at a sample of postcodes (i.e. groups of on average seventeen homes) at the third stage; the draw at the first and second stages being made with probability proportionate to the number of addresses in each district or sector.

The postcode file is used by Audits of Great Britain as a frame for their syndicated home audit of consumer durables, based on a large sample of households, 30,000 audited quarterly. (The sample has to be large because durables are infrequently bought.) AGB draw in two stages, having stratified by postcode area, drawing sectors at the first stage and postcodes at the second. Their interest is in households. To use the postcode as a frame for adults it would be necessary to list all the individuals at selected postcodes and then draw the required number of respondents; or to interview every adult at each of the seventeen addresses covered on average by each selected postcode. A more efficient method would be to select postcodes at random and then select respondents to fit a quota relevant to the subject of the survey, i.e. to use a random location design.

4.2.4 Geodemographic stratification

In Chapter 3, *à propos* multi-stage drawing and the clustering of calls, we recognized the importance of ensuring that the sample represented the population's variety of habit and attitude where the subject of the survey was concerned. CACI's ACORN is still the most widely used geodemographic system[6] but ACORN now has competitors.

Richard Webber, who pioneered the ACORN system for CACI, has set up CCN Systems and the classification system MOSAIC. (CCN Systems is owned by Great Universal Stores. The marketing needs of mail-order operations have stimulated development in the geodemographic field.) In addition to the variables derived from the census, MOSAIC multi-variate analysis takes into account length of residence, as shown by changes in the annual registers of electors, together with financial standing, as shown by bankruptcies and appearances in debtors' courts.

ACORN analysis produces thirty-eight types of neighbourhood (see Table 4.2), MOSAIC produces fifty-eight, Pinpoint sixty and SuperProfiles 150.

SuperProfiles (1986) offers an à la carte service as well as a general-

Table 4.2 ACORN classification based on the 1981 census of population

ACORN groups		ACORN types	
A	Agricultural areas	A1	Agricultural villages
		A2	Areas of farms and smallholdings
B	Modern family housing, higher incomes	B3	Cheap modern private housing
		B4	Recent private housing, young families
		B5	Modern private housing, older children
		B6	New detached houses, young families
		B7	Military bases
C	Older housing of intermediate status	C8	Mixed owner-occupied and council estates
		C9	Small town centres and flats above shops
		C10	Villages with non-farm employment
		C11	Older private housing, skilled workers
D	Poor-quality older terraced housing	D12	Unimproved terraces with old people
		D13	Pre-1914 terraces, low-income families
		D14	Tenement flats lacking amenities
E	Better-off council estates	E15	Council estates, well-off older workers
		E16	Recent council estates
		E17	Council estates, well-off young workers
		E18	Small council houses, often Scottish
F	Less well-off council estates	F19	Low-rise estates in industrial towns
		F20	Inter-war council estates, older people
		F21	Council housing for the elderly
G	Poorest council estates	G22	New council estates in inner cities
		G23	Overspill estates, high unemployment
		G24	Council estates with overcrowding
		G25	Council estates with worst poverty
H	Multi-racial areas	H26	Multi-occupied terraces, poor Asians
		H27	Owner-occupied terraces with Asians
		H28	Multi-let housing with Afro-Caribbeans
		H29	Better-off multi-ethnic areas
I	High-status non-family areas	I30	High-status areas, few children
		I31	Multi-let big old houses and flats
		I32	Furnished flats, mostly single people
J	Affluent surburban housing	J33	Inter-war semis, white-collar workers
		J34	Spacious inter-war semis, big gardens
		J35	Villages with wealthy older commuters
		J36	Detached houses, exclusive suburbs
K	Better-off retirement areas	K37	Private houses, well-off elderly
		K38	Private flats with single pensioners

Source: Crown Copyright/CACI Copyright

purpose classification (or menu). Subscribers are encouraged to order classifications tailored to their particular marketing needs and to access the system's computer file direct, using a microcomputer version of this together with a personal computer. (This will be common practice in due course.)

Pinpoint was launched in 1983. Pinpoint's PIN (Pinpoint Identified Neighbourhoods) is a classic example of the benefit to be derived from the electronic marriage of data from disparate sources. In a joint venture with the Ordnance Survey, and in co-operation with the Post Office, large-scale Ordnance Survey maps have been 'digitized' and used to define postcode boundaries. Postcodes and enumeration districts may be matched via the national grid references making it possible to target individual households within the census's 150 household-enumeration district blocks.

The market research industry is trying to ensure that, when the 1991 census is taken, enumeration districts will be re-coded to accord with postcode boundaries and that the postcode will be adopted 'as the main unit of spatial location'.[7]

In the meantime, the Consumer Location System developed by the Post Office[8] attaches postcodes to geodemographic neighbourhood classifications, while the TGI's large product, media and 'lifestyle' data bank (based on 25,000 self-completion questionnaires — see section 11.2.2) also holds relevant postcode and geodemographic data.

We return to geodemographic classification when discussing market segmentation in Chapter 6. In the meantime, it would be possible to draw a probability sample of households using geodemographic stratification. Taking enumeration districts for the first-stage units, the listing for the draw might be as follows:

Standard Region 1
Classified residential neighbourhood (CRN) types listed in order of, say, affluence.
Enumeration districts listed within their CRN group.

Standard Region 2
As above.

And so on until all ten regions and 125,000 enumeration districts are covered.

The populations of the enumeration districts are accumulated and districts are drawn for the sample with PPS following the standard procedure, random draw and systematic interval.

At the second stage:
Electors or their addresses may be drawn using the registers covering the selected enumeration districts.

Or streets may be drawn from within the selected enumeration districts with probability proportionate to the number of addresses in them, and quotas set relevant to the subject of the survey.

In the second case we have a random-location sample.

We have been considering the procedures used to sample consumer markets. Most consumer markets embrace a large number of households, or individuals, and these are distributed over such a wide area that it is necessary to cluster calls while ensuring that the geographical distribution of the population is represented in the sample. When drawing a probability sample it is, at the same time, necessary to ensure that every household/individual in the population has a known chance of being included in the sample.

In non-domestic markets the situation is different. Here a limited number of manufacturers or traders may account for a substantial proportion of output or turnover (see section 3.8) and it is necessary to recognize their importance in the market when designing a sample. Opportunity to apply probability methods is limited while, working with often imperfect information, construction of purposive samples requires judgemental skill.

4.3 Sampling 'non-domestic' populations

The description 'non-domestic'[9,10] is useful because it reminds us that practical considerations affecting the sample of manufacturing industries also apply to the distributive trades, government departments, local authorities and the service industries: compare Kotler's 'producer, reseller and government markets'.

In section 3.8 we stressed the need to exercise informed judgement when designing 'non-domestic' samples and said that, where it is possible to establish a complete list of firms within strata, a probability design is theoretically possible; but purposive selection of firms within strata is the more general practice.

In this section we look more closely at stratification of 'non-domestic' markets by volume/value of output or turnover, at the problem of establishing a complete list of establishments and consider the relevance of probability methods.

4.3.1 Stratification by volume/value

In consumer markets the individual purchase has, with rare exceptions, little effect on total sales. In non-domestic markets, where one or two firms may dominate, these dominating firms must be included in the sample if sampling estimates are to reflect the behaviour and attitudes of the industry as a whole (see section 3.8).

There are some markets which can be described as 'mass industrial markets',[9] markets for such items as photocopiers, automatic typewriters, and 'industrial wiping cloths'.[10] Here, buying behaviour of the individual customer is less crucial. But in any non-domestic market there is going to be sufficient variation in the demand of different-sized establishments for it to be desirable to design a sample which attaches due weight to variations in size.

Table 3.4 (p. 53) illustrates a situation in which 79.2 per cent of establishments account for only 13.3 per cent of gross output while 1.4 per cent account for 40.7 per cent. The eighty-four establishments which constitute the 1.4 per cent make a contribution to gross output out of all proportion to their numbers. Let us assume that we decide to draw a sample in which the eighty-four are self-selecting and all size categories are represented in proportion to their contribution to gross output, the constitution of the sample would be as in Table 4.3.

There is a wealth of statistical information available about the structure of manufacturing, distributive and service industries. The twenty-seven standard industrial classifications (SIC) used by the Government Statistical Service are broad (Table 4.3 is based on order III) but the twenty-seven SIC orders are sub-divided into 181 Minimum List Headings (MLH) and some of these are further divided into 'optional sub-divisions'. The closeness with which the SIC/MLH definitions fit marketing requirements varies. The mass industrial market will embrace a number of classifications. But the official statistics usually make it possible to define a non-domestic population in terms such as those used in this example.

The official statistics enable us to set quotas, and the chances are that we will decide to proceed on a purposive basis, using names of establishments derived from internal records, directories and business associates to fill the quotas.

Employees N	Establishments N	%	Gross output %	Sample n	%
1– 99	4,532	79.2	13.3	27	13
100– 199	425	7.4	8.1	16	8
200– 499	459	8.0	17.7	37	18
500– 999	181	3.1	14.0	29	14
1,000–1,499	50	0.9	6.2	13	6
1,500& +	84	1.4	40.7	84	41
	5,731	100.0	100.0	206	100

Table 4.3 Constitution of the sample

To draw a probability sample we would need to acquire a complete list of establishments: a sampling frame. It is clearly desirable that we should be able to assign firms to strata before we draw: to stratify after drawing is likely to be wasteful of effort, time and money.

4.3.2   Sampling frame shortcomings

In order to draw a sample at random we need a list which is complete, up-to-date and without repetition of items. None of the generally used non-domestic frames quite meets these requirements. They are useful sources of names for a quota sample (see Appendix 1) but are likely to be inadequate for a probability sample.

> *The financial directories* (e.g. the *Stock Exchange Yearbook* and *Dunn and Bradstreet*) define the overall worth of an enterprise but may not record separately that part of the enterprise in which we are interested. They give 'no indication of the geographical location, size or activity of individual plants'.[9]
>
> *Kompass Register* relates enterprises to standard industrial classifications, but subsidiaries may be omitted and information relating to financial standing and to size may be inadequate for the purpose of stratification.
>
> *Trade directories* vary in their effectiveness. Omissions within and duplications between directories occur.
>
> *Trade associations* are not necessarily supported by important enterprises.
>
> *The classified Yellow Pages computer file* is invaluable when it comes to making contact with establishments selected for the sample, but it does not include information about the size of establishments. To use the *Yellow Pages* file as a sampling frame necessitates telephone screening.
>
> *Records built up over time* from representatives' reports, the financial press, industry and trade association sources together with previous research are valuable sources of marketing information. But they are unlikely to be sufficiently complete for a probability sample.
>
> *The Post Office 'Large User' File of Addresses with Unique Postcodes* is a useful sampling frame for products and services widely distributed across 'non-domestic' markets (see sections 4.2.3 and 4.3.3).

Knowing the size structure of a market, and being able to relate establishments to the size structure, are crucial to sound estimates of market size.

It is possible to project from sample estimates to the real world with confidence in the results if the following conditions are met:

- The market in question fits the SIC/MLH classification system.
- There is a complete, up-to-date and unduplicated listing of establishments available.
- The source of information has been located within establishments.
- Unambiguous answers have been given to survey questions.

There are usually a good many 'ifs' and 'buts' attached to the projections: so much so that, particularly in a market extending over several industrial classifications (e.g. heating and ventilating equipment) there may well be a case for the sequential approach:

1. Decide what return (e.g. in terms of return on investment or contribution to profit) is required to make the venture viable.
2. Translate this into minimum demand for the product or service.
3. Estimate its potential popularity in terms of market share, taking account of viable marketing expenditure.
4. Sample the market until sufficient potential has been located.

4.3.3 A probability procedure

In large-scale consumer surveys cost-effectiveness is achieved by drawing the sample in more than one stage with PPS so that calls are clustered (see section 4.2.1). It is possible to apply a similar procedure to non-domestic markets when these are of a 'mass industrial' nature.[9,10] McIntosh has appraised the valuation lists as a sampling frame.[10] Rating authorities, after regional stratification, would be the first-stage units. They can be drawn for the sample according to their total rateable value, or according to the nature of the rated premises which are classified as 'industrial', 'shop', 'office', 'other commercial' and 'domestic'.

The official statistics, 'Rates and rateable values' in England, Wales and Scotland, are published annually. The rating authority's records are regularly updated (as might be expected) and the valuation lists are 'with very few exceptions'[10] available for inspection and copying at local authority offices.

The rating statistics make it possible to do the following:

- List rating authorities within Economic Planning Regions, accumulate rateable values and attach to each authority a range of numbers representing its rateable value (instead of electorate, see section 4.2.1).
- Draw sufficient rating authorities to allow for regional variations (more marked in non-domestic markets than in consumer markets) using the PPS procedure.
- Use the valuation lists as a sampling frame for this first-stage sample of rating authorities (which may serve as a master sample).

The valuation lists give the names of the ratepayers, types of premises and rateable values. The rateable value is based on an assessment of the rental value of the premises. It is 'a good indicator of the physical size of an establishment'.[10] In order to construct a list of firms from the valuation lists as a frame it would probably be necessary to make some telephone calls, or to refer to the *Yellow Pages* computer file. Drawing in more than one stage makes this a practical proposition. Screening calls are a big item in non-domestic research costs.

Also by concentrating research in certain carefully drawn rating authorities, data accumulate as surveys are carried out. Accumulation and filing of data make a significant contribution to non-domestic research.

The assumption is, of course, being made that rateable value indicates a firm's substance in the market concerned. The correlation must depend on the nature of the market; it would be close for floor coverings and strip lighting.

To complete the probability draw, it will be necessary to stratify firms according to their value and to draw from the strata at random, probably using variable sampling fractions. Purposive selection of firms within strata would probably be more cost-effective.

4.4 Conclusion

Use of a probability procedure to draw a sample of individuals, householders, firms or other 'unit of enquiry' has two advantages:

- It makes it possible to measure sampling error when translating sample estimates into population values.
- It ensures that human likes and dislikes do not influence the selection or rejection of units for the sample.

It is possible to cluster calls while still ensuring that every item in the population has a known (and non-zero) chance of inclusion in the sample. Drawing in more than one stage with PPS reduces fieldwork costs and makes for improved supervision: but this procedure, as we have seen, is quite a complicated and lengthy one.

The procedure when it is used to draw a master sample is likely to be cost-effective in consumer markets and there are certain non-domestic markets of a 'mass' nature offering opportunities for the use of a master sample drawn in more than one stage with PPS.

Drawing in more than one stage makes it possible to concentrate the sampling frame for the final draw, for example to draw from a comparatively small number of registers. This concentration is particularly valuable where non-domestic surveys are concerned, because sampling frames do not come ready-made in non-domestic markets. It is usually necessary to construct them.

The advantages to be derived from probability sampling are dearly bought. In non-domestic surveys it is usually necessary to compromise and in consumer survey work there is a cost-effective case for drawing sampling locations at random and then setting quotas relevant to the nature of the enquiry.

Sources and further reading

1. A.S.C. Ehrenberg, *Frequency Distributions* (New York: Wiley, 1975), Chap. 12.
2. M. Collins, 'Sampling', Chap. 4 in R.M. Worcester and J. Downham (eds), *Consumer Market Research Handbook*, 2nd edn (Wokingham: Van Nostrand Reinhold, 1978).
3. A.S.C. Ehrenberg, *Data Reduction: Analysing and Interpreting Statistical Data* (London: Wiley, 1975), p. 291.
4. *Postal Coding*, London: The Post Office.
5. D. Chilvers and R. Longford, 'Research techniques to isolate the separate segments of the Post Office letter market', *MRS Conference Papers* (1982).
6. A. Garrett, 'How to home in on the target market', *Marketing Week* (29 May 1987), pp. 57–60.
7. P. Mouncey, 'Making sense of the census', *MRS Newsletter*, no. 261 (Dec. 1987), pp. 16–18.
8. D. Chilvers and M. McManus, 'New media are coming, but are existing media fully exploited?' *ADMAP* (Nov. 1983), pp. 602–8. (Describes The Post Office's consumer location system.)
9. A.R. McIntosh and R.J. Davies, 'The sampling of non-domestic populations', *Journal of The Market Research Society* (Oct. 1970).
10. A.R. McIntosh, 'Improving the efficiency of sample surveys', *Journal of The Market Research Society* (Oct. 1975).

See also

• P.E. Green and D.S. Tull, *Research for Marketing Decisions*, 4th edn, Chap. 7 (Englewood Cliffs, NJ: Prentice Hall, 1978).

- P.N. Hague, *The Industrial Market Research Handbook*, 2nd edn (London: Kogan Page, 1987).
- G. Hoinville, R. Jowell and Associates (eds), *Survey Research Practice*, Chap. 4 (London: Heinemann Educational Books, 1978).

Problems

Faced with the following assignments: (a) what type of sample design would you propose in each case?; (b) what data sources would you use to establish the population parameters?; (c) what breakdowns would you provide for when calculating sample size?

1. A survey of voting intentions at a general election.
2. A survey to establish where and in what way gardening tools are selected by the population of an expanding town in the south-east, a town served by a variety of traditional and modern retail outlets.
3. A survey to establish car accessories in use on the vehicles of private motorists, together with those not on the vehicle but desired.
4. A survey to show regional differences in the use of equipment by commercial laundries.

Describing markets: collecting data by means of questions

5

As we have seen in section 3.4 there are two broad ways of collecting descriptive data about consumer behaviour: observing and questioning. We return to observational methods when comparing the data yield of consumer panels and retail audits in Chapter 10; and when considering the development of pack designs, the pre-testing of advertisements and the measurement of TV viewing.

This chapter focuses on question and answer as a means of finding out about the habits, awareness and attitudes of consumers *vis-à-vis* the products and services available to them and the needs these products and services are designed to meet. The chapter proceeds from a general discussion of types of questionnaire and kinds of question to a detailed examination of the stages in the development of a questionnaire and consideration of the questions themselves, 'the art of asking questions'.[1]

Methodological research funded by the MRS suggests that more than half of the questions asked in surveys of the adult or housewife populations are attitude questions. These are given a separate section at the end of the chapter (section 5.5.7). There are certain techniques in common use for measuring attitudes and these are best considered in isolation; but, in a descriptive survey, attitude questions are likely to be introduced into the questionnaire as and where relevant to questions of behaviour and awareness.

The influence of technological developments on the asking of questions and recording of answers is considered in Chapter 3.

5.1 Why describe?

The descriptive function is far-reaching. It embraces the following:

- Description of consumer behaviour: what is bought, where it is bought and how it is used.
- Description of consumer awareness: awareness of available products, services, brands; their characteristics and the claims made for them.

- Description of consumer attitudes: towards the relevant activity (motoring, clothes washing, shaving) and the products, services, brands available for pursuing the activity.

However, description is not an end in itself. We describe markets in order to locate opportunities (see Chapter 6 on market segmentation) and, more frequently, in order to keep track of 'our' performance in relation to the performances of competitors (see Chapter 11 on evaluating performance and predicting). In the last analysis the questions about behaviour, awareness and attitude are asked so that future behaviour may be anticipated.

So why do we not just ask consumers what they are going to do? Questions about intentions, such as intentions to buy (or to invest capital) can usefully be asked if sufficient data have been collected over time to establish relationships between intentions as expressed and actions as actually taken.

Many research enquiries are 'one-off' (*ad hoc*), designed to aid the making of a particular and immediate decision. Lacking trend data we arrive at hypotheses regarding future behaviour as follows:

- By first asking questions about present experience of the product or service: about what is being bought, used, owned or done now.
- We then ask questions about past experience in order to determine whether present behaviour is habitual.
- Lastly, answers to awareness and attitude questions, taken together with answers to the behavioural ones, help us to decide what the respondent's future behaviour is likely to be.

An attitude is a learned pre-disposition to respond in a consistently favourable or unfavourable manner with respect to a given object.

An opinion is the expression of an underlying attitude. An individual might hold the attitude that smoking is anti-social and express the opinion that people who smoke in non-smoking carriages should be put out at the next station.

The distinction is a fine one and the terms are often treated as interchangeable.

Attitudes are the product of experience (what has happened to the respondent), awareness (what has been noticed and learnt) and volition (what is wanted or willed). Attitudes are recorded to help explain behaviour so that informed assumptions may be made about future behaviour. (For techniques used to elicit and measure attitudes, see section 5.5.)

5.2   Kinds of questions and types of questionnaire

The 'shorthand' used when discussing questionnaire design is summarized below:

Coding: A numerical code is allocated to each type of response to facilitate data processing. All possible answers may be listed and coded in advance of the interview and, in surveys of any size, this is done wherever possible. When responses cannot be allocated to a range of possible answers, coding takes place after the interview. (See section 5.3.5 and Appendix 2, 'Principles of analysis'.)

Closed questions: The respondent chooses between possible answers to a question. If there are only two possible answers (apart from 'don't know' (DK) or 'no preference') the question is dichotomous (either/or):

Is your mower a rotary mower?	(Code no.)
Or a cylinder mower?	(Code no.)
DK.	(Code no.)
(The mower has to be one or the other.)	

If there are more than two possible answers, apart from DK, the question is multi-choice:

Is you mower driven by petrol?	(Code no.)
Mains electricity?	(Code no.)
Battery?	(Code no.)
Human effort, unaided?	(Code no.)

Open-ended questions: The respondent is left free to answer in his or her own words and the interviewer is required either to write down the answer verbatim, or to allocate the reply to a range of possible answers set out and coded on the questionnaire. Verbatim answers demand subsequent coding. Answers to the question 'would you tell me why you chose a rotary mower?' might receive 'open' treatment.

Direct questions: The respondent is asked about his/her own behaviour without equivocation, as in the questions given above.

Indirect questions: The respondent's own behaviour or attitude is inferred from answers to questions about the behaviour or attitude of other people: 'Why do you think people have pets?' or 'Why, would you say, do people go to church?' (Respondent reluctance to give true answers can also be overcome by using a projective technique such as 'sentence completion' or 'word association': see section 5.4.3 on projective techniques.)

Most survey research data are collected by means of structured questionnaires using direct questions:

Structured questionnaire: The order in which questions are asked together with their wording are laid down. The interviewer must not alter or explain questions. Many questions are closed and the possible answers to most questions are pre-coded so that all the interviewer has to do is to ring a code number. (For coding see section 5.3.5.)

Unstructured questionnaire: Most of the questions are open-ended. The interviewer is free to change the order of asking questions and to explain them. The questionnaire may take the form of a check-list for discussion. The unstructured questionnaire is used in 'depth' interviews, group discussions and in non-domestic surveys.

Electronic data processing (EDP) puts a premium on questionnaire 'structuring' and this may be counterproductive, impeding instead of facilitating data collection. Both the interviewer and the respondent have suffered from the computer revolution. The practice of recording answers on grids and scales, which are easy to analyse, causes boredom and frustration in the interview situation, unless the subject is absolutely riveting.[2]

By making the processing of data so fast and effortless EDP removes or weakens two obstacles to the lengthy questionnaire, sometimes leading to an increasingly turgid and irrelevant questionnaire, more and more sections of which had their genesis in that terrible phrase 'we might as well add it'.[3]

On the other hand, EDP makes it comparatively easy to put a question to one-half of a sample in one form and to the other half in another, or to show the effect on results of a change in question order.[4]

5.3 Design of a structured questionnaire

We are going to consider the stages in the development of a structured questionnaire from the formulation of hypotheses during exploratory research (Chapter 2) to the pilot test in which the proposed questionnaire is tried out on members of the survey population. (The proposed sampling method may be tried out at the same time.) These stages are illustrated in flow-chart form in Figure 5.1.

By the time that we come to design the questionnaire we should know what topics are relevant to the decision-making task, and from what population the sample is to be drawn. We ought to have arrived at tentative ideas (hypotheses) about behaviour and attitudes in the market; and we should be clear as to the conclusions we are going to need to be able to draw, depending on whether our hypotheses are accepted or rejected.

In order to do this we have to decide the following:

1. In what detail we need to ask questions about the survey topics — the level of generality (see section 5.3.2).
2. How we are going to relate answers to respondents — the plan of tabulations (see section 5.3.3).

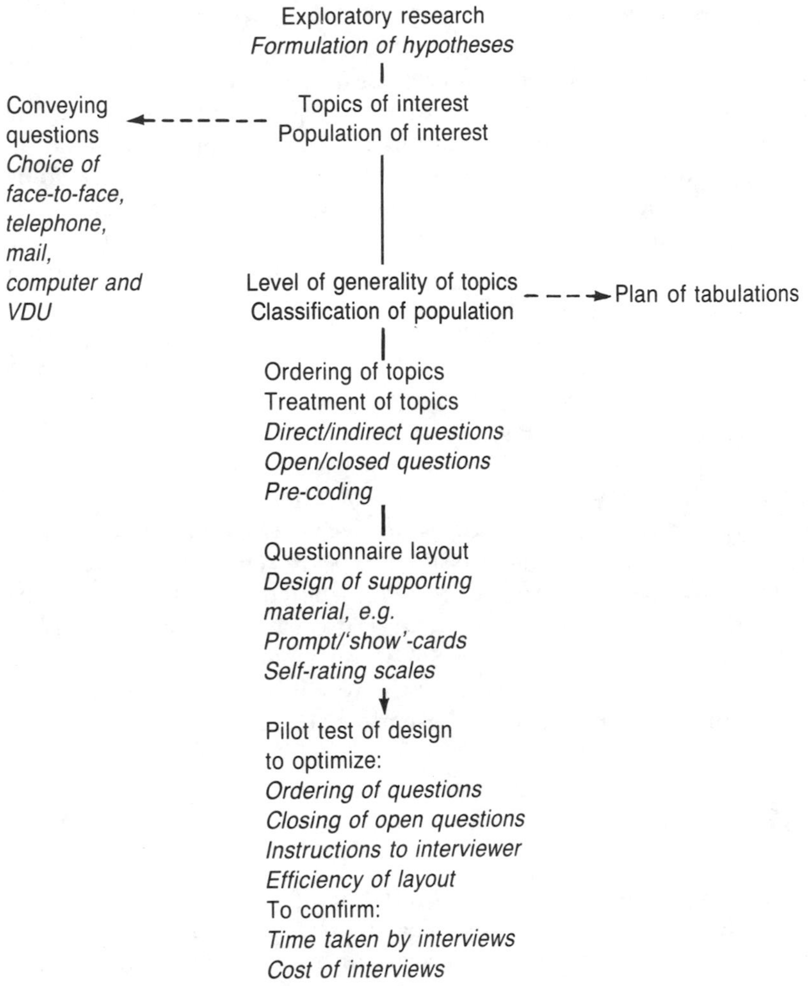

Exploratory research
Formulation of hypotheses
|

Conveying   ← – – – – – –   Topics of interest
questions   Population of interest
Choice of
face-to-face,
telephone,
mail,
computer and   Level of generality of topics – – – → Plan of tabulations
VDU   Classification of population

Ordering of topics
Treatment of topics
Direct/indirect questions
Open/closed questions
Pre-coding
|

Questionnaire layout
Design of supporting
material, e.g.
Prompt/'show'-cards
Self-rating scales
↓

Pilot test of design
to optimize:
Ordering of questions
Closing of open questions
Instructions to interviewer
Efficiency of layout
To confirm:
Time taken by interviews
Cost of interviews

Figure 5.1
Stages in the
development of
a questionnaire

5.3.1 Formulation of hypotheses

Considering what conclusions we may want to draw does not mean that we are pre-judging the answers: we are just making sure that, when the time comes to draw conclusions, the data are available, and available in sufficient detail, for us to be able to accept or reject our conjectures about the market we are describing (see section 2.9). The intellectual effort involved is illustrated in the case of a possible demand for works transport at the end of this chapter (see pp. 105–7).

5.3.2 Levels of generality

Oppenheim has described the survey design process as 'an arduous intellectual exercise'.[5] We have to make decisions not only about the topics to be included in the questionnaire but also about the detail in which they should be covered. We must be careful not to leave some critical aspect out, but the questionnaire which provides for every possibility puts off respondents, demoralizes interviewers, wastes time and therefore money, and antagonizes decision-makers. The data must be actionable (see section 2.1).

In designing the questionnaire it is also necessary to take into account how we are going to break down the survey population. When it comes to making decisions, what groups are going to be critical? The sample should be designed to yield enough individuals in each critical group for us to be confident that they represent this group in the population. On the other hand, each interview costs money. The group's behaviour and attitudes must be relevant to the decisions we anticipate having to make. The best way of deciding what classifications are relevant is to take each survey topic in turn and consider the importance of each group in the survey population in relation to it. (The relationship between topics and population is developed in section 5.3.3). A detailed picture of the kind of decisions that have to be made by the research planner at this stage is given in the case described at the end of this chapter.

5.3.3 Plan of tabulations

The topics have been listed in the required detail and the population has been classified into relevant groups (see Figure 5.1). This is a good point at which to plan the tabulations, bearing in mind that too much detail is as counter-productive as too little detail. We need to take each topic in turn and to decide which groups in the survey population warrant individual attention when it comes to discussing *this* topic.

The agreed classification of respondents may usefully be applied to every answer, but this is not invariably the case: and we are likely to want to consider other groupings, such as of those whose answers to the questionnaire show them to be alike in their behaviour.

Taking an example from the 'works transport' case, it goes without saying that we are going to put questions about a particular mode of travel, say its advantages and disadvantages, to those who use it. But in planning tabulations we may still have to make a number of decisions. Take those who come to work by car:

- Do we put these attitude questions to all of them, passengers as well as drivers?

- To those who come all the way as well as those who come part of the way?
- Or do we focus on drivers who have used no other mode of travel to work during the period covered by the survey?

Tabulations need to be decided upon before the questionnaire is written because the wording of the questionnaire must make it crystal clear whose answer is required to each question. This applies when an interviewer is putting the questions in a personal or telephone interview, and when the questionnaire has been mailed to a respondent for 'self-completion'.

Decisions about the tabulations also affect sample size. Particularly crucial for the calculation of sample size is the decision whether to break down the behavioural groupings by a demographic classification. Where 'getting to work' is concerned we might hypothesize that the 'shop-floor' attitude towards driving to work is sufficiently different from that of the 'staff' to warrant this further breakdown of the car drivers. The further breakdown would necessitate a larger sample and the additional cost might not be justified.

It may be helpful, when considering tabulations, to set up a matrix with topics in detail down the side and standard demographic and other groupings across the top. The plan of tabulations can then be seen at a glance, and we will have ensured that nothing of importance is left out. The code frame should include a description of the question and a description of who should be answering it.[6] (For a more detailed treatment of this subject, see Appendix 2.)

5.3.4 Ordering of topics

It is good common practice to follow these principles:

- Open with one or two general, bland questions which the respondent is expected to find easy to answer.
- Then explore present behaviour in the market before delving into the past, i.e. to focus on what is being done, used, bought, eaten *now* before asking about earlier experience.
- Record behaviour before putting attitude questions. Answering behaviour questions concentrates the respondent's mind on the topic in question so that he/she is ready to express an opinion about it, or to take up a position on a self-rating scale (see section 5.5 on attitude measurement).
- Take topics in a logical order so that the respondent is not confused.
- Withhold topics that might be embarrassing until the personal or telephone interview is under way or, in the case of a mailed questionnaire, until the respondent's interest may have been aroused by the earlier questions.

- Be prepared to try more than one place in the questionnaire for the 'difficult' topic, at the pilot stage.
- Try to avoid boring sequences in the questionnaire, e.g. a run of multi-choice questions or too many rating scales one after the other.
- In a personal or telephone interview, make sure that the topics are ordered in such a way that ideas, influencing answers to later questions, are not put into the respondent's head. The mailed questionnaire is likely, if filled in, to have been read right through first.

Classification questions are often embarrassing or difficult, but they can be left until the end in the case of a probability sample, for the respondent drawn at random must be interviewed. In the case of a quota sample, some classification questions need to be asked at the outset, because it is necessary to establish that the respondent fits into the quota set (see section 3.6.2).

In a postal survey classification questions are reached at the end of the questionnaire. They are unlikely to be as disturbing as they would be in an interview because the respondent is not always asked to fill in his or her name and address.

'Show cards' are often used to take the embarrassment out of age and income questions, the respondent being asked to point at the slot they fit into. An example for age might be, depending on the requirements of the survey:

'Would you show me on this card your age last birthday?'

15—24
25—44
45—64
65+

One hesitates to give an example for income because it is necessary first to define income and then to distinguish between weekly, monthly and annual income. Also, the figures soon become out of date. Here again, respondents are normally shown a card.

In the case of a mailed questionnaire the respondent ticks in the appropriate box, while in a telephone interview age and income brackets, if used, must be kept few and broad.

It is clearly desirable that questions designed to classify respondents should, as far as possible, be standardized so that the results of surveys can be compared. The Market Research Society set up a working party in 1971 'to consider whether the use of standard questions in survey research should be encouraged, and if so to put forward recommendations'. The recommendations, based on research agency practice, are summarized in *Standardized Questions: A Review for Market Research Executives*.[7]

5.3.5 The treatment of topics

We are going to consider the actual wording of questions in section 5.4, but, before writing the questionnaire, we need to decide whether we should treat the topics in an 'open' or 'closed' way, and in a 'direct' or 'indirect' way.

In survey research there is a practical case for pre-coding, and also for closing as many questions as possible. The respondent is given a choice of answers plus 'don't know'. The interviewer has merely to ring the code number alongside the respondent's choice of answer. Too many closed questions may bore the respondent but interviews and data processing take less time than they would if the question were open and the answers had to be put into coding categories *after* the interview. Also the closed pre-coded question is more likely to yield valid data: there are fewer opportunities for lapses of memory on the part of the respondent and for the incorrect recording of answers by the interviewer.

Open: 'What extras and/or accessories were already fitted when you bought your car?'
(The respondent tries to remember; perhaps goes out to look at the car. The interviewer writes down items as they occur to the respondent.)

Closed: 'Which of these extras and/or accessories were already fitted when you bought your car?' [SHOW CARD]

	Col. 9
Wing mirrors	1
Seat belts	2
Radio/tape recorder	3
Heater	4
Head rests	5
Fog lamps	6
Reversing lights	7

We need to distinguish between questions which are pre-coded and closed (as in the car accessories example) and questions which are pre-coded but put to the respondent as if open; in both cases the respondent answers and the interviewer rings the relevant code number, but in the first case all possible answers are put to the respondent and memory is stimulated.

There is evidence that respondents react differently to the two types of question, as if they are being asked to perform two different answering tasks. In the open situation the respondent is required to generate and define items relevant to the question, in the closed to choose or judge between relevant items already selected. It has been shown that, when the same question is put to matched samples of respondents,[8] responses vary with the approach used.

The importance of this finding depends on the nature of the question being asked. In the car accessories example the respondent is being asked a strictly factual question and the closed question is clearly more likely to produce a true answer than an open one. When attitudinal or 'why' questions are being asked, there is room for doubt. This is illustrated in Belson's 'Comparison of open-ended and check-list questioning systems'.[9]

Belson's comparison of open-ended and check-list questioning systems

During survey work in five different product fields an experimental 'why' question was asked. The five samples were split so that one half received the experimental question open and the other closed. One half were required to volunteer reasons for liking, disliking or using as the case might be; the other half were given a list of reasons to study. The items on this check-list were derived from 'preliminary open-ended research'.

Example: 1,521 interviews with 'bath additive' users in Great Britain dealing with reasons for using a bath additive.

The check-list system
'You've said you have used ... (READ OUT ALL RESPONDENT CLAIMS TO BATH ADDITIVES USED) in your bath. I would like to know *all your reasons* for using this/these.
(PAUSE)
Here is a list of possible reasons.'
   PASS CARD AND SAY:
'Please go through it and call out all that apply in your case.'
   WAIT FOR RESPONDENT TO FINISH WITH THE LIST.
   WHEN HE/SHE HANDS IT BACK, SAY:
'What other reasons do you have for using this/these bath additives?'

The open-ended system
'You've said you have used ... (READ OUT ALL RESPONDENT CLAIMS TO BATH ADDITIVES USED) in your bath. Please tell me *all your reasons* for using this/these.' (PROBE FULLY, USING PROBES SUCH AS: 'What else?'/'What other reasons?'/'Uhuh', followed by a waiting silence.)

Findings: The five samples yielded six experimental treatments (one sample was asked first about things liked and then about things disliked). The following findings are based on all six sets of data.

- The check-list stimulated a substantially higher overall level of response.
- Check-list respondents offered fewer 'other reasons', suggesting that the use of the check-list has a dampening effect upon the volunteering of any further items.
- The frequency with which individual reasons are given by the two halves of the samples varied (from 0.93 to 0.02), i.e. rank order is not stable between the two systems.

- Reasons only quoted once during the preliminary research scored frequently when on the check-list: e.g.

From bath additive study % endorsing/volunteering each reason:	Check-list (760 cases)	Open-ended (741 cases)
To ease my feet	22.1	5.4
It has a clean smell	9.3	0.1

The check-list questioning system stimulates memory and it may put into words ideas which the respondent was not conscious of having, or introduce new ones. The check-list also draws attention to items which the respondent might not have considered worth mentioning when asked an open-ended question: i.e. the two questioning methods cannot be assumed to produce the same result.

Data capture is streamlined and full advantage is taken of electronic data processing when questions are closed and pre-coded. In survey work it is common practice to use the open-ended system at the exploratory stage and then to reduce the list of items and close.

We need to remember that the two questioning methods are likely to produce different data sets; and that, when we reduce the list by discarding less frequently mentioned items, we are making the assumption that ideas voiced infrequently are less important in determining behaviour than those voiced frequently.[10] The Survey Research Centre has conducted a major methodological study in this area.

In order to pre-code questions it is necessary to anticipate the possible answers. For standard classification questions (such as age, class, sex) and when providing for such regular items as 'DK' 'no pref.' 'anything else'/'any other', pre-coding is a straightforward matter. But in order to pre-code answers to most survey questions, prior knowledge of the range of possible answers is needed. Exploratory research will have suggested what answers are to be expected and the pilot test will confirm the completeness of the list, provided an 'anything else?' is included and respondents are given time to think whether or not there is 'anything else'.

A questionnaire consisting entirely of 'closed' questions is boring for both respondent and interviewer. Open questions break the monotony. But when designing a survey to describe a market as many questions as possible should be pre-coded and open questions necessitating hand-written answers kept to a minimum.

If a closed question means choosing between more than three possible answers, it is best to list the choices on a show-card. This assumes a personal interview. On a mailed questionnaire they would be set out alongside the printed question. There is evidence that some 45 per cent of questions use show-cards.[11]

If a topic proves to be 'difficult' or embarrassing at the exploratory stage, we may decide to approach it indirectly when it comes to formulating survey questions. In survey research we need the comfort of numbers, so our treatment of the subject must be a *quantifiable* one. We might ask a 'third person' question such as 'why do you think people . . . ?' (It is becoming increasingly difficult to think of a 'difficult' or embarrassing topic!) We return to this subject in section 5.4.

5.3.6 Questionnaire layout

Apart from the questions relating to the survey topics, we have to provide for the following:

- Identification of the job by means of a reference number.
- Identification of each individual questionnaire by means of a reference number.
- Identification of the interviewer in the case of a personal interview.
- Introductory remarks.
- Classification of respondents, plus, in some personal interviews, the respondent's name and address.

The job may be one of many being handled by a research agency. In addition, it may be necessary to identify the filed data long after the job is finished. In the case of a personal or telephone interview it is good practice to check a proportion of calls. Alternatively, quality may be controlled by comparing the answers recorded by one interviewer with those recorded overall.*

In a personal interview, a card (complete with the interviewer's photograph) introduces the interviewer (provided the research supplier is a member of the MRS Quality Control Scheme), but it is still important to explain to the respondent why his/her privacy is being invaded. This applies whether the data are being collected face-to-face, over the telephone or by mail.

In a structured survey the words used will be standard so that each respondent is introduced to the subject of the survey in the same way. These introductory remarks often appear at the beginning of the questionnaire, but if the questionnaire is mailed the introductory remarks are more likely to be the subject of a covering letter.

---

*The MRS Quality Control Scheme now has a membership of fifty companies supplying research. 'These companies all operate above, or at least to, the standards laid down by the Scheme. All have been visited by QCS inspectors, who have required access to all their documentation relating to training supervision, quality control and the office procedures and records that are kept by each company. At the end of the inspection companies have compiled a short summary describing their field-work operation.'

> Good morning/afternoon/evening.
> SHOW INTERVIEWER CARD**
> I am from Researchplan. We are conducting a survey on do-it-yourself activity
> and the sort of jobs people do around the home, and would be grateful for
> your help.

We discussed the placing of the classification questions and the ordering of topics in section 5.3.4. Here we are concerned with the effect of the layout of the questionnaire on the respondent in the case of a mailed questionnaire and on the interviewer in the case of face-to-face and telephone enquiries.

> The questionnaire layout must clearly distinguish questions from instructions. It is good practice to use upper and lower case letters for questions and capitals for instructions, as in the example shown above.
> There must be no doubt as to who is to answer the question, e.g.:
>
> ASK THOSE WHO WENT BY AIR
> 'Did you get there on time?'
> or, for a mailed questionnaire:
> 'If you went by air . . . '

This extract from a questionnaire illustrates the following 'ground rules':

- Questions are best clearly separated from answers in the layout of the questionnaire.
- The route through the questionnaire should be immediately clear (see Q.1 'SKIP to Q.3'.
- The interviewer must be told whether to read out the pre-coded answers (compare Q.2 and Q.4).
- And when to show a card (the instruction at Q.4 might have been SHOW CARD instead of READ OUT).

In this example we assume that the first four columns are allocated to classification data.

		Col. 5
Q.1	Do you own an electric drill?	Yes 1
		No 2 SKIP TO Q.3

**We assume 'Researchplan' is a member of the Quality Control Scheme.

		Col. 6
Q.2	What brand or make of drill do you own at the moment?	Black & Decker 1
		Wolf (and so on) 2
		Other 8
		Col. 7
Q.3	Do you use a drill in your day-to-day work?	Yes 1
		No 2
	IF NOT A DRILL OWNER NOR A USER AT WORK, CLOSE INTERVIEW	
		Col. 8
Q.4	About how often do you use some sort of power drill?	READ OUT
	Less than once a week	1
	At least once a week	2
	At least every two weeks	3
	About once a month	4
	Less than once a month	5

The interviewer must be left in no doubt as to whether or not to read out coded answers. By reading out the answers as coded the interviewer stimulates the respondent's memory. If some memories are stimulated and others not, bias is introduced.

Finally, in an open-ended, uncoded question ample space must be left for taking down the respondent's answer in the respondent's own words.

5.4　The art of asking questions

This is the title of a classic work on the subject.[1] Here we would overload the text if we attempted to do more than set out some generally accepted principles, together with examples. What follows is for those who have to accept or reject questionnaires, and for those who have to answer examination questions about questionnaire design. If you are engaged in writing questionnaires professionally, the sources quoted at the end of this chapter will give you further guidance.

The content of the questionnaire is, of course, determined by the research objectives as laid down in the research proposal (see section 3.1). The way in which the questions are put will be influenced by the following:

- The nature of the survey population.
- The method chosen to convey the questions to the survey population (see section 3.5).

There is, of course, interaction between these two factors. If our research objective were to predict demand for private motor cars, we might well decide to focus our enquiry on the behaviour and attitudes of new car buyers and to send questionnaires through the post because the subject is of particular interest to this survey population. (We would, of course, need to define 'new' and to take account of new cars, other than outright 'company' cars, whose funding is aided by employers. It would also be desirable to repeat a survey of this kind at regular intervals to establish trends!)

We have determined the topics to be covered and in what detail individual topics should be investigated. Now, as we formulate each question, we need to ask ourselves the following:

- Has the respondent got the information?
- Will the respondent understand the question?
- Is the respondent likely to give a true answer?

5.4.1   Has the respondent got the information?

It is easy to assume that the respondent has had the experience necessary to give a valid answer to your question. You ask a respondent 'which do you prefer for cooking, gas or electricity?' and he/she may well answer 'gas', having had no experience of electricity. He/she may, of course, use solid fuel, or may not cook at all.

Or the respondent may give you an opinion about packaged tours without having been on one. On the whole, respondents feel they *ought* to have an opinion. They also, on the whole, aim to please the interviewer by having an opinion to give in return for the question.[5]

The respondent may not have the information because he/she is not the right person to ask: the respondent may not know how the house is insured; the professional buyer, or purchasing officer, may not know why this particular piece of laboratory equipment is being used.

> It is good practice to find out about a respondent's actual experience of a product or service before putting questions about how it is used or regarded.

5.4.2   Will the respondent understand the question?

At the pilot stage we may find that a commonly used word is variously interpreted. Everyday words like 'lunch', 'dinner' and 'tea' can be ambiguous. 'Tea' may be confused with 'supper', 'dinner' may be a midday meal or an evening one, and 'lunch' may be a 'bite' or a sit-down meal. If you want to find out how and when bacon is used, it is safer to pin the questions to 'midday meal', 'evening meal' and 'main meal'.

Words such as 'generally', 'regularly' and 'usually' are a common source of ambiguity. Faced with a question about what they generally/regularly/usually do, respondents either describe their recent behaviour or answer in terms of the way in which they like to think of themselves behaving, and perhaps do, *sometimes*.

It is better to be flat-footed and ask in the first instance about the current or most recent occasion ('how did you get to work this morning?').

An unfamiliar word in a question either leads to misunderstanding or puts the interviewer into the undesirable position of having to interpret the question. Words such as 'faculty', 'facility', 'amenity', 'coverage' are not helpful in an 'everyday' context, though they would be appropriate if the respondents were academics, insurance brokers, hoteliers or media planners. The following example was given on an MRS course.[12]

> Are there facilities for your cat to urinate indoors?

The recommended wording was:

> Is there a dirt tray for your cat indoors?

It is easy, but of course wrong, to ask two questions in one:

> Do you think Tide gets clothes clean without injuring the fabric?

and to ramble on, so that the thread of the question is lost:

> Do you buy your dog any dog treats — by dog treats I mean any item that is outside the dog's normal diet, is consumable at one occasion (i.e. excluding rubber toys) and is not fresh food, e.g. human biscuits or fresh bones?

Instead of trying to define 'dog treat' in the question it would be better, as recommended, to list all the items regarded as 'dog treats' on a card and SHOW CARD.

5.4.3   Is the respondent likely to give a true answer?

Given that the respondent has the information and understands the question, what are the chances of the question eliciting a true answer?

There are three outstanding hazards:

1. The respondent may find it difficult to verbalize.
2. The respondent's memory may be defective.
3. The respondent may be reluctant, or unwilling, to answer the question.

The respondent may find it difficult to verbalize

The respondent has an answer to give but cannot find the words to put it into; or the respondent is so slow that the interviewer records 'don't know' and moves on to the next question. This hazard is avoided when questions are closed and the respondent has merely to choose between possible answers. If the question is open but pre-coded, the interviewer may be tempted to read out the code answer categories to hurry the interview along. This is not desirable!

The respondent's memory may be defective

Memory varies from one individual to another, and with the importance of the event. Questions about the new car are more likely to get true answers than questions about the brand of motor spirit last bought. Three practical measures which help to ensure true answers when the answer depends, as many do, on remembering are the following:

(a) Recall can be aided by means of a check-list.
(b) The respondent may be asked to keep a diary.
(c) A recording mechanism may be installed, for example the 'set meter' used in TV monitoring.

The diary and the mechanical device properly belong to observation as a means of collecting data (see section 3.4). The check-list is a question-naire component. We have met it in the form of the closed question.

By showing a card or reading out a list we are stimulating memory and we have to be sure that this is what we want to do. Ask a respondent what electrical appliances there are in the house and you will probably get an incomplete answer. (He/she may, for example, overlook the power drill in the garage.) Show him/her a list of appliances and, provided the list is complete, the answer stands a good chance of being true. If we need to know what comes to mind unprompted, we can always ask the open question first (unaided recall) and then SHOW CARD.

The respondent may be reluctant, or unwilling, to answer the question

We all have ideas as to what is expected of us by other people. We all have a self-image which we aim to preserve. We do not want to give ourselves away or show ourselves in a poor light.

Oppenheim quotes five barriers to true answers:[5]

(a) The barrier of awareness: 'People are frequently unaware of their own motives and attitudes.'
(b) The barrier of irrationality: 'Our society places a high premium on sensible, rational and logical behaviour.'
(c) The barrier of inadmissibility.
(d) The barrier of self-incrimination.

(c) and (d) are two aspects of the same problem, the problem of reconciling our everyday behaviour and attitudes with those we consider desirable (c) and those we consider acceptable (d). (We may fancy ourselves as being able to carry our liquor but be wary of revealing our actual consumption of alcohol.)

(e) The barrier of politeness: 'People often prefer not to say negative, unpleasant or critical things.' (The respondent may be motivated by kindness, the interviewer 'is only doing his/her job', by a desire to get the interview over as quickly as possible, or by fear of repercussion.)

Oppenheim's barriers are, perhaps, more critical in social than in marketing research, but research at the exploratory stage may alert us to a sensitive area in our survey.

> Association of the consumption of animal fat with coronary risk means that today spreading margarine on bread, buns, scones, etc., is not only socially acceptable but even an indication of a prestigious, because stressful, life. Not so long ago to spread margarine was regarded as an indication of lower-class poverty. It was difficult to get respondents to admit that they spread margarine instead of butter. One questionnaire adopted the following approach: 'Respondents have been telling us that they use butter and margarine for different spreading purposes for their family.' Having suggested that some respondents admitted to using margarine as a spread, the respondent was then taken through 'spreading purposes' (toast, sandwiches, etc.), the use of 'butter or margarine' featuring in each question.

A disarming approach of this kind can be effective when it is necessary to ask questions which imply standards of behaviour such as how often teeth are cleaned, or hair is washed. Another way of softening the challenge is to ask the respondent when he/she last *happened* to go to the pub, to take the dog for a walk, etc.

Projective techniques have been developed by clinical psychologists to enable their patients to express motivations which come up against Oppenheim's 'barriers'. Projective techniques are sometimes used in marketing research to uncover motivations behind the opinions expressed about products or services and the communications designed to advertise them. The more commonly used techniques are as follows:

Sentence completion: The respondent is asked to complete a series of sentences without 'stopping to think'.

Word association: Here the stimulus is a word and the respondent is asked to give the first word that comes into his/her head. It *might* be 'cholesterol' in response to 'butter'.

Thematic apperception test (TAT): The respondent is shown illustrations of critical situations and is asked to describe what is going on.

Cartoon test: Similar to the TAT except that the characters have balloons coming out of their mouths or heads, and one balloon is waiting for the respondent to fill it in.

In each case the respondent is being given an ambiguous stimulus. The stimulus is meaningful to the psychologist but not to the respondent who is being given opportunities to express his/her own behaviour and attitudes without self-censorship. Interpretation of the data collected can also be ambiguous. This also applies to the responses to 'third person' questions. The respondent, on being asked 'why do you think people . . . ', may well give what he/she believes to be the behaviour or views of 'people', and fail to project his/her own.

5.5   Asking questions about attitudes

In section 5.1 we defined *attitude* as:

> a learned predisposition to respond in a consistently favourable or unfavourable manner with respect to a given object

and *opinion* as:

> the expression of an underlying attitude.

We said that the distinction between 'attitude' and 'opinion' was a fine one. In this section we do not attempt to draw the distinction, using 'attitude' throughout, as is common practice.

Respondents hold attitudes about general subjects (or 'attitude objects') such as motoring, and about specific objects, such as a Range Rover. Where specific objects are concerned attitudes can be held about physical or functional properties, like acceleration and petrol consumption, or about subjective and emotional ones such as the kind of lifestyle suggested by Range Rover ownership.

Attitudes are the product of the respondent's experience to date: what he/she has become aware of, and what he/she has come to want. They are, of course, influenced by the respondent's view of what society regards as desirable and this influence depends on the extent to which he/she is inclined to conform.

We ask respondents about the attitudes they hold to help us predict their future behaviour in the market. In making predictions we are careful to relate the attitudes expressed to the respondent's present and past behaviour (see section 5.1).

5.5.1   Establishing the 'universe of content'

When we ask an attitude question we sample a 'universe of content':[5] the body of ideas held by the relevant population about the 'attitude object', say driving or running a car. 'Depth' interviews or group discussions during exploratory research will have generated a variety of statements about products or services in the market we are investigating and the contexts in which they are used. We can be reasonably sure that we have spanned the dimensions of the attitude when we no longer meet fresh ideas about the attitude object, but we cannot, of course, be entirely sure.

In order to quantify the results of this qualitative work we need to arrive at a list of statements representing the universe of content. If exploratory research has been adequately thorough we have the following in the transcribed recordings of 'depth' interviews and/or group discussions:

* The ideas held about the attitude object by the population we are going to survey.
* The expressions used by the population when talking about these ideas.

The same basic idea may be expressed in different ways by different respondents and the compilation of an attitude battery requires considerable skill. Decisions have to be made about the order in which ideas (or topics) are put, and the number and variety of attitude statements associated with each topic.

When constructing the battery, and when analysing the responses, it is important to recognize that, among the statements listed, some are likely to be more important to the respondent than others. A respondent might agree strongly with both of the following statements:

Convenience foods are a necessity to the modern housewife.
Convenience foods make it possible to give more time to the family.

However, the second statement might count for more than the first with the respondent concerned.

It is also important to bear in mind the fact that, in agreeing with a statement such as 'Convenience foods are a necessity to the modern housewife', the respondent may be either expressing a belief ('I accept this as a true statement') or making an evaluation ('I identify with this point of view').[7] (See Belson's 'Comparisons of open-ended and check-list questioning systems' in section 5.3.5.)

5.5.2 Choosing the type of scale

We have now to decide in what form to administer the attitude statements to the respondent. At the simplest we put the statement, in words or in writing, and ask the respondent whether he/she 'agrees' or 'disagrees' with it, or neither:

Convenience foods are a necessity	Agree 1
to the modern housewife	Disagree 2
	Neither agree nor disagree 3
	DK 4

This is a nominal scale. We sum the responses by adding up the number in each of the four categories and, for each statement, comparing the 'agree', 'disagree', 'neither' and DK numbers. We could, of course, compare the individual statement scores with the scores for the battery as a whole.

To establish the relative importance in rank order of the attitude statements we might construct an ordinal scale. If we were investigating attitudes towards biological detergents we might, for example, ask respondents to rank statements such as 'removes stains', 'saves time', 'no need to soak', 'gets clothes cleaner', 'the modern way', in order of importance. To summarize the responses we would allocate a number to each rank. Given five items to be ranked, the first/top position scores five, the second scores four and so on down to the fifth which scores one.

The ordinal scale lacks sensitivity. The rank order gives no indication of the intensity with which attributes are viewed. The attribute ranked first may, for example, be far and away first for the respondent who may not find much to choose between the rest. This limitation also applies to the nominal scale. We have no indication of how strongly those who reply 'agree' do agree, nor how strongly those who reply 'disagree' do so.

In order to get an indication of the strength or weakness with which an attitude is held, we need to construct rating scales. We are going to consider two commonly used types of rating scale:

- Likert summated rating scales.
- Osgood semantic differential scales.

5.5.3 Likert scales

A statement is put to the respondent and the respondent is asked 'please tell me how much you agree or disagree with . . . ' It is common practice to give the respondent the choice of five positions on the scale ranging from 'strongly agree' to 'strongly disagree'.

The scale may be put to the respondent in the form of words printed on a card, or on the questionnaire in the case of a postal survey; or it may take the form of a diagram. For the verbal rating scale The Market Research Society's working party[7] suggested the following approach.

> I am going to read out some of the things that people have said to us about . . . . Please tell me how much you agree or disagree with each one (SHOW CARD); pick your answer from this card.
>
> Agree strongly
> Agree slightly
> Neither agree nor disagree
> Disagree slightly
> Disagree strongly

For a postal survey the approach would, of course, need to be modified ('Here are some of the things . . . '). Whether in a personal interview or through the mail, respondents rate themselves. These are self-rating scales.

The diagrammatic rating scale based on the Likert approach is as follows:

Strongly agree	Slightly agree	Neither agree nor disagree	Slightly disagree	Strongly disagree
0	0	0	0	0

The statement is read out by the interviewer, or written on the questionnaire in the postal survey. The respondent is invited to point at the position that expresses his/her feeling in response to the statement, or to tick in the appropriate position in the case of a postal survey.

In a personal interview the interviewer has the scale with him/her to show to the respondent. It is a form of show-card.

The words used to denote varying strength or weakness of attitude are not immutably those quoted so far. A Likert-type scale might range from 'very true' to 'very untrue' or from 'a very important reason for . . . ' to 'an unimportant reason for . . . '.

The responses are analysed by allocating weights to scale positions. Given five scale positions we might allocate 5 to 'strongly agree', 3 for the mid-position, 1 for 'strongly disagree', or vice versa: it does not matter provided we are consistent. If the scale battery includes both positive and negative attitude statements, as most do, we have to make sure that 'strongly agree' for a negative statement rates 1 and not 5.

We are going to want to be able to compare the sample's total response to individual statements with its response to the battery as a whole, remembering that the statements have been chosen to span the dimensions of this attitude object, i.e. to represent 'the universe of content'. We are also going to want to be able to compare the summed scores of individual statements, to see how responses to statements correlate. We return to this subject in Chapter 6 when, under market segmentation, we discuss psychographic groups.

5.5.4 Semantic differential scales

Likert-type scales are commonly used to investigate general subjects such as motoring, do-it-yourself, clothes washing. They are also used to rate agreement/disagreement with the specific attributes of individual models of motor car, makes of power drill, or brands of detergent. But in practice, scales of the semantic differential type are found to be easier to administer and more meaningful to respondents when it comes to rating responses to statements about the specific attributes of named products and services.

A product or service is designed to have certain desirable attributes. We want to find out whether or not, and how strongly, these desirable attributes are associated with our product, as compared with the competition. Let us assume that our product is a motor car and that we want to investigate attitudes towards power, styling, driver's image, petrol consumption and reliability in relation to our make/model and others in the market. Following Osgood and his colleagues we might construct the following double-ended scales:

Good acceleration	0 0 0 0 0 0 0	Poor acceleration
Up-to-date styling	0 0 0 0 0 0 0	Out-of-date styling
Thrusting driver	0 0 0 0 0 0 0	Sluggish driver
Extravagant consumption	0 0 0 0 0 0 0	Economical consumption
Reliable	0 0 0 0 0 0 0	Unreliable

The respondent is asked to rate each model in turn on these attitude dimensions. It is important that the order in which the cars are named, whether by the interviewer or on a postal questionnaire, is rotated so that, for example, the Allegro is not always considered first.

Semantic scales can be either mono-polar (sweet . . . not sweet) or bi-polar (sweet . . . sour). With bi-polar scales it is important that the two poles should be perceived as opposites by the survey population.

5.5.5 Kelly's 'personal constructs'

'Depth' interviews and group discussions centred on general subjects, such as clothes washing, tend to be more fruitful of attitude statements than those centred on the attributes of specific products or brands. (The car market is probably an exception. Discussion of individual motor cars can generate as much interest as discussion about motoring in general.)

A structured 'depth' interview procedure, based on Kelly's theory of personal constructs, helps respondents to express their views about individual brands, products, models:

- The product (or service) field is represented by names on cards, photographs of models or of packs, or by the packs themselves, depending on what stimulus is most appropriate. (We will assume a pack of cards.)
- The respondent is handed the pack of cards and is asked to discard any brand, name or model that is unfamiliar.
- The retained cards are shuffled by the interviewer who deals three to the respondent.
- The respondent is asked to say one way in which two of the brands or models named on the cards are the same and yet different from the third.

The answer is the respondent's personal construct and it can be used to form a semantic scale: for example, faced with cards showing three shampoos, a respondent might make one of the following responses:

'These two are scented, that one isn't.' (mono-polar semantic scale)
'These two are for greasy hair, that one's for dry hair.' (bi-polar scale)

The shuffling and dealing of triads goes on until 'the respondent can no longer think of any reason why two items are different from the third' — the procedure is fully described by Sampson in the *Consumer Market Research Handbook*[13] and by Green and Tull.[14]

5.5.6 Some further considerations

It has been found that too many scale positions confuse respondents and demand too much of their capacity to discriminate. However we need at least five, because there is a tendency to avoid the extreme scale positions, especially the negative one.

Giving the respondent an even number of scale positions to choose from forces choice; there is no middle position to accommodate uncertainty. Opinions vary as to whether this is a desirable practice or not. When choice is forced, a more clear-cut verdict 'for' or 'against' is delivered but this may, of course, be dangerously misleading.

If a product or service is liked, the respondent may automatically rate it high on all attributes (the halo effect): and, in the course of scoring his/her own attitude on a large number of attitude scales the respondent may get into the habit of going for the same position on the scale.

This tendency to go for the same position on the scale is less likely if favourable (positive) and unfavourable (negative) statements are interspersed.

When attaching weights to responses to attitude statements it is important to discriminate between favourable and unfavourable statements and to maintain a consistent direction. This requirement is well illustrated by Green and Tull.[14]

Consumer attitudes towards the advertising industry
Item 1: Advertising contributes very importantly to America's industrial prosperity.
Item 2: Advertising merely inflates the prices I must pay for products without giving me any information.
Item 3: Advertising does inform the public and is worth the cost.
Item 4: The American public would be better off with no advertising at all.
Item 5: Advertising old products is a waste of the consumers' dollar.
Item 6: I wouldn't mind if all advertising were stopped.
Item 7: I wish there were more advertising than exists now.

Three of these scale items (or attitude statements) are favourable towards the advertising industry (1, 3 and 7), and four are unfavourable (2, 4, 5 and 6).

A Likert-type scale is used:

| Strongly approve | Approve | Undecided | Disapprove | Strongly disapprove |

and each subject (or respondent) underscores 'the description that most suits his/her feeling' toward each statement.

Green and Tull use the following weights:

+2   +1   0   −1   −2

(The procedure is the same if weights running from 5 for 'strongly approve' down to 1 for 'strongly disapprove' are used.)

For items classified as favourable these weights are used without modification. For items classified as unfavourable, the order of the weights is reversed so as to maintain a consistent direction.

Application of the weights is illustrated in the following example, based on the responses of one subject to the seven items:

Item	*Response*	*Weight*
1	Strongly approve	+2
2	Disapprove	+1
3	Approve	+1
4	Strongly disapprove	+2
5	Disapprove	+1

6	Strongly disapprove	+ 2
7	Strongly approve	+ 2
	Total score	11

(As a matter of interest, it is assumed by Green and Tull that these seven items are taken from a scale battery of 100 items.)

The data derived from weighted responses to rating scales are used as the basis of sophisticated statistical analyses (see Chapter 6, where the application of multi-variate techniques to market segmentation is discussed). It is important to remember the following:

- The scale positions and the weights attached to them are arbitrarily fixed.
- With the scales in common use in marketing research, distance between positions appears equal, but for the respondent this is not necessarily the case: e.g. the distance in strength of feeling between 'approve' and 'strongly approve' may well be different from the distance between 'disapprove' and 'strongly disapprove', but responses are weighted as if the distances were equal.

The rating scales in common use give us useful assessments of the way in which consumers respond to attitude statements about products and services and the needs these are designed to meet. The statistical data derived from rating scales enable us to make comparisons and draw useful conclusions: but they are not, strictly speaking, measurements.

5.5.7 Some MRDF findings

> Sampling error is understood, measurable and predictable . . . non-sampling error is a much greater source of survey error.[11]

The 1984 April issue of the *Journal of the Market Research Society* is devoted to methodological research financed by the Market Research Development Fund into the types of question asked by market researchers and the words used in framing these. The interviews analysed were with 'all adults' or 'all housewives'.

Twenty-eight research agencies with turnovers of more than 1 million each were asked to supply one randomly selected page from five of their questionnaires. Twelve agencies responded and 570 questions were analysed. These fell into the following categories:

$n = 570$	% of answers
Factual questions	5
Behaviour questions (past, present, future)	33

| Awareness, knowledge | 8 |
| Attitudes, opinions, beliefs | 54 |

Note: Research agencies were asked to exclude pages containing questions classifying respondents: i.e. the 'factual' total is depressed.

Questions designed to explain behaviour dominate.

Attitude measurement was seen to rely on scales and on lists of possible answers (show-cards). Hundred per cent literacy is assumed in the survey population, while 'true answers' depend on the respondents' understanding of the task set and the words used.

Computer analysis of the research vocabulary used in the sample showed that, taking Payne's coding of difficult and ambiguous words as a yardstick,[1] one-fifth of frequently used market research words were potentially problem ones. O'Brien concludes:

> . . . if questionnaires are designed without qualitative input, if the timetable does not allow for pilot testing, if nobody has thought about the potential for ambiguity or misunderstanding of the words in each question, then we are probably introducing a whole range of error into our measurements.[11]

5.6 Conclusion

The questioning techniques discussed in this chapter may be applied to a wide range of descriptive surveys, from a simple recording of products, services and brands in current use to the collection of data about how these were acquired, how they are used, why they were chosen and how far they go to meet felt needs.

Asking questions remains the most fruitful way of collecting statistical data about consumer behaviour. From an examination of the relationships between habits, awareness, attitudes and needs revealed in answers to questions it is possible to arrive at a sufficiently robust understanding of consumer behaviour to formulate hypotheses as to 'what might happen next', or 'what might happen if'.

The marketing decisions arrived at have ultimately to be put to the test (see Chapters 7–10); but first the extent to which analysis of descriptive data can reduce uncertainty about the requirements of the market is considered in the next chapter.

Possible demand for works transport: extracts from a case history to illustrate deciding levels of generality with regard to a survey topic, in this case 'means used to get to work' (see section 5.3.2), classification of respondents (see section 5.3.3) and choice of sample design (see section 3.7).

The management of a labour-intensive firm with works on the outskirts of a large town is considering whether to provide transport for its employees. The board want to be able to predict who might use the firm's transport without, at this stage, committing the company to setting it up. The personnel director suggests that a 'getting to work' survey should be commissioned for publication in the house journal. The survey would describe transport used, routes taken and costs incurred together with opinions held about the transport means available.

A research agency was employed. The research officer assigned to the job observed traffic at the firm's car parks and bicycle sheds, held three group discussions, listed question topics suggested by this exploratory research and discussed the detail in which means of getting to work should be recorded. Was a two-way breakdown sufficient?

Private transport   *Public transport*

What about on foot, all the way? (Public transport would mean some walking!) The effects of railway strikes and of petrol cost and shortage had come up during the group discussions. It was decided that getting to work should be recorded in a less general way:

Private transport	*Public transport*
Motor car	Bus
Motor bike/moped	Train
Bicycle	
On foot all the way	

Suppose more than one means of transport were used: car to station, then train, or train then bus. And what about variations in habit? It was decided to stratify calls by day of the working week and to ask a question about getting to work today: then to find out if today's journey had been different in route taken and transport used from other journeys to work in the rest of the previous week. Use of 'generally', 'regularly', 'usually' could then be avoided (see section 5.4).

Observation of traffic into the car parks at the exploratory stage had revealed that lifts were given, car owners taking it in turn to act as chauffeur. The effect of increased petrol costs had, the group discussions suggested, developed the habit of sharing transport. Company cars and car allowances also came up. It was hypothesized that sharing costs and company funding might affect reactions to attitude statements on the questionnaire.

It was finally agreed that data about the topic 'means used to get to work' should be collected in the following detail:

Private transport	Public transport
Motor car, driver	Bus
No passenger	Train
With passenger(s)	
Company car/allowance	
Motor car, passenger	
Motor bike/moped, driver	
Motor bike/moped, passenger	
Bicycle	
On foot all the way	

There were, of course, other topics on the list. We move onto classification of the survey population. Company cars apart, was there likely to be a relationship between means of transport used and job done? Would a simple dichotomy be sufficient?

Staff	Shop floor

Or would it help management to decide whether to introduce a transport service if employees were classified in more detail, so that the habits and attitudes of smaller groups towards getting to work could be compared? The following classification of respondents was considered:

Staff	Shop floor
Management	Supervisory
Sales	Wage-earners
Clerical	Piece-workers

But it was soon agreed that the following classification would be more relevant to the survey objectives:

Staff	Shop floor
Itinerant, i.e.	By 'shop'/department, e.g.
sales representatives,	paintshop,
service engineers	despatch
On the spot	

The decision to distinguish the 'itinerant' group from the 'on the spot' group was taken because it was hypothesized that those who had to get to the office every day would have different attitudes from those who came in and out at irregular intervals, while the irregular habits of the latter would confuse the overall 'staff' behaviour data.[*] The decision to relate 'means of getting to work' to shops or departments in the works was determined by the management's desire to know where bus or train strikes or a petrol shortage would be most damaging, should there be marked variation in habit from one department to another. (Since all employees and their jobs were recorded on a computer file, it was possible to draw a stratified probability sample, using a variable sampling fraction (see section 3.7). Shop-floor employees far out-numbered staff and some shops were very much larger than others. A disproportionate design therefore made more efficient use of the research allocation than a proportionate one.)

[*]It was recognized that all the 'itinerant' group would have company cars, but so, of course, would some of those who worked 'on the spot'; while the reasons for isolating the 'itinerant' group still held good.

Sources and further reading

1. S.L. Payne, *The Art of Asking Questions* (Princeton: Princeton University Press, 1951). The classic text on this subject. Excerpts are quoted in J. Seibert and G. Wills (eds), *Marketing Research*, (Harmondsworth: Penguin, 1970).
2. V. Farbridge, Introduction in 'Fieldwork and Data Processing', supp. to the *MRS Newsletter*, no. 177, (Dec. 1980).
3. L. England, 'The dangerous dialogue in fieldwork and data processing', supp. to the *MRS Newsletter*, no. 177 (Dec. 1980).
4. J. O'Brien, 'Two answers are better than one', *MRS Conference Papers* (1987).
5. A.N. Oppenheim, *Questionnaire Design and Attitude Measurement* (London: Heinemann Educational Books, 1970).
6. *Guide to Good Coding Practice* (London: The Market Research Society, 1987).
7. A.R. Wolfe (ed.), *Standardised Questions: A Review for Market Research Executives*, 2nd edn (London: The Market Research Society, 1984).
8. J. Morton-Williams and W. Sykes, 'The use of interaction coding', *Journal of The Market Research Society*, vol. 26, no. 2 (April 1984).
9. W. Belson, 'A comparison of open-ended and check-list questioning systems', *MRS Conference Papers* (1982).
10. Dr William Belson in a letter to the author dated 24 June 1988.
11. J. O'Brien, 'How do market researchers ask questions?', *Journal of The Market Research Society*, vol. 26, no. 2 (April 1984).
12. G.J. Read, 'Asking questions about behaviour', MRS course (1977).
13. P. Sampson, 'Qualitative research and motivation research', Chap. 2 in R.M. Worcester and J. Downham (eds), *Consumer Market Research Handbook*, 2nd edn (Wokingham: Van Nostrand Reinhold, 1978).
14. P.E. Green and D.S. Tull, *Research for Marketing Decisions*, 4th edn (Englewood Cliffs, NJ: Prentice Hall, 1978).

See also

- W.A. Belson, *Validity in Survey Research*, (London: Gower, 1986).
- M. Collins and G. Courtenay, 'The effect of survey form on survey data', *MRS Conference Papers* (1984).
- *A Handbook for Interviewers* (London: The Market Research Society, 1974).
- J. Macfarlane Smith, *Interviewing in Market and Social Research*, (London: Routledge and Kegan Paul, 1972).
- J. Morton-Williams, 'Questionnaire design', Chap. 5 in R.M. Worcester and J. Downham (eds) *Consumer Market Research Handbook*, 3rd edn (Amsterdam: North-Holland, 1986).

Problems

These problems relate to Chapter 3 as well as to Chapter 5.

You are designing the questionnaire for a face-to-face usage and attitude survey of the in-home wine-drinking habits of the British population.

1. (a)   Define the population of interest (the survey population) and prescribe population breakdowns, taking account of the statistical data quoted below.

   (b)   Draft classification questions and pre-code these.

2. List topics of interest and construct a flow chart to illustrate the ordering of topics and the route taken through the questionnaire by the interviewer.

3. Draft the questionnaire, including introductory comment and instructions to the interviewer.

4. Pre-code answers wherever possible.

Users of table wine (base all adults)

Heavy users	3–5 bottles a month	7.5
Medium users	1–2 bottles a month	20.0
Light users	Less than 1 bottle a month	29.5
All users		57.0
Non-users		43.0

Demographic profile (base all users)

Men	47.4	15–24	18.7	AB	23.9
Women	52.6	25–34	21.2	C_1	27.2
		35–44	18.5	C_2	29.0
		45–54	14.5	D	14.1
		55–64	13.3	E	5.8
		65 & +	13.8		

Source: BMRB/TGI (1983)

6 Market segmentation

To 'segment' is to 'divide into parts' (*OED*). In the marketing context these parts may be groups of consumers with like requirements or groups of products/services with like attributes.

A marketing company may adopt a segmentation strategy for two main reasons:

1. To locate a new opportunity, a 'gap' or unfulfilled (or only partly fulfilled) need in a market.
2. To position its brand (or brands) *vis-à-vis* competitive brands so that the company brand is favourably placed within the product field.

A market researcher is likely to approach design of a segmentation study from one of two angles:

1. Collection and analysis of data relating to the habits, attitudes and needs of consumers with a view to sorting consumers into homogeneous groups differentiated by their lifestyles and buyer behaviour (*consumer typology*).
2. Collection and analysis of data relating to the products/services/brands available in the market, focusing on how these are perceived by consumers, with a view to sorting the brands into groups of those with like attributes in consumer eyes (*product differentiation*).

The 'gap' or new opportunity sought by the marketing company may be located (if it exists) using either of these research approaches. Product positioning is more closely associated with the second approach: but, since in both cases the data are derived from descriptions of consumer habits, attitudes and perceptions, the distinction between the two is by no means 'hard and fast'. Given the structure of this book, segmentation is of particular interest as a means of locating new opportunities (see section 1.4); but marketing companies necessarily devote most of their attention to the reinforcement of existing branded lines and many segmentation studies are designed to help a company improve the competitiveness of an existing product.

During the 1960s and into the 1970s most segmentation studies were carried out by individual marketing companies for their own strategic purposes. Esso's 'motorists' typology' (section 6.7) is a good example of a custom-built, product-specific typology.

Today, a marketing company is more likely to buy into one of the services offered by the large market research agencies. These consumer typologies take account of the behaviour, beliefs and values of consumers and so add flesh to the traditional demographic variable used in market and social research: social class.

Segmentation systems which divide the population into general lifestyle categories are useful indicators of social change when the longer-term future is being planned,[1] but for more immediate marketing purposes 'lifestyle or attitude classifications provide the greatest discrimination when they are designed to address specific markets'.[2]

There is on computer file and available to subscribers a mass of data relating to the buying, viewing and reading habits and attitudes of consumers, together with detailed data about where they live. When these data are filed on an individual or 'single-source' basis, the construction of 'own-label' classifications is possible. The spread of personal computers can be expected to encourage the DIY habit.

In the meantime, the relative validity and usefulness of social class (which provides the essential link between databases), lifestyle and life-stage systems are being debated as well as the contribution to market planning of the geodemographic classifications (section 6.2.2).[3]

In this chapter we first consider the basic classification variables, and then review the segmentation services available to subscribers. But we ought first to ask ourselves 'why segment?'

6.1   Why segment?

On the face of it, to segment a market flies in the face of economic theory. What about economies of scale, the long production run for a mass market?

The segmentation approach to market planning developed in the United Kingdom in the late 1950s and became fashionable in the 1960s. The development was associated with the end of rationing and the revival of competition as a marketing force. Acceleration of technological progress following the end of the war, together with increased social mobility and growth in the variety of wants felt by consumers, encouraged competitive marketing activity, while the UK market is now open to EC products and brands.

Marketing interest in the changes taking place in the habits and attitudes of consumers was further stimulated by the need to counter the growing power of retail enterprises. The producer's strength at the point of sale was eroded by the abolition of resale price maintenance in 1976, removing the producer's right to specify the price at which the product should be sold to consumers. A more critical factor was the development of 'own-label' branding by retailers.

Manufacturing for the retail trade is now 'big business' and many important manufacturing companies create competition for their branded lines by supplying the retail trade with 'own-label' brands which usually compete with the manufacturer's brand on price. Market segmentation makes it possible for the manufacturer (or marketing company) to sidestep competition from 'own label', while preserving and developing his brand identity at the point of sale.

By meeting the requirements of those whose wants are not being satisfied, by concentrating marketing effort on a market segment, the manufacturer can expect to create a loyalty sufficiently strong to counteract the appeal of generics and low-priced brands, and in particular of the retailer's 'own label'. In addition, by consistently focusing effort on a target segment, a satisfactory relationship between marketing costs and sales revenue can be achieved. But the mere fact that a market segment is not being served, or is being served poorly, is not sufficient. Three additional conditions must be considered.[4]

Kotler's three 'conditions' are as follows:

1. Measurability: we must, of course, be able to establish the size of the segment characteristics.
2. Accessibility: it must be possible to distribute to the segment and to communicate with it through the media.
3. Substantiality: the segment must be sufficiently large and demanding to generate an adequate contribution to profit.

Having located this measurable, accessible and sufficiently substantial area of want, it is, of course, necessary to develop a product or service to which both consumers and distributors respond. Research funds are laid out with maximum cost-effect when the target segment and its wants have been established, for it is then possible to work to an unequivocal brief specifying both of the following:

- The kind of people to be asked to discuss ideas about product and communication (concept testing); and to take part in experiments to help determine final choices.
- The grounds for choice: i.e. the criteria to be used in the design of concept tests and experiments, and in the interpretation of results.

6.2   Segmentation variables

In the search for a target segment we consider the ways in which those in the market vary. These variables are summarized in Figure 6.1. They fall into two broad categories:

1. Variables which are descriptive: the geographic, cultural, demographic and 'behaviour in the product field' groups.

```
Geographic
Cultural
Demographic
    Social–economic group
    Income
    Age
    Terminal education age (TEA)
    Family life-cycle

Behaviour in the product field
    Heavy, medium, light purchasers
    Brand loyalists, switchers

Social–psychological
    Innovators . . . late adopters      ⎫
    Reference groups                    ⎬  Academic origin
    Personality, standardized inventories ⎭

    Principal benefit sought            ⎫
    Psychographic groups                ⎬  Marketing origin
        Consumer typology/lifestyle     
        Product differentiation         ⎭

(Variables used in non-domestic markets:
    Geographic, cultural
    Application, e.g. SIC
    Organizational buying behaviour
    see section 4.3)
```

**Figure 6.1
Segmentation
variables**

2. Variables which are explanatory; the social–psychological group.

The two categories are not entirely discrete, for the geographical and demographic variables are necessarily used to locate and delimit the social–psychological groups derived from attitudinal and lifestyle studies. Most segmentation approaches involve the multi-variate computer analysis of data.

6.2.1 Geographical and cultural

In Great Britain these two groups of variables 'hang together'. Among the native population television has minimized regional differences in habit and attitude, while the motor car has blurred distinctions between town and country dwellers. Wants tend to be 'like', but geographic concentration of vulnerable industries (e.g. steel, textiles, cars and trucks) creates areas of economic hazard and so constrains buying behaviour.

Immigrant populations are geographically concentrated and culturally distinct and these populations represent significant segments in the markets for food, toiletries, cosmetics, air travel and packaged holidays.[5]

Outside Great Britain, in the EC as well as further afield, cultural differences are more significant. (Great Britain is deliberately referred to here rather than the United Kingdom, which embraces Northern Ireland.)

Geodemographic systems are included here because they relate to the geographical distribution of the population as revealed by the census.[6] As we saw when considering stratification of the population for the purpose of drawing samples (section 4.3) ACORN, the pioneer geo-demographic system, has been followed by MOSAIC, Pinpoint's PIN and SuperProfiles. All four systems relate population characteristics recorded in the census to the enumeration districts from which the data are collected. Statistical analysis reduces this mass of data to meaningful clusters. As Twyman said of the pioneer system: 'ACORN is basically a method of mapping geographically the concentrations of particular types of people where those types are likely to be related to the housing characteristics of their district.'[7]

The four systems vary in the census and other variables fed into their computer programs, in the statistical procedures used to cluster these, in the number of residential types emerging from the statistical treatment and in the descriptions attached to the types (see Table 6.1).

It has been said that 'geodemographics amount to a massive argument for direct marketing':[8] i.e. promotion ('below-the-line') as compared with advertising ('above-the-line') expenditure. Indeed the original impulse came from the requirements of mail-order houses.

Geodemographic systems tell us in what types of neighbourhood a brand is doing well/badly, and where, once a target has been defined, development research might usefully be carried out. But geodemographics do not define a target segment in terms of consumer behaviour in the product field, nor do they take account of consumer attitudes which help to explain that behaviour. Geodemographics are not helpful to those who create advertising campaigns.

Table 6.1 Geodemo-graphic systems	Input variables Number	Residential types Number
ACORN	40	38
MOSAIC	54	58
Pinpoint's PIN	104	60
SuperProfiles	90	150

6.2.2 Demographic

Social class (or social grade)

'This occupation-based system of classification remains the standard for both market and social research despite criticisms that have been brought against it.'[10] The occupation-based system in common use is that used in the continuous random-sampling procedure followed for the National Readership Survey (NRS). The class categories derived from this are summarized on p. 48. 'The current convention is to use a socio-economic grouping based exclusively on "occupation of head of household" ',[9] (or chief wage-earner).

The social-class classification enables data to be related across a wide range of sources, including the media series discussed in Chapter 9 (the segment must be accessible!). Criticisms of the occupation-based system were accordingly addressed by the MRS in 1981 and in 1987.

The 1981 enquiry studied the validity of the system in some depth and drew the following four conclusions:

1. Analysis of data covering product field penetration, weight of use and brand use shows that, over all, social grade provides satisfactory discriminatory power.
2. None of the alternative standard classification variables examined was found to provide consistently better discriminatory power.
3. No one classification variable works 'best' across all product fields or data types.
4. No evidence was found to show a decline in the discriminatory power of social grade over the last ten years.[10]

The 1987 enquiry endorsed the use of the head of household (HOH) or chief wage-earner (CWE) convention but felt that 'this area should continue to be monitored as it was an area of some concern'.[11] The committee issued a guide to the identification of HOH and CWE, and gave broad descriptions of the social classes, including a grading of the new 'hi-tech' occupations.

The 1987 committee paid particular attention to the continued use of HOH/CWE at a time of social change. An analysis of NRS data showed that about one-half of women working full-time would have had their classification altered by using their own occupation as against that of HOH/CWE. 'This is so despite the number of working women in one-person households and those who are themselves HOH/CWE, for whom a different classification cannot by definition arise.'[12] 'However the HOH/CWE occupation still seemed to be the best indicator of household "style", so we decided that we should have to recommend the continued use of HOH/CWE for household related purchases.'[11]

The discriminatory power of social class was compared with

classifications based on life-stage and lifestyle in a survey based on 1,380 fifty-minute interviews carried out in January 1987. (For information about life-stage and lifestyle see 'Family life cycle' and 'Psychographics and lifestyle' later in this chapter.) Respondents were asked about twenty items, such as having a home computer, taking holidays abroad, having an interest-earning cheque account. The results endorse the discriminatory power of social class across a range of subjects. The life-stage classification also performs well. Lifestyle does best when applied to attitudinal subjects (as might be expected): i.e. results confirm conclusions 2 and 3 of the 1971 committee.

However, when a sample of those originally interviewed was asked the same classification questions ten months later, but by different interviewers, social class showed a 41 per cent change in the allocation of respondents to class, compared with 16 per cent for life-stage. It is suggested that life-stage is a more stable classification because it is based on factual data of a kind easier to collect and less open to misinterpretation than social class; and that, unlike social class, 'it can be applied consistently at an international and cross-cultural level'.[3]

Income

This was among 'the alternative standard classifications' studied by the 1981 joint industry working party. Income (and more especially disposable income) is difficult to establish, not only because of reluctance to give the information (this is reduced by asking the respondent to point to a figure on a card). The main difficulty is establishing what income is, as the standard question shows:[9]

> Which of these comes closest to your total take-home income, from all sources, that is after deducting income tax, national insurance, pension schemes and so on? SHOW CARD

(And what about mortgage repayments? And the controversial 'poll tax'?) It is, of course, necessary to keep the annual, monthly and weekly lists of earnings on the show-card up-to-date.

In many surveys the data relate to buying for a family by the housewife. Here, definition of income is further complicated by the fact that family income often derives from more than one wage packet. A full and accurate investigation requires a whole questionnaire with documented cross-checks.[9]

Age

This is an important discriminator in many consumer markets (and it is a useful check on the representativeness of samples, for the age distribution of the population is well documented). Two methods of establishing the respondent's age are in common use: a straight question, 'what was your age last birthday?' or by means of a show-card with age brackets. As with income, this may reduce reluctance to answer the question.

Terminal education age (TEA)

TEA, type of school or college attended and examinations passed have gained in significance as segmentation variables with the rapid development of silicon-chip technology. The standard TEA question is 'how old were you when you finished your *full-time* education?'[9] This definition of TEA begs some questions, particularly at present, when there is increasing emphasis on vocational training which is often 'day release' or part-time. In the current disturbed state of our educational system, collection of data relating to type of school or college attended and educational qualifications requires 'definitions and explanations which cannot conveniently be given on the questionnaire and therefore require a feat of memory on the part of the interviewer'.[9] (And Scotland is different!)

Family life cycle

With or without marriage, the family remains a basic social unit in Great Britain. Demand for many products and services is related to the stage reached in the family life cycle. These stages are commonly defined as:

Young	Young, single, no children	Young couple, youngest child under six	Young couple, youngest child six or +	Older couple, with children 18+ at home	Older couple, no children at home	Older, single

The life-stage classification mentioned above under social class takes account of employment in the family as well as the family's composition, increasing the marketing relevance of this segmentation variable.

SAGACITY, developed by Research Services Limited (RSL), is a segmentation based on a combination of life cycle, income and occupation.[13] (See Figure 6.2.)

Life cycle: includes age and situational variables.
Income: takes account of spouse's employment status, i.e. full-time/part-time/unemployed.
Occupation: divides ABC_1 (white collar) from C_2DE (blue collar).

'Treating demographics multi-variately in this way generates sharper discrimination in some areas, groups that mean something in social terms, and is clearly an advance on using single demographics.'[7] The robustness

The basic thesis of the SAGACITY grouping is that people have different aspirations and behaviour patterns as they go through their life cycle. Four main stages of life cycle are defined, which are sub-divided by income and occupation groups:

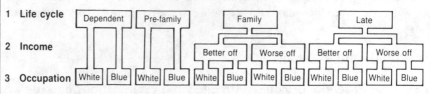

Descriptive notations for each of the twelve groups are described below together with their size as a percentage of total adult population.

Dependent, white (DW) 6.5 per cent
Mainly under 24s, living at home or full time student, where head of household is in an ABC_1 occupation group.

Dependent, blue (DB) 9.0 per cent
Mainly under 24s, living at home or full time student, where head of household is in a C_2DE occupation group.

Pre-family, white (PFW) 4.5 per cent
Under 35s who have established their own household but have no children and where the head of household is in an ABC_1 occupation group.

Pre-family, blue (PFB) 4.7 per cent
Under 35s who have established their own household but have no children and where the head of household is in a C_2DE occupation group.

Family, better off, white (FW+)
7.9 per cent
Housewives and heads of household, under 65, with one or more children in the household, in the 'better off' income group and where the head of household is in an ABC_1 occupation group. (63 per cent are AB).

Family, better off, blue (FB+)
7.9 per cent
Housewives and heads of household, under 65, with one or more children in the household, in the 'better off' income group and where the head of household is in a C_2DE occupation group. (80 per cent are C_2).

Family, worse off, white (FW−)
5.6 per cent
Housewives and heads of household,

under 65 with one or more children in the household, in the 'worse off' income group and where the head of household is in an ABC_1 occupation group. (70 per cent are C_1).

Family, worse off, blue (FB−)
12.4 per cent
Housewives and heads of household, under 65, with one or more children in the household, in the 'worse off' income group and where the head of household is in a C_2DE occupation group. (53 per cent are DE).

Late, better off, white (LW+)
6.1 per cent
Includes all adults whose children have left home or who are over 35 and childless, are in the 'better off' income group and where the head of household is in an ABC_1 occupation group. (61 per cent are AB).

Late, better off, blue (LB+)
6.4 per cent
Includes all adults whose children have left home or who are over 35 and childless, are in the 'better off' income group and where the head of household is in a C_2DE occupation group. (72 per cent are DE).

Late, worse off, white (LW−)
9.6 per cent
Includes all adults whose children have left home or who are over 35 and childless, are in the 'worse off' income group and where the head of household is in an ABC_1 occupation group. (67 per cent are C_1).

Late, worse off, blue (LB−)
19.3 per cent
Includes all adults whose children have left home or who are over 35 and childless, are in the 'worse off' income group and where the head of household is in a C_2DE occupation group (72 per cent are DE).

Source: Research Services Ltd (1987)

**Figure 6.2
The twelve
SAGACITY
segments**

All adults %	Index	Dependent DW	DB	Pre-family PFW	PFB	Family stage FW+	FB+	FW−	FB−	Late stage LW+	LB+	LW−	LB−
Package holiday taken abroad in last 12 months													
10.3	100	154	109	208	117	156	92	100	36	200	129	108	44
Owns cheque book													
52.9	100	105	57	169	114	171	111	146	73	162	91	132	46
Refrigerator acquired in past 2 years													
14.0	100	—	—	173	168	130	117	109	106	103	91	74	54
Moved home in past 2 years													
14.7	100	—	—	502	340	109	86	115	115	69	44	54	50

**Table 6.2
Market-
penetration
data**

Source: P. Cornish, 'Life cycle and income segmentation — SAGACITY', *ADMAP* (Oct. 1981), pp. 522–6

of the SAGACITY segmentation is supported by the 'it stands to reason' nature of the market-penetration data in Table 6.2.

The SAGACITY databank is kept up-to-date and the twelve segments have been used in special analyses of NRS data. Development work at RSL includes a projected life cycle, which takes account of changes due in the next six months, changes such as leaving home, marrying, birth and retirement.

6.3 Behaviour in the product field

Price is a segmentation variable familiar to economists, and price is, of course, an important determinant of consumer choice. In many markets, from motor cars to pet foods, products are tailored to fit into specific price segments. But, from the marketing point of view, price is one element in the marketing mix, and interest is focused on the inter-relationships between variables affecting ultimate choice and extent of use, such as the relationship between size of family, social grade, housewife gainfully or not gainfully employed and the extent to which variously priced brands are bought and used. (Price as a product attribute is considered in section 7.5.)

Given adequate data, users of products/services can be divided into 'heavy', 'medium' and 'light' user categories according to amount bought and frequency of buying. This kind of analysis is best based on trend data derived from consumer panels, whether the data are recorded in diaries or by means of regular audits. We need to remember that those who buy the product are not always those who use it, and to distinguish between data based on household panels (e.g. the Attwood consumer panel and the television consumer audit) and data based on panels of individuals (e.g. the motorist's diary panel and AGB's personal purchases index).

Apart from 'heavy', 'medium' and 'light' buying, it is also possible to sort the individuals on panels into 'loyalists' and 'switchers' according to how their buying moves between brands. All these 'buying-behaviour' groups can be described in geographic and demographic terms.

Micheal Head of Heinz has put the view 'that big brands are often trying to sell to everybody, or everybody with certain situationally determined product requirements (like having children for example) and that classification data were useful descriptively but not as a basis for creating typologies. For many brands the important typologies were created by existing buying patterns.'[7]

> The segmentation approach is used with a view to reinforcing the position of ongoing brands as well as in the search for new market opportunities.

Moving away from fast-moving consumer goods to washing machines, refrigerators, electric fires and other durables, trend data are less essential, though once-a-quarter auditing (as in the AGB home audit) establishes first acquisition and subsequent replacement of durables more conclusively than an *ad hoc* survey can.

(For a durable product geography may be important, e.g. truly rural areas do not have piped gas, while hardness or softness of water can also influence marketing decisions. Family life cycle and whether or not the housewife works outside the home count in segmentation studies relating to durables.)

6.4 Search for explanatory variables

The segmentation variables considered so far are important for 'measurability' and 'accessibility'. They help to define the size of segments and how best to reach them through the media. All these variables are, however, descriptive: they do not explain behaviour. We can observe associations between the demographic variables and those relating to behaviour in the product field and we can infer reasons for the behaviour, but the observed associations tend to be rather obvious ones, such as that large families are heavy users of breakfast cereals.

It was for a time anticipated that procedures developed and tested by anthropologists, sociologists and, more particularly, psychologists might be applied to the segmentation of consumer markets, for example:

- Division of the population into innovators (2.5 per cent), early adopters (13.5 per cent), early majority (34 per cent), late majority (34 per cent) and late adopters (16 per cent) following the 'diffusion of innovations' theory.

- Or establishing the kind of individuals with whom consumers sought to identify themselves following the 'reference group' theory.

- While the psychologists' standardized personality inventories looked particularly promising as a source of segmentation variables, since these standard lists of attitude and behaviour questions were designed to sort individuals into homogeneous personality groups.

The personality inventories developed by Eysenck in the United Kingdom and Cattell in the United States, to quote two outstanding examples, have been extensively tested for validity and reliability. (Do answers to this list of questions indicate an individual's membership of a distinct personality group? Does this list of personality questions stand up to use over time with different individuals?) Given that there were available personality inventories which had been tested for validity and reliability, was it not wasteful, indeed frivolous, to start again from scratch when seeking to group consumers for marketing purposes?

Attempts to apply academic theories to marketing added to the understanding of consumer behaviour but they were not sufficiently focused on the marketing context to provide usable techniques. As an example of the kind of problem encountered, Russell Haley quotes application of the Edwards personal preference schedule to the consumer market for toilet tissue.[14]

The Edwards scales are designed to reveal personality traits such as 'autonomy', 'dominance', 'order', 'endurance'. In the toilet-tissue case it was found that purchases of single- and double-ply tissue correlated with consumer responses to the Edwards inventory. Knowing about the personality traits of single- and double-ply toilet-tissue users might well inspire the creative group in an advertising agency, but questions relating to the 'measurability', 'accessibility' and 'substantiality' of the segments remain to be answered.

It was generally found that responses to standardized inventories did not correlate well with consumer behaviour, while the 'rather abstract relationships' established were of only marginal help when it came to making marketing decisions.[14]

6.5 Benefit segmentation

The 'benefit' approach to segmentation focuses on product or brand use but introduces psychological variables into the segmentation study. Consumers are grouped according to the principal benefit they seek when they make buying decisions. Table 6.3 reproduces Russell Haley's benefit segmentation of the toothpaste market. Haley pioneered the 'principal benefit' idea and this is now a classic example.

Michael Thomas comments on benefit segmentation as follows.

> The goal of benefit segmentation is to find a group of people all seeking the same benefits from a product. Each segment is identified by the benefits being sought. It is not unusual for various segments to share individual benefits. The major factor is the amount of importance each segment places on each benefit.[15]

**Table 6.3
Russell Haley's
benefit
segmentation
of the
toothpaste
market**

Segment name	The sensory segment	The sociables	The worriers	The independent segment
Principal benefit sought	Flavour, product appearance	Brightness of teeth	Decay prevention	Price
Demographic strengths	Children	Teens, young people	Large families	Men
Special behavioural characteristics	Users of spearmint flavoured toothpaste	Smokers	Heavy users	Heavy users
Brands disproportionately favoured	Colgate, Stripe	Macleans Plus White Ultra Brite	Crest	Brands on sale*
Personality characteristics	High self-involvement	High sociability	High hypo-chondriasis	High-autonomy
Life-style characteristics	Hedonistic	Active	Conservative	Value-oriented

*i.e. on offer.

Source: R.E. Haley, 'Benefit segmentation: a decision-oriented research tool', *Journal of Marketing* (July 1968), pp. 30–5

The 'benefit' approach to segmentation is particularly relevant to market planning for existing brands. It effectively describes, and begins to explain, the branded product field as it is. Haley's analysis takes note of segmentation variables other than benefit sought, as Table 6.3 shows; but the criterion for segmentation is principal benefit sought. As Haley points out, 'the benefits which people are seeking in consuming a given product are the basic reasons for the existence of true market segments'; but consumers do not always find it easy to define the benefits they seek or to give true answers (as we saw when discussing Oppenheim's 'barriers'; see section 5.4.3).

6.6 Psychographics and lifestyle

The answer was to develop personality inventories based on attitudes expressed by consumers when discussing:

- The relevant activity: i.e. motoring, leisure, feeding the family, housekeeping, shaving, insuring against risks.
- The products, brands, services available for carrying out the activity. Which did consumers know about and how well did these meet the demands of the activity?

In a segmentation study the attitude statements forming the inventory (or battery) of scales are elicited from group discussions, depth interviews or Kelly 'personal construct' interviews as described in section 5.5. As a general rule the statements are put to consumers in the form of either Likert-type, or semantic differential scales, depending on whether the segmentation study is designed to type consumers or to group products according to the ways in which consumers perceive them.

A segmentation study will necessarily include questions of a demographic and product-use nature as well as the attitude battery. The range of questions will depend on how far it is intended to explore the lifestyle of those in the market. Do we intend to collect data about consumers' needs, values, activities and interests outside the product field and the context in which products (or services) are used? The answer depends on whether preliminary research suggests that the more far-ranging data will be relevant, interpretable and actionable.

The main stages in a psychographic segmentation are commonly as follows:

Exploratory or preliminary research

A company embarking on a segmentation study is likely to have a good deal of descriptive data on file and to know what kind of consumers to invite to group discussions or depth interviews.

Exploratory or preliminary research ───────────┐
   A list of attitude statements. (Qualitative research.)
Questionnaire piloted ─────────────────────────┐
   Reduction of attitude statements to a critical short-list.
                              (Quantitative research + factor analysis.)
Main survey ───────────────────────────────────┐
   Clustering of consumers or of products/brands as perceived by them.
                              (Quantitative research + cluster analysis.)

(Section 2.7 covers this question of 'whom to invite' in greater detail.) Qualitative work goes on until we are satisfied that we have collected a good (if not exhaustive) pool of consumer ideas relevant to the market.

Taped recordings are transcribed, consumer statements sorted into groups according to topic, and attitude scales constructed. There may be 60 to 100 attitude statements on the original questionnaire.

Piloting the questionnaire

The battery of attitude statements is likely to be long and repetitive, especially if we are seeking to type consumers. The same attitudes can be expressed in more than one way; and some statements count for more than others when it comes to accounting for consumer variability.

With a limited number of attitude statements it would be possible to establish associations between consumer responses by drawing up a correlation matrix; but it would clearly be difficult to 'read' a 60×60 correlation matrix (in segmentation studies scale batteries can run to more than sixty items). We therefore need the means to deal with the interrelationship of many variables quickly.

> Statistical techniques which simultaneously examine the relationships between many variables are known as multi-variate statistical procedures.[16]

Provided it is done on an adequate scale (say 200 calls) the pilot test gives us the opportunity to use the multi-variate technique called *factor analysis* to reduce the battery of attitude statements to a small number of factors each made up of a group of highly correlated scales representing a particular dimension of the overall attitude. In the following example four factors were found to account for most of the variability shown in the answers of respondents to questions about saving.[17]

Exploratory stage: Depth interviews generated a list of some twenty-five attitude statements.

Pilot stage: These statements were put to 130 members of the public in the form of scales, and weights were attached to their responses (section 5.5).
Factor analysis: Multi-variate analysis of the scores derived from the responses of the sample to individual statements yielded four factors. Each of these factors represents a different dimension of the overall attitude towards saving:

Factor 1. Temperamental difficulty in saving (e.g. 'I have never been able to save').
Factor 2. Sense of solidity (e.g. 'If you've got a bit of money saved you are not so likely to be pushed around').
Factor 3. Concern with independence (e.g. 'I hate to feel I might have to ask someone for financial help').
Factor 4. Feeling of financial security (e.g. 'I feel it's unlikely I shall have any financial emergencies in the near future').

Let us consider Factor 1 more closely. It is associated with five attitude statements compared with four for Factors 2 and 3 and three for Factor 4.

Factor 1.
(a) I have never been able to save.
(b) Unless you have some specific reason to save, it's better to spend and enjoy it.
(c) I believe in enjoying my money now and letting the future take care of itself.
(d) I don't feel it's necessary to save just now.
(e) I can't help spending all I earn.

The survey

The object is to locate homogeneous clusters of consumers, or of products as perceived by consumers. The clusters must do two things:

1. Fulfil the three conditions for market segments of 'measurability', 'accessibility' and 'substantiality'.
2. Be sufficiently distinct one from another to offer choices of marketing strategy.

We now use a large sample, say 1,500, and a multi-variate procedure called *cluster analysis*.

- Factor analysis examines correlations between variables across respondents.
- Cluster analysis looks for correlations between respondents across the segmentation variables.

> The cluster characteristics will depend on the nature and range of the questions put to respondents. As with all survey work it is necessary to develop hypotheses before going into the field.

As an example, let us assume that we are clustering drinkers according to their use of, and attitudes towards, alcoholic drinks. Qualitative work at the exploratory stage may have suggested that there are at least four types of drinker: social, compulsive, restorative and self-compensating. Unless our questionnaire includes items which make it possible for respondents to reveal these proclivities, cluster analysis will neither prove, nor disprove, this hypothesis.

It would be helpful if the statistical procedure were to show a definitive association between the level of response to one particular attitude statement and membership of a particular cluster. In practice, it requires the responses recorded in answer to something like twelve statements to establish the membership of one of four or five psychographic clusters.

This adds to the space on the questionnaire needed for 'classification of respondent' questions, for any marketing company undertaking a segmentation study is likely to want to be able to use the segmentation criteria routinely in subsequent surveys, just as questions are routinely asked about occupation, age, etc.

If the psychographic questions produce psychographic types who show consistent results over time in terms of buying behaviour, or response to advertising campaigns, the reliability of the procedure used to type consumers is confirmed.

Consumer panellists are classed according to their psychographic type and behaviour in the product field is analysed by psychographic as well as by demographic criteria. An early segmentation study was made by Attwood Statistics. This sorted housewives on the Attwood consumer panel into types showing the following characteristics:

- Conscientiousness related to housework.
- Economy consciousness.
- Conservatism in brand choice.
- Traditionalism in housework.
- Willingness to experiment in shopping.

Knowing that a majority of the purchases of their brand was regularly made by housewives in the 'traditional' group would suggest to a company marketing household cleaners that plans for changing the product and its communication should be viewed with doubt, but that there would probably be a case for introducing a second product designed for the more experimental.[18]

6.7 A motorists' typology

Table 6.4 shows a brief summary of a comprehensive and carefully planned survey of motorists' behaviour and attitudes carried out by

Table 6.4
The five types
of motorist

1. The uninvolved

Very low interest or involvement with car or with motoring. This group seldom tinkers with the car and does very few repairs; does a low mileage, has little technical ability, and gets little satisfaction from maintaining the car.

Likely to be older white collar; this group includes most women motorists. This group relies heavily on the garage and will follow the dealer's advice in the choice of motor oil.

2. The enthusiast

A high degree of interest and involvement with the car and with driving and working on it. This is almost the reverse of the uninvolved group. These people do many repairs, have high technical ability and obtain much satisfaction from maintenance. They have many accessories on their cars, enjoy talking about cars, and are interested in motor sport. Nearly all are male and an above-average proportion, about half, are working class. They have a high level of driving experience, and are likely to own an older, second-hand car.

Nearly all change and top up the oil themselves and have strong opinions about brands. Have a strong tendency to buy from non-garage outlets, especially motorist accessory shops.

3. The professionals

These are highly involved with driving and with the car, but only as a necessary part of the working life. Mainly use the car for business, do high mileage, but do little of the servicing or repairs themselves.

Likely to be male and white collar, driving relatively new car — often a company car.

Mainly concerned with keeping the car on the road, they leave servicing to the garage, and tend to buy petrol company brands of oil.

4. The tinkerer

Through a combination of economic necessity and enthusiasm, are more involved in working on the car than in driving it. Much the reverse of the professional group, they get much satisfaction from maintenance work and tinkering, but although they do many repairs they have low mileage.

Tend to be male and working class, very often skilled. Car likely to be old, second-hand, used mainly for pleasure and driving to work.

They do most of the minor work on the car but may leave bigger jobs to the garage. Tend to top up and change oil themselves, but are brand-conscious.

5. The collector

An enthusiasm for collecting trading stamps is the distinguishing characteristic of this group, which tends to be normal in most other respects. They tend to be young and inexperienced.

Source: England, Grosse and Associates (1969)

England, Grosse and Associates for Esso Petroleum. The survey was first made in 1969 using a quota sample of 2,000 motorists. It was repeated three times and, as will be seen, the research design produced a stable typology.

Preliminary work

'Considerable preliminary work, both qualitative and quantitative, ... enabled the input variables to be selected with reference to a broad preliminary idea of the kind of typology we expected to find.'[19]

Main survey

Cluster analysis of answers to fourteen input variables yielded five motorist types.

Size of cluster groups, percentage of total sample

		1969	1971	1972	1975
1.	Uninvolved	27	19	22	23
2.	Enthusiast	20	19	20	20
3.	Professional	15	27	23	25
4.	Tinkerer	24	22	20	24
5.	Trading-stamp collector	14	13	15	8

The five segments are described in Table 6.4. ('Company cars' and the effect of incomes policy on this benefit are shown in the Type 3 estimates; decline in the popularity of trading stamps in the Type 5 estimates.)

Variables used in the cluster analysis

Significant in the solution:
- Number of accessories on car.
- Mileage driven per week.
- Self-assessment of driving ability.
- Frequency of 'tinkering' with car.
- Extent to which servicing work is done personally.
- Self-assessment of technical ability.
- Satisfaction from working on the car.
- Trading stamps as criterion of garage choice.

Insignificant in the solution:
- Use of car for work or pleasure.
- Liking of driving.
- Loyalty to petrol brand versus loyalty to garage.
- Frequency of polishing car.
- Petrol brand as criterion of garage choice.
- Quick service as criterion of garage choice.

The kind of questions asked

The following are examples of the questions asked to collect data about the variables listed above:

Number of accessories on car: (SHOW CARD A) 'Which of these extras and/or accessories were already fitted when you bought your car and which ones have you fitted since you bought the car? (Multi-choice, closed question.)

Self-assessment of technical ability: 'How would you rate your technical ability and knowledge of motor cars? Would you say it was well above average, above average, average, below average or well below average? (Five-point verbal scale of the Likert type.)

Trading stamps as criterion of garage choice: 'Suppose you moved your home to a new district and had to find a garage. What would you look for in choosing a garage?' (Open-ended question.)

All the questions are focused on the car and the motorist's relationship with it.

The motorists' typology is an excellent case of a segmentation study designed to sort consumers into homogeneous groups. The value of the segmentation approach is particularly well put.[19]

- By maximizing the differential between segments we create a powerful tool for discriminating in terms of attitudes, buying behaviour, media exposure and so on.
- By maximizing the homogeneity within segments we can create a typology. For each segment we can describe a stereotype in consider-able detail. We, and the marketing people, can study these stereotypes in the round and try to understand them. This can be a considerable help to marketing planning in helping us to predict reactions to marketing activities or to changes in the market environment.

6.8 Social value groups

The motorists' typology relates to a particular consumer activity. Taylor Nelson's social value groups derive from an annual survey of social change, MONITOR (now operated by Applied Futures Ltd). There is now more than a *decade* of data on file. The trends revealed are of especial value when business and social strategic plans are being made, always provided that the trends are interpreted by those who understand the data[20] (see section 1.5).

The seven social value groups are 'founded on shared values and beliefs'[21] but the members of each group also share distinct patterns of behaviour: e.g. questions about respondents' attitudes towards health and nutrition are accompanied by questions about their behaviour in terms of keeping fit and playing sports. This association of attitude and behaviour questions is important because the object of the segmentation process is, of course, to aid in the prediction of behaviour.

The seven social value groups are typified in Table 6.5. The way in which the seven clusters are arrived at is summarized by Dr Nelson[21] below.

**Table 6.5
The MONITOR
social-value
groups**

1. Self-explorers
'I am what I am': Personal fulfilment through self expression. Creative individuals looking for intellectual and emotional satisfaction.

2. Social resisters
'Society needs changing to my way of thinking': Critics of the way Britain has developed, although still patriotic and loyal. Active in local community and charitable causes.

3. Experimentalists
'I'll try it': Fashion followers looking for novelty, fun and excitement. Ambivalent over social issues.

4. Conspicuous consumers/achievers
'Look at me': Status-conscious, acquisitive and emulative. Concerned with superficial appearance more than with inherent quality.

5. Belongers
'My family comes first': A future-orientated, self-sacrificing, achievement-directed group. Few interests or concerns outside the home or workplace.

6. Survivors
'The working class is *my* class': Conventional, conservative, chauvinistic. Rigid thinkers along sex/class stereotype lines.

7. Aimless
'I couldn't care . . . less': Social casualties − demoralized, goal-less, apathetic. Blame their plight on convenient scapegoats. Without hope for the future.

Source: C. Bunting *et al.*, 'Social change analysis: A new area for the application of research', *MRS Conference Papers* (1982).

Some 150 items are included each year in our MONITOR survey based on 1,500 adults. We included all 150 items in a factor analysis and found that 15 dimensions covered the vast majority of the variance. We then took the 15 dimensions and subjected them to a cluster analysis, using the normal method of two split halves: a cluster analysis of two samples each containing 750 people. In both analyses, the seven-cluster solution was the best solution.

This means that we can go back to the original 15 dimensions and take the item which is most strongly correlated with each dimension. We can then administer the 15 items to a fresh sample and allocate each person in that sample to a cluster.

In this case the starting point is a large-scale survey; but the 150 items in the MONITOR survey will themselves have been the product of the preliminary qualitative work which starts off the psychographic procedure summarized in section 6.6.

The discriminatory power of the social value segmentation is illustrated in Table 6.6[21] in which respondents concerned about the level of

All concerned 31 per cent					
By social class		**By age**		**By social value group**	
	%		%		%
AB	37	15–24	27	Self-explorers	43
C₁	36	25–34	35	Social resisters	40
C₂	27	35–44	38	Experimentalists	34
DE	28	45–54	30	Conspicuous consumers	33
		55–64	31	Belongers	26
		65–74	29	Survivors	24
				Aimless	19

Table 6.6 The discriminatory power of social-value segmentation

artificial flavourings and colourings in food are classified by social class, by age and by social value group.

6.9 Relevance of lifestyle and social values

There has been considerable debate about the practical usefulness of general lifestyle classifications; i.e. about classifications not specifically related to a particular product field (see the introduction to this chapter and notes 2 and 7).

In a seminar paper 'Lifestyle and values: The European dimension', Moorcroft comments on the limited life of product-focused typologies and makes a case for the deeper and longer-term view:

> By looking at more fundamental beliefs — values — and how they are developing within the population, we are able to look much longer term — as far as some 20 years ahead, while obviously still being in touch with the here and now. We are also able to move between product areas, applications and countries, as well as time frames.[1]

She refers to a typology of five food-types and how the distribution of these differs in France, West Germany and the United Kingdom. Increasing involvement in Europe, together with the strategic planning stimulated by this, supports the case for generalized typologies such as those being developed by the International Research Institute on Social Change.

6.10 The TGI and OUTLOOK

The TGI databank houses buying, viewing, reading and listening data derived from 25,000 self-completion questionnaires. These data have been continuously collected since 1968 and the method used is described in Chapter 11 on evaluating performance and predicting. The critical fact to remember is that these data are disaggregated so that the buying and media habits of an individual may be correlated.

More recently a lifestyle section has been added to the TGI questionnaire. Agreement/disagreement with 192 attitude questions is recorded. Clusters of individuals may be derived from these responses using the statistical methods introduced earlier in this chapter. 'Having determined attitude similarities, the groups can then be analyzed against demographics, media and brands to produce an overall "perspective".'[22]

As pointed out in the introduction to this chapter, access to wide-ranging, disaggregated data based on a large sample opens the way to DIY target segment-building by advertisers, advertising agencies and by management consultants.

OUTLOOK, based on the TGI data, is described as 'a generalized lifestyle system'[23] and it has been attacked as such.[24] But the exponents of the OUTLOOK segmentation claim that the size and disaggregated nature of the TGI databank make it possible to produce a psychological classification which achieves the following:

1. Discriminates on product usage at least as well as other systems.
2. Discriminates amongst media in order to make it possible to reach target audiences.
3. Produces groups which have 'face validity'.
4. Produces groups which are replicable over time.

The six OUTLOOK groups have defined and disparate characteristics: trendies (15 per cent of sample); pleasure seekers (15 per cent); the indifferent (18 per cent); working-class puritans (15 per cent); social spenders (14 per cent); moralists (16 per cent). Creative people in advertising shy away from stereotypes such as these, however soundly based.[24]

6.11 Use of 'segment-membership predictors'[25]

The consumer typologies considered in sections 6.7 and 6.8 have been seen to be stable over time. It is desirable that it should be possible to use the critical 'predictor' items as classification questions, along with social grade, age and so forth, in a variety of surveys. But research carried out by J. Walter Thompson in the United States shows that the stability of consumer typologies should not be taken for granted[25] for responses to the short-listed attitude statements may be affected by variation in the interviewing methodology used in different surveys. Inclusion of standard behavioural questions is a necessary control.

6.12   Product segmentation or brand mapping

Had the objective been to cluster products rather than consumers, and product differentiation rather than consumer differentiation, the segmentation procedure would commonly follow the three stages described in section 6.6:

1. Exploratory or preliminary research.
2. Piloting the questionnaire.
3. Survey.

However, the focus would be on consumer use and perception of types of product or service and, more especially, brands.

At the exploratory stage groups and individuals would be stimulated to talk about specific brands, their advantages and disadvantages according to purpose (e.g. spreading and cooking in the case of margarine). Depending on the point of view of the researcher, the ideal product would be talked about. (Some consider this adds richness to the data, others doubt the validity of statements about the ideal.) Kelly constructs might be used to help elicit scale items (see section 5.5).

At the pilot stage attitude statements are more commonly put to respondents in the form of semantic differentials than as Likert-type scales. As in consumer typing, results of the pilot are likely to be factor analysed in order to extract the most influential attitude dimensions and to reduce the criterion variables to a manageable number.

At the survey stage the main difference comes in the way in which the results are presented. In place of descriptions of consumer types our attention is focused on brand maps.

It is easy to visualize brand positioning based on consumer responses to one semantic differential scale. Let us assume a soft-drinks market containing seven brands, A—G. Consumers have been asked to rate these brands on a seven-point scale running from 'refreshing' to 'cloying'.

A mean score is computed for each brand and the positions are plotted on the continuum, refreshing to cloying. If no two brands scored equally on this dimension we might get a result like this:

refreshing   A F   E G D   B C   cloying

If we had asked consumers to rate their ideal brand on the same dimension, the result might have been as follows:

refreshing   I   A F   EGD   BC   cloying

the scores for the seven named brands representing their distance from the ideal. (When questions related to specific attributes are asked about the ideal brand as well as about available brands, the respondent's answers are more meaningful than when a general question is asked about 'your ideal soft drink'.)

It is also a simple matter to plot responses to two semantic differentials: let us assume 'economical to use' to 'extravagant to use' for the second dimension. (See Figure 6.3.)

Let us assume that *F* and *E* are two brands marketed by the same company, and that strategic planning decisions are being based on responses to these two semantic differential scales.

There is a clear case for re-positioning one of these two brands which consumers perceive as much the same. The re-positioning might be achieved by making one brand more economical than the other, say by moving *F* closer to *I*, the ideal. A more 'value-for-money' image could be attached to the brand by modifying the formulation, changing the type of container used, or altering the advertising campaign (a re-launch if all three measures were taken).

Figure 6.3 shows that brand *A* is in a strong position because of its closeness to the ideal as perceived by consumers; *B* scores on 'economical in use' but is seen to be 'cloying'.

In some product fields 'extravagance' can be a plus quality but perhaps not for soft drinks. Theoretically, there is a gap in this market for a cloying rather than a refreshing product which tends to be extravagant in use: but it will be a long way from the ideal. The gap is a 'non-starter' and in some circumstances this may in itself be a significant finding.

In evaluating responses to attitude statements, it is, of course, necessary

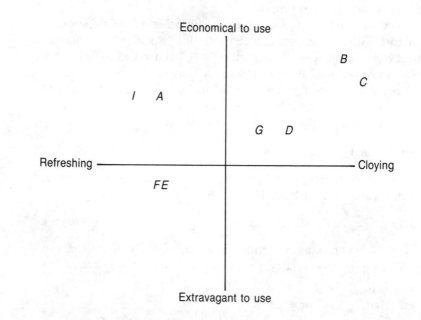

**Figure 6.3
Brand
positioning**

to take account of the fact that some attributes will count for more with the respondent than others. The respondent may rate two product qualities favourably on two attitude scales, but one favourable response will be more important than the other (see section 5.5.1).

We have been considering the relationship between two attitude dimensions. It is more difficult to conceive of a 'map' showing the interrelationship of a number of product attributes in multi-dimensional space. The fact remains that it is possible to chart the position of brands, taking account of interaction between all the criterion variables, and for the map to show the following:

- Whether a company's existing brands are competing with each other.
- Whether there is a gap in the market waiting to be filled.

If the company's brands are seen by consumers to be much the same, it may be possible to move them apart so that perceived differences are maximized; price, packaging and advertising being brought into play with, possibly, product modification and a complete re-launch.

If consumer perceptions of the ideal carry conviction, the position of the ideal brand may suggest ways in which an existing brand might be modified in formulation and/or presentation.

Finally, the map may show a gap, but the observed gap may not make marketing sense. There is a gap in the automobile market for a high-performance car at an economic price.

When collecting data about consumers' perceptions of products, services or brands it is, of course, essential to establish the consumer's demographic characteristics and product experience. This is because:

- The perceptual map of ABC_1 consumers may differ from that of C_2DE consumers.
- The perceptions of 'loyal' users of a brand may well differ from those of 'switchers'.
- Demographic and user groups may vary significantly in their perceptions of the ideal.
- Knowledge of the demographic characteristics of target consumers is essential for media planning.

6.13 Conclusion

A segmentation study carries application of the marketing concept an important step forward: the outcome of the segmentation study is a strategic plan focused on the declared needs of a target in the market which has been carefully defined. This applies whether the study is made with the object of initiating a new product or of improving the positioning of one or more brands already in the product field, and both research approaches ('consumer typology' and 'product differentiation') yield the required data about consumers, their needs and perceptions.

The segmentation study provides the blueprint for the development, or improvement, of a brand; the product as perceived by consumers being an integrated mixture of formulation, packaging, price and communication, i.e. it is a brand.

Sources and further reading

1. S. Moorcroft, 'Lifestyle and values: the European dimension', *ADMAP* (May 1987).
2. T. Bowles, 'Does classifying people by lifestyles really help the advertiser?' *ADMAP* (May 1987).
3. S. O'Brien and R. Ford, 'Can we at last say goodbye to social class?', *MRS Conference Papers* (1983).
4. P. Kotler, *Marketing Management, Analysis, Planning and Control*, 4th edn (Englewood Cliffs, NJ: Prentice Hall, 1980), Chap. 8.
5. P. Hodgson, 'Sampling racial minority groups', *Journal of the Market Research Society* (April 1975).
6. See J. Rothman (ed.), special issue on geodemographics, *Journal of The Market Research Society*, vol. 31, no. 1 (Jan. 1989).
7. T. Twyman, 'Re-classifying people: the ADMAP seminar', *ADMAP*, (Nov. 1981), pp. 568–71.
8. P. York, 'Should grown men be allowed to play with dollies?', *ADMAP* (May 1987).
9. A.R. Wolfe (ed.), *Standardised Questions: A Review for Market Research Executives*, (London: The Market Research Society, 1987).
10. Joint Industry Working Party, *An Evaluation of Social Grade Validity* (London: The Market Research Society, 1981).
11. J. Bound, 'The use of socio-economic grading', *MRS Newsletter* (Dec. 1987).
12. 'Social economic grading', report of a sub-committee of the MRS Technical and Development Committee (1987). (Free to members).
13. P. Cornish, 'Life cycle and income segmentation: SAGACITY', *ADMAP* (Oct. 1981), pp. 522–6.
14. R.E. Haley, 'Benefit segmentation: a decision-oriented research tool', *Journal of Marketing* (July 1968), pp. 30–5.
15. M. Thomas, 'Market segmentation', *The Quarterly Review of Marketing* (Autumn 1980).
16. C. Holmes, 'Multivariate analysis of market research data', Chap. 13 in R.M. Worcester and J. Downham (eds), *Consumer Market Research Handbook*, 2nd edn (Wokingham: Van Nostrand Reinhold, 1978). See also P.E. Green and D.S. Tull, *Research for Marketing Decisions*, 4th edn (Englewood Cliffs, NJ: Prentice Hall, 1978), Chaps. 12–14.
17. J. Morton-Williams, 'Research on the market for national savings', case study no. 5 in M.K. Adler (ed.), *Leading Case Histories in Market Research* (London:

Business Books, 1971). (Quoted in R.M. Worcester and J. Downham (eds), *Consumer Market Research Handbook*, 2nd edn (Wokingham: Van Nostrand Reinhold, 1978), Chap. 5.)

18. A. Lunn, 'Segmenting and constructing markets', Chap. 14 in R.M. Worcester and J. Downham (eds), *Consumer Market Research Handbook*, 2nd edn (Wokingham: Van Nostrand Reinhold, 1978). (Source of these conjectures).
19. D. Lowe-Watson, 'Segmentation: application in motoring', MRS course, (February 1976).
20. C. Bunting, E. Nelson and S. Thomas, 'Social change analysis: a new area for the application of research', *MRS Conference Papers* (1982), pp. 225–35.
21. E.H. Nelson, in a letter to the author (11 November 1982).
22. 'The plain man's guide to the TGI', *BMRB* (1989).
23. K. Baker and R. Fletcher, 'OUTLOOK: a generalized lifestyle system', *ADMAP* (March 1987).
24. J. Ward, 'Lifestyles and geodemographics: why advertising agencies shun a single-source approach', *ADMAP* (June 1987).
25. S. Yuspeh and G. Fein, 'Can segments be born again?' *Journal of Advertising Research*, vol. 22, no. 3 (June/July 1982), pp. 13–21.

See also

• U. Becker and H. Nowak, 'The everyday life approach as a new research perspective in opinion and marketing research', ESOMAR Congress, Vienna (Amsterdam: ESOMAR, 1982) pp. 269–89.
• G. Oliver, *Marketing Today* (Hemel Hempstead: Prentice Hall, 1980), Chap. 6.

Problems

1. (a) What segmentation procedure(s) would you adopt when seeking to locate an opportunity for a new or modified product/service in the following fields:

    (i)   domestic laundry equipment;
    (ii) packaged holidays;
    (iii) cooking oil;
    (iv) car accessories.

    (b) How would you collect and process the required data?
    (c) How would you apply the results of your segmentation study?
2. (a) In what ways does the application of multi-variate statistical treatment of data collected in segmentation studies further the development of marketing plans?
    (b) How may the data be treated and to what marketing ends?
3. Does the use of these statistical techniques (a) diminish the scope for using human judgement, or (b) enhance it?
4. Discuss the extent of the contribution to segmentation studies made by developments in information technology.

7

Developing a branded product or service

The marketing research process has reached the point where a market of interest has been explored, described and segmented, and a promising target or niche located. We now develop a product or service that appears to meet the needs which the research has uncovered. Our concern is to develop a brand:

> The difference between products and brands is fundamental. A product is something that is made, in a factory; a brand is something that is bought, by a customer. A product can be copied by a competitor; a brand is unique. A product can be quickly outdated; a successful brand is timeless.[1]

The next two chapters of this book hang together. They consider research methods used to specify the ingredients of the brand and how these are best packaged and priced (the present chapter), together with the application of advertising research to the development of the brand image (Chapter 8). As we will see, division between the content of Chapters 7 and 8 is by no means hard and fast. Selection of the media to carry the advertising campaign follows in Chapter 9.

Research planner's dilemma

The expression 'hang together' is used advisedly because the brand-development programme is confounded by two fundamental considerations:

1. The whole is greater than the sum of its parts. In the classic case of the Ford Edsel, individual car parts were meticulously tested and the preferred one was adopted in each case. The whole model, which had not been pre-tested, failed.
2. The measurements on which choices were evaluated, as in the Edsel case, are not scientific measurements. They record the way in which consumers perceive the attributes of a product or service. We are in the area of psychophysics and are in the business of comparing psychological responses to physical stimuli.[2] Response to the stimuli is influenced by the context in which they are met.

We can test the relative popularity of the various attributes that go to make up a packaged holiday — distance from the sea, local cuisine, ancient monuments, discos, etc. — the ultimate decision is made not only on the importance of these aspects to the individuals planning the holiday but also on how the total mix is presented, (plus, of course, a number of practical considerations such as cost and point of departure).

It is accordingly difficult to draw a line between the product concept and the advertising concept which will establish the product as a brand when developing and testing hypotheses in what is commonly referred to as 'NPD' (new product development).

Emphasis on qualitative research

During recent years greater emphasis has been placed on the usefulness and validity of qualitative methods when new branded products or services are being developed: 'The findings from qualitative research should have a truth that goes beyond the research context to a truth founded in the world.'[3] Indeed, there are those who contend that richer ideas and more meaningful decisions derive from a carefully designed programme of group discussions, extended individual interviews and other qualitative techniques than from a meticulously designed series of controlled experiments to which statistical tests can be applied.

Ground covered in Chapter 7

The value of qualitative work at the development stage, when hypotheses are being formulated and exposed to target consumers, is generally accepted. Accordingly this chapter opens with a discussion of the threats to validity which those who work in the qualitative field seek to guard against. Next, we discuss scientific method as applied in experimental design, together with examples of experimental procedures in common use during the development of a branded product.

Chapter 7 concludes with a review of developments in pricing research (such as Research International's brand/price trade-off model) and this introduces the use of individual, as opposed to aggregated, data in simulated test markets when making the final go/no-go decision (see Chapter 10).

7.1 The qualitative approach

7.1.1 The validity of qualitative methods

In qualitative work the findings derive from the experience, perceptions and ability of a small number of target consumers, say four groups of eight individuals, or thirty extended interviews, or a mix of the two. The setting of quotas for the recruitment of these individuals is clearly critical. So are the methods used to stimulate and focus discussion, the stimulus material, the role of the moderator or interviewer and the way in which consumer behaviour and opinions are recorded and presented.

7.1.2   Selection of participants

If a segmentation study has been carried out, the demographic, behaviour-in-the-product-field and lifestyle of those in the market of interest can be modelled, the characteristics of a potential target group defined and a quota representative of this group set.

The above applies to both quantitative and qualitative sampling as commonly practised. Martin Collins has spoken on the relationship between quantitative and qualitative sampling: 'most quantitative research today is model-based, in the same way that all qualitative research can be said to be.'[3]

In a qualitative research design the setting of the quota for participant recruitment is especially important. Indeed it is generally agreed that the validity of qualitative research rests substantially on 'highly purposive sampling'.[3]

Validity also rests on recruitment. Suitable subjects are recruited by interviewers, who are generally required to find quota members who have not been contaminated by previous group experience: 'The trend is towards more difficult quotas.'[4] It is not easy to locate suitable participants when working to a quota which may represent only 5 per cent of the total population, while meeting standards set by the MRS and the Association of Users of Research Agencies.[5]

The respondent's experience in the use of the product/service concerned is usually material when quotas are set, whether for qualitative or for experimental work. How the product is used can have a marked effect on choice as Table 7.1 shows. The three brands 'were considered very similarly by the whole sample but differently when the sample was

Table 7.1 Preference of spirits and relationship to use with a mixer or not

Brand	Total	Mixer	Neat
A	2.86	3.12	2.62
B	2.86	2.84	2.88
C	2.91	2.68	3.02

Source: M. Callingham, 'The psychology of product testing and its relationship to objective scientific measures', *Journal of the Market Research Society*, vol. 30, no. 3 (July 1988)

broken down by the way they used the spirit',[2] the 40 per cent who took the spirit neat preferring C, which was least preferred overall.

The number of groups,' or of individual interviews, in the research design depends — research budget apart — on the definition of the target. Were the hypothesized product/service for international or EC markets — as is, of course, increasingly the case — the design needs to accommodate cultural/geographic variations as well as demographic and product-use ones.

7.1.3 Choice of stimulus material

Stimulus material is a thing, article or item that is used to convey a product, pack or advertising idea to the consumers or to trigger their responses to a particular area of enquiry.[6]

Stimulus materials in current use are summarized in Table 7.2. The type of material chosen to start a group discussion (or extended interview)

		Table 7.2 **Stimulus** **material**
Concept boards:	Single boards on which the product, pack or advertising idea is expressed verbally and/or visually.	
Storyboards:	Key frames for a commercial are drawn consecutively, like a comic strip. The script may be written underneath and/or played on a tape-recorder with special sound effects.	
Animatics:	Key frames for a commercial are drawn and then filmed on video with an accompanying sound track. The effect is of a somewhat jerky TV film, using drawn characters to represent live action.	
Admatics:	A development of animatics, changing crudely animated storyboards into something nearly approaching the level of a finished commercial by using computer-generated and manipulated images.	
Flip-overboards:	Key frames for a commercial are drawn as above but, to avoid the respondents reading ahead, are exposed one by one by the interviewer in time to a taped sound track.	
Narrative tapes:	An audio tape on which a voice artist narrates the dialogue and explains the action of the commercial and describes the characters. The tape may be accompanied by key visuals.	
Photomatics:	A form of animatic using photographs instead of drawn key frames, thus showing the characters and scenes more realistically.	

Source: W. Gordon and R. Langmaid, *Qualitative Research — a Practitioner's and Buyer's Guide* (London: Gower, 1988)

is clearly going to influence the views expressed by participants. Choice of material, including degree of finish, demands professional judgement based on experience and training in the behavioural sciences.

The material used will, of course, relate to the stage reached in the development of the product/service, from the initial concept or idea to presentation of the brand in an advertisement. The concept may be introduced to those taking part as a simple statement on a board: the eventual brand presentation as a photomatic (see Table 7.2).

Gordon and Langmaid ask three basic questions:[6]

1. What do consumers *see* when shown stimulus material?
   'Consumers evaluate all research stimuli as advertisements: most find it difficult to deal with concepts or ideas.'
2. How 'rough' or 'real' should the stimulus material be?
   'Consumers do not see "rough ideas" when shown stimulus material: they see a finished execution.'
3. How do consumers create meaning from, or de-code, stimulus material?
   The material may convey an idea or message very different from the one intended: the classic cigarette campaign 'You are never alone with a Strand' misfired for this reason.

7.1.4   Qualitative compared with experimental approach to NPD

NPD makes considerable demands on company resources. The modification of a going brand with a view to increasing its popularity, or sustaining its life, may make less demand on resources: but here there is the additional hazard of putting off existing supporters.

During the development stage, choices need to be made with confidence. To rely entirely on qualitative methods demands faith in the research supplier and understanding of the rigour with which qualitative methods may be applied. It is easier for a marketing company to have confidence in the experimental approach. The setting of quotas and the recruitment of those taking part are as critical to the design of experiments as for qualitative work. But if the standardized methods are duly followed it is possible to subject the results of experiments to statistical tests. For the decision-maker there is comfort in numbers.

Given an experimental approach the collection of data is less open to bias, and the results less open to mistakes of interpretation. On the other hand, the opportunity for a new product breakthrough may be missed; while experimental data lack the stimulus of qualitative findings when the brand presentation is being designed.

In order to design experiments it is necessary to have hypotheses to test! Qualitative research is a valuable source of hypothetical ideas and the two approaches to NPD may be combined with advantage.

7.2 The experimental approach

7.2.1 From description to experimentation

An experiment has been defined as 'a way of organising the collection of evidence so that an hypothesis may be tested' (Jahoda). To arrive at any hypothesis which is both meaningful and relevant it is necessary to have to hand data about the consumers and products in the market. The data will often have been collected by descriptive studies and, if a segmentation approach has been used, the company is well placed to design experiments, for detailed knowledge of the market makes the following issues more pertinent and thus effective:

- Choice of hypothesis to be tested.
- Decisions regarding the criteria to be used when measuring and analysing results of the experiment.
- Control of environmental factors.
- Selection of the subjects to take part in the experiment.

For an ongoing brand, or for a new brand in a familiar market, 'detailed knowledge of the market' is likely to be derived from previous product research and from monitoring of own and competitors' achievements in the product field (see Chapter 11). Kotler's diagram showing 'the experiment as a system' is a useful introduction to the forces at work in an experiment:

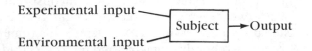

In many texts, the experimental input is called the 'independent variable' and the output is called the 'dependent variable'. The environmental input is made up of extraneous variables, some of which can be foreseen, others not, i.e. some of which are controllable variables and others uncontrollable variables. The experimental input is the treatment applied to subjects whether this is one variable, e.g. sweetness, or a combination, e.g. sweetness plus colour in a soft drink.

7.2.2 Focus on theory

An understanding of the theory associated with experimental design will help us to explain and evaluate the procedures commonly practised when products are being developed for the market.

Threats to validity

'History', 'maturation', 'instrument effect' and 'testing' or 'learning' effect are considered at greater length in Moser and Kalton[7] and Green and Tull.[8]

History: Outside events may affect the dependent variable during the course of the experiment. Clearly, the longer an experiment goes on the greater the risk of history contaminating results.

> Let us assume that we have designed an experiment to test the effect on sales of brand X paint of a home-decorating campaign. If there were a prolonged strike in the test area during the course of the experiment, and if this strike affected a substantial number of workers, results of the experiment might be deceptively encouraging, enforced 'leisure' having stimulated home decorating. In this situation, increased sales would not be attributable to the campaign, and the experimental results would be spurious.

Maturation: This effect relates to changes in the test subjects in the course of the experiment. They may, for example, get tired.

> If we were comparing the effects of two sales training programmes we might find that test subjects 'played back' what they had learnt better at the beginning of the day than at the end. If we were aiming to compare two training methods, and failed to arrange that both groups contained comparable proportions of 'fresh' and 'stale' subjects, the results might then be spurious.

Instrument effect: As might be expected, this relates to inconsistent or faulty instruments and in experimentation the instrument is often a questionnaire administered by an interviewer. Mechanical instruments are also used: tachistoscopes, psychogalvanometers and projectors feature in experiments described in this chapter and in Chapter 8.

> Continuing with the sales training example, we might expect the training officer to suffer fatigue too, so that the questionnaire is administered less effectively towards the end of the day.

Testing or learning effect: This is particularly relevant to company image, public relations and advertising research.

> Let us assume that we have been commissioned to create a campaign to improve the image of a company in its employee catchment area. We decide to do a 'before and after' test: to ask a sample of local people what they know about the kind of work the company offers, the amenities it provides and so forth; then to run the campaign, going back at a later date to see

what effect the campaign has had on the experimental group's view of the company.

We cannot attribute greater awareness and changed opinions to the campaign because the respondents' attention will have been drawn to the company and its activities by the first call. What they learn at the first call may stimulate the sample to pay more attention to the campaign than they would otherwise have done, and to pick up information about the company which might otherwise have passed over their heads.

For this reason we either use an 'after-only' with control design when testing communications (see below); or we take the 'before' measurement on one group and the 'after' on a group matched to the first (i.e. we use matched samples).

Selection of test subjects: This is not just a matter of ensuring that those who receive the experimental treatment represent the target for whom the product is designed. We also have to ensure that experimental and control groups are matched. (For the role of the control group see below.)

Before designing an experiment it is necessary to know what demographic and product-use characteristics are critical. Experience in the product field often acts as an initial filter: for example, if we were developing a medicated bubble bath we would need to know whether the target consumers were bubble-bath users, users of medicated bath products or both. Age and class might be critical demographic variables when it came to setting quotas for the experimental and control groups. To attempt to match the groups by age within class (or vice versa) as in an interrelated quota (see section 3.6.2) adds to the time needed to recruit and to the cost of the experiment. It is common practice to sort the test subjects into age and into class strata, then to use a random process when assigning members from within these age and class strata to either the experimental or to the control group. If combinations of age and class are found to differ from the experimental to the control group, or from one experimental group to another, it is possible to standardize results by weighting, as in a disproportionate sample.

Depending on the context, there are other effects to be taken into account, and an extended list will be found in Moser and Kalton,[7] pp. 216–20.

Control: experimental groups

A control group is used in an experimental design to make it possible to discount the effect of unforeseen extraneous variables. The control group is matched to the experimental group. It is questioned, or observed, at the same time as the experimental group; but the control group does not receive the treatment, nor, of course, is it asked those questions which relate to the experimental treatment.

Control groups are not always used in marketing experiments. Decision may be based on the responses of two or more matched experimental groups to alternative product formulations, pack designs or advertisements.

In comparative tests, especially in tests to decide product formulation, control may be exercised by setting a standard against which alternatives are assessed: for example, one group may be given the existing product and another the formulation which is thought to be an improvement on it, both products being wrapped and presented in the same way. In this case the control group receives a treatment but it is one against which the experimental treatment is judged. But when two possible advertising treatments are shown to two matched groups we have a design based on two experimental groups.

However well designed an experiment may be, there is always a risk that an observed difference may be due to sampling error, and not to the effect of the treatment. The statistical procedures used to establish the significance of the differences observed are summarized in Appendix 3, at the end of this book. Unless subjects have been assigned to groups at random, or groups to treatments, these calculations should, strictly speaking, not be made.

7.2.3 Experimental designs in common use

The designs set out in Table 7.3 are the basis of most of those in common use. The notation developed by Campbell and Stanley (in Green and Tull)[8] is a useful shorthand which helps to concentrate ideas about experimental procedures. The following comments relate to Table 7.3.

After-only without a control group. This is not a true experiment but it is not uncommon for an increase of sales over target to be attributed to some marketing tactic, such as a sales promotion or increased advertising, when other factors have contributed. In other words, the collection of evidence has not been organized 'so that an hypothesis may be tested'. (But it is sometimes possible to guard against spurious results by asking questions: claimed awareness of an advertisement can be validated in this way.)

After-only with control. Given that the experimental and control groups are well matched, that observations are made at the same time and that the environmental input is the same for both, we can use the control group to discount factors other than the treatment as contributing to the result shown by the experimental group.

Before–after. By observing the experimental group at a suitable interval

**Table 7.3
Experimental
designs in
common use**

Notation: X exposure to the experimental treatment
O measurement or observation taken
Sequence of events from left to right

Design				Measurement*
After-only	X	O		O
After-only	X	O_1		$O_1 - O_2$
with control		O_2		
Before–after	O_1	X	O_2	$O_2 - O_1$
Before–after	O_1	X	O_2	$O_2 - O_4$
with control	O_3		O_4	$(O_2 - O_1) - (O_4 - O_3)$

Time series†

$O_1 O_2 O_3 O_4$	X	$O_5 O_6 O_7 O_8$	Mean of 4 post-treatment observations − mean of 4 pre-treatment observations‡

Time series with control

$O_1 O_2 O_3 O_4$ X $O_5 O_6 O_7 O_8$

$O'_1 O'_2 O'_3 O'_4$ $O'_5 O'_6 O'_7 O'_8$

$$\left(\begin{array}{c} \text{Mean of } O_5 \ldots O_6 \\ \text{minus} \\ \text{Mean of } O'_5 \ldots O'_6 \end{array} \right) - \left(\begin{array}{c} \text{Mean of } O_1 \ldots O_4 \\ \text{minus} \\ \text{Mean of } O'_1 \ldots O'_4 \end{array} \right)$$

Cross-sectional

			Matched groups
	X_1	O_1	$O_1 \ldots O_n$ compared
	X_2	O_2	(see section 7.2.3)
	.	.	
	.	.	
	.	.	
	X_n	O_n	

Randomized block
Latin square   See section 7.2.3
Factorial

* We assume a positive result throughout.
† The number of observations taken pre- and post-treatment will not necessarily, of course, be four as here.
‡ The mean of the observations is taken when the effect of a particular treatment, e.g. of a sales training programme, is being measured.

before and then after it receives the treatment we get a less ambiguous measurement than with an after-only design, but where there is danger of the respondent learning from the pre-test an after-only design is to be preferred.

But *before–after with control* makes it possible for us to allow for any contamination of the experimental result (as in the case of after-only with control).

Time series is an extended 'before–after' and it may be used with or without a control group (or area). In 'real-life' market tests it is common practice to take a number of observations before and after introduction of the new product, pack, price or advertising. The interval between observations is related to the rate at which the product is purchased by consumers, and the data are often derived from consumer panels. The repeat buying rate is an important factor in brand-share prediction. (See Chapter 10.)

With 'going' brands it is common practice to predict what would happen, if the experimental treatment were not introduced, on the basis of the trend data collected 'before'. The effect of the experimental treatment, say a pack change, is then measured by comparing the actual 'after' observations with the 'after' predictions. The AMTES model is designed to measure what would happen if a change in the marketing mix were not made (see section 10.5.2).

Cross-sectional. Different levels of treatment such as different prices, levels of advertising and incentives to sales representatives are applied to a number of matched groups at the same time. The main problem is matching the groups.

Randomized block. So far we have assumed that the only difference between groups is the kind of treatment they receive: in other words that, having matched groups on critical characteristics, the environmental effects will be the same for all groups. It may well be that previous research has alerted us to differences, for example of region or location, which may influence results.

Blocking is stratification applied to experiments. Use of stratification to reduce sampling error in surveys was discussed in section 4.1.5.

Let us assume that we need to measure the effect on sales of three pack designs.* A supermarket chain has agreed to have the experiment staged in some of their branches. Previous research has suggested that there may be regional differences in consumer reaction to the three packs. We accordingly do the following:

- Stratify by region, say North, South and Midlands.
- Arrange for the test to be made in, say, three branches in each region.
- Use a random process to assign pack design to branch in each region as follows (*T* stands for treatment).

Region	Three branches in each region		
North	T1	T2	T3
Midlands	T1	T2	T3
South	T1	T2	T3

*The following example is based on one quoted by Cox and Enis.[9]

The product is on sale in all three pack designs in each region. We are assuming that the supermarket branches do not have distinct regional characteristics. The statistical figure-work (analysis of variance) is shown in Appendix 3. Briefly, the design makes it possible for us to isolate the between-regions source of error so that we are left with a smaller residual error to take account of when considering the between-treatments results: i.e. the design is cost-effective because we can use a smaller sample than would be the case if we had not 'blocked' (or stratified).

Latin square. The randomized block design illustrated above controls one extraneous variable. If the product were one which sold through more than one type of retail outlet, we might have decided to use a Latin square design. The Latin square is a cost-effective design which makes it possible to allow for two extraneous sources of variation, in our case region and type of retail outlet.

In the Latin square design it is conventional to think of the two extraneous sources of variation as forming the rows and columns of a table. Treatment effects are then assigned to cells in the table randomly, subject to the restriction that each treatment appears once only in each row and each column of the table. Consequently the number of rows, columns and treatments must be equal, a restriction not necessary in randomized block designs.[9]

The finished design might look as follows:

Three Regions, Three Types of Retail Outlet (*A*, *B*, *C*)
Three Treatments (T1, T2, T3)

Region	Type of Retail Outlet		
	A	*B*	*C*
North	T2	T3	T1
Midlands	T1	T2	T3
South	T3	T1	T2

The Latin square is an economical design for the measurement of main effects, in this case variation due to region and to type of retail outlet. Each treatment (in the case we have been considering, a pack design) is tested in each type of retail outlet and in each region. We can estimate error due to these two sources of variation using analysis of variance (see Appendix 3): but we are assuming that the treatment effects will not be contaminated by interaction between them. We allow for the effects individually but not as the one (here region) influences the other (retail outlet).

Factorial design. If it is necessary to take account of the interaction of variables, as opposed to measuring main effects, a factorial design is used. Anticipating product testing, let us assume we are developing a soft drink. We may expect that, in a taste test, there is likely to be interaction between the colour of the drink and the amount of sweetener in it: that the more acid the yellow of a lemon drink, the sourer the response to taste.

Say we are experimenting with three variations of colour and three degrees of sweetness, then the factorial design would be as follows:

Sweetness		Colour	
	a	b	c
A	Aa	Ab	Ac
B	Ba	Bb	Bc
C	Ca	Cb	Cc

Every possible combination of colour and sweetness is allowed for in the design, which requires nine matched groups of testers.

This can be an expensive design and we may find that we have not used a sufficiently large sample when it comes to considering the significance of results. If there is any doubt on this score the test should be replicated so that there are sufficient testers' judgements to warrant the drawing of firm conclusions. Replication may avoid the waste incurred when an unnecessarily large sample is drawn in the first instance: but it extends the time taken up by the test and there is always the possibility, of course, that time itself may affect results.

So far this chapter has served as a general introduction to experimental design. As the examples given show, the theory covered applies both to experiments of a 'laboratory' type and to those carried out in the open market, which are the subject of Chapter 10.

From now on the chapter focuses on the use of experiments to optimize brand characteristics before exposure on the open market. This pre-testing stage is concluded in Chapter 8, where advertising is more closely considered.

It is assumed that research resources may now be devoted to the development of a product, or service, concept and that this concept (or idea) fits company resources and aspirations. Many companies have a laid-down procedure for screening suggestions at the outset, well before company funds and staff time have been invested in them: see, for example, Kotler's 'product-idea-rating device'.[10]

7.3   Pre-testing branded products and services

7.3.1   The whole and its parts

Market description may suggest introduction of a new product or modification of an existing one. Analysis of data about consumer behaviour and attitudes may yield tentative ideas, or hypotheses, about the kind of product required, the way in which the product should be packaged and priced, and how it should be brought to the attention of potential consumers.

Before considering ways of testing hypotheses about these individual components we have to recognize that, once the product is out on the market, consumer perception will be influenced by the interaction of all four, as well as by environmental factors such as the actions of competitors and distributors, not to mention the state of the world at the time.

Product formulation, packaging, pricing and communications are likely to be the subject of separate experiments on the way to 'real-life' testing in the market of the complete offering: first, on the grounds of cost; and second, to help assess the contribution made by constituent parts to the overall performance.

With regard to cost: even a small-scale test in the market makes notable demands on resources. The product must be available in sufficient quantity to meet demand and it has to be associated with properly finished packaging and advertising.

> A product development programme will, therefore, include experiments specifically designed to aid decisions about formulation, packaging, price and communication: but it is likely also to include attempts to assess the interaction of these components.

The product concept may be introduced to the experimental group in the form of a rough advertisement before the product is tried and responses to the product both before and after actual trial are compared. Pack designs may be presented to testers along with designs for advertisements, while questions about selling price are likely to be asked at every stage. The fact that the whole may well be different from the sum of its parts is taken account of in this chapter and in Chapter 8.

7.3.2 Having and trying out ideas

Most 'new' products or services derive from what is already available to consumers. The true innovation is rare indeed and, if successful, soon copied, as with the biro.

In a key speech at the 1983 conference of The Market Research Society Stephen King said:

> I believe that part of our national failure to innovate has come through trying to use market research not as an *aid* to innovators, but as a *system* that ideally reduces all personal judgement to a decision as to which of the two numbers is larger.[11]

And he instanced the 'trade-off' approach in which the respondent is asked to choose between a series of options.

The trade-off technique is based on the concept that 'obtaining a desired product quality (say efficiency) will require the consumer to sacrifice — trade-off — some other desired quality (say gentleness).'[12]

This use of the multi-variate approach has, of course, been stimulated by the speed with which a long list of 'trade-off' choices can be processed; easy for the computer, exhausting for the respondent (see Len England's comment in section 5.2). However, the respondent finds the questioning procedure less tedious when operating a microcomputer.

So how can research aid innovation? In the first instance by supplying 'background knowledge';[11] and it clearly helps if that background knowledge is the result of thoughtful, rather than mechanistic, description of consumer habits and attitudes.

Research cannot 'have the idea' but it can usefully 'try the idea out' in concept tests. This raises the question 'how should the idea be presented to those it is supposed to appeal to?' (We began to answer this question when considering the increasingly important part played by qualitative methods in the development of NPD (see the introduction to this chapter and section 7.1).

This book follows a scenario in which one research stage leads to another as follows:

Market description————————————►Definition of a target segment
Definition of a target segment———►Hypothesizing about its requirements
Formulation of hypotheses————————————►Trying out of concepts
Trying out of concepts————————————►A programme of experiments

This ordering of events is not, of course, hard and fast, particularly when the product field is familiar to the marketing company as in the well-presented case of Seagram's 'baby bottle' brand Crocodillo.[13]

- Research on file about the drink market suggested that 'young female uncommitted drinkers aged 18–24' might be 'looking for new drink experiences'.
- After this desk research it was decided to do qualitative research among this target group. Depth interviews were used, because the women in the age group had such varied lifestyles (factory workers, students, young mothers, etc.), and it was thought that groups would be 'superficial in quality and inhibiting for the respondents themselves'.
- The product concept grew out of the transcripts of the forty 'depths': 'This idea of a new slightly sparkling wine-based drink not too strong and certainly not too sweet, but clean-tasting and refreshing . . . ', i.e. a drink

suitable for 'on-premise' drinking and, as further research showed, one helpful to the drinker's self-image.
- There followed a series of 'blind' product tests 'to see to what extent the drink itself was acceptable' before the benefits of the marketing package were added.
- After exposure to pack and advertising, 52 per cent 'certainly wanted to try' the drink. After sampling, this figure shot up to 72 per cent.

This necessarily condensed account focuses on the idea-generation stage. The full research programme, through to monitoring performance after launch, is an excellent example of research in action.[13]

7.3.3 'Lab.' v. 'field'

A carefully controlled experiment, conducted in 'lab.-like' conditions, yields results which are unambiguous. The experiment has internal validity. But the conditions in which the test is carried out are not those in which the product would normally be chosen or used and the lab.-like experiment lacks external validity.

The field or market test, on the other hand, is conducted in a real-life context. The findings have external validity but they may well have been distorted by market influences or local happenings so that they are ambiguous and difficult to interpret. The more that is known about the forces at work in the market from descriptive work, the easier it is to control them or to allow for them when drawing conclusions.

Table 7.4 shows a comparison of laboratory and field product-testing procedures based on an analysis which draws on Unilever experience.[14]

	Lab.-type (internal validity)	Field (external validity)
Place	Testing centre/hall/mobile van	Where product normally used, kitchen, bathroom, garage, etc.
Treatment	Atomistic (usually)	Holistic (usually)
Length of trial	On the spot assessment	Normal use
Subjects	Expert panel	
	Ad hoc sample(s)	*Ad hoc* sample(s)
	Test panel, both normally drawn from the target group	Test panel, both normally drawn from the target group
Design	Comparative or monadic	Monadic

Table 7.4 Lab.-type conditions compared with field conditions

7.3.4   Monadic v. comparative tests

In a monadic design the respondent experiences only one test product. In a comparative test the respondent is given more than one product to try: the products may be given to the respondent simultaneously, or they may be given in sequence.

Comparison sharpens perception and so comparative tests are more sensitive than monadic tests: but the comparative procedure is further removed from real life than the monadic procedure. In real life products are usually judged in the light of current or recent experience of a similar product. In a monadic test responses to the test product are similarly based on current or recent experience in the same product field: with the critical difference that the test product is likely to be in a plain package without benefit of pack design and advertising support.

In section 7.3.9 we describe how General Foods, who have followed a programme of monadic testing, aim to get closer to real life by simulating pack design and advertising support before asking respondents to try products. Meantime, one would expect respondents to favour known and properly 'dressed' products over anonymous 'blind' ones, but this is not necessarily the case (see section 7.3.6).

If the test programme is based on a series of paired comparison experiments, one test product can stand as a control throughout. The control product may be the market leader or the leader in a particular market segment. If a brand is being re-positioned, the control can be a product it is desired to move closer to in terms of consumer perception. If a product is being relaunched, the existing product is the control product.

Since, at the outset, all products are likely to be tested 'blind', the difference in dress and communication between the test product and a product actually on the market is obviated. If the same individuals make all the tests, sampling error is reduced (but we must, of course, ensure that learning from test experience does not contaminate results).

It may be that there is no obvious control product and a number of possible product formulations are to be compared. This situation might arise if a range of prepared foods was being developed, say. In this situation a *round robin* would be an efficient design to choose. Given four different fillings *A*, *B*, *C*, and *D*, the procedure would be to test:

    A v. *B*   *B* v. *C*   *C* v. *D*   *A* v. *C*   *A* v. *D*   and   *B* v. *D*

If the tests were made by six matched groups of fifty from a sample of 300, each filling would be tried by 150 respondents.

7.3.5 Use of testing panels

Companies continuously engaged in product testing, such as Heinz, Spillers and Unilever, place products with panels of consumers. Demographic and product-use characteristics of panel members are recorded and the computer is programmed to retrieve experimental and control groups suitable for the test concerned. Test products are distributed by hand, or through the post, to panel members and the proportion returning the test questionnaire through the post is usually substantial (over 70 per cent).

There is a risk that panel members may learn from their testing experience and cease to be typical. But when the panel is a large one and the research supplier covers a wide range of product fields, it is possible to maintain the interest of panel members without running the risk of conditioning them.

7.3.6 The 'friendliness effect'

There is some evidence that respondents are biased in favour of the test product: that faced with a 'blind' product to test against their 'usual' product they will tend to choose the test product. In a test for Proctor and Gamble, housewives were asked to compare a test detergent with the detergent they were using. The 'blind' test product was in fact identical with the product in use, but 59 per cent favoured the test product.[15]

At an ESOMAR conference in 1969, Dr Johan J.M. van Tulder reported on a series of tests using Biotex designed to establish 'the level of the friendliness effect'. Testers were given cues as to which product was the test product: the stronger the cue the greater the degree of preference shown.

The friendliness effect is particularly relevant to monadic testing. In an interesting article on 'The monadic testing of new products' this propensity is attributed to 'gratitude' and 'novelty appeal': the respondent has been singled out to try something new.[16] (This article also describes methods used by General Foods to add realism to monadic testing; see section 7.3.9).

7.3.7 Order effects

In comparison tests care is taken to ensure that the trial order is rotated. This is easy to control in a test centre or if products are placed one after the other. If two products are distributed at the same time, the tester is told which one to try first, half the sample being told to try one first, and half the other.

It is hoped that the instruction will be followed, because there is evidence that preference is biased in favour of the product tried first. Some of this evidence is summarized in Table 7.5. In all these tests the order of testing had been rotated.

It has been suggested that 'the first product pre-empts the favourable response', that it achieves 'the level of sensible enthusiasm' the respondent is prepared to reach. As Oppenheim points out, 'our society puts a premium on sensible behaviour.'[17]

'Testing' or 'learning' effect (pp. 144–5) may also be at work.[18]

> When testing razors we found that the first razor used in a paired comparison test was generally much preferred, and we thought at the time that this might be due to the respondents having learned, by the time they were testing the second razor, what a new razor could do for them. In this context the second razor did virtually nothing compared with the first, while the first had done a great deal compared with their old razor.

Table 7.5
Order effects
in taste tests

Six taste tests with cakes and breakfast cereals, items systematically rotated, summary of results:*

Preferred first tried	66%†
Preferred second tried	31%†
No preference	3%

n = 472

A typical example from among 50 canned soup tests, controlled temperature, identical utensils, order rotated; variety the same in each test, i.e. tomato v. tomato, oxtail v oxtail.‡

	Tried *A* first %		Tried *B* first %		Total %	
Prefer *A*	51		28		40	
Prefer *B*	47		67		57	
No preference	1	'100'	5	100	3	100
n		152		152		304

* From D. Berdy, 'Order effects in taste tests', *Journal of the Market Research Society* (October 1969).
† Difference significant at the 99 per cent level.
‡ From P. Daniels and J. Lawford, 'Effects of order in the presentation of samples in paired comparison tests', *Journal of the Market Research Society* (April 1974).

7.3.8 Preference and discrimination

The consumer's propensity to prefer the test product in monadic tests and the first tried in comparative tests arouses doubt in the stability of responses. If money and time were no object there would be a strong case for repeating product tests, as in the Pillsbury Mills case reported by Boyd and Westfall.

> Two cake mixes were tested 'blind' on the same sample. The code numbers on the packs were altered and the sampler was asked to try another two mixes, the two pairs of test products being identical.
>
> 50% preferred the same cake mix in both tests: 50% switched their preference. It could be argued that this was just a case of 'heads I win', but among the stable preferrers there was a 3:1 vote in favour of one of the two mixes.[19]

In most product tests a definite preference is being sought. It is hoped that new A will be preferred to old B: or that there will be a significant difference between the preference score of new A (1) and that of new A (2). But occasions arise when it is hoped that respondents will not notice any difference. This occurs when a product is established on the market and either substitution of another ingredient reduces production costs and so contributes to profit, or a source of supply is interrupted and an alternative source has to be found.

The substitute ingredient will not be used unless those concerned with the marketing of the product are satisfied that users will not notice the difference. Testers are reluctant to show lack of discrimination: many are going to guess and there are two types of error to be avoided. If there *is* an observable difference, but the experiment does not reveal this, the position of an established brand may be undermined. If there is *not* an observable difference, and the results of the experiment suggest that there *is* (a more likely happening), we pass up the opportunity to make a cost saving or to ensure supplies.

The triangular discrimination test, developed in the brewing industry, is one way of approaching this problem. There are two test products, new A and existing B. The sample is split in half. Each half is given three products to test: one gets triad AAB, the other ABB. The products are presented 'blind' with ambiguous code numbers (A and B would certainly not be used).

The respondent is told that one product is different from the other two and is asked to find the different one. It is assumed that a third of the respondents will guess right and that the measure of discrimination is the percentage correctly picking the modified product, less 33.3 per cent. If 40 per cent picked correctly, the measure of discrimination would be $[(40 - 33)/0.67]\%$, i.e. of the order of 10 per cent instead of 7 per cent, because we have assumed that one-third of the testers will guess right.

Discrimination tests are not always triangular. Respondents may, for example, be told that, out of a group of five products, two are of one type and three of the other. This is a more severe, but perhaps rather intimidating, test of discrimination.

7.3.9 Perceptual wholes are more than the sum of their parts

This is the atomistic v. holistic dilemma referred to earlier on. The problem is illustrated in a methodological test carried out by J. Walter Thompson.[20]

Two matched samples were asked a straight question as to which they preferred of two products: one sample was given two products out on the market and the other the same two products in plain packs with only a code to differentiate them. The results were as follows:

	'Blind' (%)	'In normal packs' (%)
Preferred brand A	27	39
Preferred brand B	47	40
No preference/DK	26	21

In the 'blind' test the products were being judged on taste or performance (we do not know the product field). In the 'normal pack' test previous experience (which could, of course, be taken into account), packaging, price and advertising message all come into play.

In a monadic test respondents deliver verdicts on a 'blind' product in the light of their experience and knowledge of the product field. They are often asked what brand they use and are then encouraged to compare the test product with this brand. The test product has the advantage of being new and different, and the possible disadvantages of not being supported by pack design and advertising message.

General Foods and their research agency have expressed the view[16] that, whatever the difficulties of interpretation, research is only relevant if it attempts to simulate the situation in the market place.

Comparative tests are further removed from 'the situation in the market place' than monadic tests. Is it possible to bring monadic tests closer to the market place? This is the objective of the procedure followed by General Foods for convenience desserts.[16]

1. Housewives are recruited for a hall or mobile-caravan test according to product use and demographic criteria.
2. The testers are shown a videotape film, or story board, illustrating the product concept. They are also shown a pack design.
3. The testers are questioned about their reactions to these communications about the product, which they have not as yet tried.
4. The test product is taken home and tried.

5. In an interview a week later the housewife is asked the same questions as after the concept test, so that it is possible to compare response to the product after use with response to the idea of the product conveyed by advertising message and pack design.
6. Responses are measured as follows:

   (a) on a general evaluation scale ranging from excellent to poor;
   (b) in a purchase-intention question, at a quoted price, on a scale ranging from 'I would definitely buy it' to 'I would definitely not buy it';
   (c) likes, dislikes and perceived similarity to other desserts are recorded;
   (d) the test product (and sometimes the respondent's 'ideal' product) is rated on a number of attributes.

This type of procedure goes some way to reflect the circumstances in which new products are actually encountered by introducing advertising message and pack design, together with an idea of price, before the product is tried.

It follows that, as in real life, response to the product will be influenced by the way in which it is introduced. It is, of course, possible to try out more than one message and more than one pack design, not to mention price, together with a particular product formulation. The programme of tests could be rather expensive because testing or learning effects make it necessary to test each combination of elements on a separate sample, while results may be affected by the degree of finish of advertisements and packs. We return to the subject of concept testing in Chapter 8, where we focus on the procedures used to pre-test advertising messages.

The decision whether to test the components of the perceived product individually, or in combination, is a vexed one. A company such as General Foods draws on a considerable experience of product tests. By consistently following standard procedures a company accumulates normative data: it is able to compare pre-launch test results with post-launch performance and it is in a better position to construct pre-test models (see section 8.5).

7.4 Pre-testing packs

7.4.1 Function, impact and image

Packaging, both 'inner' and 'outer', is a significant item in the costing of a product; and packaging research is a wide-ranging subject involving studies carried out by R & D, production, distribution and the suppliers of packaging materials, as well as those commissioned by marketing among distributors and consumers.

We need to distinguish between tests to assess the functional efficiency of a pack, its visual impact at the point of sale and the image of the product conveyed by the packaging.

7.4.2 Functional testing

To give a product the best possible chance of success its pack must function well in the following conditions:

- On the production line.
- As bulked quantities travel along the distributive channel to the point of sale.
- At the point of sale after bulk has been broken.
- When being used by the consumer.

The pack has to protect the product from deterioration and from pilfering. It must stand up to handling and the shape should lend itself to efficient stacking, wrapping and palletization. At the point of sale how the pack behaves compared with the competition is important. Does it 'hog' shelf space, or fall over? When it reaches the consumer, ease of opening and of closing (if not used up at once), of dispensing the contents, together with being steady on its feet, are critical variables to be considered in experimental design.

The suitability of the materials used and of the method of construction are tested by R & D, production and by the suppliers of containers. Suppliers such as Metal Box, who make plastic as well as metal containers, are so close to the consumer market that it serves their purpose to carry out research among consumers as well as among manufacturers and distributors.

The supplier has to satisfy the manufacturer that his/her product will not deteriorate and that it will reach the point of sale in good order. Suppliers of packaging materials are particularly interested in consumer responses when introducing an innovation, such as the aerosol and the ring-top opener for cans. The innovation is likely to involve a considerable investment: the research findings help to persuade manufacturers to adopt the innovation, as well as improving it.

Distributors' complaints and the reports of sales representatives are the usual sources of information regarding the behaviour of the pack before it makes contact with the consumer at the point of sale. Here our concern is with the product as it presents itself to the consumer.

If the product is used up in one go, as with a can of beer, and the critical factor is ease of opening and dispensing, the experiment can be staged in a hall, mobile van or research centre; and the data are best collected by means of observation.

Some consumers get fussed when faced with an unfamiliar method of opening or dispensing, and it is necessary to create a relaxed atmosphere.

This is difficult to achieve if the tester's efforts are being closely watched and recorded by an observer, and a method used by Metal Box has much to commend it.

> When the ring-top can-opening device was introduced as an alternative to the tear-off tag, consumers were invited into a mobile van to try one against the other. A hidden camera filmed the way in which the consumers approached and handled the cans.

The camera can also be used to record whether or not consumers read instructions, and whether one form of instruction appears to be easier to follow than another. (See p. 27 concerning use of hidden cameras.)

Individuals vary in their dexterity and with tests of functional efficiency there is a case for using a comparative design, with each respondent trying both types of opening, assuming there are two to be tried. It is probably sounder to allow for the learning effect by rotating the order in which packs are tried, than to rely on samples being matched not only on product use and demographic criteria but also on handiness; but this is a matter of opinion.

If the product is used, closed and then re-used, the experiment needs to be carried out where this goes on — kitchen, bathroom, garage, etc. — and data are likely to be collected by means of a questionnaire. In this context variations in dexterity are less critical, though still material. They are less critical because results will be based on how easy/difficult the respondent finds the opening, closing and dispensing: on consumer perception rather than observed behaviour.

To isolate the effect of function it is, of course, necessary to use plain packs as in a 'blind' product test. If the opportunity is taken to test 'visuals' at the same time, response to visual effects may contaminate response to functional efficiency. On the other hand, we have to remember that when the product reaches the market, consumer response will be conditioned by the visuals. We are back to the atomistic/holistic dilemma.

7.4.3 Visual impact

As we all know, products have to speak for themselves at the point of sale. There is usually no one around to make the introduction.

The term 'impact' is used here to mean 'stand-out' value. Tests of 'stand-out' value are usually based on observation by means of the tachistoscope, or, as in William Schlackman's 'find-time' procedure[21] with a slide projector.

The tachistoscope enables an image to be exposed for controlled lengths of time. Lengths of exposure likely to be used in a pack test are from 1/200 of a second up to 1/10. The respondent is either looking into a box-like instrument or at a screen. After each exposure the respondent is asked what, if anything, was seen.

This simple procedure is useful for comparing the visual impact of elements in a pack design, such as colour, brand name or message: but it does not simulate the context in which the respondent is going to meet the pack. A closer approach is made to reality in the following conditions:

- The respondent is shown the test pack along with two or three control packs, care being taken to simulate the size of the packs as they might 'loom up' on the shelf at the point of sale.
- After each timed exposure the respondent is asked to pick the three or four packs out from a display which reproduces the company in which the pack is likely to find itself on the self-service shelf.

In a test of this kind results are likely to be contaminated by learning and it is advisable to use matched samples. If responses to the control products are of the same order for both samples, we are reassured that the samples are matched for acuity (i.e. speed of perception and response), as well as on the more obvious criteria.

When designing experiments to measure visual impact it is necessary to take into account variations in sharpness of eyesight and the speed with which individuals respond to the image. They may, for example, be required to press a button as in the 'find-time' design described below.[21] Organizations specializing in pack testing use standard acuity tests.

When recruiting for an experiment it would be time-consuming to take acuity into account as well as product use and demographic characteristics. It may be necessary to weight results when the acuity of matched samples is found to differ; but acuity is affected by age and familiarity with the product field, so matching on these variables may obviate the problem.

In the 'find-time' procedure (Table 7.6) pioneered by William Schlackman[21] matched samples are used and the respondents are allowed to familiarize themselves with a test pack. They are told that this may or may not be present in the displays which will be projected onto a screen.

- Some nine displays, typical of the product field at the point of sale, are photographed and the photographs are prepared for slide projection.
- In about six of the nine slides the test pack is among its competitors, in six different positions. It is absent from the other three slides.
- The slide remains on the screen until the respondent presses a button to signal that the test item has been found, or has not, as the case may be.
- The measure of 'stand-out' value is the time taken to find the test pack when it is present. This is automatically recorded when the button is pressed.

Test items: two versions of a new pack design for a confectionery product (*V*1 and *V*2) plus the current pack (*P*).
Design: Monadic using three matched samples of 50.
Procedure: Each sample is shown nine slides of which six contained *V*1, *V*2 or *P*.

Table 7.6
A 'find-time'
experiment

Pack	Mean reaction time in sec.	t-test* value	Significance level
*V*2 *P*	1.77 1.59	1.99	not
*V*1 *P*	1.98 1.59	3.71	0.001
*V*2 *V*1	1.77 1.98	2.05	0.05

In this table results are compared for the three possible pairs. Clearly, neither new version is an improvement on the current pack design.

*For statistical tests, see Appendix 3.

7.4.4 Image of the product in the pack

The product has been designed to meet the requirements of a target group in the market. If a segmentation study has been made, the characteristics of the group, and the benefits wanted by it, are certainly known. The pack has to tell these consumers that it contains a product with the desired qualities.

In a programme of image tests respondents are asked for their perceptions of the product in the pack before they have tried it.

The following test was carried out on members of a test panel in a test centre:

At the test centre, panel members were asked what products they usually used for their main wash and for their light hand-wash. If they used a washing powder they were introduced to the experiment as follows:

'I am going to show you two different packets of a washing powder called Coral. The manufacturer is considering two different versions of the product, and would like to know what housewives think about them.'

(The interviewer was instructed: SHOW FIRST PACK. ALTERNATE AT EACH INTERVIEW).

'I would like you to tell me what you think about the product in this packet by indicating where you think it would come on this scale. If you point to the largest box you strongly agree with the statement. If you point to the smallest box you think the statement applies very slightly to the product.' (There were seven sizes of box.)

The respondent then rated each pack in turn on the following criteria without having tried the product:

Suitable for all modern fabrics.
Gets white nylon really white.
Suitable for machine and handwash.
Washes thoroughly but gently.
Cares for delicate fabrics.
Up to date.
I would buy.

When a consumer meets a new product at the point of sale, the decision whether to try it is influenced by ideas about the product conveyed by its pack.

Having carried out this concept test, the marketing company concerned might well have put the same questions to the test panel after actual trial. Comparison of the responses would show whether or not the product came up to expectation: if it exceeded expectation, the pack design might need modification.

The pseudo-product test (Table 7.7) is designed to measure what William Schlackman describes as 'symbolic transference'.

Influence of the labels on taste perceptions is further evidence of the importance of testing the whole as well as its parts.

**Table 7.7
The pseudo-
product test**

Test items: 'A mild beverage', two labels: *L* and *M*.
Design: Simultaneous comparison test (i.e. two bottles were 'placed' at the same time). Four days' trial.
Procedure: Respondents asked to use one bottle first, then, on completion, the second. Order rotated. Consumers told the interviewer would be returning to ask them about their experience.

	L	M	DK	Total
Product found most acceptable	20	75	5	100
Product which was mild	25	65	10	100
Product most bitter	70	28	2	100

n = 200

Conclusion: '*M* moves the product more effectively in the direction of the marketing intention than does *L*'

Source: W. Schlackman and D. Chittenden, 'Packaging research' in R.M. Worcester and J. Downham (eds), *Consumer Market Research Handbook*, 3rd edn (Amsterdam: North-Holland 1986)

7.4.5 The brand name

Marketing companies may apply the company name to all their products, as in the case of 'Heinz'; or give each branded line a distinctive name, the practice pursued by the Unilever marketing companies and by Beecham.

Ideally, the brand name should convey or support the product concept. If the product has a 'unique selling proposition' (USP) the brand name should, if possible, reiterate this: for example, 'Head and Shoulders' for an anti-dandruff shampoo. If the packaging and promotion are being designed to convey an emotional benefit in the context of a 'brand image', the name will be chosen to support the image, as in 'Close-up' for a toothpaste. (For 'USP' and 'brand image' see section 8.3.3.)

Before brand names are tested for their power to communicate the nature of the brand, it is necessary to establish the following:

- The name is available for registration in the countries in which the brand is going to be marketed.
- The name has no dubious or unhelpful associations in these countries.
- The name is easy to pronounce, read and remember.

Ease in pronouncing the name may be tested by asking consumers to read over a short list of names, taking note of hesitations and of any variations in emphasis. A tape recorder makes it possible to play back responses.

The 'stand-out' value of the name is likely to be tested as a component of the pack design, after the 'runners' have been reduced to a few, perhaps in a tachistoscopic test or in a 'find-time' test (see section 7.4.3).

The communicative power of the name is tested by establishing its associations in the mind of consumers:

- In the first instance by means of 'free association', consumers being asked to say the first word, or thought, that comes into their head on hearing the name.
- Then by asking consumers to associate kinds of product with the brand names as these are read over.
- And/or by asking consumers to associate the brand names with product-attribute statements.

When designing research of this kind three factors need to be taken into account:[21]

1. Respondents should be given a trial run before the critical names are put to them. This applies in particular to the 'free-association' test.
2. The order in which names and/or statements are put to respondents should be rotated.
3. The time taken to respond must be recorded.

As pointed out in the introduction to this chapter, when a target segment and its wants have been defined, it is possible to work to a clear brief regarding the kind of people who should be recruited for experiments and the criteria for judging the acceptability, or otherwise, of brand characteristics. This applies to the brand name as well as to the other characteristics considered so far: product formulation and packaging.

7.5   Pre-testing price

7.5.1   The right price

A product's retail selling price is constrained by the cost of materials, company philosophy about returns on investment or contributions to profit, government policy, the cost of competitive products and the cost of marketing it. If the product is out on the market there is little room for manoeuvre. If it is a new product, attempts are made to anticipate what consumers would regard as a suitable price, and to establish a relationship between selling price and product image.

Soundings are taken as the product develops, at the concept stage, when the product is tried, as part of pack tests and (as shown in Chapter 8) during advertising research. The soundings usually take the form of 'intention to buy' questions related to quoted prices.

When the product goes on sale in a store test, or in a full market test, a credible verdict may be delivered depending on the length and sensitivity of the test. The purpose of taking soundings on the way to a market test is as follows:

- To see what kind of price consumers associate with the product and how this varies between types of consumer.
- To try out the effect on price perception of changes in the product, its packaging and advertising.

When questions about 'intention to buy' at a stated price are regularly asked, companies accumulate normative data. By comparing intentions with eventual buying behaviour it is possible to get close to a correction factor to apply to the experimental findings.

7.5.2   Pricing research, objectives and methods

The willingness of consumers to buy at different prices can be used as a measure either of price elasticity in the brand field or of the value to the consumer of individual elements in the brand mix as, for example, packaging. We are going to consider three methodological approaches to the price-setting problem:

1. Gabor and Granger's 'buy–response' method, which uses price as a measure of quality.
2. Frappa and Marbeau's use of conjoint analysis to measure the comparative importance to consumers of brand elements including price.
3. Research International's 'brand/price trade-off' model (BPTO), which estimates brand shares across a range of prices for the new brand and its competitors.

Proposed retail selling price is also, of course, a critical element in the market simulation models, such as Burke's BASES series, which will be encountered in Chapter 10, 'Out in the open: the final go/no-go decision'.

When setting quotas for pricing research it is common practice to establish what brand the respondent is using, whether this is his/her usual brand and what is his/her average rate of consumption. The following considerations also need to be borne in mind: Ehrenberg's work on panel data has shown that 100 per cent loyalty to a brand is rare and that many consumers have a brand repertoire from which they choose; it is also advisable to establish what type of retail outlet the respondent habitually uses, because the retail trade segments on price.[22]

We are going to ask respondents to deliver verdicts based on their buying experience to date as well as on the research treatment they are about to receive.

7.5.3 The buy–response method

The buy–response method derives from the work of Jean Stoetzel, Professor of Social Psychology at the Sorbonne, on price as an indicator of quality. The method has been validated and applied commercially by the Nottingham University Consumer Study Group.[23] The tests are usually carried out in halls, i.e. they are of the 'lab.-type' variety.

The idea of price as an indicator of quality has long been associated with durables and luxury goods. Methodological research has shown it to be relevant to fast-moving consumer goods. Too low a price is risky ('it would be dust at that price' of tea) while a high price may be 'too dear'. The buy–response curve (Figure 7.1) shows the limits within which a selling price would not be a barrier to acceptance, while the shape of the curve shows where the most generally acceptable price is likely to fall. In addition, a comparison between the shape of the 'price last paid' curve and the buy–response curve may indicate an opportunity: e.g. in Figure 7.1 it would seem that brands priced at 12p do not enjoy their potential share.

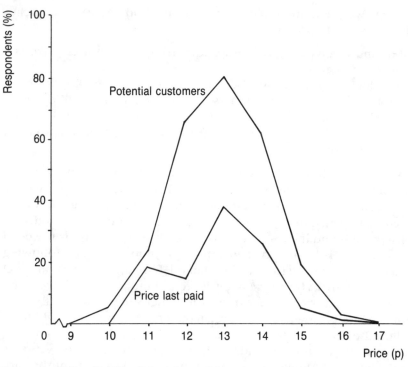

**Figure 7.1
'Buy–response'
and 'price last
paid' curves**

Source: A. Gabor, *Pricing: Principles and Practices* (London, Heinemann Educational Books, 1977)

The usual procedure is as follows:

- The range of consumer selling prices in the product field is recorded and not more than ten prices are chosen for testing.
- The respondent is shown the product, its pack or its advertising and is asked 'would you buy *X* at . . . ?' The price first quoted will be near to the average for the product field. The other prices will be quoted at random so that upper and lower limits are not suggested to the respondent.

  Alternatively, if there is a risk of confusing the respondent with the number of possible prices, the sample may be split in half, one half being taken down through the possible prices from top to bottom, and the other being taken up through the list.
- The responses are summed for each price accepted by respondents and the acceptable prices are charted as shown in Figure 7.1. Respondents are also asked prices last paid, and here again the distribution is charted. (There is, of course, only one 'last paid' to a number of 'would buys' for each respondent.)

It is possible to use the buy–response method to compare the effect on consumer price perceptions of different product formulations, different packaging and different communications.

If a consumer target has not been defined, it is also, of course, possible to compare the responses of different segments of the market.

In the buy–response interview the respondent meets an isolated test product. In real life new products are encountered alongside their competitors: consumers' reactions to price are comparative ones. The shop display used in the BPTO procedure is designed to meet this problem.

7.5.4 Price importance and 'trade-off'

Frappa and Marbeau drew a distinction between 'price acceptance' and 'price importance' at the 1982 ESOMAR Congress.[24]

> Price-acceptance research seeks to answer the question 'are the considered price levels for a particular product going to be accepted by a sufficient proportion of the consumer target group to make the new product viable?'

'Intention to buy' measures price acceptance.

> Price-importance research seeks to measure the importance to the target consumer of different levels of price compared with different levels of other attributes, e.g. a range of car prices compared with a range of miles per gallon / maximum speeds / different lengths / numbers of seats / countries of origin.

Trade-off, or conjoint measurement, can be used to arrive at each individual's best-liked combination of product attributes. 'In conjoint analysis we are concerned with the measurement of utilities — how people make trade-offs in choosing among multi-attribute alternatives.'[8]

The simplest way to present the alternatives is in pairs, as shown in Table 7.8 but, as Green and Tull point out:[8]

> While the two-factor-at-a-time approach makes few cognitive demands on the respondent and is simple to follow, it is both time-consuming and tedious. Moreover, it is conducive to respondents' losing their place in the table or developing some stylized pattern, just to get the job done. Most importantly, however, the task is unrealistic; real alternatives do not present themselves for evaluation on a two-factor-at-a-time basis.

A more meaningful alternative is to construct a series of cards, each card representing one of the possible mixes of attributes. The respondent is then asked to order the cards from most-liked combination to least-liked. In a trade-off covering the multi-variable relationships of all product attributes, instead of just price versus the others, the number of cards is likely to be too large for sorting in one operation. A preliminary sort

**Table 7.8
Trade-off
applied to price**

There are times when we have to give up one thing to get something else. For each of the following questions please write in the numbers from 1 to 9 to show your order of preference for your new car.

	Miles per gallon				Top speed		
Price of car	25	30	40	Price of car	70 mph	80 mph	100 mph
£4,600				£4,600			
£5,300				£5,300			
£5,900				£5,900			

In this case price is a constant attribute and the respondent would be presented with only five grids to complete, given five attributes other than price. If all possible combinations of all six attributes were set out on the questionnaire there would be 15 grids to be completed.

Source: P.E. Green and D.S. Tull, *Research for Marketing Decisions*, 4th edn (Englewood Cliffs, NJ: Prentice Hall 1980)

into 'definitely like', 'neither definitely like nor dislike', 'definitely dislike', followed by ranking within each of the three groups, helps to concentrate the respondent's mind. Care is, of course, needed to ensure that all possible combinations of attributes are represented by the cards.

7.5.5   Brand/price trade-off (BPTO)

The Research International model focuses on two attributes: the brand and its price. It is assumed that brand elements other than price have been tried on potential consumers and that there is now available a finished presentation to be displayed alongside likely competitors. (If two brand presentations are level-pegging the sample may be split into two matched halves, but this requires a larger sample and two sets of expensive artwork.)

The respondent is shown a display of brands. Each brand, including the test brand, is priced at the lowest level to be considered for the brand. For the sake of simplicity Table 7.9 shows four brands and three price levels. A BPTO exercise might cover as many as eight brands at ten price levels.

BPTO lends itself to computer administration. This way of conveying questions to respondents is described in Chapter 3.

The BPTO procedure may be used either to *diagnose* or to *predict*. This decision affects the sample used, the range of brands shown to respondents and the use of 'correction factors'. If the object is to predict actual brand share, the sample taking part and the brands displayed will mirror the real market as closely as possible and correction factors will

The respondent is asked: 'If these were the prices of the brands in your usual shop, which of them do you think you would be most likely to buy?' *When a brand is chosen, its price is raised to the next level.*

**Table 7.9
Brand/price
trade-off
procedure**

Brand		A	B	C	D
Start	- - - - - - - - Level	1	1	1	1
Round 1.	B chosen	1	2	1	1
Round 2.	B chosen again	1	3	1	1
Round 3.	B now too pricey, and D chosen	1	3	1	2
Final round	*Either* respondent refuses to purchase any brand at the prices displayed. *Or* the range of prices has been exhausted.				

Source: R.P. Morgan, *Brand/Price Trade-off: Where We Stand Now* (Research International, 1988)

be applied to offset the total awareness and total penetration/distribution enjoyed by the brand in the test situation. Effective calculation of these factors depends on the accumulation on file of data relating to distribution and brand awareness in the field (a subject further discussed in section 8.5.1).

If the object is to diagnose, say, brand-switching patterns, there is a case for drawing the sample of respondents from among those making frequent purchases in the product field and for excluding from the array of brands those which are bought infrequently. In this case the object of the BPTO exercise is to obtain useful insights into the elasticity of price changes.

7.6   Conclusion

Much of the content of this chapter applies to services as well as to products. Services have also to be formulated, presented/packaged and priced.

After a review of theory applicable to both lab. and field experiments, the chapter focuses on pre-testing, the object being to bring the best mix of attributes to trial in the real world.

The designer of a pre-testing programme is faced with two dilemmas:

1. It is possible to achieve 'internal validity' in lab.-type conditions but the conditions are, to varying extents, unreal and the respondents

know they are delivering judgements. Would the results be the same in normal circumstances? Has the experiment 'external validity'?
2. In the real world the consumer perceives the whole product formulation + packaging + price + the 'added value' of advertising. It is, therefore, necessary to devise a programme of experiments which seeks to optimize individual elements, such as formulation, but which attempts to take account of their interaction.

We focus on pre-testing the brand mix at the end of the next chapter, after we have considered research procedures used in the development of the brand image.

Sources and further reading

1. S. King, *Developing New Brands*, 2nd edn (JWT, 1984), (Quoting from introduction to 1st edition.)
2. M. Callingham, 'The psychology of product testing and its relationship to objective scientific measures', *Journal of The Market Research Society*, vol. 30, no. 3 (July 1988).
3. 'Reliability and validity in qualitative research', report on an MRDF Seminar in the *MRS Newsletter*, no. 268 (July 1988).
4. P. Feldwich and L. Winstanley, 'Qualitative recruitment: policy and practice', *MRS Conference Papers* (1986).
5. 'Standards for qualitative research', (London: Association of Users of Research Agencies, [1981]).
6. W. Gordon and R. Langmaid, *Qualitative Research: A Practitioner's and Buyer's Guide* (London: Gower, 1988).
7. C.A. Moser and G. Kalton, *Survey Methods in Social Investigation* (London: Heinemann Educational Books, 1971).
8. P.E. Green and D.S. Tull, *Research for Marketing Decisions*, 4th edn (Englewood Cliffs, NJ: Prentice Hall, 1978).
9. K.K. Cox and B.M. Enis, *Experimentation for Marketing Decisions* (Glasgow: Intertext, 1973).
10. P. Kotler, *Marketing Management, Analysis, Planning and Control*, 4th edn (Englewood Cliffs, NJ: Prentice Hall, 1980).
11. S. King, 'Applying research to decision-making', *MRS Newsletter*, no. 208 (July 1983), pp. 28–33.
12. R. Westwood, A.J. Lunn and D. Beazley, 'The trade-off model and its extensions', *Journal of The Market Research Society* (July 1974), vol. 16, no. 3.
13. P. Hill and S. Woodward, 'The Crocodillo launch: the market research contribution', *MRS Conference Papers*, (1982), pp. 343–52.
14. J.C. Penny, I.M. Hunt and W.A. Twyman, 'Product testing methodology in relation to marketing problems', *Journal of The Market Research Society* (Jan. 1982).
15. A.A. Clarke, 'Propensity for the participant to react over-favourably to the test product', *Journal of The Market Research Society* (July 1967).

16. G. Brown, A. Copeland and M. Milward, 'The monadic testing of new products', *Journal of The Market Research Society* (Apr. 1973).

17. A.N. Oppenheim, *Questionnaire Design and Attitude Measurement* (London: Heinemann Educational Books, 1970).

18. E.J. Davis, *Experimental Marketing* (London: Nelson, 1970).

19. H.W. Boyd and R. Westfall, *Marketing Research: Text and Cases* (Itaska, Illinois: Irwin, 1972).

20. S. King, 'What can pre-testing do?', *ADMAP* (1968).

21. W. Schlackman and D. Chittenden, 'Packaging research' in R.M. Worcester and J. Downham (eds) *Consumer Market Research Handbook*, 3rd edn (Amsterdam: North-Holland, 1986).

22. R.P. Morgan, '*Ad hoc* pricing research: some key issues', *Journal of The Market Research Society* (Apr. 1987).

23. A. Gabor, *Price as a Quality Indicator in Pricing: Principles and Practices*, (London: Heinemann Educational Books, 1977).

24. J.P. Frappa and Y. Marbeau, 'Pricing new products at better value for money: the ultimate challenge for market researchers', ESOMAR Congress, Vienna (Amsterdam: ESOMAR, 1982), vol. II, pp. 171–95.

See also

• M. Baker, 'Innovation: key to success', *Quarterly Review of Marketing*, (Jan. 1982), vol. 7, no. 2.

• S. Day, 'Clover new product development', paper no. 3 in U. Bradley (ed.), *Applied Marketing and Social Research*, 2nd edn (London: John Wiley, 1987).

• L. de Chernatony and G. McWilliam, 'Clarifying the difference between manufacturers' brands and distributors' brands', *Quarterly Review of Marketing* (1988), vol. 13, no. 4.

• C. Greenhalgh, 'Research for new product development', Chap. 15 in R. Worcester and J. Downham (eds), *Consumer Market Research Handbook*, 3rd edn (Amsterdam: North-Holland, 1986).

• F.A. Johne, 'Innovation in the marketing of high technology products', *Quarterly Review of Marketing* (Apr. 1984), vol. 9, no. 3.

• 'Producing a winner', *Survey* (an MRS publication), (spring 1987).

• 'Research into pricing', a special issue of the *Journal of The Market Research Society*, vol. 29, no. 2, April 1987.

Problems

1. What experimental designs would you advocate in the following circumstances? How would you recruit the test subjects? What treatment would you apply to the subjects? How would you measure results? (You are pre-testing.)

   (a) Acceptability of a cooked breakfast cereal which (it is claimed) does not stick to the saucepan.

   (b) Response to an addition to a confectionery counterline popular with junior schoolchildren.

   (c)   Perceived effectiveness of a shampoo for cars with a protective ingredient.

   (d)   Response to a range of selling prices for a new range of gourmet foods.

   (e)   Alternative packaging for a range of frozen desserts.

2. 'Whatever the difficulties of interpretation, research is only relevant if it attempts to simulate the situation in the market' (Brown, Copeland, Milward). Discuss this statement, focusing your answer on the pre-testing of a branded, fast-moving consumer product/service of your choice.

3. You have been asked to design an experiment to show which (if either) of the following two courses of action is more likely to increase the total of a bank's transactions with its customers (the bank has branches in major population centres throughout Great Britain):

   (a)   Saturday morning opening; or

   (b)   provision of 24-hour cash points.

What experimental method would you use? How would you measure effects? How would you seek to achieve external validity?

Establishing the brand identity and pre-testing the whole

8

In the last chapter we considered how uncertainty may be reduced while a branded product is being developed for the market.

We stressed the fact that the brand — the product or service as perceived by consumers — is a mixture of intrinsic qualities (such as colour, taste, consistency) and of the way in which these qualities are packaged and priced.

Consumer perception is also, of course, influenced by the way in which the brand is presented in advertisements, while whether the message is actually conveyed to the consumer depends on the size of the advertising appropriation and the efficiency with which media choices are made when the advertising schedule is planned.

This chapter focuses on the creative aspect, while media selection is reserved for Chapter 9: but the relationship between the message and the medium used to convey it is necessarily a close one, and the most cost-effective results are achieved when creative work and media planning proceed simultaneously and with joint consultation.

The need to reach target consumers as often and as forcefully as possible within the financial resources available will largely determine media selection. This overriding consideration may, for example, prescribe use of television to communicate the message, and this decision will have a critical effect on creative thinking. On the other hand, the need to present a benefit, or create an image, as persuasively as possible will influence the length of commercials, the size of print advertisements and the choice of supporting media.

Communications research is a large subject. Figure 8.1 sets the scene by summarizing the stages in the development of an advertising campaign and relating these to the relevant chapters in this book.

The 1980s have seen increasing emphasis on the role of the account planner in advertising agencies. The claim is made that 'the account planner creates a dialogue between the consumer and the process of creating advertisements' and that:

> This responsibility for setting advertising in its real-life context is what
> differentiates the account planner from, on the one hand, the market

175

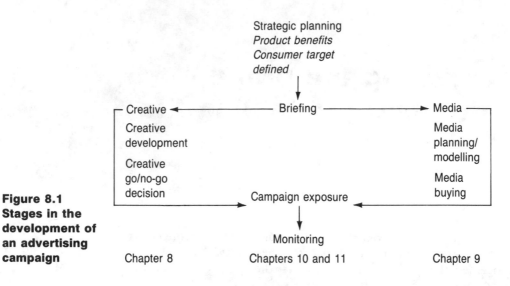

**Figure 8.1
Stages in the
development of
an advertising
campaign**

researcher, and, on the other, the account handler [or account executive].
The market researcher is there to *answer* questions, the planner is there
to ask them and to interpret the answers.[1]

There is clearly room here for role confusion and territorial
manoeuvring but this focus on the importance of consumer behaviour,
beliefs and values makes a major contribution to British advertising. It
has been associated with the systematic use of qualitative research and
has fuelled the debate between the claims of qualitative and quantitative
methods.

Advertising budgets represent substantial investment in a brand, and
scientific measurement techniques add the weight of numbers to choices
and serve as input for econometric models.[2]

In order to construct an econometric model it is, of course, necessary
to be able to put a value on each of the marketing variables such as price,
distribution and advertising, which 'best explain variations on the key
dependent variable: sales'.[2] These values derive from time series such as
consumer panels, retail audits, media expenditure reports, and there must
be 'enough points in the time series to provide a sound basis for multiple
regression'.[3]

Econometric modelling features in case studies published by the
Institute of Practitioners in Advertising (IPA) under the advertising
effectiveness scheme; see for example TSB's school-leaver campaign and
the Andrex story in the 1986 series.

The IPA objective is 'to isolate the contribution of advertising to sales
and profits over and above that of the marketing mix'.[3] Obstacles to the
achievement of this objective will be encountered in this chapter which
is concerned with the pre-testing of advertisements.

But in order to put the subject in perspective it is necessary first of
all to do the following:

- Distinguish between marketing objectives, advertising objectives and creative tasks.
- Review the chronological stages in the advertising research programme.
- Consider some theories as to how advertising works.

8.1 Advertising objectives and creative tasks

We need to distinguish between marketing objectives, advertising objectives and creative tasks. The marketing objective is, in the last analysis, to improve the contribution to profit of a particular brand or to maintain its contribution for as long as possible. The profit contribution can be achieved by improving or maintaining sales value or, in the shorter term, by reducing marketing costs, and this generally means the advertising appropriation. The following made-up case illustrates the relationship between marketing objectives, advertising objective and creative task:

> *The marketing objective* is to increase the market share of the brand by x per cent. The client's promotional budget, which embraces trade deals and consumer promotions as well as the advertising appropriation, is related to this objective. Study of disaggregated panel data shows that, among those who buy the brand, there is a group of individuals who return to the brand time and again without being entirely loyal to it. The data describe the demographic characteristics of this group and indicate that the segment is sufficiently large to warrant further attention.
>
> *The advertising objective* is accordingly to stimulate the loyalty (or to improve the repeat-purchase rate) of a consumer target defined as housewives with children at home who are working full- or part-time outside the home. The social class and age classification of the segment is known and this is important for media planning.
>
> *The creative task* may be determined by qualitative work among women representative of the segment. 'Depth' interviews or group discussions may suggest that, in this product field, the target consumer is anxious to maintain her home-making role in spite of the demands of outside work. The creative task might then be defined as supporting the domestic confidence of these hard-pressed women. There is, of course, more than one way of doing this in an advertising campaign!

If advertising objectives are agreed between client and agency at the outset, and if the creative task is defined at an early stage, there are defined standards for experimental and, finally, monitoring purposes.

8.2 Stages in the advertising research programme

The creative research programme we are going to follow is based on Stephen King's cycle of advertising research.[4]

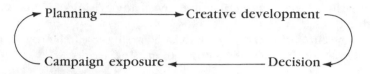

8.2.1 The strategic planning stage

The data considered range from clients' sales figures, through trend data derived from subscription to consumer panels and/or retail audits, to repeated attitude surveys tracking consumer responses to brands on the market: tests carried out during the development of the product, descriptive surveys including segmentation studies and qualitative work on file. This listing does not include the media statistics, which we will be discussing in Chapter 9.

The wealth of data made available by electronic data-processing has created a developing role for planners in advertising agencies: to help ensure that the available data are effectively digested and to act as purveyors of the relevant and stimulating findings of research. The purveyor role is especially important when it comes to briefing creative people. To do this effectively requires a rare combination of the analytical and creative faculties. The advertising objective(s) are defined at this stage and the creative group briefed.

If the marketing company has studied consumers in sufficient detail (if, for example, it has carried out a segmentation study), the consumer target and the benefits to be conveyed to the target can be sharply defined when media and creative groups in the advertising agency are briefed.

As with product testing, definition of target and benefit(s) specifies the type of consumer to be involved in qualitative and experimental work, and what perceptions of the product should be used as measures of advertising effectiveness.

8.2.2 The development of creative ideas

Let us assume that the creative task has been defined during the strategic planning stage and that the creative group has been effectively briefed. At this early stage of creative development qualitative work is commonly used to try out ideas. A limited number of target consumers is shown creative ideas in an unfinished form. The degree of finish is a matter of judgement. The demands of time and cost suggest as rough as possible: what is wanted is response to ideas. These may be conveyed by, say, sketched layout plus headline, or perhaps typed copy for print advertisements; storyboard or mocked-up video treatment for television commercials. (See Table 7.2.)

This material is used as a stimulus for discussion in groups or in individual interviews. The discussion or interview is taped so that the creative group (who should in any case be involved in the research work) can play it back. In some agencies, videotape or one-way mirrors are used so that 'body language' may be observed by the creative staff.

No attempt is made to count heads. The numbers taking part in this qualitative work are sufficient to generate a good range of ideas and reactions, but not for statistical analysis. Content of the tapes is analysed in terms of the following:

- Ideas about the product derived from the advertising stimulus, including ideas about the kind of people who might be expected to use the product.
- The extent to which those taking part associate themselves with the product and the context in which it is shown.
- Features ignored, which may indicate either that the message is unclear or that those present are dissociating themselves from this aspect.

8.2.3 Eliminating non-starters

It may be necessary to give statistical support to the agency proposal or to choose between more than one approach. What is now wanted is 'a quantified measurement of future performance in real conditions'[5] without incurring the cost of the complete marketing effort and before meeting competitors in the market place.

Debate has for a long time centred on the validity of the measures used in pre-exposure testing, measures such as the recall of advertisements and their contents and expressed intention to buy the branded product. Once a pre-tested brand is out in the real world it is, of course, possible to compare actual performance with estimated performance: to establish the relationships between recall of advertisements in the pre-test and awareness of the advertising after exposure, between expressed intention to buy and actual sales, and to arrive at correction factors which enable predictions to be made with more confidence.

The estimation of correction factors is, however, 'a most difficult and expensive exercise. Moreover, it is only achieved through complex mathematical equations (e.g. the "geometric stretch function").'[6]

The once hard and fast distinction between pre- and post-testing has been blurred. Greater confidence in the meaning of pre-test results, access to databanks and computer programs plus disenchantment with the cost and necessary duration of the traditional test market have stimulated interest in research approaches designed to simulate the responses of the target segment before exposure to the market, which may well take the form of a rolling launch. The marketing-mix test (section 8.5.1), the mini-test market (section 10.5.1) and the simulated test-market models (section

8.5.2) are approaches designed to eliminate non-starters and to bring the new brand to market more speedily.

A promising brand has to be developed before the test in the market may be simulated. Following on from Chapter 7, this chapter adds the critical communication element to the brand. To complete the cycle of advertising research, section 8.2.4 briefly looks ahead to the advertising research role after the advertising campaign is launched.

8.2.4 Campaign exposure

Once the creative campaign is out and about in the media it becomes difficult to distinguish the effect of the creative work from that of the media selection. After exposure, advertising research is often used to see whether the opportunities to see/hear the creative message, offered by the media selected, are in fact being taken by the target consumers. Results of the recognition checks and campaign penetration studies considered in Chapter 10 are used (a) to monitor performance and (b) to refine future media scheduling, for the process is a circular one.

Of course what we would like to be able to do at this stage is to relate the advertising costs to sales achievement. A simple cause-and-effect relationship between advertising and sales *can* be observed when response is direct, as in mail order. In most cases other marketing factors intervene. Has the sales force, perhaps aided by dealer incentives, been able to achieve not only distribution but 'stand-out' value for the brand? What level of competitive activity is the campaign provoking? We discuss the research methods used to help answer questions such as these in Chapter 10.

In the meantime, the grey area is shrinking with the increasing availability of disaggregated data — 'within person' and 'shop by shop' — and the associated development of computer programs which examine relationships between the brand and media consumption of individuals over time: while the availability of 'shop by shop' data will in due course make it easier to establish the effect of distributive, as opposed to advertising, tactics. We return to this subject when considering monitoring procedures in Chapter 11.

The problem of separating the effect of the creative work from the effect of the media planning remains.

8.3 How advertising works

Ideas as to how advertising works influence the research methods used when advertisements are tested: it is now generally accepted that there can be no one all-embracing theory because advertising tasks are so varied.

To take two extreme cases:

1. In 'direct-response' advertising the goods are sold to the consumer in an advertisement and delivery is direct from manufacturer/marketing company on receipt of cash or credit-card number. The Sunday supplements carry many advertisements of this kind.
2. In 'corporate image' advertising the objective may be to protect profit growth from attack by political and social pressure groups; and the advertising task to keep the public informed about technological achievements of benefit to the community. ICI's 'path-finders' campaign is an example of 'corporate image' advertising.[7]

In the direct-response case, sales are substantially attributable to an advertisement in a particular medium (provided the print advertisement, television or radio commercial has a code attached to it, and the purchaser refers to the code!).

In the corporate-image case, the effect of the campaign is likely to be measured by asking members of the public awareness and attitude questions in *ad hoc* surveys carried out at regular intervals, say once a year. By asking a standard core of questions in each survey it is possible to keep track of changes in the image of the enterprise held by the general public. Brand images are similarly monitored (Chapters 10 and 11).

In the direct-response case, advertising can be said to *convert*: in the corporate image case, to *reinforce*. Let us now see how these two conceptions of the advertising task, conversion and reinforcement, arose.

8.3.1 The early models

The earliest model is probably AIDA (attention, interest, desire, action). This model postulates a simple relationship between advertising and selling.[8] Provided the advertising succeeds in attracting attention, arousing interest and stimulating desire, the result is a sale:

$$\text{Attention} \longrightarrow \text{Interest} \longrightarrow \text{Desire} \longrightarrow \text{Action}$$

Colley's DAGMAR model is more sophisticated in its approach, but the advertising process is still seen as one of step-by-step conversion. DAGMAR stands for 'defining advertising goals for measured advertising results,'[9] the goals being to achieve the following in the consumer:

$$\text{Awareness} \longrightarrow \text{Comprehension} \longrightarrow \text{Conviction} \longrightarrow \text{Action}$$

Lavidge and Steiner's 'hierarchy-of-effects' model[10] draws on the theory that an attitude embraces three elements or states — cognition (knowing), affect (evaluation) and conation (action); but the advertising process is still seen as one in which, for the potential consumer, a change of attitude will precede a change in behaviour:

Conation	Purchase	↑
	Conviction	
Affect	Preference	
	Liking	
Cognition	Knowledge	
	Awareness	

The assumption that attitude change precedes change in behaviour ignores the implications of Festinger's theory of cognitive dissonance. Individuals aim to achieve consonance or harmony in their thinking and feeling. Choosing (as between products, brands and services) threatens a consumer with post-decisional dissonance.

> The magnitude of post-decision dissonance is an increasing function of the general importance of the decision and of the relative attractiveness of the unchosen alternative.[11]

It has been shown that car buyers are more likely to look at advertisements for the car they have just bought than for those they did not choose: while Ehrenberg's work on disaggregated panel data has proved beyond doubt that advertisements for fast-moving brands are more likely to be perceived by those who buy them.[12]

In other words, it is now generally accepted that a change in attitude may either precede or follow action: that the relationship may work in either direction.

Attitude ⟶ Behaviour
⟵

8.3.2 The reinforcement role

Dissonance theory suggests that advertising has a reinforcement role to play, for, by reassuring consumers that they have made a sensible choice, loyalty to a particular model or brand is reinforced.

Ehrenberg's rigorous examination of disaggregated panel data has shown that, in many product fields, 100 per cent loyalty to a brand is rare indeed; on the other hand, choice is not haphazard.

> Let us assume that a typical shopper's short list is of three brands, E, F, G: that his/her habitual pattern of buying is E, E, F, G: and our brand is G. It would clearly improve our brand share if this shopper's buying of G were sufficiently frequent in relation to E and F to create an habitual buying pattern of G, E, F, G. The advertising task might then be to reinforce the attraction of G for those who already use the brand from time to time.

For established brands, sales increases represent only a small proportion of total sales in any one period and reinforcement of the status quo is essential to the maintenance of profit contribution. But consumers die, move out of the country or get too old for the product, and, as Corlett pointed out: 'Brands grow partly through attracting new buyers, partly through increased frequency of buying among existing users.'[13]

The relative importance of these two roles, conversion and reinforcement, will depend on the nature of the market and the position of the brand in the market.

> New users (converts) are essential to the baby-food market. But this is a field in which cognitive dissonance is particularly painful, and reassurance, through reinforcement of the choice made, a powerful weapon for good (or ill, as in some developing countries).

Finally there are, of course, situations in which advertising is used to defend a brand's position and the advertiser is satisfied if market share is maintained without any increase in advertising or other marketing costs.

8.3.3 USP and 'brand image'

These two models were developed in New York advertising agencies in the early 1960s: the 'unique selling proposition' (USP) by Rosser Reeves and the 'brand-image' concept by David Ogilvy.

The unique selling proposition (1961)

In the rare case of a product with a unique, and desirable, attribute, definition of the USP is a straightforward matter. But integral differences between brands in a product field are often marginal and a USP is likely to be suggested by study of consumer habits and attitudes in the product field: to quote a classic example, use of toothpaste + fear of bad breath = 'the Colgate ring of confidence'. The USP, once defined, must be adhered to in every communication about the brand. This is a behaviourist approach to 'how advertising works' and, as with Pavlov's dogs, repetition is of the essence. Time is needed to condition the consumer to associate the proposition with the brand.

Brand image (1963)

David Ogilvy's concept of the 'brand image' has proved more fruitful in the development of creative advertising. Consumers buy brands (not products or services) and by developing a personality for the brand (as opposed to attaching a proposition to it) the brand is made more meaningful to the consumer and this added value strengthens loyalty. The consumer is treated as a rational being with conscious ends in view and a defined self-image. Brand loyalty is strong when there is empathy between the brand's image and the consumer's self-image.

Recall and awareness are likely measures to use when assessing the effectiveness of a USP campaign; while attitude measurement and the tracking of changes in attitude over time are essential to 'image' studies.

8.3.4 Fishbein and buying intention

'Intention to buy' (or 'try') questions are now accepted as valid indicators of consumer response to products and the advertising associated with them. The answers have been shown to have predictive value. As a result of Fishbein's work on attitude theory and measurement, investigations into consumer habits and attitudes now often include attitude questions relating to *the act of purchase*.[14]

Fishbein postulates that behavioural intention (BI) is the product of how we feel about the act ('attitude towards the act', Aact) — and in our context the act is buying a brand — plus how we feel about society's attitude towards the act (SN, a subjective norm). In the formula given below, w_1 and w_2 are weights representing the strength of our wanting to carry out the act (buying or trying the brand) and the extent to which this might be modified by social considerations:

$$BI = Aact_{w_1} + SN_{w_2}$$

There is a lucid and helpful analysis of Fishbein's model in Tuck's *How do we Choose?*[15] The Fishbein finding that 'simple behavioural intention can give a good indication of the trend of mass consumer behaviour in the relatively short term' is supported by Unilever experience. Two Unilever associates did extensive work in this field, Lintas and Research Bureau Limited (RBL, now Research International Limited).

Lintas asked 'housewives and heads of households' in 492 households whether they would buy/use over the next three years

more	less	about the same

of a large number of goods and services: 'when compared with data later released by the Central Statistical Office, the predicted overall trend was confirmed.'[16]

RBL has long made a practice of asking 'intention to buy' questions. The data have been systematically filed and (where possible) correlated with actual purchase data. Experience has shown that 'intention to buy' scores indicate how far the total message effect adds up to a feeling of wanting to buy the brand (as opposed to, say, just enjoying the advertisement), and this feeling is related to subsequent sales.[17]

An experimental design used by RBL to assess advertising effectiveness is described in section 8.4.2.

8.3.5 The continuing debate

During the 1960s and 1970s many papers were published on how advertising was thought to work. Joyce introduced the concept of 'added value'.[18] In addition to having certain in-built product qualities, such as softness in toilet tissue, a brand may acquire the added value of, say, social rightness or 'being a good housewife' from the creative impact of its advertising. This will add to the life of the brand for 'the effective matching of the user-image to the self-image of the potential buyers then becomes a crucial function of the advertising'. 'People choose their brands as they choose their friends. It is the total person you choose not a compendium of vices and virtues.'[19]

Towards the end of the 1970s a change in political and business attitudes prompted a more pragmatic approach and the introduction of the IPA advertising effectiveness awards.

> In the advertising business we all know that the ultimate test of any advertising campaign is the sales result to which it contributes. . . . The Institute of Practitioners in Advertising is now setting out to remedy this situation with a unique competitive award scheme that will be based solely on the assessment of the *effects* of advertising campaigns in any media. It will aim to achieve three things:
>
> 1. A better understanding of the crucial role advertising plays in marketing.
> 2. Closer analysis of advertising effectiveness and improved methods of evaluation.
> 3. A clear demonstration that advertising can be proven to work, against measurable criteria.'[20]

Five volumes of case histories have been published to date.[20]

It is, of course, possible to measure effects without knowing what motivates those who buy the brand, and those who do not:

What motivates people to buy my brands? For centuries . . . academics have puzzled about what goes on in the human mind. They have reached no sort of common conclusion. Rather little of this academic work has filtered through to the world of marketing, probably because it is not sufficiently action-orientated. Perhaps the best bridge comes from the anthropologists. Mary Douglas, in particular, has written about why people buy goods, saying 'Goods are for thinking with'. In a splendid piece called 'Beans meanz thinks' she wrote, 'Consumption decisions are a vital source of the *culture* of the time. . . . The individual uses consumption to *say something* about himself and his family and his locality.

This passage was quoted by Stephen King in his key speech at the 1983 MRS conference 'Applying research to decision-making'.[21]

8.4 Measures of advertising effectiveness

Before discussing experimentation at the go/no-go decision stage (see section 8.2.3) we ought perhaps to remind ourselves of two points:

1. Our concern is with the target consumer's response to the brand and to the kind of people seen as likely to use it: we are not asking for artistic verdicts.
2. Qualitative work at the creative development stage (see section 8.2.2) will have indicated whether or not target consumers understand what the advertising is trying to convey, and how far they associate themselves with this message.

It is unlikely that qualitative work will have been carried out with a sufficiently large number of target consumers to bear statistical analysis, and the reassurance of numbers may be wanted. (Much depends on the nature of the client and the authority of the creative group within the agency.)

The validity of pre-tests is often debated: experiments are carried out in unreal circumstances; results are often based on comparison between individual advertisements representing different approaches to the creative task.

> Are lab.-type experiments which compare the effects achieved by individual advertisements, valid predictors of the response to be anticipated to a series of advertisements appearing in the media over a period of time?

In addition, there is doubt about the validity of the measures used to assess advertising effects, whether these be verbal measures such as recall, physiological responses recorded by instruments such as the psychogalvanometer (see section 8.4.3) or behavioural measures such as coupon redemption. In most experiments, the measures used are verbal ones, and they are often referred to as intermediate or indirect because they fall short of measuring sales.

8.4.1 Verbal measures

At the pre-testing stage, i.e. before campaign exposure, the most commonly used measures of creative effectiveness are the following:

- Recall, unaided and aided.
- Attitude towards the product/brand and its likely users.
- Intention to buy.

Questions relating to the respondent's habitual behaviour in the product field will often help to determine whether the respondent is a suitable participant in the test. They will also contribute to interpretation of the answers to recall, attitude and intention-to-buy questions.

Impact is the result of the following:

- The information conveyed to the respondent (usually measured by recall).
- The respondent's emotional response to the brand (measured by attitude questions).
- The strength of the respondent's desire for the brand (as indicated by intention-to-buy questions).

We are close to the hierarchical models* with their cognitive, affective

*The US Marketing Science Institute which carried out methodological research to identify 'Today's top priority advertising research questions',[22] 1980–82, suggests that each step in the hierarchical advertising models has one or more measures associated with it:

Cognition:	Recall
	Recognition
	Belief strength
	Awareness
	Comprehensive of main copy points
Affect:	Attitude regarding product's features
	Product preferences
	Extent of match of product with self-image
	Internalization of message
Conation:	Purchase intent
	Intent to try product (trial)
	Intent to adopt product (commitment)
	Actual purchase behaviour

But 'hierarchy of effects might apply more to high-involvement than to low-involvement products'.[22]

and conative components (see section 8.3.1) but with two important differences:

1. We recognize that attitude change can be the effect as well as the cause of a change in behaviour, that it can be 'post-' as well as 'pre-' action.
2. We distinguish between attitudes towards the brand and those who might use it, and attitudes towards the act of purchasing or behavioural intention.

Once the campaign is out in the real world, recognition is an important measure. Recognition checks whether or not an advertisement has been noticed. This will, of course, depend on the effectiveness of the media planning and buying as well as on the creative impact.

Awareness, *campaign penetration* and *salience* are other terms used when discussing advertising research after campaign exposure (post-testing). Awareness covers a range of responses from mere recognition to unaided recall of the attributes the advertising seeks to associate with the brand. Campaign penetration and salience measures help to establish whether the opportunities to see, view or hear offered by the media schedule are in fact being taken.

8.4.2   Testing before campaign exposure: three methodologies

The folder or reel test — a lab.-type experiment

Let us assume that the creative group has come up with two possible solutions to the creative task.

> *The test material:* two folders or videotape reels are prepared containing a selection of advertisements with which the proposed advertisements will have to compete for attention. The competitive advertisements are likely to represent a variety of product fields. The two folders/reels are identical except for the test advertisements, assigned one to each, and placed in the same position relative to the rest of the content. It is, of course, important that the test material be of the same degree of finish as the rest of the content.
> *The design:* monadic, using two matched samples of 50–100 members of the target population.
> *Procedure:* the respondents are asked to go through one of the folders or to watch one of the tapes. They are then asked which advertisements they happen to have noticed. Given that the brand is an established one (as is often the case in advertising research) the test advertisement will not stand out as being of special interest to the interviewer. Once unaided recall has been recorded, a list of the brands in the test is shown

to the respondent as a memory trigger. The respondent may be asked which was most liked and which was liked least, or which 'you would most like to talk about'. Procedures vary, but essentially attention is gradually focused on the test advertisement and recall of its content.

Recording of aided recall must of course be differentiated from unaided recall, and the order in which advertisements and product attributes are mentioned is likely to be significant as a measure of salience.

Measurement of results: Applying the notation used in Table 7.3 we have an after-only design based on two matched experimental groups, here E_1 and E_2:

Group	Treatment	Observation	Measurement
E_1	X_1	O_1	O_1 compared with O_2 in a controlled context
E_2	X_2	O_2	O_2 in a controlled context

The basis for comparison is not likely to be limited to recall. Attitude and intention-to-buy questions may also be asked: while behaviour in the product field will be taken into account.

Testing in the field before campaign exposure

If the brand is on sale it is possible to pre-test in the field by arranging for the run of a publication to be 'split', so that different areas receive issues with different advertisements; or by arranging for different transmitters to put out different commercials. Here again the context is controlled: same television programme, same publication; the independent variable being the advertisement.

Here again the measures used to determine the relative effectiveness of the alternative advertising approaches are recall (unaided and aided), attitude questions, intention to buy (if not already doing so) in the light of experience to date in the product field.

The setting up of this kind of experiment is straightforward enough; publishers and independent television contractors offer standard packages as part of their own sales promotional activity.

The main procedural difficulties are the following:

- Contacting suitable, i.e. target-group, respondents.
- Matching experimental groups on critical product use and demographic criteria.
- Making sure that respondents have in fact been exposed to the test material.

A question relating to editorial content of the issue, or in the case of television, about adjacent programmes, is the usual way of establishing that the responses recorded relate to the advertisements whose impact we are trying to assess. It is possible to use the media to test the effectiveness of a new advertising approach if the brand is 'ongoing' and in distribution. Were the media to be used to finalize advertising for a new brand it would be necessary to have produced the product in sufficient quantity, packed and priced to meet the demand created; and the competition would be alerted.

An 'after-only with control' example

When we pre-test the effect of communications we would like to be able to take a 'before' measurement and to base our conclusions on observation of the changes effected by the advertising material on the respondent's awareness, attitudes and intentions with regard to the brand. But we know that questions asked at the first interview are likely to influence responses at the second (see section 7.2.2).

Research Bureau Limited (now Research International) have validated a procedure which sidesteps this difficulty:

* Two samples of about 100 target consumers are matched on about two demographic characteristics and, where relevant, on some aspect of brand or product field usage.
* The experimental group receives the advertising test material *plus* some other prompting stimulus such as a pack shot.
* The control group receives the other prompting stimulus *without* the advertising material.
* The two samples are questioned about the brand and the added value of the advertising material is appraised by comparing the responses of the experimental group with those of the control group. As we saw in section 8.3.4, RBL attach considerable importance to the intention-to-buy measure.[17]
* The design (using the notation shown in Table 7.3) is, given X = advertising test material and Y = the other stimulus:

Group	Treatment	Observation	Measurement*
E	$X + Y$	O_1	$O_1 - O_2$
C	Y	O_2	

*It is possible, of course, that some of the verbal measures used may not show a positive result for E, the experimental group, and that the overall result may not show value being added by the advertising.

In an 'after-only with control' design sampling error will be greater than it would be if both sets of measurements were taken on the same sample of respondents, as in a before—after design. In order to avoid the possible bias due to the learning effect, communications research relies very often on a comparison of responses from more than one group, whether these be two experimental groups, as in our first example, or an experimental group with a control group. Matching of the groups is critical and it is advisable to ensure that test and control samples . . . use the same interviewers in matched locations.[17]

When commercials are being tested, the location is likely to be a van, suitably equipped, or a hall.

8.4.3   Pre-testing with instruments

There is a good case for using mechanical means of observation when testing the stand-out effect of pack designs (see section 7.4.3). For a time lab.-type experiments using mechanical observation were fashionable in communications research; but the following considerations now count against the use of 'ironmongery' to measure advertising effects:

- Use of measuring devices such as the tachistoscope or psychogalvanometer restricts the venue for the experiment to a test centre or mobile van and adds to the cost of data collection, for the ironmongery is expensive and the procedure likely to be time-consuming.
- Artificiality of the circumstances in which the advertising material is exposed to target consumers reduces belief in the external validity of their responses.
- It is usually necessary to ask questions in order to interpret the meaning of the physiological observations recorded by the instruments.

We are going to consider two devices: the tachistoscope and the psychogalvanometer.

The tachistoscope is relevant to the testing of posters for stand-out value, and it could be claimed that the more speedily perceived of two advertisements has the better chance of being noticed in the press or during the commercial break on ITV. But, posters apart, experiments based on verbal measures are likely to produce richer and more actionable data at less cost. It is always possible, of course, to combine the physiological and verbal procedures: to record the speed with which elements in the advertisement are perceived and then to ask the recall, attitude and intention questions.

As for the psychogalvanometer, the case for physiological measurements rests on doubts about the capacity of researchers to ask meaningful questions and of consumers to give true answers. Response to an advertising stimulus when attached to the psychogalvanometer (or 'lie detector') is involuntary. Electrodes attached to the hands measure sweat levels, an autonomic indicator of emotional arousal. Provided the temperature of the research centre, or van, is kept stable, comparison of fluctuations with a base measurement will show how the respondent reacts to the development of a commercial, or to the sight of a press advertisement or sound of a radio commercial. The emotional responses are duly recorded but the nature of the responses, whether these are favourable or unfavourable, has to be elicited by means of questions.

8.5 Pre-testing the brand mix

> But where research, or much of research, probably fails the new product development function is an adherence to techniques that are patently not up to providing adequate guidance to management, and in the refusal to adopt newer techniques that, although not infallible, are better able to meet management's needs in the area of marketing mix evaluation and sales forecasting.[23]

'Over the last few years there has been a dramatic growth in the use of the group of techniques we term Simulated Test Markets.'[24] We have arrived at a point where a useful distinction can be made between *test market* models and *pre-test* market models.'[25] We are going to consider four approaches to marketing mix evaluation: the total package or marketing-mix test,[26] Research International's (RI)[24] SENSOR simulated test market and their predictive model, MicroTest, together with Burke Market Research's simulated test market system 'for evaluating new products and new concepts'.[23]

Godfrey and Wilkinson include town tests and RI's mini-test (or van test) in the category of simulated test markets. Here, town tests are included in Chapter 10 for, once a brand is on sale, even if in a limited area, a commitment has been made to produce and package the product and to distribute it to the trade in sufficient quantity to meet demand.

The mini-test market is also included in Chapter 10 (section 10.5.1). In terms of pre- compared with post-exposure, the case for allocating the mini-test to Chapter 10 is less clear-cut. The mini-test records sales to two panels of housewives (representing North and South) who use a van shopping service. The need to sell in to the trade is obviated, but the housewives do not see themselves as testers. They are taking advantage of a door-to-door retail service and sufficient product must be produced to meet demand.

The mini-test also differs from the total package/market-mix test and the simulated market model used by RI and Burke's BASES system in that panel members must not be asked usage and attitude questions; otherwise the panel would be contaminated. (Usage and attitude questions are put to a separate but matched panel.) The four mix-evaluation procedures treated here allow for usage and attitude data to be collected and so yield valuable diagnostic data when brands are being 'fine-tuned'.

8.5.1 The market-mix test

In section 7.3.9 we looked at a monadic test procedure developed for General Foods. This type of design, in which the product idea is introduced in some, often unfinished, form before the product is tried, is now a commonly used one.

The design considered here moves the go/no-go decision for a new brand as close to market commitment as is possible in lab. pre-testing conditions.[26]

The communication plus product design developed by Gordon Coulson Associates is of particular interest for the following reasons:

- The test conditions are made as 'real-life' as possible.
- A 'likelihood of buying' measure is used (see section 8.3.4).
- Concept and 'in-use' responses are used, suitably adjusted, to predict penetration and repeat purchase. (We meet these two important predictors of brand share in Chapter 10.)

The experimental design can also, of course, be used to compare different combinations of communication, pack design and product and price: but, as we shall see, real-life simulation must add to research costs; and to avoid the learning effect the design would need to be a monadic one with groups of testers matched.

To get as close as possible to real life the following conditions are met:

- Advertising and pack are 'finished' — they may not be final but they appear so.
- The pack is of a size it is intended to market.
- The target consumer tries the product where it would normally be used (kitchen, bathroom, garage, etc.).
- Sufficient time is allowed for a thorough trial by all who might share in the use of the product.
- The brand is introduced as being on the market elsewhere.

In addition to the likelihood-of-buying question, questions are asked about the product and the kind of people who would use it, how it would be used and its price, both at the concept stage (i.e. before it has been tried) and after trial.

Responses to the likelihood-of-buying question sort respondents/testers into either three or four groups: three if the trial of the product is limited to those who say they are likely to buy after seeing advertising and the pack; four if all those who are willing to try the product are given the opportunity to do so, even if they have said they are unlikely to buy. As can be seen, extending the trial to those who would be unlikely to buy it has diagnostic value (see Table 8.1).

**Table 8.1
Likelihood of
buying**

Group	Pre-trial	Post-trial	Marketing implications
1	Yes	Yes	All clear
2	Yes	No	Product does not live up to expectations
3	No	Excluded	'Idea' of the brand does not engender initial buying
If 3 not excluded			
3	No	Yes	Presentation of the 'idea' needs rethinking
4	No	No	Brand (as it stands) a non-starter.

If our objective is choice of one advertising creative approach as compared with another, we recruit two matched-test samples, vary the communication but hold other elements, such as price, steady.

If we want to predict penetration from the pre-trial results and repeat-buying from the post-trial results we have to allow for the fact that the consumer's introduction to the brand has been 'hothoused' in two respects: 100 per cent awareness of the brand and its advertising plus 100 per cent distribution has been achieved.

In a well-researched market, given a known advertising appropriation and sufficiently advanced media plans, it is possible to estimate the probability of awareness being achieved: indeed, as we shall see in Chapter 9, cost-effective media planning depends on estimation of the likelihood of opportunities to read/view/hear being taken by the target market.

Similarly, given access to trend data relating to retail distribution in the product field, it is possible to estimate how effective the distribution of our brand is likely to be, given the strength of the competition and the promotional support planned for our entry. This subject is covered in more detail in Chapter 10.

A model for relating expectations to performance was presented at the 1977 MRS conference by K. Clarke and M. Roe.[27]

8.5.2 Simulated test markets (SENSOR)

Research International's SENSOR Model, presented by Godfrey and Wilkinson at ESOMAR's 1983 Barcelona conference, simulates encounter with the new brand at the point of sale:

- Respondents are 'recruited to central locations'.
- Respondents are exposed to advertising.

- Respondents are taken to a simulated shop display including the new brand and its competitors.
- Respondents are given coupon money to spend on products in the display.
- Those who buy the test product are given it to use at home under natural conditions.
- After a suitable interval trialists are called on and asked brand preference questions.
- Prices are discussed using the 'trade-off' procedure (see section 7.5.4).
- The respondent is given the opportunity to buy the test brand using his/her own money.

Prediction is based on estimates of penetration and repeat purchase using the Parfitt and Collins equation (see section 10.4.3). Penetration derives from the percentage choosing the new product in the simulated shop, initial repeat-buying rate from the percentage of triers buying the brand with their own money. Data derived from the brand-preference questions and from the 'trade-off' answers are used to arrive at an estimate of the level at which repeat buying will settle. A Markov modelling procedure is used to calculate the brand-switching probabilities.

Simulated test-market tests have the following features:

- They have the advantage of speed for both penetration and repeat buying are 'hothoused'.
- They provide for 'extensive diagnostic questioning'.
- They depend on neither attitude measurement scores nor the availability of trend data.
- They provide opportunities to explore the effects of modifications to product formulation, pack, price and advertising.
- They 'can eliminate the need for much of the hitherto necessary separate testing of elements such as advertising, pack and product'.[24]

SENSOR is a macro-model, in contrast to MicroTest and BPTO. The SENSOR data are stored and processed on an individual basis but the modelling is done at the aggregate level, using aggregate parameters derived from the research.

It is important that the shop display should represent the retail context in which the brand will be competing in the real world. Success in meeting this criterion depends on the nature of the product field. If the brand and its competitors are sold through one type of retail outlet and if they are located all together at the point of sale (breakfast cereals would be an example), then the selling situation to be simulated is clearly defined.

If brands in the product field are sold through more than one type of retail outlet (consider crisps and soft drinks), there are two courses of action: to concentrate on simulating the type of outlet through which most sales are made; or (if one type of outlet does not predominate) to set up parallel tests, taking account of any difference in the nature of the shoppers who may represent different sub-segments of the market.

Those who design any simulated market test need to know the parameters of the product field in which the new brand is to compete (do canned soups compete with packet soups?), current merchandising practices at the point of sale, as well as the current advertising and sales promotional activities of competitors.

Of the three simulation programmes mentioned by Godfrey and Wilkinson, SENSOR and ASSESSOR follow similar modelling procedures; and both 'lay great stress on disguising interest in the new brand to avoid biases due to gratitude effects'.[24] None depends on attitude scale measurements or norms based on past experience in order to predict sales or market share.

8.5.3   MicroTest: a predictive model

SENSOR estimates market share. The model assumes that the size of the market (as revealed by shop audit, consumer panel or omnibus data) will remain much the same; but 'the marketing task in many cases is to establish a place for the brand in individual shopping baskets or purchasing repertoires'[28] and 'a measure of absolute volume sales' is needed.

The MicroTest model is illustrated in Figure 8.2. Some of the inputs are self-explanatory (availability, advertising, brand visibility, concept acceptability, product acceptability, frequency of purchasing, weight of purchasing, fidelity), but others require definition.

Brand 'heritage' is an important factor *if* the new product is associated with a brand or manufacturer's name familiar to the respondent.

Experimentalism measures the respondent's predisposition to try a new brand at two levels. First, general willingness to try new brands is explored by asking attitudinal questions. Then, the respondent's likelihood of risking the purchase of a new brand in the particular product field in question is established as follows: respondents are shown cards listing recently launched brands and they are asked which they have bought and which they are currently using. This technique is appropriate to high-penetration product fields where micro-modelling is especially relevant.

Trial: Calculation of the probability of trial derives from the now substantial SENSOR databank and from other research projects including 'simulated shop purchasing'.

Adoption is 'a measure of penetration achieved in a time period relative

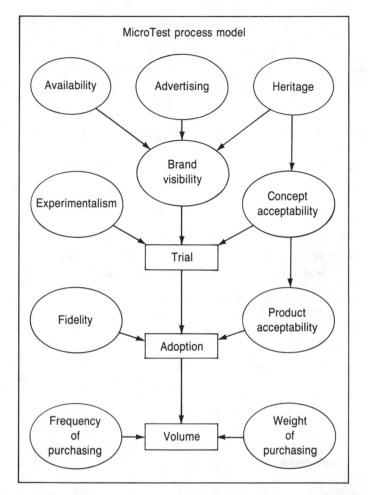

Source: B.C. Pymont, R.P. Morgan and J.R. Bond, 'The application of micro-modelling to predicting total market mix potential', *Journal of Marketing Management* vol. 3, no. 3 (1988)

**Figure 8.2
MicroTest
model**

to the usage rate of the product field', an important predictor of long-term volume for each respondent. 'The model compares the post-trial scores with the pre-trial ones and calculates the probability of adoption according to the differences between them.'[28]

Volume: Brand consumption of individual respondents is estimated by asking the following:

1. How often they ate/drank/used . . . a particular brand when it was in the house.
2. How often it was 'in-home'.

All predictive models depend not only on the inputs selected but also on the relative weights attached to these. Refinement of the model depends on access to databanks and on opportunities to try the model out. Large international research suppliers such as Research International and Burke have these opportunities.

8.5.4 The BASES simulated test-market system

The main difference between BASES and SENSOR is that BASES has the following features:

- It does not require a simulated 'test shop' purchase of a product 'as marketed'.
- It is a sales decomposition/recomposition model based on a diary panel concept — whereas SENSOR is two models — a simulated purchase model and a constant sum evaluation of a set of brands (evoked set).

In diary panel reconstruction 'no attempt is made to create a laboratory shop environment. Target respondents are shown concept material (print or TV commercial) for the test product alone. Only those expressing a positive interest to buy are given the product for in-home use. One recall interview is made'.[25]

In a 'convenience-food product' example discussed by Factor and Sampson the input data are classified as shown in Table 8.2.[25]

**Table 8.2
The input data;
total
parameterization**

1. **From the survey (before and after use)**
    (a) Purchase intention
    (b) Product evaluation
    (c) Value for money
    (d) Purchase frequency
    (e) Average number of units would purchase
    (f) Competitive/substitute usage.

2. **From management**
    (g) Distribution build across first four quarters and maximum distribution at end of years 1, 2 and 3
    (h) Awareness build (same)
    (i) Out-of-stock positions
    (j) Target market size (households)
    (k) Likely promotional activity, sampling scenarios

3. **Market-place variables**
    (l) Seasonality factor
    (m) Geographical factor
    (n) Category-development factor.

In order to provide the management input, marketing management must have access to trend data relating to the product field which the brand is to enter — data from retail audits/consumer panels/tracking studies; while tentative decisions about investment in the promotion of the brand will need to have been made. Most marketing companies operate in familiar markets, have access to trend data and are used to deriving forecasts and predictions from these. The research methods used to produce these 'input parameters' have been in use for a long time. The 'newer techniques that, though not infallible, are better able to meet management needs'[23] rely on intelligent choice of input parameters and decisions as to the form in which each input should be represented in the model. Computer technology makes it possible rapidly to try out many scenarios, such as the effect of different levels of distribution and awareness.

The simulated test markets discussed so far are also described as 'pre-test market models' because they are designed to precede, and possibly to obviate, testing in the open market. The case for/against testing in the open market is discussed in Chapter 10, 'Out in the open: the final go/no-go decision'. By this time the new brand will have attracted a substantial injection of company resources and once in the open it runs the risk of alerting the competition and, if unsuccessful, of dissipating retailer goodwill. BASES tracking for estimating sales in test market is discussed in Chapter 10, together with Frost International's Sandpiper, Research International's mini-test market and AMTES as pioneered by Michael Stewart.

8.6 Conclusion

In order to create effective advertising it is necessary to consider how advertising can work to further the marketing objective, and so to arrive at a definition of a specific advertising objective.

Given an adequate advertising appropriation, successful achievement of the advertising objective depends on a combination of effective media planning and the capacity to create persuasive advertisements.

Advertising is a substantial marketing cost, especially where branded consumer products are concerned. With considerable sums at stake (see Chapter 9) advertisers are not, as a rule, happy to take creative work entirely on trust; while advertising agents, including their creative staff, seek reassurance that they are on the right lines.

The usefulness of qualitative work to stimulate creative thinking and to try out ideas is generally accepted (see section 8.2.2). The external validity of creative pre-tests and the reliability of intermediate measures are often debated (see section 8.4).

It may be thought necessary to commit resources to an experiment in the field and to run this experiment for an adequate length of time to arrive at the forecast of response to the brand mix of formulation + presentation + communication (see Chapter 10). But the new information technology encourages the development of predictive models designed to reduce the need for overt experimentation in the field.

The predictive value of these models depends on corporate experience in the market, the existence of trend data and the care with which preliminary research, such as hall tests, is designed and interpreted. John Davis stresses:

> There is a need to remember the extent to which the results may be sensitive to changes in the inputs to the models. [However] under suitable conditions these Simulated Test Market procedures may be useful in eliminating non-starters, in helping to 'fine-tune' the brand mix, and they may make it possible to treat the conventional Test Market as the first phase of a rolling launch.[29]

Sources and further reading

1. D. Cowley, (ed.), *How to Plan Advertising*, (London: Cassell, in association with the Advertising Planning Group, 1987).
2. T. Prue, 'Where is the "scientific method" in the measurement of advertising effect?', *ADMAP* (Dec. 1987).
3. C. Channon, *Advertising Works*, 4th edn (London: Cassell for the IPA, 1987).
4. S. King, 'Can research evaluate the creative content of advertising?', *MRS Conference Papers* (1967).
5. S. King, 'What can pre-testing do?' *ADMAP* (Mar. 1968).
6. P. Sampson, Technical Director of Burke Marketing Research Ltd, in a letter to the author dated 13 Dec. 1984.
7. R.M. Worcester and E. Mansbridge, 'Tracking studies: basis for decision making', *Journal of The Market Research Society* (Oct. 1977).
8. E.K. Strong, *The Psychology of Selling* (Maidenhead: McGraw-Hill, 1925).
9. R.H. Colley, *Defining Advertising Goals for Measured Advertising Results* (New York: Association of National Advertisers, 1961).
10. R.J. Lavidge and G.A. Steiner, 'A model for predictive measurement of advertising effectiveness', *Journal of Marketing* (1961).
11. L. Festinger, *A Theory of Cognitive Dissonance* (Stanford: Stanford University Press, 1957).
12. A.S.C. Ehrenberg, *Repeat-buying: Theory and Applications* (Amsterdam: North-Holland, 1972).
13. T. Corlett, 'How can we monitor the influences of advertising campaigns on consumers' purchasing behaviour?' MRS Conference (1977).
14. M. Fishbein, *Readings: Attitude Theory and Measurement* (New York: John Wiley, 1967).
15. M. Tuck, *How do we Choose? A Study in Consumer Behaviour* (London: Methuen, 1976).

16. G. de Groot, 'Changes in consumer attitudes and behaviour and its consequences for marketing and research in the 1980s', MRS conference (1980).

17. W.A. Twyman, 'Designing advertising research for marketing decisions', MRS conference (1973).

18. T. Joyce, 'What do we know about the way advertising works?', ESOMAR seminar (Amsterdam: ESOMAR, 1967).

19. S. King, *Developing New Brands*, 1st edn (London: J. Walter Simpson, 1973).

20. S. Broadbent (ed.), 'Advertising works', 1 and 2, in *Cases from the IPA Advertising Effectiveness Awards* (London: Holt, Rinehart and Winston, 1981). Awards were made in 1980, 1982, 1986 and 1988.

21. S. King, 'Applying research to decision-making', *MRS Newsletter*, no. 208 (July 1983), pp. 28–33.

22. D.H. Schmalensee, 'Today's top priority advertising research questions', *Journal of Advertising Research*, vol. 23, no. 2 (Apr./May 1983), pp. 49–60.

23. P. Sampson, 'BASES: a way ahead for new product development', *ADMAP* (Nov. 1983), pp. 594–600.

24. S. Godfrey and J. Wilkinson, 'Predicting the sales potential of new products: a review of current methods and their applicability to different new product types', ESOMAR Congress, Barcelona (Amsterdam: ESOMAR, 1983), pp. 45–66.

25. S. Factor and P. Sampson, 'Decisions about launching new products', *Journal of The Market Research Society*, vol. 25, no. 2 (1983).

26. G. Coulson, 'Total package (or marketing mix) research for a new brand', supp. on new product development to *MRS Newsletter* (March 1980).

27. K. Clarke and M. Roe, 'The marketing mix test: relating expectations and performance', MRS conference (1977).

28. B.C. Pymont, R.P. Morgan and J.R. Bond, 'The application of micro-modelling to predicting total market mix potential', *Journal of Marketing Management*, vol. 3, no. 3 (1988).

29. E.J. Davis, *Experimental Marketing* (London: Nelson, 1970).

See also

- S. Godfrey, 'The Sensor simulated test market system', *ADMAP* (Oct. 1983), pp. 534–40.

- G. Greenway and G. de Groot, 'The qualitative–quantitative dilemma: what's the question?' (a case history demonstrating the integration of qualitative and quantitative research in the definition of creative strategy and the guidance of creative expression), *MRS Conference Papers*, 1983, pp. 437–63.

- S. King, *Developing New Brands*, 2nd edn (London: J. Walter Thompson, 1984).

- P. Kotler, in Kassarjian and Robertson (eds), *Perspectives in Consumer Behaviour* (Glenview, Illinois: Scott, Foresman, 1973).

- *Market Researchers Look at Advertising*, ESOMAR papers 1949–79 (Oct. 1983), which includes M. Tuck, 'Practical frameworks for advertising research' (1971).

- M. Sutherland and J. Galloway, 'Role of advertising: persuasion or agenda setting', *Journal of Advertising Research*, vol. 21, no. 5 (Oct. 1981), pp. 25–9.

Problems

1. 'In the advertising business we all know that the ultimate test of any advertising campaign is the sales result to which it contributes'. Does this statement imply that attempts to pre-test advertising campaigns are irrelevant?

2. 'Consumption decisions are a vital source of the *culture* of the time. . . . The individual uses consumption *to say something* about himself and his family and his locality'. Does this statement by an anthropologist answer the question, 'what makes advertising work?'

3. A marketing company, fearing 'me too' action by competitors, is hesitating to test-market a shampoo which includes an ingredient to improve hair 'rinsibility' after shampooing. You have been asked to review and evaluate the method(s) whereby the impact of the total mix (formulation, package, price and communication) might be assessed without alerting the competition. Propose a suitable research design.

Conveying the brand message: media planning

UK advertisers spend over £3,000 million a year on advertising in national newspapers, consumer magazines and on television (60 per cent on television, 30 per cent in national newspapers, 10 per cent in consumer magazines). It is not surprising that the advertising industry (advertisers, advertising agents and media owners) finance carefully designed and expensive research into the reading and viewing habits of the UK population. Radio, posters, cinema and cable are also monitored but not so continuously as the main national media.

The media scene has been fluid during the 1980s and there are more changes to come, especially for television research. With new printing techniques press media, especially magazines, have proliferated and this faced the Joint Industry Committee responsible for the National Readership Survey with a challenge. This challenge was met in 1984 when, after a carefully controlled experiment, the list of NRS publications was extended from some 120 titles to 200, necessitating a change in questioning technique.

Measurement of television audiences (BBC plus ITV, C4, S4C) and of viewers' reactions to television programmes is currently (Nov. 1988) controlled by the Broadcasters' Audience Research Board (BARB), which is jointly owned by the Independent Television Association and the BBC. The contract for the audience-measurement service is held by Audits of Great Britain (AGB), while the BBC's Broadcasting Research Department, acting for BARB, provides the audience-reaction service.

The government's (Nov. 1988) white paper, *Broadcasting in the 90s: Competition, Choice and Quality*, envisages the following changes to the current broadcasting structure:

- An Independent Television Commission (ITC) takes over from the IBA and the Cable Authority and assumes control of Direct Broadcasting by Satellite (DBS).
- The ITC's role is that of a licensing authority.
- Licences are awarded for ten years (and may be renewed) to the highest bidder subject to limited conditions.
- ITV becomes Channel 3 and the current regional structure is open to review.

- A fifth terrestrial channel opens by 1993.
- Government-licensed British Satellite Broadcasting (BSB) launches three satellite channels in 1989.

Independent Television Commission

Terrestrial channels	*Cable*	*Satellite channels*
3 4 5	(currently available in 11 areas, mostly S.E.)	BSB 3 channels

BARB will be reviewed in 1991 when the AGB contract lapses. It is probable that the distinction between 'audience measurement' and 'audience reaction' shown in Figure 9.1, 'The structure of BARB', will be retained (the BBC's contract does not run out until 1996), but that the representation of broadcasting interests will be expanded. Direct satellite broadcasting (DSB) will, of course, be represented on the board as will cable television.

The immediate future is likely to bring new television options to UK advertisers and to viewers — a fifth terrestrial channel, more cable franchises, three BSB channels. BSB's satellite is due to start transmitting by the end of 1992; meanwhile, the Luxembourg consortium which owns Astra is leasing broadcasting facilities to Murdoch, Maxwell and other entrepreneurs of television packages. Will the revenue generated by advertising and subscription, (and the licence for the time being in the case of the BBC), be sufficient to meet programming requirements?

It is unlikely that either satellite broadcasting or cable will account for a substantial share of advertisers' UK budgets for some time: but the need to monitor developments is critical. At an ESOMAR seminar held in April 1988, media experts faced the research-design problems that arrival of DSB will bring. Twyman, in his paper 'Towards a European standard for television audience measurement', points out that 'satellite by direct reception will be expensive initially and is likely to be scattered thinly across all geographical areas cable will grow on a highly specific localised basis as new generation cable is laid'.[1] We shall be better able to appreciate the audience-measurement problems presented by small, scattered and diverse audiences after we have considered the research methods used in the United Kingdom to collect the data on which media planning, monitoring and assessment are based.

Research is commissioned by BARB for television, by the Joint Industry Committee for National Readership Surveys for the NRS, and by JICRAR for radio-audience research. Cable-audience research and research into traffic-past posters are also controlled by joint industry committees. The data may be collected in face-to-face interviews, as for the National Readership Survey; by means of metered sets and peoplemeters, as in AGB's panel operation for BARB; in self-completion structured diaries such as those annotated by members of the Broadcasting Research Department (BRD) television opinion panel or by means of a pencil-and-paper diary together with a VDU and electronic transmission as in one of the diary methods studied by the Diary Panel Technical Study Group for JICNARS. Self-completion diaries are also used in radio-audience research. The data may be collected continuously throughout the year as for the NRS and BARB; or for limited periods as has been the case of JICRAR for Independent Radio. More options will fragment the viewing audience (and the listening one). This will aggravate the problem of sample size. Will research budgets be adequate? Would not a European Standard for Television Audience Measurement[1] help to reduce pressure on research budgets?

At this point it may be helpful to refer back to Figure 8.1, 'Stages in the development of an advertising campaign', and to get familiar with the media terminology currently in use (see pp. 238–40).

9.1 What the media planner needs to know

The media planner will, of course, need to know the advertising objectives as agreed between client and agency. He/she will, more specifically, need the information listed in the following paragraphs.

Definition of the target in the market

Demographic characteristics of the target are of first importance because most of the industry data are classified by sex, social grade, age group, whether a housewife and by region. The Target Group Index (TGI) is a useful source because it relates product/service and brand choice to 'media consumption' (see section 11.2.2).

The JICNARS data include classification of readers by a range of lifestyle indicators: 'car-owning households', 'chief petrol-buyers', 'owners of cheque books', 'holiday takers', etc. Ownership of a range of durables is also recorded. The BARB data are based on the standard demographics. As we saw in Chapter 6, a market segment is not viable unless it is accessible and in consumer markets this means accessible through the media. For media planning purposes it is necessary to translate psycho-graphic classifications and product-use classifications into demographic terms. In order to do this, it is necessary to record respondents' demographic and product use characteristics when collecting data about their wants, perceptions and attitudes.

Regional strengths and weaknesses

A brand may be more successful in, say, London, and south-east ITV areas than in the north-west, Yorkshire and the north-east. This may be peculiar to the brand or it may apply to the product field as a whole. Given variation in share by area the media planner needs to know whether the advertising objective is to be achieved by building on strength, counteracting weakness or by means of a judicious combination of the two.

The decision will influence the allocation of the media appropriation as between areas and it may determine the choice of media category. Television and the regional press, together with radio, posters and cinema can be scheduled on a regional basis. In general, national newspapers and magazines are not so flexible (though special arrangements can sometimes be made in test markets).

Seasonal nature of the product

Given a product or service with seasonal appeal the tactical decision 'from strength' or 'against weakness' still applies when allocating the appropriation. Should we concentrate expenditure in the high season or seek to extend demand by showing the product (which might be soup or ice cream) to be appropriate outside its season: for example by popularizing ice cream as a year-round pudding.

The nature of the creative task

If the product has a demonstrable benefit, use of the television medium is indicated. Television is a 'natural' for the advertising of gas for cooking because, among fuels, gas alone offers the immediate control, up or down, which cooks need on occasion.

On the other hand television is a less discriminating medium than the print media, especially magazines which can be selected for the special interest, authority or ambience conveyed by their editorial content and presentation.

The competitive advertising

How much the competition is spending and in what media can be monitored by subscribing to MEAL (Media Expenditure Analysis Limited) or the Media Register; or deduced for television from the BARB weekly reports. Confrontation or guerilla warfare? For a major advertiser the decision is likely to be confrontation: but it may be possible to plan a schedule which sidesteps the competition while offering effective reach, or coverage, of the target.

The size of the appropriation

This is usually determined in advance of media planning but in the rare cases where an unmodified 'objective and task' method is being used to determine the appropriation, the media planner will play an important part in fixing the appropriation. Whether the appropriation is laid down or arrived at in consultation with the media planner, the criterion of success in media planning is the achievement of the optimum mix of

reach (or coverage) $\times$ frequency $\times$ length/size

the last being influenced by creative considerations (see section 9.2).

Conversion, reinforcement or both

This basic objective will affect how the appropriation is laid out over time. When a brand is launched, frequent appearances in the media, longer commercials and larger spaces may all be used to achieve penetration of the market in the shortest possible time so that the brand breaks even and makes a profit as soon as possible. With an established brand, reinforcement of existing usage may be more critical and a steady 'drip' rather than a 'burst' be required. Or there might be a case for combining the two, bursts linked by drips. It all depends on where the brand stands in its life cycle, the size of the appropriation and the advertising task. (One part of the task may be to ensure shelf space for the brand.)

9.2   Achieving cost-effectiveness

It will help us to appreciate the relevance of the audience research data if we consider what planning for cost-effectiveness involves before summarizing the content of the reports and the methods used to collect the data.

It is comparatively easy to program a computer to rank media vehicles according to their coverage of the target market, and to relate coverage to rate-card cost.

It is comparatively easy to program a computer to tell us how many opportunities to see our advertisement can be bought with a given sum of money in a list of possible media.

The task gets more formidable when we seek to take account of duplication between, say, television and print media, or between newspapers and magazines, or between the individual publications we are considering for a particular schedule. The National Readership Survey provides valuable input data about duplication as between the readers of different publications, and the survey collects information about ITV viewing and about listening to local radio (LR). These data indicate the intensity with which readers of specific newspapers and magazines also view television or listen to radio.

But to achieve cost-effectiveness it is necessary to consider whether the opportunities being given to the target market to receive the advertising message are likely to be taken, and the probabilities will, of course, vary as between the broad media categories and as between the specific publications and viewing times being considered.

Whether or not the opportunities to see are effective and the message is received depends on the following:

- The frequency with which the advertisement appears.
- The period of time over which it appears.
- The frequency with which target readers see issues of publications and viewers view.
- The creative impact achieved by the campaign.

If the creative work effectively conveys the product benefit, and if the media planning has been successfully focused on the target consumers in the market, we can expect selective perception to work in our favour.

The model developed by Dr Simon Broadbent may help to concentrate our minds:[2] he uses the expression 'valued impressions per pound' (VIP) (compare Kotler's 'rated exposures'.[3])

$$VIP = \frac{\text{coverage of the target} \times \text{market weight(s)} \times \text{media weight(s)}}{\text{cost (£)}}$$

Let us consider the individual inputs in turn:

Coverage of the target

If we are advertising to a middle class ABC_1 audience, we can ignore C_2DE readers or viewers when relating coverage to cost.

Market weights

We may want to refine our estimate of effective coverage by taking account of the relative importance of groups in the target market. A company marketing baby food might well be particularly interested in reaching women aged 15–34. But older women sometimes have babies; also, as experienced mothers, older women may influence the decisions of younger women. Here it would be reasonable to apply a weight of 1 to the prime target, women aged 15–34, but to discount the value of reading/viewing of older women by applying a weight of, say, 0.5 to the reading/viewing coverage recorded for them.

Media weights

The chance of an advertising campaign attracting the attention of members of the target group is clearly influenced by the readership of the publications on the schedule among members of the target group and, in the case of television, by their viewing habits. We can allow for the frequency with which respondents claim to read, view and listen when programming VIP and can apply weights to this end.

As we shall see, however, reading and viewing are ambiguous concepts in media research. Reading a publication can mean anything between reading it from beginning to end and glancing through it, while those recorded as viewing during our time slot may well miss our 30-second commercial.

We are on debatable ground when we attempt to weight media vehicles according to the probability that they will actually convey the message to the target group. In fact it is only worthwhile attempting to apply weights to take account of the probability of opportunities to see being taken if sound normative data are available.

If an advertiser is established in a particular product field, if campaign penetration has been monitored regularly in terms of recognition or awareness levels achieved, and if it is possible to relate this achievement to individual media vehicles, then there might be a case for giving good carriers of the message preferential weights in the computer programming.

Weighting for ambience and/or authority is even more debatable since the weights are determined by judgement, unless post-exposure campaign monitoring has yielded statistical data sufficiently robust to warrant this refinement.

Cost

This is not necessarily the rate-card cost. Indeed for print media it might pay us to run the computer program using market weights only and to use the resultant ranking of newspapers and magazines as a bargaining counter.

In 1987 total advertising expenditure, excluding direct mail, was £5,781 million (Table 9.1). Expenditure on the national press (national newspapers and consumer magazines) was £1,258,000 and on television £1,872,000, making a national advertising total of £3,130,000. Regional press accounts for £1,280,000. As the percentage breakdown shows, television is the dominating medium, while poster and transport, together with radio and cinema act as 'support media'.

**Table 9.1
'Adspend' in
1987**

Total advertising expenditure (excluding direct mail) by medium (% of £5,781 m)−1987		
National press:		
National newspapers	16.6	
Consumer magazines	5.2	21.8
Regional newspapers		22.1
Business and professional,		
(including directories)		12.4
(Press production costs		5.3)
Television		32.4
Poster and transport		3.7
Radio		1.9
Cinema		0.4 100.0

Source: A A Advertising Statistics Yearbook 1987

9.3 Television-audience research

9.3.1 BARB: objectives and structure

The independent television companies need to monitor audiences in order to sell time to advertisers and their agents, while the publicly accountable BBC needs audience figures when negotiating the licence fee on which it still depends. The audience ratings indicate the relative popularity of programmes and aid scheduling decisions. But these descriptive data do not meet an important requirement of the 1977 Annan Committee on the Future of Broadcasting which preceded the setting up of BARB (Figure 9.1). The Annan Report deprecates 'the treadmill of audience measurement' and stresses the need to evaluate the responses of viewers to programmes.[4]

Under BARB the audience-measurement contract is held until 1991 by AGB, who have been recording television viewing since the arrival of commercial television. There has been a substantial technological

**Figure 9.1
The structure
of BARB**

Broadcasters' Audience Research Board
BBC + ITVA

'Head counting'	Finance	'Evaluation'
Audience-measurement	Finance	Audience-reaction
management committee	sub-committee	management committee
BBC, ITV, C4, S4C*, TV-AM	BBC + ITVA	BBC, IBA, ITV, C4, S4C*
IPA, ISBA		

*The Welsh Channel 4

investment in this field. The audience-reaction data are collected and processed for BARB by the BBC's Broadcasting Research Department. The corporation set up a department to monitor audiences and their reactions as early as 1936. The BARB contract comes up for review in 1991, and a new government white paper on the future of broadcasting has just been published (November 1988).[4]

9.3.2 BARB's electronic audience-measurement service

The one-set family is fast becoming a thing of the past. Over 40 per cent of households now have more than one television set, while one in three have a video cassette recorder (VCR) (see Table 9.2). A system was required which had:

> first the ability to measure multi-set usage more efficiently and in finer detail; second, some measure of how the VCR was used, particularly showing whether live programmes were being watched using the VCR as a tuner, or whether recorded materials were being viewed. Third and most important of all, some means of measuring individual viewing was required as the fragmentation of viewing and the growth of multi-set households made the old diary technique increasingly incapable of following the more complex viewing habits of different members of the household.[5]

AGB met the challenge by equipping every domestic set with a 'slave' meter. The slave meters communicate with a master meter through the existing electrical mains. The master meter is linked to the domestic telephone line and the day's electronic data are passed every night to the AGB computers 'which can and do have the viewing figures processed on the following morning'.[5]

Recording of the viewing of individuals is by means of the peoplemeter, a remote-controlled push-button device which communicates with the master meter.

Metering of VCRs has made it possible to distinguish between use as a tuner for viewing at the scheduled programme time and use as a

Household penetration (%)	1976	1980	1986
Colour sets	44	62	88
Multi-set H/H	7	22	43
VCR	—	2	36
Remote control	—	9	37
Teletext	—	—	15

Table 9.2 Changes in TV characteristics (UK)

Source: S. Buck 'Television audience measurement research — yesterday, today and tomorrow', *Journal of the Market Research Society*, vol. 29, no. 3 (July 1987).

recording device. The meters at present in use in the United Kingdom are unable to identify the content of playback from video recordings. However, a new generation of meters 'fingerprints' the signal for a programme recorded off-air with a day and time code which enables the content to be identified when the tape is played back. Meters of this type are already in use in the United States and in a number of European countries, and one version has been tested in the United Kingdom.

Sample design

The sample design and data collection method used by AGB for BARB has three advantages:

1. Electronic observation is less susceptible to mistaken recording than 'day-after' recall.
2. Audience measurements are very soon available to those who need them.
3. When the same, or virtually the same, sample is being surveyed every day of the week the trend data are less susceptible to sampling variation than would be the case if a different sample were recruited in respect of each day's viewing.

The AGB design, based on area panels of television homes, makes it possible to monitor the dynamics of television viewing using comparatively small samples, always provided that the panels are representative of the survey populations area by area and that panel membership remains reasonably loyal. The cost of the hi-tech electronic methodology developed by AGB makes sample size a critical consideration.

The Establishment Survey

Before setting up panels to monitor television viewing and in order to control the panels it is necessary to establish the reception and viewing characteristics of the thirteen television regions into which the United Kingdom is divided, i.e. it is necessary to define the survey population. A large-scale survey ($n = 25,000$) is carried out once a year.

The Establishment Survey does the following:

• Defines the geographic area reached by each transmitter and delimits overlap areas served by more than one (an important marketing consideration) (Table 9.3).

Area	Profile net of overlap %	Area	Profile net of overlap %
London	19.95	North-East	5.16
Midland	15.20	East	6.41
North-West	11.91	South-West	2.87
Yorkshire	10.26	Ulster	2.26
Central Scotland	6.10	Border	1.17
Wales and West	7.59	North Scotland	2.09
South and South-East	9.03	Network	100.00

Table 9.3 Distribution of ITV homes

Source: JWT Media Research Unit, media information card (Spring 1988)

- Records the number of homes with TV and the number of sets in each home.
- Records the penetration of VCRs and of remote-control pads, together with data about ancillary uses such as teletext.
- Collects data about the demographic characteristics of household viewers, family size, incidence of children, age, social economic status of the head of the household; and about the intensity of BBC and ITV viewing.

Intensity of viewing is an important panel control. Viewers are assigned to high, medium and low viewing categories according to the number of days in an average week, and the number of hours in an average day, they say that they view BBC and IBA television.

The Establishment Survey contributes to the making of marketing plans because it establishes regional variations in the viewing population and 'the viewing population' is in effect 'the total population' since 98 per cent of households have television. But its primary purpose is to give credence to the data derived from the viewing panels by defining the regions they represent and providing a pool of addresses. The area panels vary in size from 100 for Ulster, Border and North Scotland to 350 for London, 380 for south and south-east which includes the Channel Islands. In the week ending 9 October 1988 the reporting panel samples totalled 3,030.

The weekly reports

BARB issues two weekly reports to subscribers, a green volume and a blue volume. The data are also available on line, in many cases via

Donovan Data Systems, who host all the major media series for most of the advertising agencies (see p. 236 below).

The green report lists the following by day of the week within area:

- Commercial spots in chronological order: time and duration (seconds), television ratings (TVR), homes viewing (000s).
- Programmes, ITV, Channel 4, BBC1 and BBC2 with numbers of homes and of individuals viewing for all four channels, with quarter-hour by quarter-hour breakdown for the commercial channels together with viewing rates.
- In addition, minute-by-minute TVR are shown graphically for the BBC stations as well as for ITV and Channel 4.

The blue report displays the data by day of the week within area by product field. Advertisers and their agents can see the following:

- How their 'adspend' compares with competitive spending and scheduling (always assuming rate-card charges operate!).
- How effectively their campaign is reaching its target, given the demographic classifications used in the report, and assuming that target individuals are actually viewing when their commercials are screened.

The audience is defined as housewives, adults, men and children. More detailed demographic data are in the databank, but sample size becomes a consideration when broad categories are broken down.

The BARB audience-measurement service is a very sophisticated head-counting operation, but the lifestyle dimension is missing (see, for example, J. Whitehead on 'BARB: the last geodemographic hurdle').[6]

Conclusion

The BARB Audience-Measurement Service is based on a considerable investment in the electronic collection and rapid processing of viewing data. It is primarily designed to meet the advertising industry's need for a reputable currency. The service is open to attack from two directions:

1. Increased opportunities to choose among programmes and the growing popularity of VCRs, leading to fragmentation of programme viewing.
2. The movement away from mass to target marketing.

The way in which VCRs are used is particularly critical from the marketing point of view. Is the VCR being used to store television programmes as broadcast? Are the commercials on record? If so, will they be seen close to the date on which they were broadcast and in the day-of-the-week, time-of-day context in which it was planned they should be seen? 'Presence' remains a critical question when advertising campaigns are monitored.

The advertiser buys opportunities for his campaign to be seen. There is no guarantee that the audience represented by his/her TVR purchase will be present and watching when his campaign is screened; and no certainty that the audience recorded was entirely present and watching when the advertisements were shown.

The introduction of the peoplemeter has improved the quality of the data relating to the viewing of panel members, for with the push-button handset the presence of the individual viewer is electronically recorded as viewing takes place. Nevertheless, there is always the chance that a panel member will leave the room during a commercial break without pressing his or her button on the handset. However, 'a set of display lights indicates to the family what data has been recorded and is used as a reminder device to ensure that the data are correct.'[7] Any attempt to establish actual, as opposed to potential, presence necessarily involves us in research studies designed to measure the impact of advertising campaigns using such measures as 'recognition' and 'awareness' in *ad hoc* studies, tracking studies or by subscription to a service such as TABS (tracking advertising and brand strength). We return to the subject in Chapter 11.

9.3.3   BARB television opinion panel (BRD)

The sample

The BBC's Broadcasting Research Department operates the television opinion panel for BARB. Electronic observation is a reliable method for counting viewers but it leaves questions unanswered about their responses and opinions.

BRD has been operating an audience reaction service for BARB since 1982. The service was expanded in March 1986 and the data now derive from panel samples large enough 'to meet the needs of all BARB broadcasters — including the regionally based ITV companies and Channel 4'.[8]

There is a national panel of 3,000, on which the thirteen ITV regions are represented according to population size (from thirty-four panellists for Border to 571 for Thames/LWT); and regional panels, on which numbers are boosted to 500 for each region. The national panel reports once a week; the regional panels once every four weeks. Panellists sign on for a maximum of two years. The average response rate each week is 65 per cent and, when recruiting, it is estimated that 100 letters will be required to generate sixty panel members.

The panels are administered by post, but the source of names and addresses is the BRD Daily Survey of Viewing and Listening based on 1,000 face-to-face interviews a day, during which the characteristics of respondents are recorded. Data from four weeks' interviewing are used, providing a base for the television opinion panel of some 28,000 names and addresses.

These names and addresses are derived from a sample of constituencies stratified by BBC and ITV region and by ACORN type. Within constituencies wards and streets are drawn with probability proportionate to size using a fixed interval from a random start: i.e. the sampling points are randomly located. Stratification by ACORN type obviates the need to set social-grade quotas. Age, sex and, for adults, working status are quota-controlled. In other words, the bank of addresses used for the television opinion panel is carefully drawn to be representative of the population — aged twelve and over.

The names drawn within each area are distributed among an eighteen-cell matrix, (3 × 3 × 2):

Groups

Total weight of viewing (hours viewed per week)	= 3
Channel preference (hours ITV/Channel 4 viewed out of 10)	= 3
Social class (ABC_1/C_2DE)	= 2

This matrix controls the national panel and each of the regional panels.

There are in addition four marginal controls: sex, age, presence of children and size of household. The panels are tightly controlled to ensure that they are representative of the viewing public and so that they yield comparable data.

The data

These are collected in a pair of booklets designed to cover seven days' programmes, running from Monday to Sunday. The national panel receives these booklets every week, the regional panels every fourth week. The programme diary lists programmes alongside a six-point rating scale on which the panellist marks his/her evaluation of the programme. The second booklet asks more detailed specific questions about selected programmes.

The appreciation index (AI)

Panelists are asked to watch as they would normally watch and to rate the programme watched (see Table 9.4). The attitude statement 'interesting and/or enjoyable' embraces two measures of appreciation and the statement is, on the face of it, asking two questions in one. The statement is flexible, because panelists may be rating an information programme (in which case 'interesting' is particularly relevant) or an

6 =	5 =	4 =	3 =	2 =	1 =
Extremely interesting and/or enjoyable	Very interesting and/or enjoyable	Fairly interesting and/or enjoyable	Neither one thing nor the other	Not very interesting and/or enjoyable	Not at all interesting and/or enjoyable

Table 9.4 The appreciation index

To sum the panellist's appreciation of a particular programme positions on the scale are scored as follows:

100	80	60	40	20	0

The AI is calculated by dividing the total score for each programme by the total number of panellists reporting.

entertainment programme (when 'enjoyable' is a more suitable measure of appreciation).

Validity of the standard AI question was tested in 1981 in the north-east region for the IBA, which pioneered this questioning technique.[9] The experimental design was a monadic one using three parallel random samples of 250−500 adults: one experimental group rated programmes on a six-point scale ranging from 'extremely interesting' to 'not at all interesting'; another on a six-point scale ranging from 'extremely enjoyable' to 'not at all enjoyable'; while the third was asked the standard AI question.

All three groups were asked to score their reactions during the same period of time: i.e. the same mixture of informative and of entertaining programmes was available to the three groups. Their responses to the three different attitude statements have been averaged in Table 9.5.

	Information programme	Entertainment programme
Interesting index	74%	69%
Entertainment index	66%	71%
Appreciation index	74%	72%

Table 9.5 Validity of the standard AI question

Source: A.S.C. Ehrenberg, G.J. Goodhardt and D.S. Kerr, 'Two notes on television audience appreciation and audience behaviour', *ADMAP* (May 1982) pp. 308−11

In a paper which won the prize for the best technical paper at the MRS 1987 conference ('Audience appreciation: a different story from audience numbers')[10] Peter Menneer demonstrated the following:

- AIs are a crucial and necessary complement to estimates of audience size in evaluating channel and programme performance.

- AIs average at about 75. Twenty per cent of programmes are high performers exceeding AIs of 80; 20 per cent yield AIs below 70.
- AIs have a useful value in predicting and later explaining a series' audience delivery.

Menneer concluded: 'Measures of audience appreciation are important in helping to sustain the range of programmes we are accustomed to find available to us. By contrast in the USA, in the ideal world of perfect competition, numbers alone call the shots.' At present (Nov. 1988) the AI data are regularly supplied to the BBC and the independent television companies but not to media planners in advertising agencies.

9.4 The JICNARS data

The JICNARS objective is as follows:

> to provide such information, acceptable to both publishers of print media and buyers of space, as will be relevant to the assessment and efficient use of the medium. Among possible measures, this requires providing a basis for estimating the numbers and kinds of people likely to receive different patterns of potential exposure to the advertisements inserted in individual publications or combinations of publications.[11]

The expressions 'likely to receive' and 'potential exposure' remind us that 'reading' can mean anything from 'reading closely' to 'just looking at': i.e. that the readership measures represent opportunities, as with television-audience measurement. The JICNARS Meaning of Reading Technical Study Group has published on this critical subject.[12]

The National Readership Survey data derive from a meticulously designed probability sample representative of the adult population of Great Britain aged fifteen and over. The fieldwork and analysis are subcontracted, to Research Services Limited.

The data are collected throughout the year and care is taken to timetable interviews so that seasonal and day-of-the-week fluctuations in the reading of newspapers and periodicals are represented in the results.

During the first half of 1984 an experiment was made to see whether it would be possible to extend the media list from some 120 items to about 200 using a different method of data collection. The extended media-list experiment was judged a success. The first NRS report using the new data-collection method was published in September 1984. This report was based on readership data averaged over the first half of 1984. The first report based on a full year's figures was published in March 1985.

In his Introduction to vol. 1 (1987), the JICNARS director, James Rothman, emphasizes:

Because of the change in interviewing method, estimates of changes over time should not be formed by comparing results after 1983 with those for earlier years.

This section on the JICNARS data does the following:

- Considers the probability sampling procedure used to contact readers of newspapers and magazines.
- Describes the 'grouped titles technique' now used to establish what readers read and how frequently they do so.
- Looks at the case for readership panels.
- Discusses the value of the NRS as a source of demographic and lifestyle information about the reading public.
- Seeks to establish relationships between reading habits and exposure to other media.

9.4.1 Sampling procedure

The sampling procedure is described in detail in an appendix to the NRS report, which is normally published twice a year, each report being based on a year's data collection. This is a useful source for anyone studying sample design.

The NRS data are based on a stratified probability/random sample drawn in two stages ($n = 28,500$): at the first stage enumeration districts are drawn within wards, at the second stage individual adults aged fifteen and over within enumeration districts.

First stage

All the wards in Great Britain are sorted into thirty-nine geographical groupings. This constitutes the sampling frame. The geographical groupings are formed by interlacing ISBA (Incorporated Society of British Advertisers) areas with Registrar General's Planning Regions. The wards are listed within each of these thirty-nine survey regions in such a way that, when a fixed interval is applied to a random start, variations in intensity of evening newspaper readership and in social grade are duly represented (see section 4.2.1 on drawing with PPS using implicit stratification). The social-grade indicator used is the number of economically active males in managerial and supervisory occupations in each ward divided by the total economically active male population. In 1987 1,728 wards were drawn from the stratified list, each ward having a probability of selection proportionate to its adult population. In the final sample each ward is represented by two enumeration districts, again drawn with PPS.

Within each of the thirty-nine geographical groupings, the profile by ACORN type of those enumeration districts drawn to represent the area in the sample, was compared with the profile of all the enumeration districts in the geographical group. Any imbalance was corrected.

Second stage

Individuals are systematically drawn from the electoral registers for the selected enumeration districts. The procedure described in section 4.2.2 is used to ensure that non-electors have a chance and a known chance of being included in the sample. The non-electors include adults aged between fifteen and eighteen.

9.4.2   The 'grouped-titles' technique

In May 1983 a new method of data collection was tested against the pre-1984 NRS method. The experimental design was as follows:

- Two matched samples representing the adult population.
- $n = 997$ for the new method, 992 for the standard method.
- Both samples drawn in the same sixty sampling points.
- To guard against interviewer bias, the same interviewer was used for both types of interview at all but three points.
- The 120 titles covered were identical for comparison purposes: there were seventy-one additional titles on the EML test.

The objectives of the extended media list[13] experiment were threefold.

1. To establish a design which would provide data for up to 200 titles.
2. To improve the stability of the readership estimates.
3. To attempt partial validation of readership claims.

The reasoning behind these objectives is as follows:

1. The Joint Industry Committee had been pressed to extend the media list. There has been a proliferation of magazine titles. A title is discriminated against if it is not included in the NRS tables. If one is included the rest of its kind must be included. 'In these days of narrow casting' there is a demand for data about a wider range of print media.
2. Using the pre-1984 method of questioning, titles were asked about in random order one at a time. The respondent did not see the subject group (or 'topic family') as a whole. 'Confronted with the long list, one title at a time (i.e. unrelated to the topic family), informants may just be unclear about whether they have heard of or recognise certain titles'; or they may plump for the first family member they meet in the interview, confusing, say, *Camera Choice* with *Camera Weekly*.

In addition, the frequency of 'reading' scale used pre-1984 related to the frequency with which the title was published. Making the mental switch from 'in an average month' (say) to 'in an average week' can confuse the respondent.

3. 'Reading a publication or looking through it is not a clear-cut un-ambiguous act as is, for example, buying a kilo of sugar or breaking a mirror. Different people will interpret reading (or "looking at") differently, and the *same* person may interpret the phrases differently in relation to different publication types e.g. "reading" the *Sun* versus "reading" *Car Mechanics*.'

The new questioning method has made it possible to record the penetration of a longer list of titles without increasing the length of the interview or decreasing response rates; and it definitely reduces order effects and so improves data stability. But exactly what 'reading' means remains open to question, although the experimental results confirm that the opportunities which the media planner schedules have been more reliably recorded.

The 'grouped-titles technique' is applied as follows in the EML experiment:

- Titles are sorted into thirty-eight topic families. Each family is represented by a card. On one side of the card the names are shown without the frequency scale, and on the other side they are shown with it (see Figure 9.2). No one card bears more than eight titles.
- The respondent sorts the cards into three piles, according to whether one (or more) of the titles on the card has been 'seen in the past year', 'not seen' or the respondent is 'not sure'. The 'not seen' cards are immediately eliminated, the 'not sures' probed. In most cases, the interview is based on nine out of the thirty-eight cards after this filtering process.

Figure 9.3 shows how the grouped-titles technique is introduced to the respondent and the care with which the interviewer is instructed. The filtering process is covered under Q.1 using side A of the show-card (Figure 9.2); frequency of reading titles 'read or looked at' during the past year, under Q.2 using side B of the show-card; average issue readership (AIR), 'the currency of press media planning', under Q.3 also using side B.

The definition of 'reading' remains all-inclusive:

> It doesn't matter who bought the publication, where you saw it or how old it was. Just so long as you can remember spending a couple of minutes reading or looking at *any* of the publications on a card it goes on this pile. (Figure 9.3, Q.1)

The difficulty remains of relating 'reading' to issues with specific cover dates. This could be done using a panel, but reading occasions would be limited to those occurring in the home where the date can be confirmed.

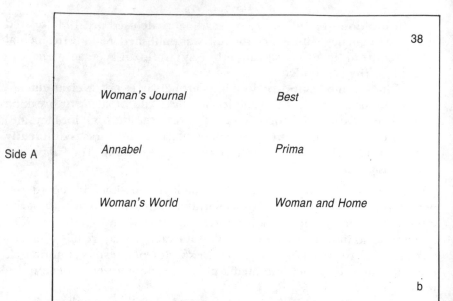

**Figure 9.2
The grouped-
titles
technique: two
sides of a
show-card**

In this example, 'b' and '38' relate to the procedure used to avoid order effects: 'b' refers to the rotation by type of publication, '38' to the placing of this topic family within the rotation.

In a volatile market it would be useful to have data related to specific issues; and to specific individuals over time, so that 'brand-switching' patterns could be extracted. In order to record the penetration of titles with modest circulations it would, however, be necessary to set up and maintain a large panel. The cost advantage offered by the lower sampling error is more apparent than real.

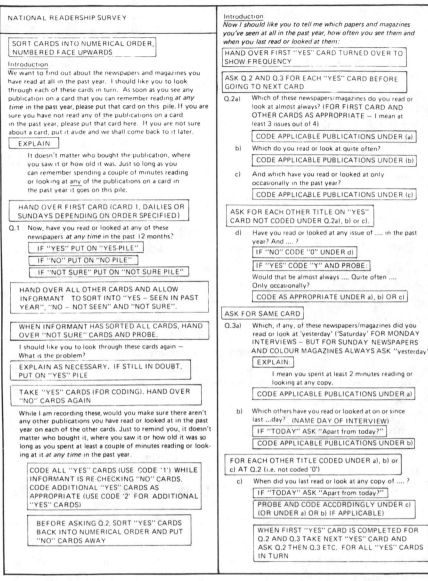

NATIONAL READERSHIP SURVEY

SORT CARDS INTO NUMERICAL ORDER, NUMBERED FACE UPWARDS

Introduction
We want to find out about the newspapers and magazines you have read at all in the past year. I should like you to look through each of these cards in turn. As soon as you see any publication on a card that you can remember reading *at any time* in the past year, please put that card on this pile. If you are sure you have not read any of the publications on a card in the past year, please put that card here. If you are not sure about a card, put it aside and we shall come back to it later.

EXPLAIN
It doesn't matter who bought the publication, where you saw it or how old it was. Just so long as you can remember spending a couple of minutes reading or looking at *any* of the publications on a card in the past year it goes on this pile.

HAND OVER FIRST CARD (CARD 1, DAILIES OR SUNDAYS DEPENDING ON ORDER SPECIFIED)

Q.1   Now, have you read or looked at any of these newspapers *at any time* in the past 12 months?

IF "YES" PUT ON "YES-PILE"
IF "NO" PUT ON "NO-PILE"
IF "NOT SURE" PUT ON "NOT-SURE PILE"

HAND OVER ALL OTHER CARDS AND ALLOW INFORMANT TO SORT INTO "YES – SEEN IN PAST YEAR", "NO – NOT SEEN" AND "NOT SURE".

WHEN INFORMANT HAS SORTED ALL CARDS, HAND OVER "NOT SURE" CARDS AND PROBE.

I should like you to look through these cards again – What is the problem?

EXPLAIN AS NECESSARY. IF STILL IN DOUBT, PUT ON "YES" PILE

TAKE "YES" CARDS (FOR CODING). HAND OVER "NO" CARDS AGAIN

While I am recording these, would you make sure there aren't any other publications you have read or looked at in the past year on each of the other cards. Just to remind you, it doesn't matter who bought it, where you saw it or how old it was so long as you spent at least a couple of minutes reading or looking at it *at any time* in the past year.

CODE ALL "YES" CARDS (USE CODE '1') WHILE INFORMANT IS RE-CHECKING "NO" CARDS. CODE ADDITIONAL "YES" CARDS AS APPROPRIATE (USE CODE '2' FOR ADDITIONAL "YES" CARDS)

BEFORE ASKING Q.2, SORT "YES" CARDS BACK INTO NUMERICAL ORDER AND PUT "NO" CARDS AWAY

Introduction
Now I should like you to tell me which papers and magazines you've seen at all in the past year, how often you see them and when you last read or looked at them:

HAND OVER FIRST "YES" CARD TURNED OVER TO SHOW FREQUENCY

ASK Q.2 AND Q.3 FOR EACH "YES" CARD BEFORE GOING TO NEXT CARD

Q.2a)   Which of these newspapers/magazines do you read or look at almost always? (FOR FIRST CARD AND OTHER CARDS AS APPROPRIATE – I mean at least 3 issues out of 4)

CODE APPLICABLE PUBLICATIONS UNDER (a)

b)   Which do you read or look at quite often?

CODE APPLICABLE PUBLICATIONS UNDER (b)

c)   And which have you read or looked at only occasionally in the past year?

CODE APPLICABLE PUBLICATIONS UNDER (c)

ASK FOR EACH OTHER TITLE ON "YES" CARD NOT CODED UNDER Q.2a), b) or c).

d)   Have you read or looked at any issue of .... in the past year? And .... ?

IF "NO" CODE "0" UNDER d)
IF "YES" CODE "Y" AND PROBE:

Would that be almost always .... Quite often .... Only occasionally?

CODE AS APPROPRIATE UNDER a), b) OR c)

ASK FOR SAME CARD

Q.3a)   Which, if any, of these newspapers/magazines did you read or look at 'yesterday' ('Saturday' FOR MONDAY INTERVIEWS – BUT FOR SUNDAY NEWSPAPERS AND COLOUR MAGAZINES ALWAYS ASK "yesterday")

EXPLAIN:
I mean you spent at least 2 minutes reading or looking at any copy.

CODE APPLICABLE PUBLICATIONS UNDER a)

b)   Which others have you read or looked at on or since last ...day?   (NAME DAY OF INTERVIEW)

IF "TODAY" ASK "Apart from today?"

CODE APPLICABLE PUBLICATIONS UNDER b)

FOR EACH OTHER TITLE CODED UNDER a), b) or c) AT Q.2 (i.e. not coded '0')

c)   When did you last read or look at any copy of .... ?

IF "TODAY" ASK "Apart from today?"

PROBE AND CODE ACCORDINGLY UNDER c) (OR UNDER a) or b) IF APPLICABLE)

WHEN FIRST "YES" CARD IS COMPLETED FOR Q.2 AND Q.3 TAKE NEXT "YES" CARD AND ASK Q.2 THEN Q.3 ETC. FOR ALL "YES" CARDS IN TURN

**Figure 9.3
The grouped-titles technique: introductory questions**

Source: NRS questionnaire form in use from 1 April 1988

The solution may be to run panels for discrete periods in order to add richness to the standard data, or to monitor the effect on reading habits of a strike, promotion or new launch.

9.4.3   The case for readership panels examined

The NRS data are moving annual averages published twice a year. The rolling sample of 28,500 adults amounts to just under 2,500 calls a month.

Given a stable print-media market and twice-a-year reporting, and the size of the sample in any one month would yield data adequate to the needs of media planners.

But the print media scene is now a volatile one and the battle to maintain, let alone increase, circulations encourages the use of promotions. Reading habits are in consequence disrupted.

In addition there has been a proliferation of titles to meet lifestyle interests; and publications with quite modest circulations are of moment to the media planner focusing on a closely defined target.

It is claimed that a readership panel would have the following advantages over the use of repeated surveys:

- Unequivocal trend data to monitor the impact of market forces.
- Frequent and quick reporting.
- Reduced sampling error, making possible a reduction in costs.
- The opportunity to relate respondents' reading to specific cover dates.

Average issue readership is especially in doubt where the less frequently published print media are concerned. Two kinds of error may occur: replicated readership, issues of an earlier cover date being returned as read in the period; and parallel readership, more than one new reading occasion in an 'issue period' being treated as one. A record of specific-issue readership could be achieved using a readership panel, because the panel could be required to record cover dates in their diaries; but there would still be doubt as to whether publications read outside the home had been correctly dated.

In 1985 the JICNARS Readership Diary Panel Technical Study Group commissioned research into three data-collection techniques:

1. A fully write-in diary, with a reference card showing the list of NRS titles.
2. A fully prompted diary, covering fifty titles, with different magazines listed for men and women.
3. An electronic view-data diary which could prompt the full NRS list of titles.[14]

Results of the three research studies indicated that the 'fully write-in diary' risked missing reading events which should have been recorded; the 'fully prompted' diary was less likely to miss reading events but the number of publications that can be covered in a prompt list diary is necessarily limited; an electronic view-data diary is less likely to miss reading events and it could cover the full list of NRS publications. But 'the cost of establishing (an electronic) panel which was sufficiently large to enable minority publications to be recorded accurately would be very high'. Rothman goes on:

It must be appreciated that the advantage the Press has over television is that advertising can be more closely targeted on particular audiences. A sample in the 10,000+ range is needed to pinpoint these audiences accurately.[14]

The electronic view-data technique was further explored in 1986 when AGB gave the JICNARS Technical Study Group access to the AGB cable and view-data panel, set up to monitor the launch of *Today*.[15]

The cable and view-data panel consisted of 1,210 individuals aged fifteen and over in 592 homes. For thirteen weeks (22 February to 23 May 1986) panel members were asked to keep a daily pencil-and-paper record of their readership of daily and Sunday newspapers, colour supplements and of six weekly magazines. Each household was equipped with a view-data terminal and panel members were required to transfer their week's readership records from diary to terminal on Saturday or Sunday, and so to the AGB host computer. Cross-checks on a sub-sample of the panel showed that most of the information was correctly transferred, although most panelists made at least one mistake.

After a detailed comparison between panel and NRS survey data, the following general conclusions were drawn:

- A panel could not supply measures of absolute readership levels as reliable as those supplied by the NRS based on a large sample.
- But the opportunities for 'week-on-week correlations in reading behaviour' meant that a panel could be a sensitive indicator of changes in reading behaviour. A panel could, for example, be a means of identifying successful marketing strategies, an important consideration at a time of new launches and promotional activity.
- Use of an electronic panel ensured rapid reporting of changes in the behaviour of panel members.

9.4.4   The NRS as a source of segmentation variables

The readership penetration tables in the NRS report are categorized as follows:

- Readership among all adults.
- Readership among heads of households/housewives (female).
- Readership among men.
- Readership among women.
- Readership among housewives (female).

Within these categories the survey population is classified with a richness of detail which interests sociologists as well as those in marketing. In addition to the familiar demographics the population is broken down as shown in Table 9.6. (These classifications may vary depending on the needs of subscribers.)

**Table 9.6
Readership
among special
groups**

Breakdown	Base
Petrol buyers, chief petrol buyers, heavy mileage	Adults/men
Terminal education age	Adults/men/women
Holiday takers, ownership of stocks and shares. Employment and occupational status	Adults
Income, tenure, car ownership, recent movers, possession of colour TV, telephone. Recent acquisition of selected consumer durables. Central heating, number of rooms	Heads of household/housewives
Sex, income, possession of power tool, tenure, number of full-time earners in household	Heads of household
Marital status, possession of power tool	Men
Marital status, working status, petrol buyers	Women
Possession of selected consumer durables, working status, household size, young children	Housewives

Source: NRS 1987

It should be remembered that the NRS is based on a stratified probability sample of substantial size and that disaggregated data are on tape, so that individual records can be correlated in many ways. The reliability of quota sampling in Great Britain owes much to the NRS as a source of quota specifications. The social-grade classifications, so widely used in quota sampling, derive from the NRS data.

In addition to the demographic and lifestyle analysis of the UK population published in the NRS reports, the NRS databank provides for special analyses by geodemographic type, Pinpoint's PIN and MOSAIC as well as ACORN; also by the SAGACITY life-stage groupings. These segmentation variables were discussed in Chapter 6 on market segmentation, and the point was made that to be viable a market segment must be measurable, large enough and accessible via point of sale and the media.

9.4.5   Inter-media relationships

In addition to establishing what kind of people read individual newspapers and magazines among a list of 200, and the numbers reading the average issue, the NRS questionnaire asks a number of questions about television viewing and radio listening. These questions probe the intensity of viewing/listening by channel or station and (for television) the equipment in use (number of sets, video recorder, remote control, video-disc player, teletext, access to subscription cable TV).

The data on file make it possible to correlate readership with listening and viewing. The TGI also has on file data about mixed-media habits. The NRS and the TGI data are of value for portraying longer-term trends when media plans are being made. But the data are collected over too long a period, and the reporting intervals are too wide, for the NRS and the TGI to reflect the effect on mixed-media habits of short-term marketing activities.

9.5 The support media

Radio, posters and cinema account for 6 per cent of total expenditure on display advertising. They are often used as local reminders of the national advertising message. As we have seen, the NRS questionnaire makes it possible to sort the population into categories according to the amount of their claimed listening to radio, and to the frequency with which they say they visit the cinema. Some of the data are included in the twice-a-year report; it is all available on the computer file and this is an important source for the support media.

9.5.1 The JICRAR data

The number of independent local radio stations increased from three in 1973 (a year after the Sound Broadcasting Act legalized independent radio broadcasting in the United Kingdom), to forty-two in 1983.[16] Between January and December 1987 the commercial network of forty-four stations reached on average 44 per cent of adults each week.[17] The number of stations is likely to increase.

Responsibility for measuring the radio audience lies with the Joint Industry Committee for Radio Audience Research (JICRAR). Cost of the research is borne by the radio stations and the contract has throughout been with Research Services of Great Britain (RSGB), a subsidiary of AGB. The JICRAR specification is summarized in the *Consumer Market Research Handbook* as follows:[18]

1. The use of radio-only diaries covering a seven-day time period.
2. Recording of listening to all radio — BBC and commercial.
3. Random samples of 1,000 or 800 individuals in each area.
4. Personal placement and collection of diaries by interviewers.
5. Response rates of 65 per cent or more.

6. The collection of listening behaviour quarter-hour by quarter-hour (with the exception of the night hours of midnight to 6 a.m. when half-hourly information was thought to be acceptable).
7. The collection by personal interview, at the diary-placement stage, of information about exposure to other media and broad radio-listening claims.

To aid station identification the type of programme broadcast by each station, together with its position on the wave band, is included in the diary, which is small enough to carry around in pocket or handbag.

Keeping the diary is simple enough (time-slots down the side, stations across the top): it is just a matter of marking off quarter-hours (or half-hours between midnight and 6 a.m.). But keeping a diary does, of course, make listeners more conscious of their listening.

It would be unreasonable to expect most listeners to keep a diary of their listening for more than a week; so it is not possible to adopt the tactic used on consumer panels of ignoring entries until behaviour returns to the normal. But some are asked to carry on for another three weeks.

Twenty-four hour recall, the method used by the BBC and by Radio Luxembourg, is cheaper to apply and free from the risk of the conditioning that is associated with keeping a diary. A sample of the general public is asked to recall its listening during the previous day and recall is aided by means of the programme. Whether or not recall is aided, the data are subject to the fallibility of the human memory and for most people listening is not a memorable activity.

> All the advantages of radio as a medium, that it supplements people's ongoing lives rather than requiring everything else to come to a grinding halt, militate against accurate memory.[19]

JICRAR sampling is spread through the seasons of the year. The samples are drawn to represent the total service area of each of the forty-four stations. Overlap areas are likely to get more extensive as new stations start transmitting. Marketing plans are sensitive to overlap areas when selling or promotional resources are being allocated.

Respondents are accordingly now asked to record all the stations they listen to if, as is increasingly the case, they can receive commercial stations other than their local one.

Radio is still on the whole regarded as a purely tactical and local medium whose strength lies in its parochialism. It serves the following purposes:

• National advertisers can make local contact, support local distributors and local promotions.
• Local retailers and suppliers of services can advertise to their catchment areas.

But the radio audience is now analysed by ITV area and by sales area as well as by the station's service area.[16]

Since 1979 a sub-sample of those completing a week's diary of radio listening has been asked to carry on for a further three weeks. A model predicting the build-up in audience occurring over four weeks has been developed, and standard analyses are available to media planners on tape.

The JICRAR specification adds up to an expensive research operation[16] and, to aid smaller stations, the minimum sample size has been reduced to 300. When the sample is as small as this, sampling errors may lead to unacceptable fluctuations in audience levels.[19] Radio stations are now free to use more than one frequency. Size and nature of the station audience(s) will depend on how this facility is used. The station audience may be divided, creating in effect two stations.

During periods of change concentrated before—after monitoring is desirable; while to establish within-station audiences it may be necessary to augment samples. Budgetary constraints suggest a more narrowly focused sampling procedure in 1989. As pointed out in the introduction to this chapter, the volatility of the current media scene creates problems of research design and of resource allocation.

9.5.2   JICPAR or outdoor advertising research

In terms of advertising expenditure, outdoor advertising is the most important of the support media (3.7 per cent in 1987); but up to 1983 research in the medium took the form of a number of *ad hoc* studies. Estimates of poster coverage relied either on observation of pedestrians and vehicles passing sites; or on asking samples of the local population whether, when last and how often they passed specific sites, using photographs and street plans to aid recall. There was an outstanding need for a national site-grading system.[20]

In the 1950s and 1960s Brian Copland estimated the potential coverage to be achieved by posters in a number of towns in Great Britain and abroad using the survey approach. For each town sampled Copland arrived at an *A* value, a measure of exposure to the poster medium, which could be applied to campaigns of varying weight and duration in that particular town:

> For each town the total OTS [opportunities to see] per head of population when plotted against the number of sites followed a straight line and the slope of this line increased as the size of the town fell ... for any town the number of OTS per head of population was the product of the number of sites (S) and a constant (A) for that town.[18]

Research recently carried out by Research Services Limited (RSL) has confirmed Copland's findings (see 'Cover and frequency in OSCAR', below).[21]

Development of OSCAR

In 1983 a census of all poster sites costing £700,000 was commissioned by JICPAR for the Outdoor Advertising Association (OAA) which represents the British poster industry, (fieldwork by NOP Market Research Limited and AGB). Ninety per cent of all poster sites are owned by members of the OAA. Since 1986 10 per cent of all poster sites have been reassessed each year. These data, based on observation, serve to update OSCAR (outdoor site classification and audience research). 'Based on individual site fieldwork, OSCAR provides, through statistical modelling, an objective method of calculating the net audience evaluation.'[22] OAA members own 120,000 OSCAR-assessed panels.

The poster market is a complex one. Many variously related factors influence the coverage estimated for any one campaign. Accordingly, OSCAR is in reality (as Derek Bloom points out[23]), eleven models (Table 9.7).

Inputs to OSCAR derive from a long and detailed check-list. They include the following:

- The physical characteristics of the site and of the poster panels associated with it. Pedestrian- and vehicular-visibility weightings are, of course, critical (Table 9.8).
- Estimates of pedestrian and vehicular traffic past the site.
- Type of location, for example 'principal shopping', 'corner shop', 'residential' (nine categories).
- Special features, such as bus routes, car parks, traffic lights.

Cover and frequency in OSCAR

We have so far been considering data collected by means of observation. In order to classify individuals passing sites and to establish the frequency of their journeys it is, of course, necessary to ask questions, and to incur

Table 9.7 Poster campaign

| | Vehicular | | Pedestrian | |
	Large town	Small town	Town centre	Other
Weekday	1	4	7	9
Saturday	2	5	8	10
Sunday	3	6	11	

**Table 9.8
Pedestrian and
vehicular
visibility
weightings**

Pedestrian visibility weightings
General visibility factor

'What proportion of pedestrians in each road have an opportunity of seeing this panel?'

Everyone	100
More than half	70
About half	50
Less than half	30
Very few people	10

Competition		**Illumination**	
0	1.0	Yes	1.25
1–4	0.9		
5–10	0.8	No	1.0
11 +	0.7		

Vehicular visibility weightings

Each panel is scored on three factors that are added together: visibility range, competition and angle. The resulting index is multiplied in turn by the score for deflection, obstruction, height from ground and illumination.

Source: D. Bloom 'How OSCAR audiences are estimated', *JICPAR* (9 May 1988)

additional research costs. These data have recently become available as integral OSCAR outputs.

In 1987 intensive questioning by RSL of 704 adults aged fifteen and over 'about their regular and occasional journeys over the previous seven days: in any part of the country, for all purposes, and by all modes of transport', taken in conjunction with site data on file, has made it possible to classify population groups 'within the limits of sample size.'[24]

On the basis of this new information the Copland model was re-formulated as follows:

$$\text{Cover} = \frac{TAM}{TAM + 1.16T + 2.84}$$

When T = campaign weeks, M = OTS per week (millions), A = a measure of exposure to the roadside poster medium.

% cover = 100(above formula)   Frequency = $TAM + 1.16T + 2.84$.

A values are available for 171 target groups taking Great Britain as a whole: twenty-one for a regional breakdown (ten ISBA regions or combined regions, and conurbations). Classification within regions is limited to broad demographics: for Great Britain as a whole it is possible to consider the poster audience in relation to other media (weight of viewing, listening, readership), together with more detailed demographics.

9.5.3 The cinema

Data relating to the number of cinema screens in the United Kingdom and the number of admissions to cinemas are published by the Department of Industry. The screen returns are published monthly broken down into the Registrar General's Standard Regions. The Cinema Advertising Association relies on NRS data for their published estimates relating to the reach and frequency of cinema-going (Table 9.9).

Cinema advertising accounts for only a fraction of advertising expenditure, 0.4 per cent in 1987; but it is a useful medium for reaching the 15–24 age group.

Questions asked during the NRS make it possible to collect information about the reach and frequency of cinema-going. (See Figure 9.4). Answers to question 1 divide the British population aged fifteen and over into seven frequency groups; answers to question 2a reveal that there is a tendency to overestimate going to the cinema 'these days': for example, some 60 per cent of those claiming to go once a month in answer to question 1 said that they had been in the last four weeks in answer to question 2a.[18] When estimates of total monthly admissions based on NRS data are compared with the Department of Industry returns, NRS estimates based on answers to question 2a are closer than those derived from answers to question 1.[18]

The Cinema Advertising Association publishes reach and frequency estimates broken down by ITV area, and by the socio-economic and media-usage characteristics of the population, based on the NRS data. Assumptions have to be made when coverage of a particular advertising campaign is estimated:

> . . . about one-quarter of those who go to the cinema in a four-weekly period visit more than one and as we move from a consideration of national coverage estimates to the coverage given by a *selection* of cinemas, we should take into account an individual's probability of visiting a particular cinema or selection of cinemas rather than any cinema.[18]

What is being shown has, of course, a critical effect on size of audience. In 1983 the Cinema Advertising Association commissioned Carrick James Market Research to undertake a series of cinema and video industry

**Table 9.9
Cinema-goers
by age group**

Profile of cinema-goers	Regular	All	GB population
15–24	67	40	20
25–34	20	24	18
35–44	6	18	17
45 +	7	18	45

Source: JWT Media Research Unit (Spring 1988)

	(23)S
CINEMA—ASK ALL	
INTRODUCE IN YOUR OWN WORDS	
SHOW CARD C1	
C1 How often these days do you go to the cinema — would it be nearer to	
once a week or more often	Y
two or three times a month	X
once a month	0
once every 2/3 months	1
two or three times a year	2
less often	3
never go these days	4
O.U.O.	5

ASK ALL EXCEPT THOSE WHO "NEVER GO THESE DAYS"

	(24)S
C2a) How long ago was the last occasion you went to a cinema?	
within last 7 days	Y
over 7 days up to and incl. 4 weeks ago........	X
over 4 weeks up to and incl. 3 months ago...	0
over 3 months up to and incl. 6 months ago	1
over 6 months ago/can't remember when	2
O.U.O.	3

	(25)M
SHOW CARD C2b	
b) Which of these films have you seen in the cinema in the last 2 or 3 years — I do not mean on video.	
Beverly Hills Cop II......................................	1
Cry Freedom	2
Fatal Attraction	3
Innerspace	4
Predator	5
Robocop	6
Snow White & The Seven Dwarfs	7
The Untouchables......................................	8
Wish You Were Here	9
Witches of Eastwick	0
None of these	Y

JN (77-80)

**Figure 9.4
The NRS
cinema-going
questionnaire**

audience-research studies (CAVIAR), based on a sample of 2,400, including 7–14 year olds. These repeated surveys make it possible to make better-informed assumptions when the coverage of a particular campaign is being estimated, because they collect data relating to the profile of audiences for specific types of film and for specific films, as well as information about respondents' cinema-going habits.

In the case of the cinema, attendence is taken to equate with opportunity-to-see the advertising despite the competing claims of soft drinks and snacks.

9.6 A note on non-domestic media research

This chapter has reviewed the most generally used research sources for media planning in consumer markets. The Business Media Research Committee, which represents print-media owners, advertisers and agents with an interest in this field, regularly commissions the Businessman Survey. In 1984 only 4 per cent of women qualified as being in occupations likely to involve the making of significant business decisions. The current survey, based on sampling between September 1987 and March 1988, found 7.5 per cent as qualifying.

The UK population is geodemographically stratified using the MOSAIC system, based on fifty-eight residential types of neighbourhood, (compared with ACORN's thirty-eight); 56,000 addresses are drawn in the neighbourhoods selected for sampling. The interviewer is armed with two occupational lists; likely occupations and unlikely ones. The unlikely are immediately discarded. Those found to be 'decision makers' after further questioning are interviewed then and there, if at home and if available for a lengthy interview; if not, interviewers are instructed to make up to eight calls. The data are collected between September and March and the survey sample of 2,000 business men/women represents 2 per cent of the population as a whole.

These business decision-makers are taken through the NRS extended media-list procedure and the intensity of their television viewing is recorded as well as their reading of 160 newspapers and magazines. The fieldwork has been contracted to Sales Research Services since 1973, and the data are, of course, available on tape. These data are a useful source of information about the demographic, occupational and lifestyle characteristics of business directors and managers, as well as about their media habits.

In planning non-domestic schedules the first problem is to locate those who influence the making of decisions, i.e. to define the target. In consumer markets it is comparatively easy to locate the target and to define the opportunities offered by the media categories and by individual vehicles within categories. The challenge comes when attempts are made to assess the probability that the opportunities provided to reach the target will be effective. The same problem arises when planning a non-domestic schedule. Will this professional journal be read, glanced at or passed straight on via the 'out' tray?

Those engaged in the marketing of industrial or other non-domestic goods tend to rely on an accumulation of readership data collected during the course of questioning about other topics: topics such as how buying decisions are arrived at and who influences the placing of contracts.

9.7 Conclusion

In this chapter we have reviewed the major research services available to media planners in Great Britain. Currently, most marketing companies make their media plans on a country-by-country basis: but the opening up of the European market and the development of direct satellite broadcasting will no doubt lead to media planning on a broader scale during the 1990s. As we saw in the introduction to this chapter, the need for a European standard for television audience measurement[1] has been expressed and interest is being shown in the statistical welding of information drawn from separate studies.

The Europeans may or may not develop an integrated media-research canon. The research methodologies described here cover the field of choice.

The media planner is faced on the one hand by more choice and on the other by pressure to focus more narrowly when allocating the advertising budget. During the 1990s there will be more viewing, reading and listening options available to consumers. Government policy apart, Britain is an inviting market for European publishing houses and television entrepreneurs. Prolonging the life and profitability of ongoing brands remains the first concern of most marketing companies, but the discovery and development of niche markets has also been of strategic interest during the 1980s.

Both preoccupations lead to a need for up-to-date and immediately available data about the media habits of target audiences, either to sharpen the schedule for an existing brand or to focus on the segment in a niche market: both demand 'narrow casting'.

As we have seen, there is a wealth of statistical data available to the media planner, not only about the media habits of consumers but also about the relationship between media habits and brand consumption (as from the Target Group Index) and about competitors' media scheduling (from MEAL and the Media Register).

These data are available to advertising agencies from one source when they are linked to a computer bureau, as most of them are: always provided that the agency is a subscriber to the original research service,

BARB, NRS, TGI, MEAL, etc. Two-thirds of all media-buying in the United Kingdom is transacted via Donovan Data Systems (DDS). DDS is on line to over 2,000 terminals in advertising agencies. BARB data are accessible on the Monday of the week following collection. Current NRS, cinema, radio and poster statistics, together with data relating to competitive spending, are also immediately on call.

Media planning, buying and billing are integrated. Progress may be monitored continuously and media schedules where necessary adjusted.

In this chapter we have concentrated on *coverage* and *opportunities* to see or hear the brand message. We investigate some of the methods used to assess the *effectiveness* of an advertising campaign, after exposure in the media, in Chapter 11 on evaluating performance and predicting.

Sources and further reading

1. T. Twyman, 'Towards a European standard for television audience measurement', ESOMAR seminar on media and media research, 'How far can we go?', reported in *ADMAP* (Apr. 1988).
2. S. Broadbent, *Spending Advertising Money*, 1st edn (London: Business Books, 1979). See also S. Broadbent and B. Jacobs, *Spending Advertising Money*, 4th edn (London: Business Books, 1984).
3. P. Kotler, *Marketing Management, Analysis, Planning and Control*, 4th edn (Englewood Cliffs, NJ: Prentice Hall, 1980), p. 508.
4. *Report of the Committee on the Future of Broadcasting* (London: HMSO, 1977). See also *Broadcasting in the '90s: Competition, Choice and Quality* (London: HMSO, 1988).
5. S. Buck, 'Television audience measurement research: yesterday, today and tomorrow', *Journal of The Market Research Society*, vol. 29, no. 3 (July 1987).
6. J. Whitehead, 'BARB: the last geodemographic hurdle', *ADMAP* (June 1988).
7. M. Kirkham 'Value from TV advertising: measurement of TV audiences', *Survey* (Oct. 1983) (published by the MRS). See also T. Rawlings, 'The hi-tech alternatives', *ADMAP* (May 1983) pp. 268−71.
8. BARB television opinion panel, 'Reference manual and user's guide', BBC Broadcasting Research Department (July 1988).
9. A.S.C. Ehrenberg, G.J. Goodhart and D.S. Kerr, 'Two notes on television audience appreciation and audience behaviour', *ADMAP* (May 1982), pp. 308−11.
10. P. Menneer, 'Audience appreciation: a different story from audience numbers', *MRS Conference Papers* (1987). See also *Journal of The Market Research Society*, vol. 28, no. 3 (July 1987).
11. JICNARS, *The National Readership Survey*, vol. 1 (1987).
12. JICNARS, *An Investigation into the Reading Behaviour Measured by the NRS* (Nov. 1985).
13. JICNARS, *The Extended Media List Experiment* (Dec. 1983).
14. JICNARS, *Diary Panels Research: A Report on Phase 1* (Nov. 1985).

15. JICNARS, *Diary Panels Research: A Report on Phase 2* (Apr. 1988).
16. D. Bloom, 'Radio: problems in measuring an invisible medium', *MRS Conference Papers* (1984).
17. JICRAR reported in JWT, *Media Information*, (Spring 1988).
18. F. Teer, 'Radio, outdoor and cinema research', Chap. 26 of R.M. Worcester and J. Downham (eds), *Consumer Market Research Handbook*, 3rd edn (Amsterdam: North-Holland, 1986).
19. W.A. Twyman, 'The state of radio research', *ADMAP* (Aug. 1976).
20. D. O'Reilly, 'Sites get their grades', *Marketing* (22 Sept. 1983).
21. C.D.P. McDonald, 'The poster model is alive and could be better', *ADMAP* (May 1981).
22. D. Taylor, 'Poster marketing: a briefing', Outdoor Advertising Association (26 Jan. 1988).
23. D. Bloom, 'How OSCAR audiences are estimated', JICPAR (9 May 1988).
24. D. Bloom, 'A short guide to cover and frequency in OSCAR', JICPAR (1 Nov. 1988).

Problems

1. A food manufacturer is planning the introduction of a range of frozen pâtés and terrines under a 'farmhouse' label aimed entirely at the consumer market. The company has a range of pies and sausages in national distribution. The board is divided between going national with the new, more up-market, range and a rolling launch; but, anticipating competitive reaction, is, on the whole, in favour of an introduction throughout Great Britain.

   The media planner concerned at the advertising agency has been asked to recommend a media strategy, given an advertising appropriation of £450,000 inclusive of production costs.

   (a) What marketing information would the media planner need in order to formulate a cost-effective strategy?
   (b) What research sources might he/she consult?

2. 'Reading a publication or looking through it is not a clear-cut unambiguous act as is, for example, buying a kilo of sugar or breaking a mirror.'

   (a) Explain why you agree/disagree with this statement.
   (b) How exactly may 'readership' be defined?

3. A company making dies for the packaging industry has recently moved from the cutting of layouts by hand to the use of lasers, resulting in greater precision, a considerable saving in time and an urgent need for new business.

   An agency with industrial experience has been appointed to advertise this 'hi-tech' development.

   (a) What information would the advertising agency need in order to plan a media strategy?
   (b) How might these data be collected?

   Assume an appropriation of £40,000.

Glossary of media terminology

Source: J. Walter Thompson Company, Media Research Unit, 'Media glossary' (Spring 1988).

average issue readership (AIR)   The number of people who claim to have read or looked at a publication in the last issue period, i.e. 'yesterday' in the case of the *Daily Mirror*, and 'in the last week' in the case of *Woman's Weekly*.

average listening hours   The average number of hours listened to a radio station. Calculated by dividing total listening hours in a week by weekly reach (total number listening in a week).

cost per hundred (CPH)   The average cost of achieving 100 TVRs against a specified audience. (*See* TVR.)

cost per thousand (CPT)   Used with reference to a specific audience, cost per thousand is a measure of the average cost of reaching 1,000 members of this audience. For example: if a spot on Thames TV reaches 400,000 men and costs £4,000, then the cost per thousand men is £4,000 ÷ 400 = £10.00.

cover (sometimes termed **reach** or **net coverage**)   The proportion of the audience having an opportunity to see the advertising one or more times. Usually measured as a percentage, but can be expressed in thousands.

cumulative cover   The increased cover resulting from taking space in more than one issue of a particular publication.

effective reach (sometimes termed **effective cover**)   The percentage of the target audience who have the opportunity to see the desired number of TV spots (or hear radio spots, or see press ads). For example: if it is desired that the target audience see between two and eight spots, then the effective reach of the schedule is the percentage with between two and eight OTS.

equal impacts   A strategy for regional allocation giving equal number of TVRs to all regions.

frequency   The average number of times the target audience has an opportunity to see the campaign measured in OTS. (OTH for radio.) Calculated as frequency = gross OTS ÷ net cover

$$\text{or} = \text{TVRs} \div \text{net cover (for TV)}$$

gross rating points   The total number of OTS achieved by a campaign expressed as a percentage of the universe. For TV this would be equivalent to total TVRs. For press, it would be the sum of individual average issue readerships. For example: a campaign achieving 70 per cent cover at 4 OTS would yield 280 gross rating points.

impacts   Impacts (sometimes termed gross impressions or messages) are the total number of separate occasions a commercial(s) is viewed by a specific audience, measured in thousands.

MPX (magazine-page exposure)   MPX scores the number of times an average issue reader of a publication looks at an average page.

net homes   Describes the number of homes in a TV area, exclusive of overlap. (*See* TV overlap.)

OSCAR (outdoor site classification and audience research) Provides classification of site visibility/quality and traffic-past site. Does not provide demographics of audience.

OTH (opportunity to hear)   The radio equivalent of OTS — the average number of times an audience is exposed to a radio commercial. 'Exposure' is defined as any listening within the clock quarter-hour.

OTS (opportunity to see)   The opportunity to see a TV commercial or a press, cinema or poster advertisement, defined as follows:

Press: Read or looked at any issue (for at least two minutes), within the publication period (e.g. last week, for a weekly).
Cinema: Measured in actual cinema admissions.
Posters: Traffic past the site.
TV: Presence in room with set switched on at turn of clock minute to one channel, providing presence in room with set on is for at least fifteen consecutive seconds.

Average OTS is measure of frequency of exposure to an advertisement: if an audience is exposed to an advertisement on average three times each, then this is equivalent to an average OTS of 3.

page traffic   The percentage of readers who 'look at' a specific page within a publication.

pass-on readership   (sometimes termed **secondary readership**) Readers of a publication other than the purchaser or his/her immediate household. For example: readership which takes place in a doctor's waiting room.

penetration   Refers to the proportion of a population who are reached by a medium.

pre-empt   A system of buying TV air-time similar in principle to an auction. The rate-card may consist of a range of many different rates.

The buyer will elect the rate desired to pay for a spot but he/she can lose the spot if 'pre-empted' by another buyer subsequently paying more for that spot. Pre-emption can occur up to midday on the day of transmission.

primary readership   The first reader of a publication or members of his/her immediate household.

readers per copy (RPC)   The average number of readers seeing each copy sold. Calculated as average issue readership ÷ circulation.

share deals   A method of negotiation designed to increase ITV contractors' share of television revenue. Discounts are given to advertisers investing a share of their budget equivalent to the TV areas' net homes share or sales share, whichever is the greater. Used until December 1987.

timeshift   Practice of recording programmes on VCR and viewing later.

TV overlap   TV overlap areas consist of districts falling within the boundaries of more than one TV area; 18 per cent of households are currently in overlap areas.

TVR (television rating)   Expressed in terms of a specific audience, e.g. adult TVRs, home TVRs, etc. For a single TV spot, twenty-one housewife TVRs mean that 21 per cent of all housewives were recorded as viewers of that spot. For more than one spot, TVRs represent the sum of individual spots. For example, a campaign of twenty spots, each of fifteen TVRs, is equivalent to 300 TVRs.

Out in the open: the final go/no-go decision

Laboratory-type experiments are commonly used while a branded product, and the features associated with it, are being developed for the market. The experiments discussed in Chapters 7 and 8 offer the benefit of internal validity but leave us unsure as to whether consumers would respond to the experimental treatment in the same way on meeting the brand in normal circumstances and when unaware that they were taking part in an experiment. We are left wondering whether these laboratory experiments have external validity.

This doubt apart, there are important elements in the marketing mix which do not lend themselves to laboratory treatment. Experiments relating to distribution, trade incentives, selling and merchandising strategies need to be staged in the field. Provided sufficient 'back data' are available, construction of a simulation model can reduce uncertainty when mix elements are being manipulated in a 'what if?' exercise. A new, or substantially changed, brand mixture demands real-life treatment.

The application of electronic technology to data capture improves the precision with which findings are recorded and the speed with which experimental effects become available: although it remains critical that the experiment goes on long enough! The implications for research design of article numbering, laser checkouts and peoplemeters are encountered in this chapter: but the discipline and caveats met in Chapter 7 under 'Focus on theory' still hold good. We open, therefore, with a consideration of the obstacles to good design inherent in the complexity of the market place.

10.1 Obstacles to the achievement of external validity

The treatment may be the complete marketing mix (as in an experimental launch) or the manipulation of individual elements, say, advertising or advertising in relation to sales promotion. The following obstacles to valid results need to be taken account of in most field experiments:

- Extraneous variables may contaminate the effect of the treatment, e.g.

uncharacteristic activity on the part of competitors or the effect on consumer purchasing of a local happening such as a strike.

- In a laboratory test it is possible to ensure that the treatment is introduced to experimental and control groups in exactly the same way. This is not always the case with field experiments: for example, in an experiment at the point of sale the positioning of items (packs/merchandising material) may well be altered unwittingly during the course of the experiment so that experimental and control groups do not receive exactly the same treatment.
- It is sometimes difficult to isolate the effect on sales of one particular element in the mix from the effect of others: for example, measurement of the effect on sales of an increase in advertising weight may be contaminated by differences in the merchandising performance of sales representatives, one area being better served than another.
- There is a risk of 'hothousing', particularly in the case of an experimental launch when reputations are at stake and there is the temptation to show too much management interest, and for sales representatives to be unduly zealous.
- The financial commitment is greater in a field than in a lab.-type experiment. Anxiety to show a return encourages hothousing and may cause the experiment to be stopped too soon. When it looks as if an experiment is proving successful, considerations of 'opportunity cost' may prompt too rapid an extension of the experiment to the wider market.

It is, however, possible in a well-designed experiment to ensure that obstacles to a valid result are anticipated and so allowed for. Given an adequate budget, the research programme will monitor competitive, and own, activity at the point of sale. A marketing intelligence system can be organized to ensure that environmental happenings are noted. Use of a control group, essential in field experiments, and, where possible, replication of the experiment, make it possible to calculate margins of error and show how precisely results may be interpreted.

Whatever the outcome, designing and interpreting the effect of a field experiment concentrate the minds of those involved wonderfully, so that they complete the operation wiser about the requirements of the market and how best to meet these.

10.2 Scope and variety of field experimentation

We need to distinguish between the following:

- Experiments related to established brands (which most are) and those related to new introductions.
- Experiments in which individual elements in the mix are manipulated

and those in which the complete mix is on trial in an experimental launch.

- Experiments which can be confined to a limited location (for example, matched groups of retail outlets or of streets) and experiments demanding a microcosm of the real world of consumers, retail outlets and media vehicles.

These alternatives are not, of course, discrete. There are inter-relationships between them:

- Experiments related to an established brand are likely to be focused on individual elements in the mix — on price/packaging/advertising/sales promotion and so on: or on the relationship between two elements, such as the effect on profit contribution of different ratios of advertising to sales-promotional expenditure. (We must not, of course, forget that, once a brand is established, manipulation of elements in the mix takes place in the context of the image created by its marketing history.)
- For a new introduction the experimental treatment in the field is likely to be the whole mix; but the experimental launch may be preceded by a pilot launch of, perhaps, the product packaged, named and priced, designed to ensure that the product behaves well between coming off the production line and reaching the consumer.
- Some elements in the mix lend themselves to field experimentation on a limited scale, whereas others demand a more extended environment. The effect of a change in pack design can be assessed by comparing sales achieved in two matched and comparatively small groups of retail outlets. To measure the effect on sales of a change in the level of advertising expenditure may involve comparison between sales achievement in two television areas.

Use of the expression 'test marketing' has been avoided in the preceding paragraphs. Test marketing covers a variety of experimental conditions and this makes for ambiguity.[1] Davis distinguishes between the following:

1. The experimental launch (or test launch) of a new or radically improved product.
2. Market tests in which 'variations are being made only to some parts of the marketing mix of an existing product'.

He further distinguishes:

- Within (1): between the projectable test launch, an experimental launch designed to yield sales data from which national sales may be predicted; and a pilot launch designed to iron out difficulties before the full experimental launch.
- Within (2): between a specific market test designed to measure the

effect of modifying 'some factor in the marketing mix to a specific new level', e.g. an increase or decrease in retail selling price; and an exploratory market test designed to arrive at a better understanding of the way in which measurable elements in the mix affect consumer buying behaviour.
* Most market tests are of the specific type but interest in market modelling has focused attention on exploratory experimentation as a source of input data.

Davis's analysis of the variety of experimental conditions covered by the term 'test marketing' is illustrated in Figure 10.1.

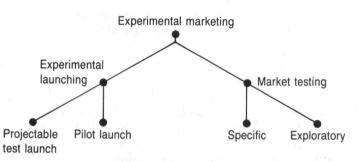

Figure 10.1 Experimental marketing classified

Source: E.J. Davis, *Experimental Marketing* (London: Nelson, 1970)

10.3   Necessary preconditions

Before going into the field it is necessary to have done the following:

* Formulated objectives and set criteria against which results are to be judged.
* Decided where the experiment is to take place, on what scale and for how long.
* Set in motion a research programme designed to monitor happenings in the market as well as to measure effects of the experiment.

We will in due course take account of the fact that technological development at the pre-test stage (e.g. market modelling) and at the point of sale (laser scanning) has reduced the need for prolonged testing in the field.

10.3.1   Formulating objectives

In most cases the ultimate objective is increased profit contribution but the immediate objective is likely to be seen in terms of sales. The situation to be avoided is one in which a 'suck it and see' approach is adopted: 'let's see what sales do'. The product of this approach would be an inadequately controlled, and probably misleading, investigation.

The 'suck it and see' spirit is unlikely to prevail when the experiment is an experimental launch: too much is at stake. Predictions of sales achievement, given various levels of marketing costs, will almost certainly have been made at stages on the road to market. It will be known that, for the proposed mix of marketing costs, a specified sales minimum must be passed. Here the main problem is projection to the wider market from the test area.

Most experiments in the field relate to individual elements in the mix, or to relationships between elements, market testing. Before setting up the test we need to have considered the criterion against which the effect of the treatment is to be judged. It is desirable that the possible benefit to be derived from the manipulation of mix elements be estimated in advance for two reasons:

1. Account has to be taken of two kinds of cost: out-of-pocket costs and (given success) opportunity costs.
2. In order to determine the size of the matched samples we are going to use we need to know not only what proportion of those in the market are likely to respond to the treatment, but also the precision with which we are going to want to consider results. The results will be estimates. What margin of error can we accept around the estimates?

These considerations determine the scale of the experiment: in how many retail outlets to put the experimental pack; through how many doors to put the promotional offer; how many people to ask awareness questions, and so on.

10.3.2   Where and for how long?

Choice of test locations

ITV areas? Sales areas? Test towns? 'In-store'? These locations account for most field experiments. Others might be circulation areas of provincial press or reception areas of local radio. The decision as to where to carry out an experiment in the field in influenced by the following factors:

- What element or combination of elements in the mix is being tested (the experimental treatment).
- How the effect is going to be measured (the dependent variable).
- The extent to which consumption and distribution of the product or brand varies in the wider market.
- Availability of suitable locations.

- The rigour with which the experiment is designed.
- The research budget.

There is interaction between these factors, but we will attempt to follow this order in considering the influences on choice of location.

The importance of television as an advertising medium means that most experiments related to the complete mix (an experimental launch) or to the advertising element in the mix have to be based on ITV areas.

In the United Kingdom small ITV areas are atypical, while larger areas, embracing a wider variety of conditions, represent a considerable marketing investment. It is difficult to design a UK experiment based on ITV areas which mirrors variations in living standards, consuming habits, retailing practices and differences in the regional strengths and weaknesses of brands, the product of past marketing history. But for planning purposes there is available a wealth of marketing information regularly published by the ITV companies.

In the United States there are many small television stations serving local markets. It is comparatively easy to represent regional differences, and to match experimental and control areas, in the experimental design. The Behaviour Scan procedure,[2] a research service on offer in the United States, combines manipulation of the commercials received by a panel of housewives with laser scanning of their purchases at the point-of-sale checkout.

Nielsen's split-transmission advertising service in co-operation with HTV, STATS SCAN, takes advantage of the fact that HTV Wales and West is served by two transmitters. Some homes receive both, some HTV Wales, some HTV West. The procedure is summarized as follows:

Area:	The Cardiff/Newport catchment area, 'geodemographically matched to the UK', where 200,000 homes receive from only one of the two transmitters, either Wales or West.
Object:	To compare the effect on consumer purchases of alternative advertising strategies, creative or media.
Methods:	To monitor the split transmitting in the area, two panels of 1,000 homes are matched demographically and equipped as follows: with hand-held scanners to record the barcodes on purchases in home as shopping is unpacked; with peoplemeters to record their TV viewing. Press, magazine and radio exposure is also monitored via the hand-held scanner.

In the United States behaviour-scan operation panelists are represented by code numbers and these are recorded when their purchases are scanned at the checkout. All the major supermarket outlets are represented in the Cardiff/Newport catchment area. The STATS SCAN procedure does not depend on their co-operation. Panelists do their own scanning. Data are retrieved via a modem linking the domestic telephone to the Nielsen computer. (Article-numbering, bar codes and laser-scanning are related to retail auditing in section 10.4.1.)

Provided the services offered prove to be sufficiently popular, the development of cable television may create opportunities for the cost-effective testing of commercials. The UK franchises relate to 'small, highly clustered geographic areas with populations not exceeding 100,000'.[3] The geodemographic classifications make it possible to define the social complexion of areas of this size with some precision; but it will, of course, be necessary to take account, when designing experiments, of variations in programme TVRs and in local shopping facilities.

For an experimental launch to be tested in more than one ITV area, the cost is likely to be prohibitively expensive. Going into the second area might, for example, represent the difference between pilot plant-production and an extension to the factory, apart from inflating all marketing costs.

It is accordingly common practice to use one ITV area for an experimental launch and to treat the rest of the country as the control area. This is made possible by the availability of syndicated trend data showing competitive brand shares within ITV areas over time, in terms of both retail sales and consumer purchases. These data are used to neutralize the effect of area differences.

For an established brand the financial burden is not of the same order as for an experimental launch. It is possible, for example, to conduct advertising weight tests in more than one area or to test a choice of, say, two sales promotion to advertising ratios in two ITV areas: but we still have to take differences between the areas into account when measuring effects.

Turning to the national press, newspapers and magazines, readership statistics are analysed on an ITV regional basis and there are also available syndicated data relating brand and media consumption (these 'single source' data are discussed in Chapter 11 on monitoring performance). It is possible to compare the effect on brand shares of different combinations of television and press advertising or to consider press alone in an ITV area. The problem is to limit the effect of the experimental treatment to the area of the experiment. It means making a special arrangement to break the print run, or, for magazines, to 'tip in'. Regional editions cover large areas of the country. Extension of the local-radio (LR) network, together with the possibility of relating groups of LR stations to the ISBA sales areas, creates opportunities for using LR to test the sales effect of promotions to encourage local stocking-up (or to discourage de-listing).

For market tests of elements in the mix other than advertising it is possible to use smaller areas and more rigorous designs. There is a wealth of secondary data available relating to the demographic and retailing characteristics of test towns and their catchment areas. These data derive from the Government Statistical Service, the provincial press and the suppliers of syndicated panel services, such as Nielsen, Audits of Great Britain and Stats MR, who offer retail and consumer panel services in test towns. In order to sell space to advertisers and to focus their editorial content, the provincial press often carry out their own research within their circulation areas. These data, published in report form, are illuminating when market tests are being designed.

For most field experiments the effect of the treatment is measured in sales. In an area test a retail audit or consumer panel is likely to be used to log brand shares, both before and after the treatment is applied. Certain elements in the mix lend themselves to 'in-store' testing: manipulations of pack and point-of-sale promotion 'ask for' an in-store design.

How are the stores chosen? A company intent on experimentation is pretty sure to have on file a record of ex-factory sales by area, by type of trade customer and by trade customers stratified by the size of their orders. The company is also likely to be subscribing to a syndicated service in order to monitor competitive market or brand shares in relation to its own.

When an in-store experiment is being designed these data will show the following:

- Whether it is necessary to include more than one type of retail outlet in the test.
- Whether it is necessary to take account of regional differences in selecting test stores.
- Whether one or more retail organizations are of critical importance.

It may well be that one particular type of outlet (say supermarkets) is so important that the experiment can usefully be confined to this type of store; and to one dominating trade customer (say Tesco). Locations in which to stage the experiment are more likely to be made available if the negotiations are carried on with one retail organization. In order to measure effect sales have to be recorded both before and after the test and over a period of time. In addition administration of the treatment must be controlled. In other words, the experiment depends on the co-operation of head office and of the managers of the selected stores.

There is a statistical reason for basing the experiment on one particular store group, where this is practicable: the selected stores are more likely to be 'like'. This reduces error deriving from extraneous variation. Randomized block and Latin square designs are frequently used in in-store experiments. These designs are described, with examples, in Appendix 3 and section 7.2.3, where the reader is referred to Cox and Enis.[4]

The effect of consumer promotions may be measured in interviews with matched groups of consumers instead of, or as well as, by recording sales in matched groups of stores.

Let us assume that a choice has to be made as between two types of point-of-sale promotion. There is no time to set up an in-store operation, or we do not want to discuss our plans with the powerful retail trade just yet: or we might want to introduce a diagnostic element into the experiment, to find out what effect the offer has had on use of the brand and attitude towards it.

In the in-store design we measure the effect of the promotional treatment by recording sales for a period before and a period after the offer is made to consumers, as well, of course, as during this period.

In the design based on consumer interviews, we use intermediate measures. We seek to establish levels of awareness of the offer, changes in use of the brand and changes of attitude towards it, but we cannot interview the same respondent before and then again after the offer has been made about awareness, use and attitude. The respondent would learn from the first interview and be more likely to notice and act on the offer.

We either use an after-only design and seek to establish past as well as present behaviour at the 'after' interview, *or*, more likely, use a larger number of respondents in matched groups, interviewing one group before the offer is made and the other after. Were we comparing two promotional treatments, the first procedure would need three groups over all — one for each offer and one control — while the second would require at least five, preferably six (since the control group may learn); and we have made no allowance for regional differences. Simulation of the shopping context would be a cheaper and less time-consuming procedure: and it would be possible to ensure that the arrangement of brands and displays remained under control (see section 8.5).

For how long?

To measure effects we need to record observations taken before, during and after introduction of the experimental treatment. The period of time to be allowed for in planning and costing a field experiment is influenced by three factors:

1. How long to allow for the experimental treatment to begin eliciting a response (penetration).
2. How quickly brand loyalty and switching patterns can be expected to develop (repeat purchase).
3. The degree of precision required in the estimate of effects.

In the case of an experimental launch the speed with which penetration is achieved will depend on the nature of the product ('Does it break new ground, like MacDougall's Pastry Mix?', discussed in section 10.5 under 'micro-marketing'; or is it a 'me too'?); weight and creative effectiveness of the advertising campaign; together with success in achieving distribution and 'stand-out' at the point of sale.

But a product can achieve a satisfactory number of triers and then flop: the extent to which triers try again is critical and the time needed to establish repeat-purchase rate in the field depends on the frequency with which the product is bought.

In order to log cumulative penetration and in order to record repeat purchase it is necessary to have available disaggregated records of consumer purchases. Analysis of back data relating to a product field and the brands in it, together with consideration of competitive expenditures on advertising over time, make it possible to predict how long an experiment may have to go on, including for how long and how often, to take observations before putting in the treatment.

Penetration and repeat purchase are discussed in more detail in section 10.4, together with the use of retail sales as a data source for prediction from experiments.

In an experiment for an established brand we have to allow for carry-over effects. The in-store test illustrates the simplest manifestation of this effect. Offers encourage stocking up and stocking up affects repeat purchase. When measuring the effect of advertising for established brands, changes in weight or in creative content, it is important to remember that present performance in the test area is influenced by the previous marketing history of the brand. We must give old effects time to die out and new effects sufficient time in which to be felt in the market.

We return to this problem when discussing the computer program developed for Beecham to predict what would happen in a test area if no change were made. (See section 10.5.2.)

If, as is to be expected, we intend to set confidence limits to our experimental results, we must then ensure that these results are based on a sufficient number of observations. A precise estimate may require that the test runs for longer than would be the case if a more generalized result were adequate.

The full test-market procedure is now less frequently used. The sophistication of pre-test procedures and the development of market simulation-modelling techniques substantially reduce uncertainty about consumer reaction to the brand mix before test in the open market. But how the brand fares is, of course, critically dependent on the treatment it receives in-store. The rapidity with which scanning data can be turned around means that go/no-go decisions may be arrived at after a shorter period of time on test than used to be needed.

10.4   Sources of data and measuring effects

The dependent variable in most field experiments is sales, and sales are usually reported in terms of brand share. The research programme for a field experiment may provide for the collection of data about other marketing factors such as level of distribution achieved, awareness of advertising and response to an offer, but the critical measurement is likely to be a sales measurement.

Ex-factory sales, however well recorded, suffer from three important limitations as a data source for experimentation in the field:

1. They do not tell us how competitive brands are performing in the experimental and control areas.
2. The 'pipeline' between the factory gate and the checkout makes it difficult to separate effects due to changes in sales from those due to changes in stocks.
3. It is difficult to isolate the volume and value of sales ex-factory attributable to the experimental and control areas.

These limitations may be overcome but subscription to a continuous service is common practice.

10.4.1   Retail audit: consumer panel

Data relating to consumer purchases may be collected either at the point of sale or in the home. The impact of article numbering, bar coding and laser scanning on retail audits and consumer panels follows a brief discussion of the marketing significance of these two information sources.

Retail audit, consumer panel or both types of data source will be used to monitor brand shares. In a test area it may well be necessary to enlarge the regular, ongoing samples of retail outlets or of consumers, or to set up special *ad hoc* ones. It depends on the choice and the size of the test area. In addition, the standard reporting interval may be shortened, but the data-collection procedures are standard.

Table 10.1 compares the data yield of these two types of syndicated service, whose main *raison d'être* is, of course, the continuous monitoring of marketing performance so that we are in effect anticipating Chapter 11. Table 10.1 shows the strengths and, by implication, the weaknesses of the two data sources.

The procedures used to predict national or broad-scale shares from area tests are similar whichever form of panel is used. However, before comparing predictive procedures there are some further details to be filled in:

- In both cases the client specifies the brands he/she wants to see recorded, usually major competitors plus an 'all others' group together with the client's brand.
- The brand characteristics to be classified individually in the regular report are also agreed in advance — type of pack, size, flavour, etc.

We are going to consider how retail-audit and consumer-panel data may

**Table 10.1
Data yield:
retail audit and
consumer
panel
compared**

Retail audit	Consumer panel

Consumer sales and brand shares:
  Units
  Sterling
  Average per shop handling
	Consumer purchases and brand shares:
	  Units
	  Sterling
	  Brand penetration
	  Consumer typology
	    Demographic characteristics
	    Psychographic characteristics
	    Buying behaviour
	      x amount bought
	      x loyalty/switching

Retailer purchases
  Units (not *sterling*)
  Brand shares
Source of delivery
  Direct/via depot/other
Retailer stocks and brand shares
  Units
  Average per shop handling
Stock cover
  Days, weeks, months
	Where purchase made
	  Type of outlet

Prices
  *Average retail selling prices at time
  of audit*
	Prices
	  Average purchase price

Promotion
  Display at point of sale
  Special offers
	Promotion
	  Offers associated purchases

	Advertising
	  *Media consumption by panel-members
	  ('Single source' data, see section
	  11.2.2)*

By type of retail outlet By ITV area	By ITV area

be used to indicate what the effect of the experimental treatment would be if it were applied to the national or broader market. We first need to distinguish between projections, which assume that all other things remain equal, and predictions, which attempt to take account of factors which vary between the experimental area and the broader market.

- The retail audit is based on samples of retail outlets which represent the volume of business going through different categories of outlet. The sample for each Nielsen index (grocery, home improvement, health and beauty services) represents the range of outlets relevant to the products covered by the industry (Table 10.2).
- The consumer panel will represent either private households with data collection via the housewife, or individuals. In addition to panels representing consumers in general, there are a number of specialist

Grocery index	Home improvement index	Health and beauty services index	**Table 10.2 The range of retail outlets relevant to products**
Independents Multiples Co-operatives	DIY multiples DIY and hardware independents Grocer superstores	Pharmacies Drug stores Grocers	
Dog food, flour, cereal etc.	Hand tools, lawn-mowers, curtain tracks and poles, etc.	Shampoo, baby napkins, razors, indigestion remedies, etc.	

panels such as the motorists' diary panel operated by Forecast (Market Research).

- The retail audit is a demanding but straightforward operation:

$$\text{Opening stock } + \text{ Deliveries } - \text{ Closing stock } = \text{ Sales}^5$$

'Opening stock' was left for sale at the close of the last audit; 'deliveries' means stock coming in since the last audit. The formula is simple, but the procedure is infinitely detailed.

- The consumer-panel data derive either from a diary, designed as a pre-coded check-list, or from an audit of household stores.

Article numbering, bar coding and laser scanning have revolutionized the collection of sales data. We are going to focus on collection at the retail outlet and in particular on the grocery outlet: always remembering that the laser-scanning of bar codes provides research data from a variety of sales outlets (see, for example, the regular scanning of records and cassettes carried out by Gallup for the music-industry record chart); while anticipating more widespread use of hand-held scanners in the home.

The laser-scanning of consumer sales is related to the work of the European Article Numbering (EAN) Association. The essential nature of EAN is that each article has a number assigned to it 'which is unique, universally recognised and can be shown in a form readable by machines as well as humans'.[6] The basic EAN is thirteen digits long, as shown in Figure 10.2.

Laser scanning of article numbers at the point of sale makes it possible to report consumer purchases in a short space of time, by brand within product field and by variety within brand (size, price, flavour, etc.). Nielsen's manually audited reports are delivered monthly. The reporting interval for Nielsen's SCANTRACK is four-weekly, with data available in weekly periods. The planning significance of the shorter reporting interval is illustrated in Figure 10.3.[7]

Manual auditing, using hand-held scanners, necessarily continues in

**Figure 10.2
The EAN
thirteen-digit
barcode**

Source: A. Wolfe and L. Cook, *The Electronic Revolution in Store* (London: Ogilvy and Mather, 1986)

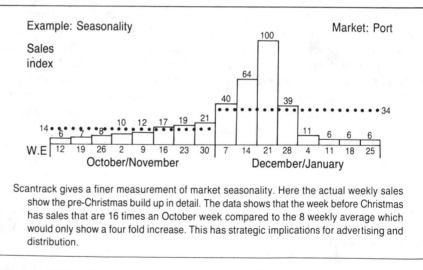

**Figure 10.3
Reporting
intervals
compared**

Source: N. Staples, 'Scanning-based services and the Nielsen contribution', *ADMAP* (1987)

order to augment the sales data collected at the checkout. Scanner stores are not as yet representative of the universe of grocery outlets. It is forecast that by 1990 50 per cent of all grocery commodity volume will be scanned. In 1987 the figure was 15 per cent, so the pace accelerates. Currently Nielsen's SCANTRACK service is based on inputs from sixty-seven supermarket operators handling 4 per cent of all commodity volume.

The rapid availability of marketing information made possible by EPOS has to be set against the fact that collection of the data depends on retail co-operation and efficiency at the checkout and on the smooth running of the computer installation (if more than one flavour is bought, are these flavours recorded individually?).[7] Merchandising support in store, critical when an experiment is under way, continues to depend on human observation, albeit with hand-held electronic assistance.

The retail audit is valuable in the experimental situation because, in addition to recording retail sales and brand shares, it monitors distribution achieved and signals the danger of 'stock-out' (a particular risk in an experimental launch dependent on pilot plant-production).

The consumer panel describes the types of consumer responding to the experimental treatment and identifies repeat purchase patterns.

10.4.2   Prediction by standardizing brand shares

Taking a simplified example, if a new brand were to achieve £100 consumer sales in an experimental area where sales of all brands in the product field totalled £1,000, it would be naive to assume that, on going national, the new brand would achieve £10,000 in a national market worth £100,000. Simple projection of the 10 per cent brand share from experimental area to total market is to be avoided because even nationally distributed and consumed brands show regional variation. The field as a whole may show little variation but individual brand shares are the product of past achievement on a number of fronts — selling and sales promotion, distribution, advertising — and it is unlikely that the marketing histories of the brands in the field will have followed, in each case, a uniform course in all areas.

The effect of marketing history up to and during the experiment is taken into account by standardizing brand shares, a technique developed by Davis.[1] When a new brand is introduced into an area market, achievement in brand share is made at the expense of other brands already there. Assuming a positive result for the new entry, some brands will resist more successfully than others. If the experiment is allowed to run long enough and provided that a competitor does not succeed in muddying the water, an estimate of national share is arrived at by applying the

**Table 10.3
Experimental
launch of
brand T into a
product field of
four brands**

| | Experimental market | | | | National market, projected | | |
| | Brand share (%) | | Lost | Loss as % of | Brand share (%) | | |
	Before	After	to T	pre-test share	Before	After	
A	30	27	−3	−10%	35	35 − 3.5 = 31.5	
B	15	10	−5	−33.3%	9	9 − 3 = 6	
C	25	25	n.c.	—	31	31 n.c. = 31	
D	30	27	−3	−10%	25	25 − 2.5 = 22.5	91.0
T	—	11	11		—	100 − 91 =	9.0
	100	100					100.0

changes to brand shares observed in the experimental area to the shares held by competing brands in the national market.

The procedure is spelt out in Table 10.3, which assumes an experimental launch (brand T) into a product field of four brands $(A-D)$. (For the statistician's formula, see footnote*.)

Had the target set for T been a 12 per cent share, the difference between the 11 per cent achieved in the experimental area and the projected 9 per cent arrived at for the national market would have been critical.

This example relates to an experimental launch. The standardization procedure could also be used when predicting the effect of changes to the marketing of an existing brand, but the impact on market testing of individual elements in the mix is likely to be less noticeable than the impact of an experimental launch. It will be more difficult to achieve statistically significant results. The AMTES (area marketing test evaluation system) econometric model is designed to meet this problem and it is further discussed in section 10.5.2.

Brand shares are the product of the historic working of the mix variables at certain fixed points in time, i.e. when the observations are taken. These data may show the relationship between area brand-sales and national sales to be a volatile one. In this case the underlying relationship is revealed by averaging the readings over a period before and after the introduction of the treatment. The length of this period will depend on the frequency with which the product is bought.

10.4.3 Brand-share prediction

The brand-share data used when taking the standardization approach can derive from either a retail audit or from a consumer panel, i.e. from shares

---

*If x_0, y_0 etc. are brand shares in the experimental area prior to the introduction of brand T, and if t_1, x_1, y_1 etc. are the brand shares after the introduction; and if X_0, Y_0 etc. are the brand shares in the wider market prior to the launch, then the projected share of brand T nationally will be T_1 where

$$T_1 = 100 - \left\{ X_0 \cdot \frac{x_1}{x_0} + Y_0 \cdot \frac{y_1}{y_0} + \cdots \right\} \%$$

of retailer sales or from shares of consumer purchases. We are now going to consider a predictive model for which disaggregated consumer-panel data are necessary inputs. This procedure, developed in connection with the Attwood consumer panel can be applied to any continuous series recording purchases by housewives, individuals, motorists, mothers or pet owners, provided the product concerned is re-purchased often enough.[8]

The brand-share prediction-model is based on three statistics:

1. Penetration: buyers of the test product as a percentage of all buyers in the product field, as they accumulate during the period of the test (P).
2. Repeat purchase rate: triers of the test product buying again as a percentage of all buyers in the product field (R).
3. Buying rate factor: a weighting factor which allows for the finding that buyers of the test product consume more or less than the average — a weight of 1 — for the field (B).

The predictive strength of the model has been proved in field experiments using generally available panel data and in the micro-market testing approach exemplified by the mini-test market operated by Forecast (Market Research). (See section 10.5.1.)

$$\frac{P}{100} \times \frac{R}{100} \times B = \textit{predicted brand share}$$

- After a time the cumulative penetration of the brand, i.e. the number of people buying the brand for the first time, shows a declining rate of increase. Once the shape of the curve is determined and a declining rate of increase is observed, it is possible to make a reasonable estimate of the ultimate likely penetration.
- The repeat-purchasing rate is calculated by taking the total volume of purchases in the product field made by people who have tried the brand under study and expressing the repeat purchases of the brand as a proportion of these total purchases. This repeat-purchasing rate usually declines in the early weeks after a first purchase and eventually begins to level off. When the levelling-off occurs it is possible to calculate what the equilibrium market-share of the brand will be.[9]

In the now classic case of Signal toothpaste, P was finally estimated at 37 per cent twenty weeks after the launch when R was levelling off at 40 per cent. (At that time B had not been introduced into the formula.) The predicted share of the toothpaste market was 40 per cent of 37 per cent, i.e. 14.8 per cent. Signal achieved this share some three or four months after the prediction was made and the brand held a share of 14 per cent to 15 per cent until the toothpaste market was radically changed by the introduction of the fluoride toothpastes.

The predictive power of the model

$$\frac{P}{100} \times \frac{R}{100} \times B$$

is shown most dramatically when an experimental launch is being observed, but the model is also applicable to field experiments involving the manipulation of elements in the mix.[9]

10.5 Simulating exposure in the field

When a brand is exposed to the market, risks are incurred:

- Unless the field experiment is conducted on a limited scale, as in an in-store test, substantial production and marketing costs accrue.
- The competition is alerted and may respond by:

  (a) going national with a copy of the product;
  (b) confusing experimental results by a counter-attack more intensive than would be possible on a national scale;
  (c) quietly monitoring the experiment while developing plans designed to spoil the national launch when it comes.

- Retail buying power is increasingly concentrated in few hands so that securing effective distribution depends on the decisions of a few individuals. Failure to perform well in the experimental area not only handicaps the brand on test, it also affects 'the manufacturer's track record' and so does longer-term damage.[10]
- Given that the sales/brand share targets set are achieved, for the duration of the field experiment opportunity costs are being incurred.

Generally speaking, to arrive at a valid estimate it is necessary to remain in the field for nine to twelve months.

There is, therefore, a need for procedures which get closer to the verdict of the market than is possible in the 'hidden' lab.-type experiment. The lab.-type experiment depends on such intermediate measures as intention to buy. What is wanted is a sales or brand-share measure without exposure to competitors and retailers. We are going to consider two approaches to this problem both now broadly available:

1. Micro-market testing, the mini-test market (developed by RBL);
2. Area marketing test-evaluation system of AMTES (an econometric model developed by Michael Stewart at Beecham).

10.5.1 Micro-market testing: the mini-test market

This procedure uses the brand-share prediction model discussed in section 10.4.3. The critical measurement is 'repeat purchasing', 'repeat buying' in the mini-market context: but, instead of diary, or audit, recording of the purchases of individual panel members, the mini-test market data are the purchases of panel members from a mobile grocery service.

The mini-test market was set up nineteen years ago to eliminate potential loss-makers before products went on trial in the market. It was limited to product testing and stood as an additional research stage between lab.-type testing and an experimental launch. It is now being used to help resolve problems associated with individual items in the mix, such as the right recommended retail selling price: to reduce the period of time during which products need to be exposed in the open market and, when exposure is particularly hazardous, to take the place of an experimental launch.

The method

The data are collected from a panel of 600 housewives in Southampton.

The panel members are card-carrying shoppers. They receive a monthly magazine in full colour carrying editorial features and advertisements. Each panel housewife is identified by a number and, provided she has spent a minimum amount, she takes part in a monthly draw.

The mobile shop is fitted out like a supermarket. It carries 1,600 items and any passer-by can use it. All van purchases are electronically recorded at the checkout.

The mini-test market shoppers must not, of course, be asked diagnostic questions if their shopping behaviour is being used for predictive purposes. The operation does, however, include a separate panel of 400 shoppers who are asked use and attitude questions as the need arises.

Validity and applications

The procedure ensures 100 per cent distribution so that penetration accumulates and levels out more rapidly than would be the case in market conditions: but the predictive value of the procedure was thoroughly tested at the pioneering stage and it is, of course, continually under test as products and strategies cleared by the mini-test market enter an area or national market.[11] Three cases are of particular interest as examples of marketing problems, apart from the mini-test market application:

Problem: To determine the optimum recommended selling price for a new introduction.

Product: Sunlight Lemon Washing-up Liquid.

The product was designed to be better and more expensive than Fairy Liquid. Two prices × two areas in a Latin square design.

Results:

	Higher price	Lower price
Cumulative penetration (of product field buyers)	42%	50%
Repeat-buying rate	13%	18%
Buying-rate index	1.0	1.0
PREDICTED BRAND SHARE	5.5%	9.0%

The 3.5 per cent difference in predicted brand share 'represented approximately £1.5m at retail value in the national market place at the time'.[11]

Appearance of a competitor prompted a national launch straight from mini-test market.

National brand-share peaked at 14 per cent after twenty-four weeks, settled at 9 per cent in the forty-eighth week.

Problem: To measure the threat launched by a competitive product undergoing experimental launch.

Product: Carousal Margarine

The product was bought in the competitor's test area (Midlands ITV). The advertising was monitored and translated into print advertisements for the mini-test market catalogue.

Results: (after six months on mini-test)

Cumulative penetration (of product field buyers	32%
Repeat-buying rate (volume)	4%
Buying-rate index	1.10
PREDICTED BRAND SHARE	1.4%

After launch by Kraft, consumer-panel data showed volume brand-shares of Carousal, predicted at 1.4 per cent, fluctuating as follows:

1973	AUG	SEP	OCT	NOV	DEC	JAN	FEB	1974
%	1.4	0.8	0.7	0.6	0.6	0.8	1.2	

Problem: To avoid being copied.

Product: MacDougall's Pastry Mix.

This was a brilliantly simple, easily copied, product concept — just add water to flour in which the other necessary ingredients had been incorporated.

It was accordingly decided to 'go national' after only twenty-four weeks on mini-test market, and this paid off.

Micro-market testing provides valid estimates of potential brand-shares; but an experimental launch has logistical purposes which demand real-life exposure. An experimental launch is a dress-rehearsal. 'What brand share can we expect?' is a critical question but other questions need to be answered: Will the product travel unspoilt from factory to the point of sale? Is the sales force geared to sell-in effectively? Are distributive and re-stocking arrangements satisfactory? Will the retail trade be moved to display the product effectively?

Questions such as these can be answered before the conventional nine to twelve months' long experimental launch is half-way through. It is the building-up of penetration and the settling-down of the repeat-purchase rate that take time. Micro-marketing hot-houses penetration and makes it possible to establish repeat-buying behaviour fairly rapidly. There may be a case for treating the area test as a logistical exercise.

10.5.2   Area marketing test evaluation system, AMTES

Before embarking on an experiment in the market it is important to decide how precisely we are going to want to interpret the effect of the experimental treatment (see Appendix 3). An experimental launch may be expected to make a significant impact on a test area, but manipulation of one element in the marketing mix may well produce an effect which cannot be measured precisely enough to give a clear verdict once confidence limits have been attached to the statistical estimate. A result of marketing significance may not be statistically significant.[12]

In area tests, ITV areas are frequently used with the rest of the country standing as a control. Examination of historic retail-audit data at Beecham Products has shown that:[12]

> sales in one area as a percentage of national sales fluctuate considerably even when no area test is being carried out.

Sales of Beecham Foods' largest brand (Lucozade) in the largest ITV area (London, with one in five of all UK homes), expressed as a percentage of national sales, fluctuated within a range of between 16.2 per cent and 21 per cent during the year to March/April 1979 (Nielsen). Many experiments relate to less popular brands tested in smaller ITV areas.

Such a volatile relationship between area market and national market indicates that, when only a small effect has marketing significance, it is necessary to do one of the following:[13]

- Either to record a large number of observations: i.e. to go into a large test area for an unduly long period of time.
- Or to remove from the estimate 'the effects due to various uncontrolled but measured variables affecting sales'.

AMTES is an econometric model: i.e. it uses aggregated data, unlike the brand-share prediction model (see section 10.4.3). The model makes it possible to establish in advance of going into the field and without alerting the competition what would be likely to happen, nationally and in the test area, if the status quo were maintained.

By comparing what actually happens during the course of the experiment with what would have happened had no change been made it is possible to interpret the experimental effect more narrowly without staying unduly long in the field, i.e. longer than about a year.

The method

The procedure has been crystallized by Michael Stewart as follows:[12]

- Draw up a list of all the variables which might have a different effect on brand sales between the test area and the control area. (The control area is usually the rest of the country.) Examples of such variables would be own and competitors' prices, distributions and advertising weights, temperatures and levels of sickness.
- Extract the data for sales and explanatory variables in the test and control areas for at least twenty periods before the start of the test — for example, four years of retail-audit data before EPOS or two years of consumer-panel data.
- Calculate, for sales and explanatory variables, the ratios of the test to control figures.
- Perform all possible subset multiple linear regressions in order to obtain an equation relating the fluctuations in the sales ratio to fluctuations in the ratios of the explanatory variables.
- As each period's data during the area test become available the actual values of the ratios of the relevant explanatory variables are put into the equation to yield an estimate of the expected ratio of sales in the test and control areas if the test had no effect. This estimate is then compared with the actual ratio of sales in the test and control areas. The difference between the two measures is the estimated effect of the area test.

> A test is applied to see if the difference is statistically significant, and confidence limits about the estimated sales effect are also calculated.

The AMTES procedure is therefore based on a combination of econometric modelling and experimentation in the field.

> *Problem*: To predict the effect on consumer sales of changing the creative concept from an association of Horlicks with a good night's sleep to an association with relaxation.

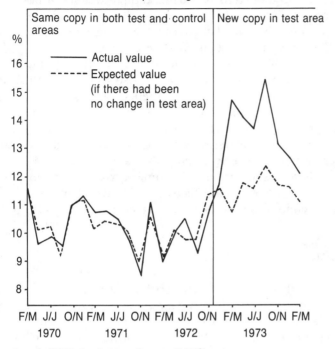

Horlicks: Yorkshire TV area copy test

Sales in test area as a percentage of sales in control area

Source: MRS Conference Papers (1976)

**Figure 10.4
An application
and its
validation**

Method: Before 'relax' was exposed in the Yorkshire ITV area, the relative importance of all possible combinations of measurable variables which might account for differences between the Horlicks performance in Yorkshire and its performance nationally was scrutinized by AMTES, and an equation which explained most of the difference was arrived at. The AMTES prediction was compared with sales as shown by Nielsen over the period of time taken into account in the development of the equation. The 'fit', as Figure 10.4 shows, validated the AMTES equation.

Results: The effect of new copy in the test area is clearly shown in Figure 10.4, the difference between 'expected value' and 'actual value' being attributed to the new 'relax' copy.

A large number of observations is required at the modelling stage. Where sufficiently extensive back data are not on file, these can often be bought from the suppliers.

The most commonly used inputs are retail selling price (the prices actually charged to consumers), advertising weight (amount spent or TVRs) and distribution (percentage of retail outlets stocking) for the test brand and its competitors, in the test area and nationally.

In a number of product fields, weather (mean temperatures, hours of sunshine) and levels of sickness will be taken into account in the equation.

The procedure can be applied to all the marketing variables. It has been shown that changes to the creative communication have a quicker and more marked effect on sales than changes to advertising expenditure. The Horlicks case illustrates the effect of creative change.

In the Horlick's case (Figure 10.4) econometric modelling is used in a field experiment. Econometric modelling is also used to control the marketing mix: to isolate individual mix elements, such as 'adspend', in order to validate investment in them.

It is, of course, necessary in the first instance to construct a database and this involves having available relevant trend data about own and competitors' performances over time. Once the database has been set up, and provision made for its updating, it becomes possible to manipulate the marketing mix to better cost-effectiveness.[14] An example of the evaluative use of econometric modelling is given in section 11.3.3.

10.6   Conclusion

We have focused in this chapter on the critical measure of marketing performance — consumer sales/brand shares: but research during the course of an experiment is likely to include criteria other than sales.

Before, during and after an experimental treatment has been introduced, repeat surveys are carried out to measure the effect on product use and on attitude towards the brand (U and A studies) of the proposed change, whether this relates to a new introduction or to an established brand.

In advertising-media experiments, changes in brand awareness are likely to be recorded, while syndicated services which relate media exposure to product and brand consumption help to validate media planning.

The main *raison d'être* of shop audits and consumer panels (see section 10.4.1) is the continuous monitoring of market performance. They are described in this chapter because an appreciation of the nature of the data is necessary to an understanding of the projective and predictive techniques discussed.

We are however, reserving discussion of the ancillary measures mentioned above for Chapter 11, because their main use is to keep track of consumer response to the brand after it has been launched.

Sources and further reading

1. E.J. Davis, *Experimental Marketing* (London: Nelson, 1970).
2. J. Malec, 'Ad testing through the marriage of UPC scanning and targetable TV', *ADMAP* (May 1982), pp. 273, 276–9.

3. J. Clemens, 'Measuring the future market for cable television', *MRS Conference Papers* (1984), pp. 33–45.

4. K.K. Cox and B.M. Enis, *Experimentation for Marketing Decisions* (Glasgow: Intertext, 1973).

5. B. Pymont and G. Welch, 'Trade research', Chap. 7 in R.M. Worcester and J. Downham (eds), *Consumer Market Research Handbook*, 3rd edn (Amsterdam: North-Holland, 1986).

6. A. Wolfe and L. Cook, *The Electronic Revolution in Store* (London: Ogilvy and Mather, 1986).

7. N. Staples, 'Scanning-based services and the Nielsen contribution', *ADMAP* (Apr. 1987).

8. J.H. Parfitt and B.J.K. Collins, 'The use of consumer panels for brand share prediction', *MRS Conference Papers* (1967).

9. J. Parfitt, 'Panel research', Chap. 8 in R.M. Worcester and J. Downham (eds) *Consumer Market Research Handbook*, 2nd edn (Wokingham: Van Nostrand Reinhold, 1978).

10. B.C. Pymont, D. Reay and P.G.M. Standen, 'Towards the elimination of risk from investment in new products', Amsterdam, ESOMAR congress (Amsterdam: ESOMAR, 1976).

11. B. Pymont, 'The development and application of a new micro-market testing technique', Barcelona, ESOMAR congress (Amsterdam: ESOMAR, 1970).

12. M.J. Stewart, 'Measuring advertising effects by area tests', *ADMAP* (Mar. 1980). (In 1981 Michael Stewart set up Abbey Management Services to provide the AMTES technique as a commercial service.)

13. D. Bloom and W.A. Twyman, 'The impact of economic change on the evaluation of advertising campaigns', *Journal of The Market Research Society* (Apr. 1978).

14. S. Colman and M. Brown, 'Advertising tracking studies and sales effects', *MRS Conference Papers* (1984), pp. 89–108.

Problems

A company marketing a premium brand of cooking oil has to decide whether to adopt a revolutionary new bottle closure. The closure, which acts as a pourer, is more efficient and hygienic than those in general use. However, its adoption would increase the price of the brand to consumers by at least 3p a bottle, irrespective of size. (The current prices are 110p for 1 litre and 68p for the $\frac{1}{2}$ litre size.)

The marketing director is anxious to get in first with the new closure but has to show what effect its adoption would have on profit contribution. A research agency is asked to establish the effect on consumer sales of price increases of 3p and 5p on both sizes. The research budget is 'flexible' but a time limit of six weeks is set.

The research agency is told that the company's brand is the leading premium brand in most parts of the country, but the consumption of premium cooking oil is higher in the south than in the north.

1. Does the research agency need a fuller brief? If you think so, make informed assumptions using secondary sources if necessary.

2. Specify the research design(s) you would use to arrive at a projectable answer in the time available.
3. Explain your choice of design(s).
4. Assume adoption of the new closure and a decision in favour of a rolling launch with television advertising demonstrating the convenience and efficiency of the closure. How would you monitor acceptance of the change?

Evaluating performance, 'What if we . . . ?' and prediction

This chapter considers how performance in the market may be monitored and suggests how the data collected by the monitoring procedures may be used to plan ahead. The monitoring/predicting process should be a continuous one; while the system adopted must, of course, aim to relate marketing costs to sales achievements.

Those engaged in strategic planning use data from a variety of 'in-house', government and other sources. Chapter 11 accordingly opens with a review of the components of a marketing information system; then discusses the contribution of research to the monitoring of individual mix activities before considering how the trend data accumulated in a database may be used to evaluate the contribution of individual marketing costs, e.g. 'adspend', to sales achievement; and finally comments on the effect of technological development on marketing research practice, now and in the future.

11.1   The marketing information system (MIS)

Marketing research data are important MIS inputs, especially those data collected continuously (trend data) or at regular intervals as in tracking studies; but effective assessment of current performance in order to plan for the future requires information from sources other than marketing research. The components of the marketing information system are represented in Figure 11.1:[1]

- We are reminded that the marketing information system should be designed to keep management in touch with environmental trends and happenings relevant to the market in which the company is operating (Kotler's 'macro-environment'),[1] as well as monitoring own and competitors' performances in the market place (the 'task environment').
- Data derived from 'the internal accounting system', 'the marketing intelligence system' and 'the market research system' are increasingly serving as inputs to a company database to which a range of management personnel have access via desktop computers.

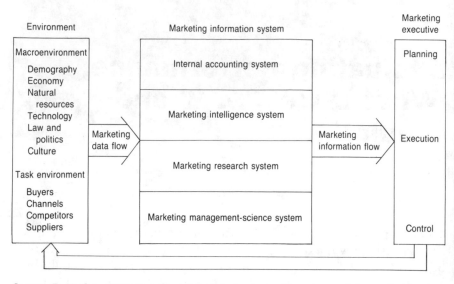

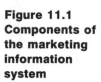

Figure 11.1 Components of the marketing information system

Source: P. Kotler, *Marketing Management, Analysis, Planning and Control*, 4th edn (Englewood Cliffs, NJ: Prentice Hall, 1980), p. 602

The setting up of an interactive data system encourages the asking of 'what if' questions as an aid to prediction: 'With direct access to the data, the researcher is able to delve into the data on a trial-and-error basis, follow through hypotheses and work with the information in a much more flexible and sensitive way.'[2]

Let us now briefly review the components in turn.

11.1.1   Internal accounting system

The importance of the internal accounting system as a data source is discussed in section 2.3, where it is stressed that the relevance of a company's accounting system to the marketing of its products indicates the strength of its orientation towards the market.

Once a brand has been successfully launched, it is required to make a contribution to profit. In the course of operating in a market, companies (especially those marketing fast-moving branded products) arrive at a norm for profit contribution often expressed as a percentage of sales revenue.

The established brand is required to generate sufficient revenue from sales for the following purposes:

- To make the required contribution to company profit.
- To cover costs associated with the production and marketing of the brand (variable costs).
- To make a contribution to company overheads (fixed costs).

The formula:

$$\frac{\text{Sales}}{\text{revenue}} = \frac{\text{Variable}}{\text{costs}} + \frac{\text{Contribution to}}{\text{fixed costs}} + \frac{\text{Contribution to}}{\text{profits}}$$

involves critical decisions:

> The procedure for determining the contribution to fixed costs is likely to be a simple but rather arbitrary one — the bigger the brand's sales the larger the share of fixed costs allocated to it.

Article numbering (AN) has facilitated the attribution of variable costs to individual company brands. AN also makes it possible to allocate shares of production, warehousing, transport and selling costs to specific sizes, scents, flavours, types of packaging within brands.

Allocation of advertising costs, often a substantial variable cost, is more straightforward; provided that the company's sales areas can be related to the ITV areas used in media planning, and provided that not more than one brand, or brand variety, is included in the campaign. Perhaps the simplest marketing activity to cost is a trade or consumer promotion.

The most critical relationship is that between the sales target and the marketing support required to achieve the target. If support were increased, would this heightened marketing activity generate sufficient additional sales revenue to more than offset increases in other variable costs (such as production costs), in contribution to fixed costs and profits? And vice versa? The internal accounting system records and attributes own costs. In order to make decisions of this 'what if' kind, data are required from marketing intelligence and marketing research sources.

11.1.2 Marketing intelligence system

Readers are referred to Chapter 2, where secondary data sources are reviewed, since these are an important component in an intelligence system.

Deciding what information should be regularly recorded, for example which of the economic indicators published by the Government Statistical Service to watch, is straightforward enough: but in designing an intelligence system there are two critical areas:

1. Determining to whom information should be circulated, in what detail and how frequently.
2. Providing for the feeding back — from the sales force, from technicians, trade unionists, suppliers — of news about significant happenings, such as the kind of circumstance which might contaminate the results of a marketing experiment.

Intelligence relating to the 'macro-environment' is required by both consumer and non-domestic companies. For intelligence relating to the 'task environment', companies marketing consumer goods tend to rely on shared-cost marketing research services such as consumer panels and retail audits, but for some consumer markets, e.g. durables, the data published by trade associations are important MIS inputs. The need to provide for news of happenings remains.

Companies operating in industrial and other non-domestic markets rely on their own intelligence-gathering and on information supplied by the manufacturing, trade or professional association to which they belong.

11.1.3 Marketing research system

Most of the data sources and procedures commonly used to monitor and predict can be classified under one of two heads:

1. Trend data derived from retail audits and consumer panels, i.e. data collected time and again from the same sample of retail outlets, households and individuals (in so far as this is possible given drop-outs).
2. Repeated sampling of a specified population, using the same questionnaire each time, or one with a core of standard questions, but selecting the individuals for questioning afresh ('tracking studies').

Data for a tracking study may be collected and financed in one of three ways:

1. Subscription to a series of shared-cost surveys specifically devoted to the tracking of images, e.g. Burke Marketing Research's BASES, the British Market Research Bureau's advertising planning index (API) or the Market and Opinion Research International's corporate-image survey.
2. By buying space in the questionnaire of an omnibus survey (in this case the context in which the questions appear on the questionnaire will vary from one survey to another).
3. By 'going it alone', say once a year, carrying the full cost.

Marketing research data are essential to the building of most marketing models.

11.1.4 Marketing management-science system

Among the decision-making techniques associated with 'management science', the use of models to help solve marketing problems is being stimulated by the following:

- Developments in information technology which facilitate the generation and manipulation of data.

- Desire to extract more mileage from the wealth of data available to marketing companies, much of it derived from marketing research sources.

Syndicated services and segmentation studies (see Chapter 6) make a substantial demand on increasingly scarce budgetary resources. Panel data, and use and attitude data, can make a big contribution to model building: marketing management and research specialists have a common interest in putting these data to work. In addition, if the model building is a shared activity, research specialists and marketing managers are brought closer together.[3]

We return to the subject of model building in section 11.3. In the meantime, we ought perhaps to remember the following:

- 'A model is a set of assumptions about the factors which are relevant to a given situation and the relationships which exist between them.'[4]
- Design of a survey is in effect a model-building exercise for, when determining the parameters of the population to be sampled and of the data to be collected, assumptions are being made — albeit informed ones — about 'the factors which are relevant' and 'the relationships which exist between them' (see Chapter 2, 'Exploring the market').
- We need to distinguish between micro-models built on disaggregated data and macro- (econometric) models built on aggregated data. Parfitt and Collin's Brand Share Prediction model is based on disaggregated data, while Beecham's AMTES is based on aggregated data.

In Chapter 8 we encountered a number of models, including Ehrenberg's NBD/LSD model, Fishbein's 'buying-intention' model, SENSOR and BASES simulated test-market models and MicroTest predictive model.

11.2 Marketing research data used in monitoring

This section focuses on the kind of marketing research data used to monitor the following:

- Selling and distributing activities.
- Media planning effectiveness.
- Impact of the advertising campaign as a whole.

11.2.1 Monitoring selling and distributing activities

A company's own records and feedback from the sales force have, of course, important contributions to make. We are going to concentrate on the use of syndicated trade research in the assessment of own performance as compared with that of competitors. (The data yield of retail audits as compared with that of consumer panels is discussed in the previous chapter, see section 10.4). A marketing company may subscribe to a full retail audit (see Figure 11.1), a distribution check or to both; but in all trade research the following sampling requirements need to be taken into account:

- We have to decide whether the product is such that one type of retail outlet predominates so that we can draw our conclusions from a sample based on, say, the grocer or chemist trade. If the product is sold through a variety of outlets, none predominant, it is necessary to use a panel reflecting this variety or to rely on the limited distributive data generated by a consumer panel. Nielsen's home improvement and health and beauty indices (see pp. 252–3) meet requirements for data derived from a mixture of relevant outlets.
- In trade research as in industrial research (see section 3.8) the sample is designed to represent the trading importance of each category (e.g. 'multiples') rather than the number of shops or establishments in each category.
- In a continuous panel operation, information regarding total turnover is more readily available than is the case with distribution checks, where repeated surveys are likely to be used. Here, as in most non-domestic research, it is necessary to assess turnover (or output) on the basis of such measures as rateable value (see section 4.3.1), number of staff employed, floor area, number of checkouts.
- The basic stratification by turnover is, of course, provided by government statistics relating to production and distribution.

Ever-growing concentration of retail power affects sample design. It also creates a critical need for research at the point of sale both to monitor own and competitor's promotional and merchandising activities, and to monitor store support given to 'our' brand as compared with the store's 'own-label' and branded competitors.[5]

For brands other than market or segment leaders there is the ever-present threat of 'de-listing'. This is a factor which has to be taken into account when the marketing budget is being constructed. How best to share budgetary resources between 'shot in the arm' promotional or merchandising activities and the advertising appropriation's longer-term effects is a critical marketing decision. Econometric modelling of trend data helps to clarify the relationships between marketing expenditures and sales achievement.

Subscription to a retail audit will provide the following criteria for evaluating distributive and, by implication, selling effectiveness:

- Own-branded sales to retailers compared with those made by competitors (volume and value).
- Whether these goods reach the retailer direct, via a depot of the chain to which the retailer belongs or by some other means (such as a cash and carry).

- Share of the total retail trade done by retailers stocking our brand compared with those stocking competitive brands (£-weighted distribution).
- Own-stock cover, given the rate at which our brand is selling, compared with the competition.
- The amount of shelf space and the display support given to our brand compared with competitors.

The data are shown for each category of outlet within ITV areas, so provided that a company's sales areas can be related to ITV areas, it is possible to evaluate sales force achievement in the light of these criteria as well as the distributive and merchandising policies being followed.

An example of a Nielsen detail table is given in Table 11.1.

Table 11.1 Example of Nielsen detail table.

PAGE.01   Nielsen grocery service   Product class Z   April 1988   Total Great Britain

Unit basis: tons — average and RSP — lbs
£ basis: thousands to IDP

	Consumer sales £ at RSP	Consumer sales	Retailer purchases	Retailer stocks	Day's supply	Distribution shop AC PC MAX %	OS %	OSF %	PUR %	MER %	Average stocks sales/M WT.sales/M	RSP P	Forward stocks
Product class Z													
Total all items	4,115.6	1,713.9	1,704.5	91.9	3.3	63	15	15	60		5.9	107.2	88.1
	100.0%	100.0%	100.0%	100.0%		93	6	6	93		54.7		100.0%
						100	3	3	100		37.1		
Brand A													
standard	764.1	307.2	305.4	13.9	2.8	18	6	6	17		3.2	111.0	13.1
	18.6%	17.9%	17.9%	15.1%		48	7	7	48		34.9		14.9%
						53	7	7	53		13.1		
Extra	710.5	268.4	267.6	13.9	3.2	12	4	4	12		4.6	118.1	13.5
	17.3%	15.7%	15.7%	15.1%		49	8	9	48		44.7		15.3%
						55	10	10	53		10.9		
Brand A total	1,474.5	575.6	573.0	27.8	2.9	19	6	6	18	*	5.9	114.3	26.6
	35.8%	33.6%	33.6%	30.3%		53	8	8	51	2	61.5		30.2%
						57	7	7	55	1	22.0		
Brand B													
standard	314.6	127.7	127.1	8.0	3.8	12	5	5	12		2.6	110.0	7.6
	7.6%	7.5%	7.5%	8.7%		27	6	6	26		20.4		8.6%
						29	5	5	28		9.1		
Extra	373.3	141.0	140.1	9.0	3.9	9	4	4	8		4.1	118.1	8.9
	9.1%	8.2%	8.2%	9.8%		36	7	7	34		32.1		10.1%
						41	6	7	40		8.0		
Brand B total	687.8	268.7	267.2	17.0	3.9	14	6	7	13	*	4.9	114.3	16.5
	16.7%	15.7%	15.7%	18.5%		41	7	7	40	1	39.0		18.7%
						45	5	6	44	1	13.3		
All other total	1,953.2	869.6	864.3	47.1	3.3	46	11	12	43		4.1	100.3	45.0
	47.4%	50.7%	50.7%	51.3%		55	7	7	53		37.7		51.1%
						63	5	5	62		31.5		

AC all-commodity value; PC product-class value; MAX maximum distribution measured; OS out of stock; OSF out of stock in forward-selling area; PUR retailer purchase; MER merchandising; SHOP number of shops handling the product during the period

A number of research suppliers include distribution checks among the services they offer. The scope is narrower than the full retail audit, being limited to what is visible at the point of sale, presence of the brand and its main competitors, shelf space allocated, promotional offers, selling prices.

The distribution check may be used because a full audit cannot be afforded, because the need to monitor distribution is felt to be a short-term one, to investigate a local problem for which the standard auditing sample would be inadequate when broken down, or to supplement distributive information from, for example, a consumer panel.

11.2.2 Monitoring media planning

The backbone of the monitoring system for media is provided by BARB and by JICNARS for the print media. These are reviewed in Chapter 9, and it will be appreciated that BARB's weekly reports monitor television buying very closely, while JICNARS, published twice a year, keep a watch on planning decisions and suggest where modifications may be advisable.

In addition, advertising agents and their clients buy into services which monitor own and competitive expenditures across all media (cf. MEAL and the Media Register), so that comparison of own costs with those of competitors is relatively straightforward. But allowance has to be made for the fact that rates are subject to offers and bargaining so that there is a margin of error around figures necessarily based on rate-card rates. Also, ambiguities inevitably arise when advertisements relate to more than one brand, or to more than one variety of a brand.

From the monitoring/planning point of view, the industry data leave two important questions unanswered:

1. Are the opportunities to receive the message being taken?
2. Is media selection based on the demographic characteristics of buyers/users as closely 'on target' (and therefore as cost-effective), as is desirable?

The OTS problem is discussed in Chapter 9, and we return to this vexed question when we consider TABS. TABS (tracking advertising and brand strength) monitors advertising awareness, and the awareness data can be related to the TVRs recorded by BARB. Awareness is, of course, dependent on creative presentation as well as 'media spend' and scheduling.

The second question brings us to single-source data. There are three ways in which a marketing company can seek to relate product/brand use to media consumption.

1. Via a consumer panel.
2. Via the Target Group Index.

3. By adding media questions to surveys about the habits and attitudes of brand users.

It is, of course, possible to ask members of a consumer panel to record their media habits as well as their purchases. The period of viewing, listening and reading covered will be limited by the demands of the panelist's regular purchasing diary — how many product fields and brands does it cover, and in what detail? — and by the specificity of the media questions. The usual practice has been to collect seven days of single-source data at intervals. Central Independent Television's 'AdLab' has succeeded in maintaining a single-source panel over time by limiting products/brands to twenty-five housewife purchases and by using personal interviews to hand out and collect the monthly diary.[6]

The Target Group Index

This is a syndicated service operated by the British Market Research Bureau, which relates product and media data across a wider product field than that covered by the TCA and Attwood panels. The TGI is rightly defined as a National Survey of Buying: 'buying' embracing, for example, leisure and financial activities.

The sample is drawn using the random-location procedure described in section 3.6.1. The data collection is designed to produce annual reports on specific product and service fields. Between reports data are available on tape for half-year periods. The sample is large (25,000) and the self-completion questionnaire long (86 pages). The questionnaire is placed by interviewers and an effective response rate of 60 per cent plus is recorded. The introduction to the 86-page questionnaire, 'How to tell us' (in answer to the title, 'What do you buy?'), explains how to answer the pre-coded questions and shows what sort of data are being collected (see Figure 11.2). The media questions follow the NRS design.

Table 11.2 illustrates the sensitivity of the relationships revealed by the 'single-source' approach. In this table the database is 'all adults'. It could, of course, be, for example, all those who buy brand X 'most often' (see Figure 11.2) or, say, readers of the *Daily Express* who buy brand X sometimes; the first being of interest if the advertising objective were to reinforce brand loyalty, the second if the objective were to persuade 'switchers' to be less changeable.

These examples show how the TGI helps to determine the selection of (a) media category and (b) media vehicles within categories. The data are also, of course, used in 'post-campaign evaluation'.

The importance of the TGI as a source of market segmentation variables is recognized in section 6.10. Market segmentation and media targeting are, of course, closely related. The demographic and lifestyle

We've worked out a simple way for you to tell us what products you buy. You will see that for each of the products listed in the following pages, there are three questions:

1. Do you <u>ever use</u> (or buy, serve, drink, take, smoke, etc.) the product?

	Yes	No

    If you DO, code the box for 'yes'

    In this case you should then go to questions 2 and 3.

	Yes	No

    If you DON'T, code the box for 'no'

    In this case, you can ignore questions 2 and 3, and go straight on to the next product.

2. If the answer is 'yes', you are asked <u>how often</u> you use it, or how much you use. Please code the box for the most appropriate answer. (An example of a completed set of questions is given on the right of the page: you can see that the person uses Adhesives about once a week.) CODE ONE BOX ONLY. If you can't give an exact answer, please give an approximate one.

3. You are then asked which <u>brands</u> you use. Please code in the first column the brand you use <u>most often.</u> (In the example, Airfix is the brand of Adhesive the person uses most often.) If the brand you use most often is a brand other than those on the list, code it in the "most often" column next to OTHER BRANDS. But before you do so, please make sure it's <u>not</u> listed. You may, in a few cases, wish to code in the "most often" column more than one brand if you use them about equally.

    Then code in the second column any other brand or brands you <u>have used in the past six months.</u> Again, if there are any such brands which are not listed, code it in the 'Others' column next to OTHER BRANDS. You can see that this has been done in the example.

If the product is one which you use more at some times than at others, please tell us how often you are using it, or how much you are using it at the <u>present time.</u>

By the way, it will help us, if you <u>do not write</u> on the questionnaire itself, apart from coding boxes and occasionally writing in non-listed brands. You will find a sheet for "Notes" at the end of the questionnaire if you want to comment, or add to any of your answers.

EXAMPLE

ADHESIVES

1. Do you ever use them?	Yes	⊂⊃ 1
	No	⊂⊃ 2

IF YOU DO

2. About how often do you use them?

More than once a WEEK	⊂⊃ 3
Once a WEEK	⊂⊃ 4
2 or 3 times a MONTH	⊂⊃ 5
Once a MONTH	⊂⊃ 6
Less than once a MONTH	⊂⊃ 7

3. Which brands do you use?	Most Often	Others
Airfix	⊂⊃ y	⊂⊃ y
Araldite	⊂⊃ x	⊂⊃ x
Bostik	⊂⊃ 0	⊂⊃ 0
Copydex	⊂⊃ 1	⊂⊃ 1
Croid	⊂⊃ 2	⊂⊃ 2
Dunlop	⊂⊃ 3	⊂⊃ 3
Durofix	⊂⊃ 4	⊂⊃ 4
Evostik	⊂⊃ 5	⊂⊃ 5
Gloy	⊂⊃ 6	⊂⊃ 6
Lepage	⊂⊃ 7	⊂⊃ 7
Uhu	⊂⊃ 8	⊂⊃ 8
OTHER BRANDS	⊂⊃ 9	⊂⊃ 9

IT IS MOST IMPORTANT THAT YOU:-

USE PENCIL ONLY (a pencil is enclosed)

DON'T MAKE TICKS OR CROSSES

PLEASE MARK THE APPROPRIATE BOX LIKE THIS: ⊂⊃

When you make an error, RUB IT OUT THOROUGHLY

Figure 11.2
TGI: 'How to tell us'

Product field	Wine (use)	Slimming (trying to)	Laxatives (once a month or more)
Base, all adults	65.6%	48.0%	8.6%
Index	100	100	100
Readers of *Daily Express*	112	103	110
Readers of *News of the World*	89	111	119
Average daily viewing of ITV:			
one hour or less	118	93	71
four hours or more	75	105	145

**Table 11.2
Selectivity of
the TGI
illustrated**

The index shows that among readers of the *Daily Express* (to take an example), the proportion of 'wine users' and of 'slimmers' is higher than the national average, for which the index is 100; while *Daily Express* readers use laxatives 'once a month or more', less than the national average.

Source: TGI, 1987

characteristics of the TGI sample of 25,000 individuals, together with their individual buying of a wide range of goods and services, may be related to their individual media habits. Access to the TGI databank, either direct or via a computer bureau, such as Donovan Data Systems, aids effective monitoring, 'what if' investigation and forward planning.

In industrial and other non-domestic markets it is common practice to attach media questions to surveys designed to establish the requirements and attitudes of those who influence buying decisions. The data are stored and used when making, and evaluating, media plans.

Media questions may also be attached to the use and attitude surveys regularly carried out by marketing companies: 'Many of our clients already commission consumer surveys into their markets. By a simple step we can sometimes double the value of these surveys at very small additional cost: by adding media questions.'[7]

This approach is appropriate when media alternatives are being compared (as in the examples quoted above), but for planning/monitoring purposes it is usually advisable to consider data drawn from the broad field of media choice, using the standard NRS questions.

11.2.3 Monitoring the advertising campaign

As pointed out in the introduction to Chapter 8, the IPA's objective for their advertising effectiveness awards is 'to isolate the contribution of advertising to sales and profits over and above that of the marketing mix'.[8] It is recognized that 'we are not talking about absolute proof here, but a balance of probabilities.'

The balance of probabilities is usually arrived at using econometric analysis techniques, of which the award-winning TSB and Andrex cases are helpful examples.[8] Econometric modelling demands trend data collected over a sufficient number of instances. These trend data derive either from a consumer panel *or* a retail audit; or from a series of tracking studies. TABS and Burke's BASES IV use tracking data.

The distinction between the two ways of collecting trend data is well put by Sampson:

> Unlike the continuous panel — a time series approach, where data are obtained from the same sample of people over a number of points in time — the tracking study is a trend design approach, collecting data from matched samples of the same population over time.[9]

Sampson confirms that 'whereas the panel allows data to be analysed for individuals . . . with the continuous tracking study, data may only be analysed in aggregate form.'

It follows that panel data can provide inputs to both micro and macro models: but, committed to aggregated data, tracking studies are by definition associated with macro or econometric models.

It is of course critical (in tracking studies) that sample designs, together with the asking of questions and recording of answers be standardized, that core tracking questions should always be asked using the same words and be put to the respondent in the same order.

We are going to consider TABS and BASES IV more closely, but it may help us to appreciate the hazards inherent in the data-collection process if we first examine three of the 'intermediate measures' used to monitor advertising effectiveness after campaign exposure: 'recognition', 'salience' and 'attitude change'.

Recognition

Recognition is more relevant to post- than to pre-testing. It attempts to measure whether the opportunity to see the advertisement has in fact been taken by the respondent. This depends, of course, on both the media selection and the creative work. In a recognition check the object is first and foremost to find out whether the respondent recognizes the advertisement: not what is remembered about it, nor the respondent's attitude towards the subject of the advertisement, just whether the respondent happened to see it.

If the respondent knows the subject of the enquiry, he/she may oblige by recognizing the advertisement. It is therefore necessary to use a procedure which either conceals the subject of interest, or one which makes it easy for the respondent to say 'no.'

Salience

'One of the principal objectives of advertising will be to bring a brand to the top of people's minds or to keep it there — to improve or maintain brand salience.'[10]

When a brand is first introduced we are concerned with the impact achieved by the advertising. Once this has been established the aim is to reinforce its position *vis-à-vis* the competition in the potential consumer's mental shopping basket.

'Thinking now of just chocolate blocks and bars, please will you tell me what products come into your mind?'

The brands are recorded in the order in which they surface and their positions are ranked, the first mention out of, say, five possibles scoring 5, the second 4 and so on. Salience scores are aggregated for own brand and for main competitors, and mean scores are calculated by dividing the aggregates by the number in the sample. Trend data based on the mean scores indicate salience standing relative to the competition over time; help to measure the effect of advertising changes in scheduling, weight and creative content.

Attitude and brand image

The attitude measures used to monitor the effect of an advertising campaign on brand image are less 'cut and dried' than recognition, as a measure of campaign penetration, and salience, as a measure of the 'stand-out' effect on the consumer's mind achieved for the brand by the campaign.

The extent to which marketing companies deliberately cultivate images for their brands, the strength of their belief in the added value of an appropriate image, varies with the product field, the management philosophy of the company and the way in which the advertising agency working on the brand approaches its task.

If advertising is being used to create and then reinforce a brand image, with a view to strengthening consumer loyalty, resisting pressure from the retail trade and extending the brand's life cycle, then there is a strong case for continuously monitoring consumer attitudes towards the brand.

If the market has been segmented, if consumers have been consulted about their needs, beliefs and perceptions and if consumers and/or brands have been sorted into groups according to the attitudes which express these needs, beliefs and perceptions, then there will be little doubt as to which attitude measures to use when monitoring the brand image.

The data are best collected for the product field as a whole, or for all substantial brands, not only for the purpose of comparing the image of our brand with those of competing brands, but also to avoid the 'friendliness effect' which questions about one particular brand might evoke.

As we have seen, being asked attitude questions is likely to increase a consumer's awareness of brand attributes. To avoid this learning effect, the population of interest is sampled afresh each time but standard questions are used.

These questions can take three forms:

1. Association of a list of attributes with a list of brands, a simple checking-off operation: e.g. Persil ticked for whiteness.
2. A ranking of attributes — e.g. Persil first out of *x* brands for whiteness — the data being processed in the way described for salience scores.
3. A rating of attributes using either Likert or semantic differential scales, e.g. 'whiteness that shows'.

When collecting brand-image data it is, of course, advisable to establish what brand(s) the respondent is using/has used/is aware of (see section 5.1).

Attitude questions can be a component in a marketing company's own 'usage and attitude' survey, carried out, say, once a year to add flesh to panel data: or a marketing company may subscribe to a 'shared-cost' service such as TABS.

11.2.4 Tracking advertising and brand strength (TABS)

The TABS databank stores answers to a standardized questionnaire placed each week with 250 housewives and 250 men who have been contacted via the NOP omnibus survey which is based on a large probability sample. Responses to the TABS self-completion questionnaire are aggregated over four weeks and an effective response rate of 650 out of 1,000 questionnaires placed is achieved for each of the two TABS samples. The service has been in operation since 1976 and over two thousand advertising campaigns have been tracked. Respondents are questioned about their media consumption as well as their product usage. There is available a volume of normative data against which to assess responses to the key brand questions illustrated in Figure 11.3.

The self-completion questionnaire is noteworthy for the 'unstuffy' way in which respondents are told what to do and for the design of the four diagrammatic scales used to record their impressions of the brand and its advertising.

The scales are introduced as follows:

- Here is a *LADDER*. You use the ladder to show your feelings about the BRAND or MAKE — in this case SPEEDY SPUDS.

'Please fill in the questions below the dotted line *EVEN IF YOU HAVEN'T RECENTLY USED THE BRAND* — it's your *IMPRESSIONS* that matter . . .'

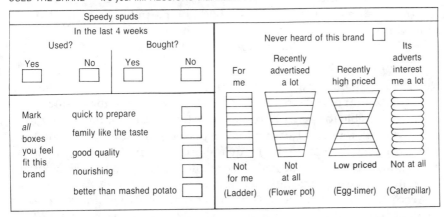

**Figure 11.3
Extract from
the TABS self-
completion
questionnaire**

- Here is a *FLOWER POT*. You use the flower pot to show how much advertising for SPEEDY SPUDS you have recently heard or seen. (Advertising includes magazines, newspapers, radio, posters, cinema, TV, etc.)
- Here is an *EGG-TIMER*. You use the egg-timer to show whether you *think* the PRICE of SPEEDY SPUDS has recently been high or low.
- Here is a *CATERPILLAR*. You use the caterpillar to show how *interesting* you feel the *advertising* for SPEEDY SPUDS is.

(The caterpillar question is used 'for some but not all brands'.) There are ten boxes in each diagrammatic scale. The respondent draws a line in pencil, from one side of a box to the other, and the position of the chosen box is scanned by an optimal mark reader. The pencil marks are converted into scores which are indexed on a scale 0—100. The scaled measures monitor brand goodwill (the ladder), advertising awareness (the flowerpot), price image or perception (the egg-timer) and how interesting the advertising is felt to be (the caterpillar). Comparison of these measures with actual weight of advertising in each medium helps to answer the question 'To what extent are the opportunities to see/hear/read actually making a real impact on the attitudes and behaviour of the target market?'

This statistical analysis also serves to validate the TABS data-collection method. 'Typically we achieve 0.9 correlations between advertising weight and consumer response, thus explaining about 81% of the variance due to advertising.'[11]

Answers to brand-usage questions, taken together with the TABS brand-goodwill measure, segment a branded market into four types of prospect:

1. Committed users: current buyer, 66—99 on the 'for me' top of the ladder (see Figure 11.3).

2. Hot prospect: not a current buyer but favourably disposed, 66−99 on the goodwill scale.
3. Cool customer: a brand buyer but not particularly well disposed towards the brand, 0−55 on the 'for me−not for me' scale.
4. No hoper: neither a buyer nor favourably disposed.

The TABS tracking samples are controlled to be representative of the British population by TV area and by weight of TV viewing. Standardization of the samples and of the procedure used to collect data makes it possible to aggregate results over four weeks for the regular four-weekly TABS report, or over a longer period when the size of the four-week sample will not support a required breakdown of results. This ability to 'roll-up' samples of adequate size is, of course, a characteristic of any carefully controlled tracking service.

According to Sampson,[9] 'The contemporary viewpoint in tracking favours, say, 100 interviews per week throughout the year, or 20 per working day in any product field being tracked.' He refers to the 'rolling four-weekly window', in which weeks 1−4 are added together and compared with the aggregation of weeks 2−5, 3−6 and so on. The data are plotted against media inputs or weekly TVRs.

11.3 Market modelling as an aid to forward planning

11.3.1 Tracking studies as inputs to market models

Tracking studies are increasingly being used as inputs to market models, whether these be pre-launch simulation models, models designed to diagnose mix-element effects as, for example, the contribution of advertising expenditure to brand share, or 'what if we . . . ?' exercises set up to aid forward planning.

Burke use tracking studies as inputs to their BASES IV and TEL-TRAC systems, together with other trend sources such as consumer panels and retail audits. Burke have accumulated a considerable volume of data relating to pre-launch claims and post-launch brand performance and they have developed a model which 'calibrates consumers' claimed responses for 'over-statement and confusion'.

It is, of course, common practice to compare performance as predicted with actual achievement. Given sufficient experience in the product field it is possible to apply a correction factor to claims such as 'intention to buy'.

Economic and competitive pressures and rising costs, especially media costs, together with the existence of a wealth of expensive trend data and the computer facility to manipulate these data, have encouraged marketing companies to treat their stored data as a company asset and to engage in market modelling. Market models draw on a wide variety of sources, including the CSO databank and the economic indicators put out by the Government Statistical Service. 'Live births', the weather, hardness or softness of water might be variables to be taken into account in the baby, home-heating and drinks market!

The syndicated services discussed in Chapter 2 on exploring the market, Chapter 9 on media planning and Chapter 10 on making the go/no-go decision are the bread and butter of market modelling.

11.3.2 Broadbent's 'adstock' model

The advertising appropriation is a large item in the marketing budget and it is advisable that advertising should be represented in an econometric model by a statistic that takes account of the fact that advertising has a lagged effect.

In 1979 Simon Broadbent published a paper 'One way TV advertisements work':

> TV advertising affects consumers' awareness that a brand has been advertised. A model is proposed for the way these two measures are related. It includes both response and decay or forgetting. It separates advertising spend from advertisement content.[12]

The database for Broadbent's model is trend data relating to the following:

- What the television budget has bought (TVRs).
- Awareness of the brand's advertising recorded by tracking studies.

The model uses aggregated data and it requires TVR and awareness readings to be synchronized. Working back from the present into the past decay is treated exponentially, greater weight being attached to 'last week' than 'the week before last'.

'Adstock' denotes the weight of advertising operating at the end of the week, fortnight or four weeks, depending on the reporting interval.

It has been shown that awareness drops between advertising bursts to a base level which shows only small fluctuations. This base level represents the historical effect of advertising and, by subtracting the amount of awareness due to history from awareness overall when a campaign is underway, it is possible to arrive at a measure of the impact of the campaign.

11.3.3 Cadbury's database and how it is used

Cadbury's had available 'accurate and reliable continuous research data going back over a long period of time'.[13] They decided to set up a database for the chocolate market's top twenty brands, Cadbury's and competitors'. The database includes time series relating to all the factors likely to affect sales and these data are analysed, using econometric techniques, to establish the contributions made by individual mix elements to sales. The data extended back over five years when the database was set up, and they are updated.

The inputs were those commonly fed into a database relating to fast-moving packaged goods: general economic data, e.g. disposable income, consumer sales data, prices at point of sale, distribution levels, out of stock, TV advertising data (thirty-second equivalent TVRs), brand and advertising awareness as recorded by tracking studies, and, in this case, adstock.

For most of the brands in the chocolate market it was possible to arrive at a regression model which explained variations in sales quite well but in each case some of the variation was left unexplained, the 'residual'. When each brand was taken in turn, correlating first price with sales, then price plus adstock, then price plus awareness the results in Table 11.3 were achieved.

Twelve major brands were analysed.[13] In nine cases 'price + awareness' explained sales variation better than 'price' alone or 'price + adstock'; in three cases the fit was the same for 'price + adstock' and 'price + awareness'.

Weight of advertising (here represented by adstock) does of course affect the extent to which advertising is recalled (awareness). The value of the 'intermediate measure' recall has often been debated. Colman and Brown show a strong relationship between awareness, as measured by recall, and sales in their paper 'Advertising tracking studies and sales effects'.

Evaluation of the contributions to sales made by individual mix items, such as adspend, over past time reduces the crystal-ball-gazing element

Table 11.3 Analysis of major brands in the chocolate market

| | R-squared | | |
	Price	Price + adstock	Price + awareness
Three best fits:			
Brand E	0.54	0.82	0.93
Brand A	0.71	0.77	0.91
Brand K	0.70	0.85	0.86
Three worst fits:			
Brand J	0.41	0.41	0.52
Brand D	0.53	0.54	0.54
Brand B	0.51	0.60	0.64

in prediction and makes it possible for marketing managers to speak with greater certainty when called on to do the following:

- Assess the size of the marketing budget required to meet planned marketing objectives.
- Allocate funds to individual mix items when the budget has been set.

Currently a good deal of effort is being devoted to the development of econometric models by manufacturing and marketing companies, by research agencies and by advertising agencies. Most of this work is specific to individual brands and procedures and results unpublished.

11.3.4 Asking electronic consumers 'what if we ... ?'

Frost International offer subscribers to its Sandpiper service unrestricted on-line access to market models which mirror the attitudes, needs, beliefs, past behaviour and present intentions of the market population. The databases relate to specific markets — durables, leisure, fast food, personal financial services, cars, cigarettes and so on — and each market is represented by the responses of some 5,000 individual consumers. The data are disaggregated and access is to individual respondents for 'what if' investigations.

The individual/discrete data are also used when estimating changes in brand share and brand switching. The data are aggregated when a statistical treatment, such as cluster analysis with a view to brand mapping, demands this.

As in the case of consumer panels, samples are regularly updated but, while they remain on the database, these electronic consumers are available for repeated questioning. The service is active in Europe, North America, South-East Asia and Japan.

The interviewing method, using portable micro-computers and VDUs is illustrated in section 3.5.4 on asking questions by means of a computer (Figure 3.2). Success of the Frost approach is largely attributable to the psychological knowledge and intensive care devoted to the design of the questionnaire. Established and innovative qualitative techniques are used to generate a comprehensive list of attributes relative to the market concerned. These fall into three categories: 'rational', 'user stereotypes' and 'corporate or brand personality'. 'Rational' attributes are typically found to account for 50 per cent of sales variation, the other two categories for 20−25 per cent each.

Qualitative research generates some 500 market features, the list is reduced to about 100. A questionnaire based on these is tested on a representative sample of consumers. Their responses are factor analysed and the analysis yields 30−40 attributes which discriminate in the market.

(We met this procedure when discussing psychographics and lifestyle in Chapter 6.)

Among the twenty-seven discriminating attributes on the cigarette list are: 'for real smokers', 'have special offers', 'suitable for all occasions', 'pleasant tasting', 'lorry drivers', 'dynamic'. What if Marlborough were seen to be more dynamic? How would an increase of, say, 5 per cent in the strength of this attribute effect Marlborough's position in terms of estimated market share *vis-à-vis* the market shares of the rest of the field?

Brand-switching details for twenty-six brands of cigarette are soon displayed on the 'explorer's' micro screen. The result looks promising; but how is it to be achieved and at what cost? And what about competitive response? Basic marketing questions remain to be answered, but the significance of this Marlborough attribute has been clearly illustrated. Now, what about 'suitable for all occasions'? The 'what if' procedure can, of course, be applied to less subjective attributes such as 'attractive pack' and 'better value for money', both on the cigarette list.

It is difficult for consumers to give a true answer as to which attribute(s) finally determine their purchase decisions. It is possible for them to rate the brands in a product field on a particular attribute, (see Figure 3.2), and to repeat the procedure taking each attribute in turn. They can also rate their ideal brand and their intentions to buy. From responses to questions such as these it is possible to infer 'importance weights' when modelling the market.[14]

> People's understanding of their own motivations is zilch, and one thing you learn is that a lot of purchase decisions are only semi-rational. What does come out, however, is the share that a given product has of the consumers' minds — and it is usually remarkably close to its actual market share.[15]

11.4 Some other approaches to modelling

It is possible to build a model without statistical data. There are 'theory-based' as well as 'data-based' models. The former utilize concepts about the working of the economy and about consumer behaviour derived from the study of economics and of the social sciences. Theory-based models feature in books on consumer behaviour. They suffer from the weakness that they cannot be proved wrong.[16] The early models of 'how advertising works' (see section 8.3.1) were theory-based. Models based on statistical data can be proved wrong and so they are susceptible to being tested.

Models may be described as 'descriptive', 'diagnostic' or 'predictive'. As we have seen, these market research functions are related to each other and this relationship is exemplified in Ehrenberg's NBD/LSD model.

Ehrenberg's rigorous examination of 'historic' panel data led him to the formulation of laws governing the buying and media habits of consumers. This diagnosis aids prediction by establishing normal behaviour.[17]

A distinction is sometimes drawn between 'behavioural' and 'statistical' models. Here again, in the marketing research context the distinction is by no means a hard and fast one. Fishbein's model is based on 'underlying assumptions about how the individual behaves', but the behavioural inputs (as when 'behavioural intention' is 'intention to buy') are the product of survey research.

Psychologists have developed a number of theories to explain the way in which choices are made by individuals[18] and some of these theories are referred to in Chapter 8. The information-processing theory of consumer behaviour[19] aims to describe and explain the means by which people absorb, structure and utilize information. In the marketing context it is accepted that consumers are constantly exposed to more information than they can meaningfully cope with. They consequently adopt decision rules — or strategies — in order to simplify the choice process.

Four consumer decision rules have been defined. For any one product field it is possible to classify consumers according to the rule they follow. An individual is unlikely to apply the same rule to all product fields (though consistency of decision-making style may emerge from the data).

1. Threshold rule: Brands with unacceptable features are eliminated from further consideration, 'irrespective of any favourable features they may be thought to possess'.[19] A too-high price (extravagant) or a too-low price (shoddy) might eliminate a brand from further consideration. (See section 7.5.3 on the buy–response method.)
2. Disjunctive rule: 'A single overwhelming advantage may determine choice.' If this advantage is associated with a particular brand, the consumer will be brand-loyal. In the margarine field the single overwhelming advantage for cholesterol shunners would be 'high in polyunsaturates, contains no cholesterol'.[19]
3. Lexicographic rule: At the point of sale, 'The first brand to demonstrate an advantage on a sub-set of key attributes, considered in order of importance, is chosen.'[19] Ehrenberg's analyses of panel data have shown that, in most product fields, consumers make their brand choices from a limited number of candidates. Few are 100 per cent 'brand-loyal'. In the toilet soap field, the advantages looked for by an individual might be scent, a luxury look and price, in that order of importance: if the purchaser is a mother, the sub-set of key attributes might be price, large size, healthy smell, in that order.
4. Compensatory rule: Choice is made after a weighing up of pros and cons, and 'the option chosen will be one which is perceived to have the best overall balance of favoured characteristics across all attributes'.[19] This decision rule is likely to be followed when a substantial or durable purchase is being made, e.g. a packaged holiday

or a television set: but its application is not limited to these. This rule is followed in the 'trade-off' model.

In order to build a predictive model it is necessary to have access to descriptive data such as the following:

- The behaviour, beliefs and attitudes of consumers in the product field.
- The extent to which they are aware of the choices available to them.
- The importance they attach to different product/brand characteristics.
- The constraints on their buying behaviour — disposable income, social and cultural pressures, availability of the brand whose future we are trying to predict.

Factor and Sampson[20] trace the history of modelling in their paper, 'Making decisions about launching new products'. In the 1960s modelling developed along two paths, which they name the 'behaviour-to-behaviour approach' and the 'attitudes-to-behaviour approach'.

During the 1970s interest focused on attempts to synthesize the behavioural and attitudinal approaches and two different routes were followed: micro-analytical behavioural modelling and sales decomposition—recomposition modelling. The first uses disaggregated data and the second aggregated. Research International's MicroTest predictive model is an example of the first. Burke's BASES IV of the second.

11.5 Conclusion

During the course of this book we have appreciated the benefits brought by developments in information technology. These facilitate decision-making at each stage in the marketing research process:

- At the exploratory stage, ready access to secondary sources.
- When describing a market, during the collection and processing of survey data (as for example in the use of optical mark reading and of micros with VDUs for the administration of attitude batteries).
- In market segmentation, by the ability to correlate the multi-variate characteristics of consumers and of brands as perceived in order to define target groups.
- While developing the brand in the procedures available for simulating the effect of mix items before exposure to the competition.
- By the use of scanners, at the point of purchase and hand-held to monitor sales; and of meters and peoplemeters to monitor television expenditure.

Finally, stimulated by technological development, there is available to market strategists a widening range of shared-cost trend, tracking and information services; together with the means readily to access these.

The benefits are associated with two hazards. Data processing is now comparatively cheap. There is the temptation to summon up and distribute information without regard to objectives — without setting objectives! The hazard of overkill. Then there is the long-recognized 'garbage-in' hazard. Qualified market researchers know the importance of qualitative work and the problems inherent in the collection of these data; the mistakes to be avoided in sample design; the dangers of bias in questionnaire design; the need to control experiments, to match samples in tracking studies and to maintain panels. In short, market researchers are trained to monitor computer input.

Market researchers are also trained to appreciate what the data will stand in the way of analysis. There is a vast volume of data available on subscription. There is the chance that those who call up and manipulate the figures will use them in unsuitable ways: thus drawing wrong conclusions and missing opportunities, while undermining the strategic significance of the market research industry. As we observed in section 1.5: ' "Hi-tech" developments present the MR industry with opportunities but, as in all industrial revolutions, these opportunities constitute challenges.'

Sources and further reading

1. P. Kotler, *Marketing Management, Analysis, Planning and Control*, 4th edn (Englewood Cliffs, NJ: Prentice Hall, 1980), p. 602.
2. D. Holmes, 'On-line databases: their role in information retrieval', in U. Bradley (ed.), *Applied Marketing and Social Research* (London: John Wiley, 1987).
3. P.A. Westwood, J.A. Lunn and D. Beazley 'Models and modelling', *European Research* (July 1974).
4. J. Rothman, 'Experimental designs and models', Chap. 3 in R.M. Worcester and J. Downham (eds), *Consumer Market Research Handbook*, 3rd edn (Amsterdam: North-Holland, 1986).
5. M. Johnson and J. Williams, 'Towards more effective point-of-sale', *MRS Conference Papers* (1984), pp. 205–33.
6. S. Moseley and J. Parfitt, 'Measuring advertising effect from single-source data: the first year of the AdLab', *ADMAP* (June 1987).
7. S.S. Segnit and S. Broadbent, 'Area tests and consumer surveys to measure advertising effectiveness' (Amsterdam: ESOMAR, 1970).
8. C. Channon (ed.), *IPA Advertising Awards* (London: Holt, Rinehart and Winston, 1984).
9. P. Sampson, 'The tracking study in market research' in U. Bradley (ed.), *Applied Marketing and Social Research*, 2nd edn (London: John Wiley, 1987).
10. J.M. Caffyn, 'Measuring effects of advertising campaigns', *MRS Conference Papers* (1977).

11. TABS manual, *Introducing the TABS National and Multi-Media Continuous Service for Tracking Advertising and Brand Strength (TABS)*.
12. S. Broadbent, 'One way TV advertisements work', *Journal of The Market Research Society*, vol. 21, no. 3 (July 1979).
13. S. Colman and G. Brown, 'Advertising tracking studies and sales effects', *Journal of The Market Research Society*, vol. 25, no. 2 (April 1983).
14. I. Grieg, 'How to get past first base', *Marketing* (6 Feb. 1986).
15. Frost, quoted in K. Gorton, 'Using a model approach', *Marketing* (6 Feb. 1986).
16. M. Tuck, *How do we Choose? A Study in Consumer Behaviour* (London: Methuen, 1976).
17. A.S.C. Ehrenberg, *Repeat-buying Theory and Applications* (Amsterdam: North-Holland, 1972).
18. R.A. Westwood, J.A. Lunn and D. Beazeley, 'The trade-off model and its extension', *MRS Conference Papers* (1974).
19. J. Palmer and J.-P. Faivre, 'The information processing theory of consumer behaviour', *European Research* (Nov. 1975).
20. S. Factor and P. Sampson, 'Making decisions about launching new products', *Journal of The Market Research Society*, vol. 25, no. 2 (1983).

See also

• N. Piercy, 'Marketing information systems, theory v. practice', *The Quarterly Review of Marketing* (Autumn 1980).
• N. Piercy and M. Evans, *Managing Marketing Information* (London: Croom-Helm, 1983).

Problems

1. (a) What inputs would you expect to find stored in the databases relating to the following fields:

   (i)   razor blades;
   (ii) car polishes;
   (iii) word processors;
   (iv) 'automatic' washing powders.

   (b) From what sources would the data originate?
   (c) For what purposes might the databases be used?

2. What do you understand by the term 'model'?
3. Choose any product or service field and specify the contribution to be expected from marketing research sources to a marketing information system covering the field.

Glossary of abbreviations

Aact	attitude towards the act
ABMRC	Association of British Market Research Companies
ACORN	a classification of residential neighbourhoods
AGB	Audits of Great Britain
AI	appreciation index
AIDA	attention, interest, desire, action
AIR	average issue readership
AMSO	Association of Market Survey Organisations
AMTES	area marketing test-evaluation system
AN	article numbering
APG	Account Planning Group
API	advertising-planning index
AQRP	Association of Qualitative Research Practitioners
AURA	Association of Users of Research Agencies
BARB	Broadcasters' Audience Research Board
BBC	British Broadcasting Corporation
BI	behavioural intention
BMRB	British Market Research Bureau
BPTO	brand/price trade-off
BRD	Broadcasting Research Department
BSB	British Satellite Broadcasting
CATI	computer-assisted telephone interviewing
CAVIAR	cinema and video industry audience-research
CRN	classified residential neighbourhoods
CSO	Central Statistical Office
CWO	chief wage-earner
DAGMAR	defining advertising goals for measured advertising results
DDS	Donovan Data Systems
DIY	do-it-yourself
DK	don't know
DSB	Direct Satellite Broadcasting
EAN	European article numbering

EC	European Community
EDP	electronic data-processing
EML	extended media list
EPOS	electronic point of sale
ESOMAR	European Society for Opinion and Market Research
GSS	Government Statistical Service
HOH	head of household
IBA	Independent Broadcasting Authority
ILR	independent local radio
IMRA	Industrial Marketing Research Association
IPA	Institute of Practitioners in Advertising
IQCS	Interview Quality Control Scheme
ITC	Independent Television Commission
ITCA	Independent Television Companies Association
ITV	Independent Television
JICNARS	Joint Industry Committee for National Readership Surveys
JICPAR	Joint Industry Committee for Poster Audience Research
JICRAR	Joint Industry Committee for Radio Audience Research
JICTAR	Joint Industry Committee for Television Advertising Research
JMRS	Journal of The Market Research Society
LR	local radio
MEAL	Media Expenditure Analysis Ltd
MIS	marketing information system
MLH	minimum list heading
MORI	Market and Opinion Research International
MR	market research
MRDF	Market Research Development Fund
MRS	Market Research Society
NBD/LSD	negative binomial distribution/logarithmic series distribution
NPD	new product development
NRS	National Readership Survey
OAA	Outdoor Advertising Association
OED	Oxford English Dictionary
OPCS	Office of Population Censuses and Surveys
OR	operational research
OSCAR	outdoor-site classification and audience research

OTS	opportunities to see
PIN	Pinpoint Identified Neighbourhoods
PPI	personal purchases index
PPS	probability proportionate to size
R & D	research and development
RBL	Research Bureau Limited
RI	Research International
RSGB	Research Services of Great Britain
RSL	Research Services Limited
SCPR	Social and Community Planning Research
SIC	standard industrial classification
SN	subjective norm
SRA	Social Research Association
TABS	Tracking advertising and brand strength
TAT	thematic apperception test
TCA	television consumer audit
TCPI	toiletries and cosmetics purchasing index
TEA	terminal education age
TGI	Target Group Index
TSB	Trustee Savings Bank
TV	television
TVR	television rating
USP	unique selling proposition
VCR	video cassette recorder
VDU	visual display unit
VIP	valued impressions per pound

Appendix 1
Access to secondary sources

Electronic desk research

Desk-researchers are increasingly using in-office computer terminals, or their own desktop micros, to gain access to secondary data. This development is being encouraged by the proliferation of host bureaux which make it possible for the desk researcher to consult a range of data sources through one supplier. Prestel, Infoline, Data-Star, Dialogue and Textline are examples of host bureaux.[1]

The information filed may be numeric, bibliographic or both:

- British Telecom's Prestel service is 'a file of some 200,000 pages of information on subjects ranging from accounts of companies to statistics on zinc production'.[1] Prestel is a numeric service.
- Pergamon Press's Infoline is a bibliographic service hosting abstracts of articles published in Dunn and Bradstreet, *Who Owns Whom*, Jordans on subjects such as chemical engineering, electronics, marketing.
- Data-Star hosts both numeric and bibliographic information.
- Textline from Finsbury Data Services abstracts articles from eighty British and European newspapers, plus 'a few journals like *Marketing* and *Marketing Week*'.

(Donovan Data Systems, as part of its service to advertising, acts as host to the media information critical to advertisers and their agencies.)

Paul Hague has an excellent chapter on 'Electronic desk research' in the second edition of his *Industrial Market Research Handbook*.[1] This covers the equipment needed (the following list is based on his text), the type of information offered by leading host bureaux, access procedures and costs, and the case for/against the electronic approach to secondary sources.

Equipment required to operate databases[1]

- An ordinary telephone with a British Telecom jack point.
- A modem or acoustic coupler to pass the data back and forth down the telephone line.
- A terminal with keyboard and VDU: 'Any personal computer or word processor will do.'
- A teletype receiver which can usually be added on to the PC.

Government statistical service

Government departments generate a wealth of statistical data critical to strategic planning. The Central Statistical Office databank offers 'regularly updated macro-economic and related statistical data in computer-readable form.'[2] The data are available 'to host bureaux for incorporation in their client services' as well as to end users.

The 1988 edition of the *MRS Yearbook*[2] includes a detailed list of the statistical series kept by government departments. This is based on

---

Government Statistics: A Brief Guide to Sources,[3] free from the Central Statistical Office, Press and Information Service, Great George St, London SW1P 3AQ (01-233 6135/6193)

Of particular interest to market researchers are the following:

- *Statistics and Market Intelligence Library*
  of the Department of Trade and Industry,
  1 Victoria Street, London SW1H 0ET (01-215 4895)
  'Provides up-to-date and comprehensive trade statistics for all countries, and general statistical publications from all over the world.'[3]
- *The OPCS Reference Library*
  Office of Population Censuses and Surveys
  St Catherine's House, Kingsway, London WC2B 6JP (01-242 0262);
  for library (01-242 2235/2237)
- *Business Statistics Office*
  Cardiff Road, Newport, Gwent NPT 1XG (0633-22 2973) (for general enquiries)

Sources of marketing data

The 1988 *MRS Yearbook* also contains 'sources of marketing data under the following headings:

- Demographics and basic statistics.
- Classification and lifestyle.
- Products and services.
- Finance.
- Retail trade.
- Media.
- Industry statistics.

Shared-cost services and databanks mentioned in *The Marketing Research Process* feature in this section of the yearbook. Research suppliers are set out in the section 'Organisations and individuals in the United Kingdom and Republic of Ireland providing marketing research services'. This register of organizations is available as a free booklet from the society.

Some business-library sources

Government Statistical Service*

CSO Macro-economic Databank, SIA Computer Services, Ebury Gate, 23 Lower Belgrave St, London SW1W 0NW (01-730 4544)
Monthly Digest of Statistics (M).
Annual Abstract of Statistics (A).
Economic Trends (M); *Regional Trends* (A); *Social Trends* (A).
Population Trends (Q). (For England and Wales. For Scotland and Northern Ireland, see the quarterly and annual publications of the appropriate Registrar General.)
OPCS Monitors, Office of Population Censuses and Surveys. Most recent census of population, 1981.
Family Expenditure Survey, (A).
General Household Survey, (A).
British Business (W).
Business Monitors prepared by the Business Statistics Office.
Production monitors (A, Q, M), service and distributive monitors (A, Q, M), miscellaneous monitors, e.g. motor-vehicle registrations (M), cinemas (A), overseas travel and tourism (Q).

Transport Statistics (A).

Government Bookshop, 48 High Holborn, London WC1V 6HB. Statistics and Market Intelligence Library, 50 Ludgate Hill, London EC4M 7HU.

Company information

KOMPASS Register, companies listed geographically and by standard industrial classification, UK and other countries.
Standard Industrial Classifications, revised 1980, CSO.
Key British Enterprises, 1984, Dunn and Bradstreet.
Who Owns Whom (A), Dunn and Bradstreet.
Stock Exchange Yearbook (A), Thomas Skinner Directories.

*M = monthly; A = annually; Q = quarterly; W = weekly.

Bank reviews

Published regularly by Barclay's, Lloyd's, Midland and National Westminster.

International

Overseas Trade Statistics of the UK (M), CSO.
UN Statistical Yearbook.
Main Economic Indicators (Organisation for Economic Control and Development,
   OECD).
General Statistical Bulletin, EEC.
Consumer Europe, 1982 (published every two years), a statistical guide to Europe's
   Consumer Markets, Euromonitor Publications.
International Directory of Published Market Research, British Overseas Trade
   Board.
International Research Directory, 1989, The Market Research Society. Gives
   details of 1,300 market research organisations in over 60 countries.

Publications of the MRS

See *The Market Research Society's Yearbook* (and section 1.5).

Some digests

United Kingdom in Figures, 1983. Free from the CSO.
Marketing Pocket Book 1984, The Advertising Association.
A−Z of UK Marketing Data, a Euromonitor Publication.
Marketing Yearbook, Institute of Marketing.
'Useful data' in *The Market Research Society's Yearbook*.

Periodicals

ADMAP (M)
Campaign (W)
Economist (W)
Marketing (W) and the *Quarterly Review of Marketing*.
Mintel Marketing Intelligence (M) and *Retail Business* (M), Economist Publications.
   These are useful secondary data sources about markets and marketing. Trade
   and published sources collected and appraised.
Journal of The Market Research Society (Q).
Survey (Q).
US Journal of Advertising Research (Q).
US Journal of Marketing Research (bi-monthly).

Sources

1. P.N. Hague, 'Electronic desk research', Chap. 18 in *The Industrial Market Research Handbook*, 2nd edn (London: Kogan Page, 1987).
2. *The Market Research Society's Yearbook* (1988), NTC Publications Ltd, PO Box 69, Henley-on-Thames, Oxon RG9 2BZ.
3. *Government Statistics: A Brief Guide to Sources*.

Appendix 2
The principles of analysis

by John Bound, BSc(Econ), FIS, full member of the MRS

Introduction

When quantitative data have been collected by marketing research methods, the data have to be analysed to turn them into information which will help in making marketing decisions. The data which may be recorded on paper forms or in a computer file have to be summarized so that their meaning may be understood. This is analysis.

This appendix treats both principles which remain unchanged, and practice which is changing rapidly. Computers enable all sorts of analysis procedures to be carried out easily, and there are at the time of writing 200 program packages available in Britain for doing different parts or sorts of these tasks, using big or little computers. We shall try to discuss methods made practicable by computing advances rather than those methods already becoming outdated, though perhaps still widely used.

The task of analysis needs a knowledge of techniques as well. For anyone who has not met the problem before, it is daunting to be confronted with a large pile of paper questionnaires, or even a computer file containing already captured data. Marketers and planners are not usually called upon to do this, but may well be expected to operate simple computing packages which make it easy to produce results, providing the user knows what is wanted. Even if a specialist analyst is employed, a knowledge of the possibilities of analysis is necessary.

Our field here is an enquiry set up to answer a particular problem, or the *ad hoc* enquiry, as it is often called.

What analysis is trying to do

The purpose of statistical analysis is to find patterns in data, and show them clearly in comparison with any previous expectations. There are thus two parts: the first is finding the patterns, and the second is seeing how well they fit any expectations. If there is previous experience of certain patterns, then the easiest thing to do is straightaway to see whether the new data are the same. To take a simple marketing research example:

if it has previously been found that big dogs eat more of a test product than do small dogs, then we look to see if the same is true, and to what extent. To say whether any patterns we find are of practical interest we need to bring in other knowledge.

The basic tool for statistical analysis is the table with rows and columns of figures. The table of this kind is one of mankind's great discoveries, enabling patterns to be readily seen and compared. Yet when a pattern is complex, involving many factors, it becomes impossible to find it or to summarize it by tables. Then multi-variate statistical methods may be used. These produce approximately correct mathematical or pictorial descriptions of complex data in terms of just a few factors. These methods also produce measures of how well the description works. Some of these procedures are mentioned below. The idea is simple: we replace a complicated explanation with a simpler one which is roughly correct, just as giving an average might make a statement which was more or less true about a lot of people, but perhaps not exactly correct about any one of them.

Techniques

General

There are some well-established routines for survey analysis. The main approach is the use of tabulations of various kinds, that is, counting the number of answers in various categories (or perhaps averaging any answers which are in the form of numbers) and putting the figures into tables.

The usual path is to start with one-way, then to go on to two-way tables, and after that to many-way tables. After this the use of multi-variate techniques may be considered. All these terms will be defined shortly. How far along this route to go depends on the objectives, the simplicity of the patterns revealed, and the amount of data.

When conclusions have been reached, suitably designed tables can then enable other people to understand both the conclusions and the way they have been derived. The tables for this are different from those we use in the initial search for patterns.

One-way tables

The first step is to produce these. A one-way table is a simple table for a question or observation giving the number and percentage of the different answers. A set of these is sometimes called a 'code-book' or 'top-line results'. Table A.1 is an example of how this may look.

Base: all respondents	460
	(100)
Prefer new	269
	(58)
Prefer old	175
	(38)
Don't know/no preference	16
	(3)

**Table A.1
A one-way
table. Q.9:
Preference for
new against
old formulation
for brand 'A'**

The heading refers to the question number and topic of the question on which the table is based. The base is the description and number of the respondents on which the table is based. Percentages to whole numbers are usual.

These results for all questions are often shown compactly in the form of a 'hole-count', which is just what it was in the days of punched cards. A hole-count is a summary table showing the code numbers representing the possible answers across the top, and the questions down the side. The entries are then the number of times each answer code occurs for any question, handily with percentages. See Table A.2.

In Table A.2, the heading 'COL' for column on a punched card indicates which question is tabulated. There may be more than one card or computer file record for one questionnaire, so the 'card of type 0' heading identifies which is in use. Some questions in the table have multiple responses, so the 'Sums' column shows the total number of responses. The layout, although based on the original punched card operation, is equally applicable to computer files.

Another useful way to present these answers is to write in the percentages for each question onto a blank questionnaire.

For some enquiries these figures give key results. In our example of a product test comparing two products, the key result might be the percentage preferring each, as shown in Table A.1.

Two-way tables

Such one-way tables are seldom enough. The results need to be shown separately for sub-groups of the sample in the form of two-way tables.

Even in the product-test example above, we would clearly want to know what sort of people preferred each product, and would have collected data about this too. So we take our one-way table of 'Product preferred', and add two other columns, one headed perhaps 'Users of A', and the other 'Users of B'. So now we have a rectangular or two-way table that looks like Table A.3.

**Table A.2
A typical
hole-count**

COL	0	1	2	3	4	5	6	7	8	9	Blank	Single	Multiple	Sums
1	0	0	0	72	0	0	0	0	0	0	0	72	0	72
				100.0								100.0		1.00
2	0	72	0	0	0	0	0	0	0	0	0	72	0	72
		100.0										100.0		1.00
3	0	0	0	0	72	0	0	0	0	0	0	72	0	72
					100.0							100.0		1.00
4	72	0	0	0	0	0	0	0	0	0	0	72	0	72
	100.0											100.0		1.00
5	9	10	10	10	10	10	10	3	0	0	0	72	0	72
	12.5	13.9	13.9	13.9	13.9	13.9	13.9	4.2				100.0		1.00
6	7	8	8	7	7	7	7	7	7	7	0	72	0	72
	9.7	11.1	11.1	9.7	9.7	9.7	9.7	9.7	9.7	9.7		100.0		1.00
7	23	20	29	0	0	0	0	0	0	0	0	72	0	72
	31.9	27.8	40.3									100.0		1.00
8	3	6	6	9	8	9	9	8	9	5	0	72	0	72
	4.2	8.3	8.3	12.5	11.1	12.5	12.5	11.1	12.5	6.9		100.0		1.00
9	0	5	11	6	3	25	22	0	0	0	0	72	0	72
		6.9	15.3	8.3	4.2	34.7	30.6					100.0		1.00
10	0	20	27	23	1	1	0	0	0	0	0	72	0	72
		27.8	37.5	31.9	1.4	1.4						100.0		1.00
11	20	44	8	0	0	0	0	0	0	0	0	72	0	72
	27.8	61.1	11.1									100.0		1.00
12	19	42	11	0	0	0	0	0	0	0	0	72	0	72
	26.4	58.3	15.3									100.0		1.00
13	0	35	36	28	31	18	22	24	30	20	0	25	47	244
		48.6	50.0	38.9	43.1	25.0	30.6	33.3	41.7	27.8		34.7	65.3	3.39
14	20	36	36	24	29	17	16	27	20	18	22	4	46	243
	27.8	50.0	50.0	33.3	40.3	23.6	22.2	37.5	27.8	25.0	30.6	5.6	63.9	3.38
15	0	33	24	17	25	4	24	19	0	0	4	30	38	146
		45.8	33.3	23.6	34.7	5.6	33.3	26.4			5.6	41.7	52.8	2.03
16	0	16	14	8	14	0	0	0	0	0	20	52	0	52
		22.2	19.4	11.1	19.4						27.8	72.2		0.72
17	0	12	20	11	10	0	0	0	0	0	19	53	0	53
		16.7	27.8	15.3	13.9						26.4	73.6		0.74
18	0	5	4	1	3	2	0	3	5	0	49	23	0	23
		6.9	5.6	1.4	4.2	2.8		4.2	6.9		68.1	31.9		0.32

STAR DDP Report WASHING POWDER: There were 72 (unweighted) cards of type 0, selected for = Total Sample

Source: IDA

These sub-group figures give a very different aspect to the figures for the total sample: a marketing decision is called for to decide whether the existing users of the brand or the users of a competitive brand are the more important in choosing the new formula. Quite a few existing users show little preference, so we shall want to look at the results for people who feel strongly, if we have thought to ask about this.

	Total	Use brand A	Use brand B
Base: all respondents			
unweighted	460	224	236
weighted	476	220	256
	(100)	(100)	(100)
Prefer new	286	83	203
	(60)	(38)	(79)
Prefer old	177	125	52
	(37)	(57)	(20)
Don't know/no preference	13	12	1
	(3)	(5)	(0)

**Table A.3
A two-way table showing both unweighted and weighted bases. Q.9: Preference for new against old formulation for brand 'A'**

Note that we conventionally show as 'base' a description of whatever group the table is based upon, and the sample size for this total and each sub-group. Since we have different weighted and unweighted bases we show both: the distinction between the two is explained below on p. 307. The percentages are worked out on the weighted base.

In the body of the table we show both the numbers of responses and their percentage of the total sample size. Sometimes we show the average of a numerical answer, and perhaps the standard deviation as well. The various sub-groups we put across the page, and the possible answers down the side. The typical survey computer printout looks like Table A.4 — useful for study, but not for communicating results. However, the two-way table is only part of the story: we may well need more complex many-way tables.

Many-way tables

These tables come in sets. Each table is based upon only part of the sample. They are needed to see the patterns when there is interaction between analysis breaks.

Interaction arises if different parts of the sample, such as people in the town and in the country, give different patterns of answers to a question. We then need a set of tables, one table for the town, and one for the country. From them we might perhaps see that people in the country with large families have different opinions from people in the country with small families, whereas in the town there is no difference between opinions according to size of families. Similarly, in discussing our example, Table A.4, we have suggested that the way in which preferences vary between users of brands may be different for people with strong preferences.

Such sets form a three-way, or three-dimensional table, but since paper

**Table A.4
A typical two-
way table with
several
analysis breaks
on the one
page**

Washing powder survey

Q.7   Agreement with statement: 'SUDSO' washes whiter

Base: all respondents

			Area		Age			Sex	
		Total	North	South	Under 25	26–40	Over 40	Male	Female
Total		72	35	37	16	9	47	36	36
		100%	100%	100%	100%	100%	100%	100%	100%
Agree strongly	(5)	0	0	0	0	0	0	0	0
		—	—	—	—	—	—	—	—
Agree	(4)	2	2	0	0	0	2	0	2
		3%	6%	—	—	—	4%	—	6%
Neither	(3)	6	0	6	1	1	4	4	2
		8%	—	16%	6%	11%	9%	11%	6%
Disagree	(2)	21	13	8	7	2	12	11	10
		29%	37%	22%	44%	22%	26%	31%	28%
Disagree strongly	(1)	43	20	23	8	6	29	21	22
		60%	57%	62%	50%	67%	62%	58%	61%
No answer		0	0	0	0	0	0	0	0
Mean Score		1.54	1.54	1.54	1.56	1.44	1.55	1.53	1.56

Source: IDA

has only two dimensions for printing, we have to make a set of tables. The third variable is sometimes called a filter variable. The number of tables in all the different possible sets escalates. In our example of a twenty-question survey, there are 380 possible two-way tables, and 6,840 three-way sets. The problem of selection is obvious. But even this is not the end: the answers people give may vary in our example not only between town and country, but also this variation may itself be different in various parts of Britain.

So we need four-way tables, and even more multi-way tables as we find more complicated patterns. We may also derive new variables: for example, we might count the number of questions for which each respondent said 'don't know', and use this as a measure of involvement with the topic. This would enable yet more tables to be formed.

There are three things which stop this process going on indefinitely. The first is that we are willing to accept a simple explanation that fits roughly, but which everybody can understand. An exact but complicated explanation might well fit only data collected in exactly the same circumstances; indeed, perhaps not even then. We would like to think our answers had a chance of applying more widely, and the simple explanation may have a better chance of this.

The second reason is that·the usefulness in marketing of complicated answers is limited. You usually just cannot sell a different product in each part of the country, or to people in the town against people in the country. If you can, then of course such knowledge is useful.

The third reason is that we run out of sample size for the bases of the many-way tables. There may be only a handful or even none at all in some of the tables for sub-sub-groups of even the biggest sample survey. That is why the government conducts a population census of all the 55 million people in Britain: the results need to be broken down in great detail. In practice three-way tables are often as far as we go.

So there are a great many tables that can be produced, and we need a way to choose which to look at.

The selection of tables

Thus for each table we have to decide the column headings. For two-way tables this is all. For many-way tables we have also to decide the filter variables for each value of which a separate table is to be produced.

Consider first two-way tables. The headings for the columns are sometimes called 'analysis breaks', 'independent variables' or 'predictor variables'. They may or may not vary from question to question: often a block of questions on the same topic will have the same breaks, and important predictor variables like age may be used for every question. A crude technique is to use the same group of analysis breaks for every question.

There are two ways of deciding which column headings to use. The better is to know already from other research or experience what sort of sub-groups are likely to vary. Age, sex and social class are most commonly found to make a difference between sub-groups. If you know the age, sex and social class of someone in Britain it is generally true that you can say much about what they buy, read and think. The advantage of this method is that if differences are *not* shown in the particular enquiry, that is a matter for comment. There is, of course, a snag: the possible predictors may not be known, or some predictors may not have been discovered.

This leads to the second method, which is often used indiscriminately. This is to try out a large number of variables, and to see which of them makes a difference, perhaps deciding on this by some statistical significance test such as the chi-squared test. But 'hunting', as it is called, has snags.

If you look at a lot of variables as potential analysis breaks, pure chance will make some of them appear important. There is no guarantee at all that any of the breaks you discover will apply to any other similar survey. What we are trying to do is to say something about the market in general, rather than to give an exact description of the particular sample. So if we come in with a theory then we can use our data to see if it is supported by the particular enquiry.

The use of significance tests also has technical problems: these do not theoretically apply if used repeatedly on different aspects of the same data, and most of them apply only to simple unrestricted probability samples which few market research surveys are. Having said this, we cannot deny that many people have used tests such as the chi-squared to find tables in which subgroups vary and have found the results useful in practice.

When we go beyond the two-way tables to three-way and many-way tables, it becomes quite impossible to produce more than a few out of the thousands which could be generated. Some theory is necessary to select which two-way tables to split further. A problem here is that a two-way table which shows no difference between sub-groups may show differences if such a table is produced separately for each sub-group of a third variable.

For instance, consumption of porridge varies little between homes with older and with younger housewives. Consumption also varies little between homes with children and homes without children. However, consumption varies a great deal between young homes with children and young homes without children. The three-way tabulation here is clearly essential to understand the market.

The selection of filter variables for many-way tables thus follows the same principles as for two-way tables. It has to be done with care to avoid producing too many tables.

We have not referred at all to graphical methods. These are of little use for understanding data based on counts of answers. On the other hand, a good chart can convey a particular point forcefully in presentation.

Table bases

Each table should show its base: that is, a description of the part or whole of the sample it covers, and the size of the sample. The size of each sub-group is also shown.

These bases vary because the table may be based upon only part of the data, and because the sub-groups analysed in the columns of tables may vary. As we said when discussing two-way tables, all tables based on samples should have this base or sample size shown for each sub-group, and also the size and description of the sample on which the table total is based. This sounds simple enough, but raises two other points which often cause confusion. They are weighting and multiple-response.

Weighting is the process of giving some responses greater weight relative to others in totalling the numbers of responses to a question. It is done because, by accident or design, there are too many or too few of some types of respondent. The effect may be to make the total number of responses shown in the table fewer or more than the number of respondents. Percentages are correctly worked out on this different 'reweighted' total, but of course it is the original number of people that forms the 'unweighted base' and enables estimates of the sampling variability of the figures in the table. Both types of base should be shown if they are at all different.

In the example in Tables A.1 and A.3 above, the weighting calculation makes little difference to the percentages in the total columns. This is as usual: indeed, big differences would raise queries. All the same, since weighting improves estimates at little effort now the computer does the calculations, it should normally be carried out.

Questions which have more than one simultaneously valid answer are known as multiple-response questions and require suitable software for recording and tabulation. The number of answers tabulated may exceed the number of respondents. The table may be based either on the number of respondents or the number of responses.

If we ask what newspaper was read yesterday, the answer may be to name none, one or several. If we want to know the number of people reading each paper, then the total of the numbers in each category will be greater than the total number of respondents, and the percentages add to more than 100. This may look odd, but is all right.

We might prefer to have the table based on the total number of newspapers read, so that the percentages would give the share of readership rather than readers. Most software packages designed for marketing research surveys will readily handle these multiple-response questions, and tabulate them on whichever base is required. Not all packages are designed to handle data in this form, and, if not, both questionnaire design and tabulation are made more complicated.

Multi-variate analysis

When the methods of tabulation starting with one-way tables, going on to two-way tables, and finally three- and more-way tables, have been fully explored we may turn to multi-variate analysis. The techniques all provide a simplified explanation of the data which is more or less correct. The results may appear as mathematical descriptions or as graphic maps.

How do we know when this point has been reached? First, the bases for the tables we want to examine may be reduced to a handful of respondents or even none at all. Second, we may be tired of examining hundreds of tables, but believe relationships exist which we have not been able to find by using either our existing theory or by 'hunting'. Third, we may suspect that relationships are too complex to be presented by tables. If our trouble is sample size we should remember that multi-variate analysis done on small samples will vary greatly in its results from sample to sample, just as will the results from tables with small bases.

Multi-variate analysis is nowadays invariably done by computer packages. These can normally be run on microcomputers, provided the data sets are not too big. They are easy to run with little knowledge of either computing systems or the statistical reasoning behind them. This does not matter very much (many people will disagree with this) if the results are taken as hypotheses, to be checked from other data gathered in other circumstances. Some understanding is required, though, if any useful insights are to be generated.

These techniques all provide a simplified explanation of the data which is more or less correct. There is almost always a trade-off between the exactness of the explanation and its elaborateness. The simpler the explanation and the more it is consistent with, or based upon, what is already known, the more likely it is that we have found something which is of more general interest than giving an exact description of the particular data which we have by chance collected. Whenever we create a model from data, we should recall that there are innumerable *other* models we might have found which would fit nearly as well, or even better if we changed our criterion of what is a good fit.

There are two sorts of these techniques. The first is the analysis of dependence, when we know which variable or variables we want to predict given the others. The second is the analysis of inter-dependence, when we want to see how all the variables affect one another. This often takes the form of drawing a map to show how people, attitudes or brands stand in relation to one another, according to some criterion.

Analysis of dependence

Multiple regression is the commonest form, but has limited use in survey analysis. It predicts a number, such as the number of packets of tea purchased, given various other numbers, such as the number of children in a family, and the income per week.

The answer takes the form of an algebraic equation, from which it may be seen how important are the various predictors, and what would happen if they were changed in value in a particular instance. For survey data multiple regression has problems. The data are usually just not in the form of numbers which can be manipulated, but are the counts of various categories. Very different results can often be produced by a slight change in technique.

This problem of categorical or ranked data may be overcome by the use of the generalized linear model, applied by, for example, the GLIM package. Although this produces complicated models, it enables individual discrepant observations to be seen. The use of the generalized linear model with appropriately transformed data is, however, not common in marketing research, but is likely to become more so.

Conjoint analysis takes the results of choices by respondents between hypothetical possibilities varying in a number of factors to estimate the relative importance of each of these factors.

Respondents might for example be asked whether they preferred a small car with medium acceleration or a large car with poor acceleration, and a series of similar questions. A deduction would then be made about the relative importance of size and acceleration. One problem of the technique is that it usually needs extensive questioning of each respondent, although programs have been developed to shorten later questions as data are successively entered on the keyboard. The appropriate questions are then presented on the screen at each stage.

Analysis of inter-dependence

If we have three observations about each of a number of entities such as people, or brands, or attitude scales we may think of each entity as a point in three-dimensional space. We could construct a model with little balls on wires from which we could see the general relationships, grouping and outlying observations. If, though, we had more than three observations about each we should require many-dimensional space which we could not represent. However, mathematical procedures have been developed which do effectively the same thing.

Principal-component analysis (PCA) is widely used. It constructs a number of factors which are weighted averages of the original measurements. A few of these factors, ignoring the rest, will often give a good description of the whole data set.

Sometimes it is called 'factor analysis', after a particular type used more often at one time. There are many variations of the method. PCA is often used with numerical responses from a sample of respondents to a series of attitude scales for each of a number of brands. The process produces uncorrelated factors each of which is a weighted combination of a number of the scales. As the factors are brought in they give an increasingly good explanation of the total pattern. The factors are then regarded as an underlying structure from which each of the scales is built up. Although there are as many factors as scales, only the first few factors are usually considered (there are rules of thumb for deciding which).

An example often quoted is that of measuring nearly rectangular parcels: if for each parcel the girth, diagonal of each side, volume etc. were recorded, PCA would show as major factors the underlying dimensions of length, breadth and height.

The technique has been criticized as showing little more than can be seen from looking at the correlations between each attitude scale. It is widely used as a method of reducing the number of attitude scales to be employed in further enquiries.

Cluster analysis seeks to put entities into groups on the basis of similarities on a number of measures. The number of groups, and the process of their formation (do you start with many groups and see what happens when some are amalgamated, or start with one group and split it successively?), are arbitrary. If the groups are distinct enough, the choice of method makes little difference, and subsequent analysis by group membership may be rewarding. The technique is applied to produce classification methods for databanks (such as the TGI) appropriate for particular product fields rather than generally. Life-stage or lifestyle variables may be used as a basis for forming clusters.

A number of techniques under the heading of multi-dimensional scaling reduce data from many dimensions to an approximate representation to fewer, in practice, to two or three. These depend on measures of difference between the entities.

These measures may take many forms, such as the difference in the number of people saying a scale applies, whether a particular scale is thought to apply at all, or whether a particular brand is seen as having more of a characteristic than another. The resulting maps, which may include points not only for each brand, but also for scales and people, require interpretation, since the meaning of the dimensions on which they are plotted must be inferred from the positions of the entities, a somewhat circular process. Correspondence analysis is a form which takes categorical data, thus needing minimal assumptions about the form of the data.

Practical processing

The application of all these ideas in practice depends on the size of the job, the time available and the hard- and software. Specialized agencies will take data from the questionnaire stage and process it to specification, and can make many helpful suggestions. They cannot, of course, work without an analysis specification as it is called. Deriving this from knowledge of the objectives and methods of the enquiry is normally the job of the research executive concerned. An experienced analyst can take a questionnaire and a set of data and turn out what is usually required, but this is akin to asking the librarian to suggest a book to read. Particularly

Particularly if the survey is large and complicated, the expertise of the professional analysts and the versatility of their equipment are often a good buy. They can work with great speed.

On the other hand, for small enquiries a personal computer or even a large flat surface can be an adequate tool. The researcher who analyses his/her own data comes to understand them in detail, and can explore them interactively. Whichever way analysis is done, it is necessary to know something about the practical considerations which the following section goes through.

Most survey data are still recorded on paper questionnaires in handwriting. This may well change.

The other possibilities are electronic recording at a visual display unit, use of a hand-logging device where data are keyed or barcodes swept as questions are asked or observations made, or paper questionnaires on which marks are made to be read electronically (optical-mark recognition). Techniques for reading handwriting are at the time of writing experimental.

The paper questionnaire requires a separate data-capture process if electronic processing is, as usual, to be used. Paper does, though, carry information beyond the words and figures it bears. All questionnaires on receipt should be examined one by one for completeness, consistency and the more elusive quality of meaningfulness. Whether there are major misunderstandings, if the document is carelessly completed, even facetious or fraudulent, may be seen by the human eye, particularly if a batch of documents from the same source is together. Rejection or correction of the data is then necessary. Personal editing is thus always needed, as well as the checks that may be made electronically.

Data capture or keying takes data from paper questionnaires to a computer. Some software is necessary to do this: many analysis packages provide a checking process. This sets up the recording so that only acceptable answers to a particular question will be read. For example, if adults are indicated at a particular point by the code 1, and non-adults by 2, any attempt to record any other code will be rejected. If multiple-response data are to be recorded, provision is made.

The layout of the questionnaire makes a great difference to the labour of data capture. If codes are clearly shown, preferably by being ringed, or clearly written in, with answers consisting of larger numbers written in boxes, the work will be done faster and more accurately. In the same way the detailed design of the questionnaire affects the work of the interviewer.

The data capture may be checked. Some packages provide a verification procedure, in which some or all of the data may be re-keyed, and discrepancies shown up.

The data in a questionnaire may require coding. That is, the answers have to be put into numerical categories, when they have been received in words. This may be done by the interviewer, with the categories set out on the questionnaire, or later in the office. The categories may not be set until after the office has received the data. These will then be in the form of a summary in words of what a respondent said, the words themselves verbatim, if not too many, or a description of what was observed (if new packaging were being offered to respondents, interviewer might record, 'broke finger-nail'). Such material is not simple to record on VDU or data-logger, so paper has an advantage. It typically arises as the answer to an open-ended question such as 'What makes this magazine article particularly interesting?'

The process of setting the categories is known as 'making a coding frame'. Usually for an open-ended question for which responses are recorded more or less verbatim, the responses in a sample of the questionnaires are examined, and meaningful categories determined. Too many are confusing, but categories can be combined later, while creating new ones during the coding process means re-coding questionnaires already processed. Not more than a dozen categories usually result. A separate frame has to be made and coding done for each open-ended question. Open-ended questions are therefore a costly form.

The next stage is to go through the questionnaires and write on each one at the answer to the particular question the number of the category. This is coding. Coding needs to be done carefully: it is easy to miss a category of mentions occurring only infrequently, but which is none the less important.

It is not necessary to have electronic equipment to analyse data. For a sample of a hundred or two, simple analysis may be done by a hand-count. This may be a preliminary operation to get top-line figures. The questionnaires are sorted into piles, each representing a combination of desired classifications. Thus if the data are to be analysed by three age groups and two sexes, there will be six piles. It is much easier if the same analysis breaks are used for every question. For each question in turn, the questionnaires are sorted into further piles, one for each answer. The piles are counted, the answers noted, and a check made that the total number of answers or respondents is correct.

An alternative is to work through each questionnaire in turn, putting a tick on a sheet in a box for the particular answer. Even more care is needed to get the totals correct. The totals have to be carefully written into tables and percentages worked out.

An intermediate stage, using a spreadsheet on a microcomputer, is suitable for small data sets where the answers consist mainly of numbers. These might be the answers to an industrial market research enquiry, where a limited number of respondents give estimates for various usages and market sizes. Such data can be incorporated in a spread-sheet. This enables ratios to be calculated for each respondent, and the original figures and the ratios compared between respondents by running the eye down the page. Totals and averages for all respondents may then be shown. Division of respondents into sub-groups may be troublesome though.

The one-way tables or hole-count will show any 'out-of-range' codes such as those denoting people aged 124, but not errors arising from the answers to two or more questions together. If a computer is being used, programs are available to carry out logical checks to find such errors. When inconsistencies are found, they may be identified for querying and correction, or the data may be automatically modified. For example, if only those saying yes in question 2 about whether they use the product are to be asked in question 8 what they think of it, the combination of the code representing no in question 2 with any code except that for not applicable in question 8 shows an error.

An arbitrary correction may then be thought best, by changing the answer to question 8 to 'not applicable'. On the other hand, a detailed examination of the questionnaire and perhaps reference to the respondent may show where the error lies. Large surveys are open to hundreds of checks of this kind, and thousands of minor inconsistencies may be revealed. Automatic correction is then almost inevitable.

It is important to 'clean' the data. Not only is accuracy desirable, but discrepancies have a way of appearing in the finished tables in a prominent and embarrassing position.

The use of computer packages

These are many. Some are menu-driven and others, usually the more powerful, require the preparation of computer files of instructions using some specialized language. They may provide a selection of data entry, data checking, data manipulation, tabulation in various forms, graphical presentation, calculation of summary statistics and tests of significance. They may further provide one or more modelling or multi-variate techniques. The data-entry modules include some for CATI (computer-aided telephone interviewing) assisting in sample selection as well as data collection. As with all software, the more widely applicable and more flexible packages are more complex to use.

The Study Group for Computer Survey Analysis publishes every two years a catalogue of software for statistical and survey analysis: the 1987 edition lists 207 items, 83 British, 112 American, and 12 from other parts of the world. Most are microcomputer-based under the PC/MS-DOS operating system.

The most complete service is provided by the specialist analysis houses referred to above. Many names appear in the Market Research Society organizations book. They will take questionnaires, code and key them, then produce tables to specification, doing all or part of these jobs as needed. They will apply multi-variate techniques to the data as directed.

Their staff can give valuable guidance in all this; as always, executive involvement costs more. We emphasize the use of these agencies because the mechanics of the earlier stages of analysis are complicated and time-consuming for those who are not practised in their use.

Time spent this way is a diversion from the main purpose of marketers. For them, *intelligent* employment of specialists is likely to be an economy in both time and money. The specialists cannot work without a knowledge of the background, objects and methods of the enquiry, so they have to be directed by people who have some ideas of the problems and possibilities of analysis. There is, though, no reason why the individual researcher or student should not do it all, given time and access to equipment. The software is a more important part of this than the actual machine.

Out of the 207 packages, many of which are intended for specialist statistical purposes outside survey research, we have selected as examples two commonly met with, which illustrate some of the possibilities. This is, of course, not to say that they are the best.

SNAP (Mercator Computer Services Ltd, Bristol): This is a micro-computer tabulation package which is largely menu-based. At each stage in operation the possible alternatives are shown on the screen, and all that is needed is to select between them. The package does tabulation, and limited data manipulation. There is a module for data entry which produces a picture on the screen of a 'card' containing the responses for one respondent, and the entries at any point may be checked for being in the legitimate range. The ability to manipulate data is limited, except by linking to other packages. There are few summary statistics or significance tests, and no multi-variate or modelling facilities at all. As in all menu-driven programs the ease of initial use soon becomes tedious: there is, however, a batch option which enables large numbers of tables to be produced by entering a few commands.

SPSS (SPSS UK Ltd, Walton-on-Thames). This is a suite available either for micros or larger machines, capable of handling and manipulating large and complicated data sets on the bigger machines. It has facilities for a wide range of modelling and multi-variate techniques as well as summary statistics and numerous statistical tests. The layout of tables is not satisfactory for scanning or presentation unless the complex add-on module is used. There is also an add-on graphics module. There are no special data-entry or logical-check facilities, but data can be manipulated in many ways.

The program is driven by creating command files in a specialized language, described in a large manual needed to cover the numerous possibilities. SPSS is popular among social scientists, who use it for prolonged examination of their data sets.

Of the many other program packages some specialize in flexible tabulation, others in model building, some in time-series analysis, some in graphics display; some are designed to produce large volumes of repetitive output, some to generate tables one by one. Some link in input and output with others, while some store their data only in forms unintelligible to any other package. The choice is wide and expanding: the only catalogue available is the listing of the SGCSA referred to above. Costs vary widely. Type of machine is not normally a restriction, although complicated operations on large data-sets usually mean a bigger machine than the micro.

The computer has made analysis both easier and more difficult. It can produce great volumes of tables: little is achieved, however, by transposing 250 questionnaires into 275 tables. Skilfully used, the computer can enable thorough and thoughtful study of data, and the eventual production of the tables which communicate in a report. The way data become information needs understanding if the marketer is to appreciate the potential and the limitations of his/her research.

Sources

Ehrenberg, A.S.C., *A Primer in Data Reduction* (Chichester and New York: John Wiley, 1985).

Green, P.E., D.S. Tull and G. Albaum, *Research for Marketing Decisions*, 5th edn (Englewood Cliffs, NJ: Prentice Hall, 1988).

Hague, P.N. and P. Jackson, *Do Your Own Market Research* (London: Kogan Page, 1987).

Study Group for Computer Survey Analysis (eds B.C. Rowe, A. Westlake and P. Rose) *Software for Statistical and Survey Analysis 1989–90* (London: The British Computer Society, 1989).

Further reading

One of the few books which deal with the principles of tabulation for both investigation and reporting is Ehrenberg's *A Primer in Data Reduction*. Practical guidance on data collation and analysis of wider application than the title suggests is given in Hague and Jackson's *Do Your Own Market Research*. The principles of multi-variate analysis are covered by Green, Tull and Albaum.

Appendix 3
Statistical tests

by E.J. Davis, BSc(Econ), FIS, full member of the MRS

The null hypothesis

When dealing with the results of experiments or surveys carried out on samples of people, shops, or whatever, it is seldom possible to *prove* results. Instead, we usually attempt to assess which of two mutually exclusive hypotheses is more likely to be true on the basis of our observed results. The general forms of these two hypotheses and the symbols attached to them are:

H_0: the hypothesis that our results do not show any significant differences between population groups over whatever factors have been measured; and

H_1: the hypothesis that differences shown in our results reflect real differences between population groups.

The first of these hypotheses, H_0, is known as the null hypothesis. If it is true it indicates that our results show nothing except chance differences between our measurements. If we can obtain sufficient evidence to refute this hypothesis with an acceptable level of confidence, then we are justified in accepting the alternative hypothesis, H_1. In effect we begin by assuming that any difference between two sample measurements is not significant and is due to chance until we can find a good basis for rejecting this assumption. If we can reject the null hypothesis we say that our result is 'significant'.

Errors of the first and second kind

In addition to setting down our hypotheses, we need also to decide on the degree of risk we can accept of being wrong in taking a result as significant when it is not. For most market research purposes we work with a level of risk of 1 in 20 of being wrong, often referred to as the 95 per cent limit or the 5 per cent level of significance. In terms of the experiments discussed in Chapter 7, this means that we devise our experiments so that we can apply tests of significance such that if they indicate a real difference, this will be a correct evaluation 95 times out of 100. As we do not normally carry out our experiments often enough to be able to think in terms of being right on 95 per cent of occasions we change the words slightly, and say that we have a 95 per cent chance of being right. From this it follows that we have a 5 per cent chance, or probability, of being wrong, and our tests are operating at the 5 per cent or 0.05 level of significance.

The level of significance here indicates the level of risk of our being wrong in rejecting the null hypothesis when it is true, and thus of accepting our experimental difference as real when it is not. Being wrong in this way is known as a Type I Error.

There is a converse risk — that of failing to detect or to accept a positive experimental result because our experimental measurements are too crude. If, say, a change in some measure, such as consumption of some food product from 30 grams per head to 35 grams per head per day would show a profitable return on some marketing expenditure, then an experiment capable only of showing a change of 10 grams or more as significant will leave the company open to such a risk.

An opportunity to take profitable marketing action may be lost because an experiment is set up which is not powerful enough to measure results with the precision needed in the particular situation. Being wrong in this way is known as a Type II Error.

Two further elements which should be taken into account when assessing the levels of significance to be used are the size of the benefits expected if successful action is subsequently taken, and the penalties expected from taking a wrong decision. In situations such as the final stages of the development and launch of a new brand, the potential benefits and potential losses resulting from decisions based on the experimental results are high. This normally calls for the design of experiments giving high levels of precision and low risks of wrongly rejecting the null hypothesis — such as 1 chance in 100 (the 1 per cent level), as opposed to the 1 chance in 20 (the 5 per cent level). But such experiments are themselves costly, and should not be used in less risky situations where the costs would not be justified. Initial testing of ideas and products is often better undertaken based on the use of significance levels of 10 per cent or more, simply because in the early stages of testing it is often unreasonable (and probably unprofitable) to insist on the more rigorous levels of significance appropriate to high-risk situations.

The problems then of interpreting the statistical results of experiments are by no means simple, nor confined merely to the use of prescribed formulae yielding magic numbers to be labelled 'significant' or 'not significant'. However, with these reservations the following statistical tests can be applied with care to a range of statistical results.

Differences between sample measurements

The range of uncertainty surrounding a measurement obtained from a sample is indicated by the 'standard error' of that measurement.

To calculate the standard error of a measurement, such as the mean price respondents say they would pay for a new product, their mean foot measurements, and so forth, we first calculate the arithmetic mean and use that as a basis for calculating the standard error. The standard error of a mean can then be calculated from this formula:

$$se_m = \sqrt{\frac{\Sigma(x-\bar{x})^2}{n^2}}$$

where n = sample size (assumed here to be at least 30);
  x = each individual measurement taken in turn;
  $\bar{x}$ = the mean of all values of x; and
  Σ indicates all values of $(x-\bar{x})^2$ added together.

When dealing with attributes such as whether a person smokes or not, whether they like the test product or whether they think they would buy the test product in preference to their usual brand, we can use a more simple version of this formula. In these cases we can put $x = 1$ whenever the respondent smokes, prefers, would buy, or whatever, and $x = 0$ if he or she does not. It is then easy to show that under these conditions the standard error of the percentage having the stated attribute can be calculated by the formula below:

$$se_p = \sqrt{\frac{p(100-p)}{n}}$$

where p = the percentage scored 1 (preferably between 10% and 90%); and
  n = sample size (assumed to be at least 30).

When using proportions instead of percentages substitute $(1-p)$ for $(100-p)$ in the formula.

Testing experimental differences involving percentages

Experimental designs such as those used for rating new products (see section 7.3.4) may involve monadic tests using independent matched samples each reporting on one variant, or comparative tests where the same sample of people report on two or more variants of the product. The procedures for testing the results vary, and are described separately.

Monadic results from independent samples

The hypotheses:

H_0: that any difference between readings p_1 and p_2 from two independent random samples of n_1 and n_2 respondents is the result of chance alone;

H_1: that the difference between the readings must be attributed to the experimental conditions.

Note that these hypotheses do not stipulate any direction for any difference, i.e. whether p_1 or p_2 is the higher percentage. Hence a two-tailed test is used, and finding a significant difference in either direction would lead to the rejection of H_0.

First calculate p, the overall percentage given by combining both samples, on the assumption that they are both drawn from the same population. This is given by

$$p = \frac{n_1 p_1 + n_2 p_2}{n_1 + n_2}$$

Then calculate the standard error of the difference $(p_1 - p_2)$:

$$se_d = \sqrt{p(100 - p)\left(\frac{1}{n_1} + \frac{1}{n_2}\right)}$$

In the special case where $n_1 = n_2$:

$$p = \frac{p_1 + p_2}{2}$$

$$se_d = \sqrt{p(100 - p)\frac{2}{n}}$$

Now calculate the absolute value of the test statistic, t, ignoring its sign, where t is defined as:

$$t = \frac{p_1 - p_2}{se_d}$$

If $t \geq 1.64$ the difference is significant at the 10 per cent level; if $t \geq 1.96$ the difference is significant at the 5 per cent level; and if $t \geq 2.58$ the difference is significant at the 1 per cent level.

If a significant difference is found at the required level it suggests that the difference between the readings p_1 and p_2 is not simply due to chance, but reflects a real difference in preferences for the test items.

In some circumstances the direction of any difference is important, as in experiments with a new version of a product expected to be preferred by more people than the old. Here we are not testing whether there is a difference in *either* direction, but whether there is a difference in *one* direction only. In such cases a one-tailed test is used and rejection of H_0 only follows if the test is significant in the appropriate direction.

Assume that p_1 measures acceptance of the old product, and that p_2 measures acceptance of the new version when they have been tested on two independent samples. Then our hypotheses become the following:

H_0: that p_2 is no greater than p_1; and
H_1: that p_2 is greater than p_1.

We calculate se_p and t as before, but now we are only interested in t if p_2 exceeds p_1. The test is now concerned with only one tail of the distribution of error, and the values of t associated with different levels of significance are changed.

If $t \geq 1.29$ the one-way test is significant at the 10 per cent level, and if $t \geq 1.64$ the one-way test is significant at the 5 per cent level, and if $t \geq 2.32$ the one-way test is significant at the 1 per cent level.

Comparative readings from the same sample

If we measure preferences for A, B, C, etc. in the same sample, then there are problems of correlation. As p_a increases so p_b may well diminish, and vice versa. Now to establish whether any difference is significant we have to take account of correlation in our formula for se_p. Our hypotheses become the following:

H_0: there is no difference between the proportions p_a and p_b preferring A and B, measured within a single sample;
H_1: there is a difference between preferences for A and B.

Now the formula for the standard error of the difference becomes

$$se_d = \sqrt{\frac{p_a(100-p_a) + p_b(100-p_b) + 2p_ap_b}{n}}$$

$$t = \frac{p_a - p_b}{se_d} \text{ as before,}$$

and the values of t apply as before for either one-tailed or two-tailed tests.

More complex tests of preference scores

Sometimes we wish to examine more complex situations, such as a preference test where the sample is broken down by some other attribute such as social class. Then the χ^2 or chi-squared test is a more useful way of proceeding.

Suppose we have the following results from a sample of 195 housewives who have each tested products X and Y and stated their preferences. Information on social class has also been collected from each respondent. The results were as follows:

	ABC_1	C_2D	
Prefer X	55	45	100
Prefer Y	35	60	95
	90	105	195

A t-test on the overall split between preferences for X and Y has shown that this is not significant. It appears that there may be differences in preferences between social classes. While it would be possible to carry out a t-test for each class a χ^2 test is more powerful and economical. Here

H_0: there is no difference between the pattern of preferences by social class;

H_1: the pattern of preferences differs between the two social classes.

If there is no difference between classes, then we would expect the same proportion of housewives in each class to prefer X, and the same proportion to prefer Y. The overall estimate of the preference for X is 100 out of 195. Applying this ratio to the 90 ABC_1 housewives, we would expect 46.2 to prefer X, i.e., $100/95 \times 90$. Similarly we would expect $95/195 \times 90$ ABC_1 housewives to prefer Y; $100/195 \times 105$ C_2D housewives to prefer X, and $95/195 \times 105$ to prefer Y.

	Observed	Expected	$O-E$	$(O-E)^2$	$(O-E)^2/E$
X/ABC_1	55	46.2	8.8	77.44	1.68
Y/ABC_1	35	43.8	-8.8	77.44	1.77
X/C_2D	45	53.8	-8.8	77.44	1.44
Y/C_2D	60	51.2	8.8	77.44	1.51
	195	195.0	0		6.40

In fact, once we have calculated one of the four expected values in a 2×2 table such as this one, the other three values are fixed because of the need for columns and rows to add to their original totals. In technical terms we have only 'one degree of freedom' in such a table.

For each cell we now have an observed (O) and an expected (E) value. We then calculate $(O-E)^2/E$ and add.

We can now consult a table of values of χ^2 for our number of degrees of freedom and level of significance, and see whether our sample value exceeds the tabulated value or not. If it does, the differences are significant at that level.

| | Degrees of freedom | | | |
	1	2	3	4
10%	2.7	4.6	6.3	7.8
5%	3.8	6.0	7.8	9.5
1%	6.6	9.2	11.3	13.3

Some values of χ^2

Comparing the calculated value of 6.40 with the table for one degree of freedom, the results are seen to be significant at the 5 per cent level but not quite at the 1 per cent level.

In general, when using χ^2:

- use frequencies, not percentages;
- cells should preferably contain five or more cases;
- degrees of freedom = (rows − 1) × (columns − 1), e.g. a table of two rows and three columns has $(2-1) \times (3-1) = 2$ degrees of freedom.

Differences involving variables

The same general procedure is followed for comparing means of variables as for proportions. In these cases, for independent samples calculate a pooled estimate of the se thus:

$$se_d = \sqrt{\frac{n_1}{n_2} \cdot se\,_{x_1}^{2} + \frac{n_2}{n_1} \cdot se\,_{x_2}^{2}}$$

$$t = \frac{\bar{x}_1 - \bar{x}_2}{se_d}$$

Null hypotheses and alternative hypotheses are set up as before, and the links between values of t and levels of significance for one-tailed and two-tailed tests are the same as for testing proportions.

Where pairs of readings are taken from the same sample, such as numbers of cigarettes smoked by individuals before and after an experiment or weights of slimmers before and after treatment, etc., the situation is most easily handled by calculating the difference, d, for each individual and $\bar{d}$, the average value of d. Then calculate se_d:

$$se_d = \sqrt{\frac{\Sigma(d-\bar{d})^2}{n}}$$

Then our hypotheses become the following:

H_0: that the value of d is not significantly different from zero; and
H_1: that the observed differences are significant.

The tabulated values of t at different levels of significance and for one-tailed and for two-tailed tests apply as before.

For more complex situations 'analysis of variance' is used

Consider the experiment described in section 7.2.3 with results in volume of sales by outlets in three areas, North, Midlands and South and with three pack designs or treatments on test.

	T1	T2	T3	Total	Average
	\multicolumn{5}{c}{Shop sales in a pack test}
N	150	220	180	550	183.3
M	90	100	110	300	100.0
S	60	70	70	200	66.7
Total	300	390	360	1050	
Average	100	130	120		116.7

The regional differences in sales are clearly seen, and on visual inspection they appear to be greater than the differences in sales between the experimental packs. It therefore becomes logical to try to separate the variation or 'variance' between treatments (pack designs in this case) from the variance between regions. Hence we undertake an analysis of variance.

Now the overall variance is given by

$$s^2 = \frac{1}{n-1} \Sigma (x-\bar{x})^2$$

where n = number of cells in the analysis;

$\bar{x}$ = the average sales level over all stores in all regions, namely

$$\bar{x} = \frac{1050}{9} = 116.67.$$

Within the total variance some part will be due to the following:

- variations in sales between areas;
- variations in sales between pack designs; and
- chance variations in sales between stores.

The statistic F is used to assess whether any observed differences in the variance contributions are significant, or probably due only to chance, and hypotheses H_0 and H_1 are set up as before.

The calculations necessary to analyse the overall variance from the experimental results into the parts due to each of these sources are as follows:

r = numbers of rows (areas)
t = number of treatments (packs)

Add up total sales and calculate average sales ($\bar{x}$).
For each area find total sales and average sales (rows) $-\bar{A}_i$.
For each pack find total sales and average sales (cols) $-\bar{P}_j$.

Calculate $\sum\limits_{1}^{r} \sum\limits_{1}^{t} (x_{ij}-\bar{x})^2$ = sum of squares total (SST).

Calculate $r\sum\limits_{1}^{r} (\bar{A}_i-\bar{x})^2$ = sum of squares, areas (SSA).

Calculate $t\sum\limits_{1}^{r} (\bar{P}_j-\bar{x})^2$ = sum of squares, packs (SSP).

As a check on arithmetic one more figure may be calculated:

$$\sum\limits_{1}^{r} \sum\limits_{1}^{t} (x_{ij}-\bar{A}_i-\bar{P}_j+\bar{x})^2 = \text{error/residual sum of squares} = \text{(SEE)}.$$

Calculate degrees of freedom (d.f.) as follows:

Total d.f.   = no. of areas × no. of treatments − 1
                            = $(r \times t) - 1$
Between areas d.f.   = no. of areas − 1
                            = $(r-1)$
Between treatments d.f.   = no. of treatments − 1
                            = $(t-1)$
Residual/error d.f.   = $(r-1)(t-1)$

Note that the degrees of freedom between areas + between treatments + residual = total degrees of freedom. Then complete the following table:

Source of variance	Sum of squares	d.f.	Mean square	Value of F
Between packs	SSP	$t-1$	$MSP = SSP/(t-1)$	MSP/MSE
Between areas	SSA	$r-1$	$MSA = SSA/(r-1)$	MSA/MSE
Error/residual	SSE	$(r-1)(t-1)$	$MSE = SSE/(r-1)(t-1)$	
Total	SST	$rt-1$		

Analysis of variance for random block design

For the shop sales data from the pack test:

r = areas = 3
t = packs = 3

$$\sum_1^r \sum_1^t (x_{ij} - \bar{x})^2 = 24,400.0$$

$$r \sum_1^r (\bar{A}_i - \bar{x})^2 = 21,666.7$$

$$t \sum_1^t (\bar{P}_j - \bar{x})^2 = 1,400.0$$

$$\sum_1^r \sum_1^t (x_{ij} - \bar{A}_i - \bar{P}_j + \bar{x})^2 = 1,333.3$$

The table then becomes the following:

Source of variance	Sum of squares	d.f.	Mean square	Value of F
Areas	21,666.7	2	10833.3	32.5
Packs	1,400.0	2	700.0	2.1
Error	1,333.3	4	333.3	
Totals	24,400.0	8		

We can now consult tables of the values of F to test whether either of the F values is significant. We enter the tables with 2 d.f. for areas and 2 d.f. for packs (the numerators in the F ratios) and 4 d.f. for the mean square error (the denominator). In tables of the values of F the degrees of freedom for the numerator are denoted by v_1, and those for the denominator by v_2.

Using $v = 2$ and $v = 4$, the tables show the following significant values for F:

$$
\begin{aligned}
1\% \text{ level } F &= 18.00 \\
5\% \text{ level } F &= 6.94 \\
10\% \text{ level } F &= 4.32 \\
25\% \text{ level } F &= 2.00
\end{aligned}
$$

This result shows, as we suspected, that there are very strong area differences, with the between-areas value of F being significant well beyond the 1 per cent level. The value of F for the packs however is only significant at the 25 per cent level — that is, we could expect such observed differences in the sales of the different packs in one experiment in four, just by chance even if the packs had no differential effects on sales levels.

The action to be taken on this result would depend on other factors in the situation, such as the relative costs of the three packs, the time pressures for a decision, and so forth. Broadly we could do the following:

- adopt pack 3, accepting the low level of significance of the experimental result;
- continue with the existing pack (if there is one); or
- carry out further experiments to get a more specific indication of the effects of packs on sales.

Analysis of variance is such a widely used method of assessing the significance of experimental results that it is included in most computer statistical packages. The programs vary in detail, but the raw data are fed in as responses to promptings by the computer program, and the completed calculations printed out or displayed in a form similar to the table above. Some programs stop at the calculation of the F values, but others go on to indicate the associated levels of significance.

It is important to appreciate what calculations are taking place to produce the analysis of variance from a set of data, but seldom necessary to carry through the arithmetic by hand.

The facilities are also normally there for handling the calculations arising from more complex experiments quickly and accurately, for taking account of more factors, and for investigating possible interactions between levels of factors. At each stage of increasing complexity the calculations expand, but following the patterns shown above.

For example, the Latin square design discussed in section 7.2.3 leads us to the table on p. 327.

The similarity in structure between the tables is seen, with the inclusion of an additional line in the Latin square results. The error/residual calculation is now

$$
\sum_{1}^{t} \sum_{1}^{r} (x_{ij} - \bar{A}_i - \bar{P}_j - \bar{O}_k + 2\bar{x})^2
$$

Source of variance	Sum of squares	d.f.	Mean square	Value of F
Between packs	SSP	$t-1$	$MSP = SSP/(t-1)$	MSP/MSE
Between areas	SSA	$t-1$	$MSA = SSA/(t-1)$	MSA/MSE
Between outlets	SSO	$t-1$	$MSO = SSO/(t-1)$	MSO/MSE
Error/residual	SSE	$(t-1)(t-2)$	$MSE = SSE/(t-1)(t-2)$	
	SST	$t-1$		

Analysis of variance for Latin square

where the $\bar{A}_i$s are the averages of the areas;
the $\bar{P}_j$s are the averages of the packs; and
the $\bar{O}_k$s are the averages of the outlet types.

Worked example of the use of a Latin square

This example follows the design set out in section 7.2.3, with three packs being tested in three outlet types in three areas. The sales figures are shown below.

	Type of retail outlet				
Region	Grocer	Chemist	CTN	Total	Average
North	122^2	114^3	139^1	375	125
Midlands	108^1	115^2	104^3	327	109
South	91^3	110^1	114^2	315	105
Total	321	339	357	1,017	
Average	107	113	119		113

Raw sales data from pack test

The indices against cell sales indicate the pack version used.
   To facilitate the calculation of the pack averages the figures may be rearranged thus:

				Total	Average
Pack 1 sales	139	108	110	357	119
Pack 2 sales	122	115	114	351	117
Pack 3 sales	114	104	91	309	103

It is now possible to calculate all the sums of squares required and to fit them into the analysis of variance table.

Source of variance	Sum of squares	d.f.	Mean square	Value of F
Packs	456	2	228	25.3
Areas	672	2	336	37.3
Outlets	216	2	113	12.6
Error	18	2	9	—
Totals	1,362	8		

These values of F can be compared with the tabulated values for v_1 and v_2 both at two degrees of freedom:

at the 5% level $F = 19.0$; and
at the 1% level $F = 99.0$.

Hence both pack figures and the area figures show significant differences at the 5 per cent level.

The fact that the figures show significant variations by pack needs careful interpretation, and reference back to the averages by pack indicates that the variation arises from one pack performing less well than the other two. There is still doubt about which of the three packs may sell best — but some progress has been made in finding that one version sells less well than the other two.

Suggestions for further reading

- K.K. Cox and B.M. Enis, *Experimentation for Marketing Decisions* (Glasgow: Intertext, 1973).
- P. Harris, 'Statistics and significance testing', Chap. 12 in R.M. Worcester and J. Downham (eds), *Consumer Market Research Handbook*, 2nd edn (Wokingham: Van Nostrand Reinhold, 1978).
- P.E. Montagnon, *Foundations of Statistics* (Cheltenham: Stanley Thornes, 1980).

Index

329